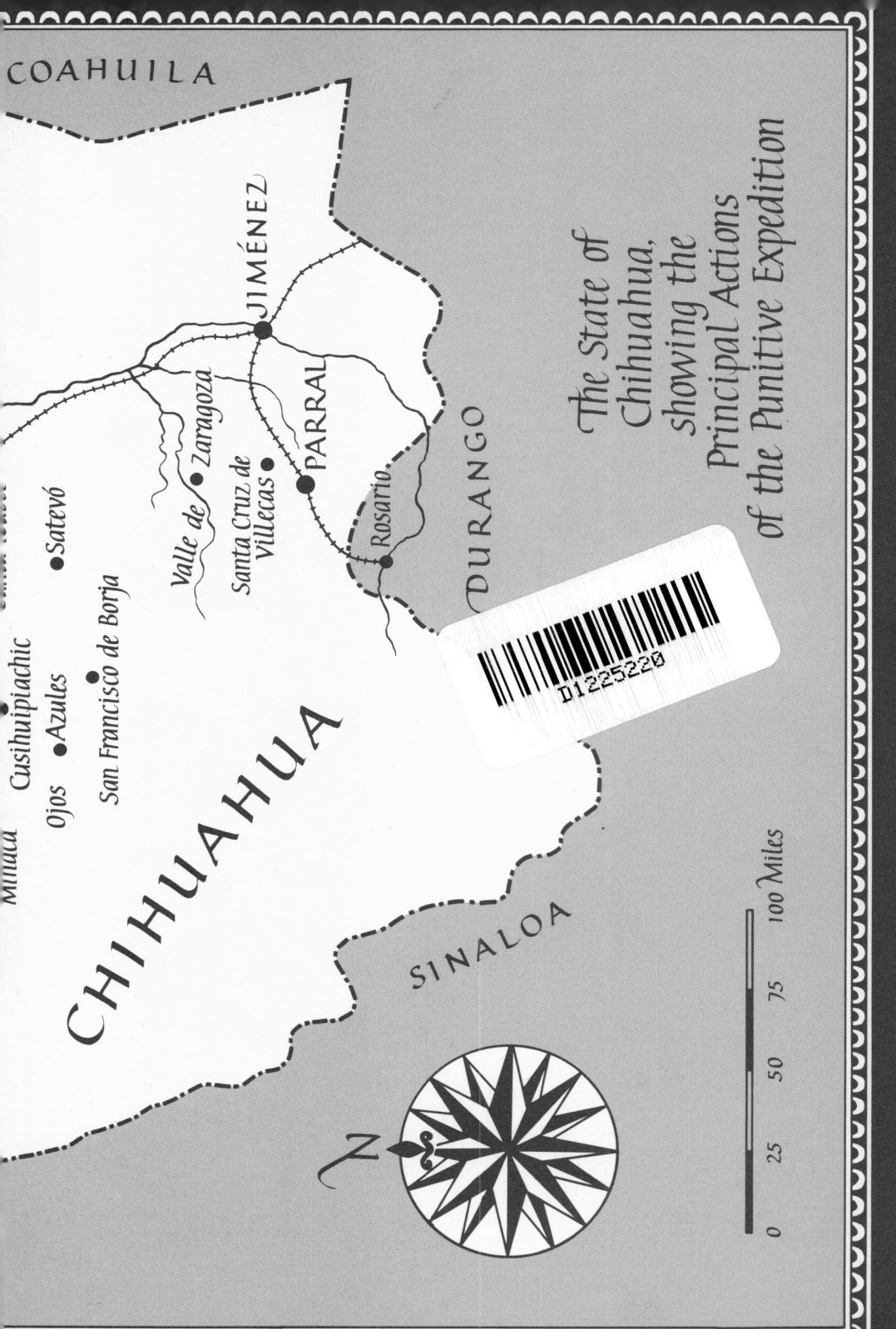

Louis Morton, *General Editor*
DARTMOUTH COLLEGE

VOLUMES PUBLISHED

HISTORY OF THE UNITED STATES ARMY
Russell F. Weigley
TEMPLE UNIVERSITY

FRONTIERSMEN IN BLUE
The United States Army and the Indian, 1848–1865
Robert M. Utley
NATIONAL PARK SERVICE

PRESIDENT WILSON FIGHTS HIS WAR
World War I and the American Intervention
Harvey A. DeWeerd
THE RAND CORPORATION

THE SWORD OF THE REPUBLIC
The United States Army on the Frontier 1783–1846
Francis Paul Prucha
MARQUETTE UNIVERSITY

BLOOD ON THE BORDER
The United States Army and the Mexican Irregulars
Clarence C. Clendenen
HOOVER INSTITUTION ON WAR, REVOLUTION, AND PEACE

VOLUMES IN PREPARATION

THE COLONIAL WARS
Douglas E. Leach
VANDERBILT UNIVERSITY

THE AMERICAN REVOLUTION
Don Higginbotham
LOUISIANA STATE UNIVERSITY

THE WAR OF 1812
R. A. Preston
ROYAL MILITARY COLLEGE OF CANADA
S. F. Wise
QUEENS UNIVERSITY (CANADA)

THE INDIAN WARS 1865–1890
Robert M. Utley
NATIONAL PARK SERVICE

THE MEXICAN WAR
Richard W. Van Alstyne
HENRY E. HUNTINGTON LIBRARY AND ART GALLERY

THE CIVIL WAR
Jay Luvaas
ALLEGHENY COLLEGE

WORLD WAR II (Pacific)
Louis Morton
DARTMOUTH COLLEGE

HISTORY OF AMERICAN MILITARY DOCTRINE
Fred Greene
WILLIAMS COLLEGE

HISTORY OF THE UNITED STATES AIR FORCE
James C. Olson
UNIVERSITY OF NEBRASKA

AMERICAN MILITARY INTERVENTIONS
Annette Baker Fox
INSTITUTE OF WAR AND PEACE STUDIES, COLUMBIA UNIVERSITY

HISTORY OF THE UNITED STATES NAVY
Raymond G. O'Connor
TEMPLE UNIVERSITY

THE SPANISH-AMERICAN WAR
J. A. S. Grenville
UNIVERSITY OF LEEDS
David Trask
STATE UNIVERSITY OF NEW YORK (STONY BROOK)

WORLD WAR II (Europe and Africa)
Hugh M. Cole
RESEARCH ANALYSIS CORPORATION

THE KOREAN WAR
Martin Blumenson

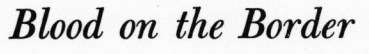
Blood on the Border

Blood on the Border

THE UNITED STATES ARMY
AND THE MEXICAN IRREGULARS

☆ ☆
☆

Clarence C. Clendenen

The Macmillan Company
Collier-Macmillan Ltd., London

Library of Congress Catalog Card Number: 69-11176

First Printing

The Macmillan Company
Collier-Macmillan Canada Ltd., Toronto, Ontario

Printed in the United States of America

Contents

List of Maps

Acknowledgments

THE OBLIGATION TO THANK those who have helped and encouraged one is always pleasant to discharge, but the duty is complicated by the number of those to whom I owe a debt of gratitude. First and foremost, I must mention the Hoover Institution on War, Revolution and Peace, of Stanford University, and express my thanks for a liberal research grant without which my project would have been infinitely more difficult than it was. I owe more than I can readily express to Dr. Thomas A. Bailey, of Stanford University, who read my manuscript, sentence by sentence, and whose suggestions and trenchant criticisms have been priceless. I, and I alone, however, am responsible for inaccuracies, omissions, erroneous statements or faulty conclusions. I am grateful to Señora Luz Corral viuda de Villa, the widow of General Francisco Villa, who graciously gave me a personal interview. With sincere gratitude and appreciation I wish to mention several veterans of the Punitive Expedition of 1916, and other border fights, who have given me freely of their time and brought out incidents and events that are either unrecorded or very scantily mentioned in the records. I am especially grateful to Colonel Charles W. Hoffman, U.S.A.R., Ret., who gave me hours of his time and wrote for me a lengthy memorandum of his experiences in and memories of the Columbus Raid. I am deeply indebted to the Reverend John Jeter, who told me in detail his memories of the Carrizal fight, and also wrote a narrative covering it. Colonel John W. Cotton, U.S.A., Ret., also granted me lengthy interviews, and made available to me his extensive collection of photographs of the Punitive Expedition and the war diary of the First Aero Squadron. I must also mention Leon B. Graves, of Ottawa, Kansas, a young man who has made a hobby of Pancho Villa and has accumulated an extraordinary collection of "Villaiana," which he generously placed at my disposal.

I am grateful, too, to several veterans of the Punitive Expedition and other Mexican-American imbroglios who made available to me materials and sources that might otherwise never have come to light. Particularly, I wish to name the following:

Colonel Carroll A. Bagby, U.S.A., Ret., who related to me his memories of the Punitive Expedition, and loaned me his personal diary;

Colonel Harrison C. Browne, U.S.A., Ret., who recorded for me a great deal of information from his memories of the Expedition;

Dr. Curtis G. Chezem, of Los Alamos, New Mexico, who told me of his experiences in following General Pershing's road into "Pancho Villa Land";

Lieutenant General John B. Coulter, U.S.A., Ret., who, at my request, wrote down his memories of the San Ygnacio fight;

Major General Donald C. Cubbison, U.S.A., Ret., who remembers much unrecorded history of the Punitive Expedition, and who also loaned me his personal diary;

Major General Robert M. Danford, U.S.A., Ret., who knew all about the famous "Yale Battery" in the mobilization of 1916. General Danford was the last Chief of Field Artillery;

Major General Ernest J. Dawley, U.S.A., Ret. who described the motor trains in Mexico;

Dr. Thorne Deuel, of the Illinois State Museum, who prepared a detailed account of his experiences as a second lieutenant in the Punitive Expedition;

Colonel Albert Dockery, U.S.A., Ret., who also told me about the motor trains in Mexico, and other experiences he had there;

Brigadier General Charles C. Drake, U.S.A., Ret., who loaned me his diary covering the Vera Cruz occupation, and his collection of photographs of that episode;

Colonel Geoffrey Galwey, U.S.A., Ret., who related to me his memories of the battle of Juarez, in June, 1919, and also loaned me his extensive collection of documents and photographs concerning that incident;

Colonel Jerome W. Howe, U.S.A., Ret., who loaned me his field diary of the Punitive Expedition, the manuscript of his unpublished memoirs, Colonel Dodd's report, and other papers, and who has evinced a continuing interest in my project;

Colonel Joseph C. King, U.S.A., Ret., who loaned me his personal diary;

Mr. Harry C. Lewis, who wrote, at my request, an account of his experiences as a soldier in the Fifth Cavalry in the Punitive Expedition;

Francis Warren Pershing, who gave me entry into his father's papers in the Library of Congress, with permission to make use of material in them;

Colonel Howard D. Queen, U.S.A.R., Ret., who gave a detailed account of his experiences in the Punitive Expedition, and particularly his memories of the Carrizal fight;

Major General Frank N. Roberts, U.S.A., Ret., who had a copy of his diary made for my use;

Dr. John Rufi, of the University of Missouri, who told me of his experiences as a soldier in the Kansas National Guard on the border;

Major General William Ord Ryan, U.S.A.F., Ret., who gave me his memories of the Punitive Expedition and also let me borrow his diary;

Major George L. Van Norman, U.S.A.R., Ret., who recalled his service as a soldier in the Seventh Cavalry in Mexico and also gave me certain pertinent papers;

Colonel Edwin T. Wheatley, U.S.A., Ret., who gave me an account of his experiences as a soldier of the Kansas National Guard in 1916;

Colonel Otis Wood, U.S.A., Ret., who gave me detailed information about his border service as a soldier in the New Mexico National Guard.

In addition to the foregoing, there are others to whom I must tender my thanks and gratitude:

The Naylor Press, San Antonio, Texas, for permission to use material in Lyman L. Woodman's *Cortina, Rogue of the Rio Grande;*

Colonel H. B. Wharfield, U.S.A.F., Ret., for permission to use materials in his published historical studies, particularly his *10th Cavalary & Border Fights;*

Edmund Wilson, for permission to quote from his autobiography, *A Prelude*, and for information he gave me;

Mrs. Virginia B. Toulmin, for permission to use material in her late husband's book, *With Pershing in Mexico;*

The Stackpole Company, Harrisburg, Pennsylvania, for permission to use the maps and other material in Colonel Frank Tompkins' book, *Chasing Villa;*

Tex Roberts and the editors of *New Mexico Magazine*, for photographs of Columbus, New Mexico, as it is today;

The Northland Press, Flagstaff, Arizona, and the late Mrs. Turbesé Lummis Fiske, for permission to use material in *General Crook and the Apache Wars*, edited by Mrs. Fiske. I am also indebted to Mrs. Fiske for calling my attention to pertinent material in her father's work, *The Land of Poco Tiempo;*

The Ames Publishing Company and Dr. Curtis Chezem for photographs and material published in *The Four Wheeler;*

The editors of the *Dodge News Magazine* for photographs of Dodge cars in the Punitive Expedition;

Major General Frederick Gilbreath, U.S.A., Ret., for permission to use information in personal correspondence that has passed between us;

Last to be mentioned, but far from least, I must acknowledge my indebtedness to Egon Weiss, the librarian of the United States Military Academy, West Point, New York. Mr. Weiss called my attention to the unpublished memoirs of the late Major General Charles D. Rhodes and allowed me to borrow the Military Academy's copy. In addition, he obtained for me photographs of Captain Charles T. Boyd and 1st Lieutenant Henry R. Adair, with biographical material on both, and has given me other items of assistance too numerous to specify.

If I have failed to mention anyone to whom I owe a debt of gratitude, I can plead only that it was unintentional, and beg for forgiveness. My thanks to all who have helped and encouraged me.

¡Hasta luego!

CLARENCE C. CLENDENEN

Introduction

THE PUNITIVE EXPEDITION of 1916 and the intervention by American forces in the battle of Juárez in June, 1919, when General Francisco Villa made his last bid for power in Mexico, were the climax of a long series of undeclared "brush-fire" wars that had continued, with occasional peaceful intervals, from before the Civil War. For the greater part of the period between 1848 and 1920 the northern part of Mexico and the southwestern part of the United States were a region that was sparsely populated and far from well explored. It was a wilderness in which frequently the only law was the law of the musket and six-shooter. The borderland was a country haunted by outlaws, both Mexican and American, and often ravaged by bands of Indians of half a dozen tribes, who raided into the United States from Mexico, then sought refuge in Mexico, or raided from the United States into Mexico and then fled northward with their captives and loot.

General Pershing's Punitive Expedition was soon so overshadowed by the entry of the United States into World War I that historians have given it scant attention, and most of those who grant it a few sentences, or a paragraph or two, are amazingly misinformed about it. As for the score or more of smaller expeditions into Mexico from the United States, in pursuit of marauding Indians or bandits, apparently the only historians who are aware that such operations occurred are those whose interests are purely local and antiquarian.

Yet the operations of small American forces in northern Mexico on numerous occasions constitute a phase of our military history that is well worth rescuing. Because they were contemporary with the spectacular Indian wars of the Northern Plains, they attracted relatively little public attention at the time. Their story offers no major battle, such as the battle of Wounded Knee or Miles's final encounter with Chief Joseph and the Nez Percé warriors, and includes no major disaster such as the Custer debacle. Nevertheless, the minor warfare in the borderlands against hostile Indians and equally hostile Mexican raiders entailed as much care and thought in preparation, was accompanied by as much hardship, and involved as much heroism as the better known campaigns farther north. The Mexican border, like the Mexican War of 1846–48, was a school in which many of the military leaders of later years gained experience, made reputations, and in some instances received their first introduction to active service. To mention only a few, Captain George Stoneman became a major general and Chief of Cavalry in the Army of the Potomac less than three years after the Cortina campaign. In the campaigns against the Apaches in the Sierra Madre of Chihuahua, captains Adna R. Chaffee and Henry W. Lawton demonstrated those military qualities that carried them to high command in Cuba and the Philippines, and the borderland was the first campaigning school for 2d Lieutenant John J. Pershing and Assistant Surgeon Leonard Wood.

A military history written from the point of view of a participant nation is necessarily one-sided; it cannot be completely objective regarding the enemy. It is a reconstruction of preparations for combat, or approaches toward combat, and of combat itself. Such a reconstruction includes characters and personalities, especially those of key leaders, along with their decisions and actions and their reasons for those decisions and actions. The commander of a military unit, whether he be an army commander with a huge headquarters and a score of divisions, or a corporal leading a squad, must base his decisions upon the information he actually has at a given moment—not upon what a scholar or historian may know half a century later. His information and beliefs about the enemy may be, and often are, erroneous, but, nevertheless, those beliefs are what determine his decision. Hence, I make no apology for having cited very few Mexican sources but I have endeavored to show, as far as possible, the basis upon which American commanders on the border formed their decisions.

This brief statement of my own attitude toward military history is in no way intended to be a rationalization of its being very difficult, in fact, virtually impossible, for an American to obtain firsthand information regarding events and activities "on the other side of the hill." Mexicans, for some reason or other, are reluctant to discuss border events with Americans. Of many letters I addressed to Villista veterans whose names and addresses I was able to obtain, only one received a reply, and that was to the effect that the questions I asked would require study. As for Mexican historians, they tend, like their American counterparts, to ignore or give a minimum of attention to border events. Thus, the Punitive Expedition of 1916 was nothing more than a disagreeable, but very minor, incident in the epic of the Mexican Revolution. Earlier American expeditions across the international boundary are either ignored or considered merely as illustrations of the gringo's aggressive imperialism and his ruthless disregard of Mexican national sovereignty.

I realize that I have included in my narrative a great deal of detail, much of which, at first glance, may seem to be trivial. The numerous expeditions into Mexico were composed of small units. Only rarely was an organization as large as a regiment involved, and not until 1916 was a force of any considerable size sent across the boundary. The borderland campaigns were fought by platoons, troops, companies, and only occasionally by battalions or squadrons. No weighty tactical or strategic problems were involved. The history of the frontier wars is a history of small units, and of the conduct and adventures of individual officers and soldiers. It is my contention that the story of the American soldier and individual officer is an important part of our military history. Only by stress upon detail can later generations see the trials, tribulations, hopes, fears, heroism and (it must be admitted) occasional misconduct of the American soldier—the soldier as he really was.

I regret that it was impossible for me to emulate a certain distinguished historian who visits every place that he expects to mention. I was already familiar, however, with much of the borderland from the region of the Lower Rio Grande Valley to the desert areas of southwestern Arizona, and I was able to make a broad survey of the country in which the Punitive Expedition of 1916 operated, and of the country in which General Crook pursued Geronimo. Of the latter, if I may be permitted a moment of facetiousness, I can say that it was not strange that an occasional pack mule fell off the trail, to be dashed to its death hundreds of feet below; the real marvel is how General Crook's packers got the mules onto the trail to start with.

I hope that my effort may contribute, if even in a small degree, to bringing to light some of the achievements of American soldiers who, over many years, sweltered, froze, marched, rode, fought and often died in the borderlands—forgotten American soldiers whose lives and careers are epitomized by a crude inscription on a tombstone in the old cemetery at Fort Clark, Texas:

> Oh pray for the soldier,
> You kind-hearted stranger;
> He has roamed the prairie for many a year.
> He had kept the Comanches away from your ranches,
> And followed them over the Texas frontier.

Stanford, California
April, 1968

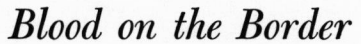

Blood on the Border

CHAPTER 1

The Background
and Beginning — the 1850s

I T SEEMS TO BE a law of history, or of human interrelationships, that when two peoples of widely differing cultural traditions and technological development come into contact with each other, they are mutually hostile for a long time. Consequently, the borderlands between different people are the historic scenes of violence and disorder; this is especially true when social conditions are primitive, where accidents of geography lend themselves to raid and retaliation and where there are few natural obstacles to limit the movements of raiders from either side. One has only to cite the long and violent history of the border between English and Scots, between Germans and Slavs, and between Spaniards and Muslims, in support of the statement. A modern example is found in South Africa, where the juxtaposition of Briton and Boer, and of both with the Bantu tribes, produced a century of bloodshed and disorder. In such regions violence ceases only after populations have increased and governments with power enough to enforce order have come into existence.[1]

Although the borderlands between the United States and Mexico do not offer a history as bloody as that of many similar regions of the world, they provide no exception to the rule. From the time, early in the nineteenth century, when Americans and Mexicans first came into contact with each other, until very recent times, the vast country lying on both sides of the international boundary, for two thousand miles from the Gulf of Mexico to the Pacific Ocean, has been the haunt of freebooters, filibusters and robbers, the scene of raids by Indians, and the field of undeclared wars and unrecorded battles. It has been the cause and source of endless disputes that brought the two nations to open war once, and to the verge of war many times. In its vastness American and Mexican soldiers have fought against each other, and have fought side by side against common enemies.

The term "Mexican Border" comprises far more than the sharp and arbitrary line delineating the political authority of the two governments. The international boundary, the Rio Grande from its mouth to a point a few miles above El Paso, and from there an imaginary line extending to the Pacific Ocean, is purely artificial. The "Border" includes the regions lying on both sides of the line; the borderlands are a region with a peculiar unity of their own, despite the dissimilarity of the populations on each side. In fact, along the Rio Grande the Mexican and American people are bound together, rather than separated by the river. On both sides they are mutually dependent upon the Rio Grande for their agriculture and a score of other necessities. Mexican and United States communities lie in pairs—Brownsville and Matamoras, Laredo and Nuevo Laredo, Eagle Pass and Piedras Negras, Del Rio and Villa Acuña, El Paso and Juarez. The pairs actually form closely connected, integrated communities, regardless of the political division between them. The signers of the Treaty of Guadalupe Hidalgo, in 1848, ending the only formal war fought between the two countries, did not know the Rio Grande well. They probably envisioned a deep, slowly flowing river with a fairly stable main channel, such as the rivers of Europe and the eastern part of the United States. They did not envision a brawling mountain torrent, two thousand miles long, that was likely to change its main channel with every spring flood, and at other times could be forded at so many places that nobody, even to this day, has ever found it possible to describe and enumerate them. In short, the Rio Grande is not an obstacle or barrier; it is a political boundary, and nothing more.

From El Paso westward to the Pacific the international boundary is even more arbitrary, artificial and undistinguishable. Marked by a series of stone monuments, in some places it is indicated by a high, tight "cyclone fence." In other places it is

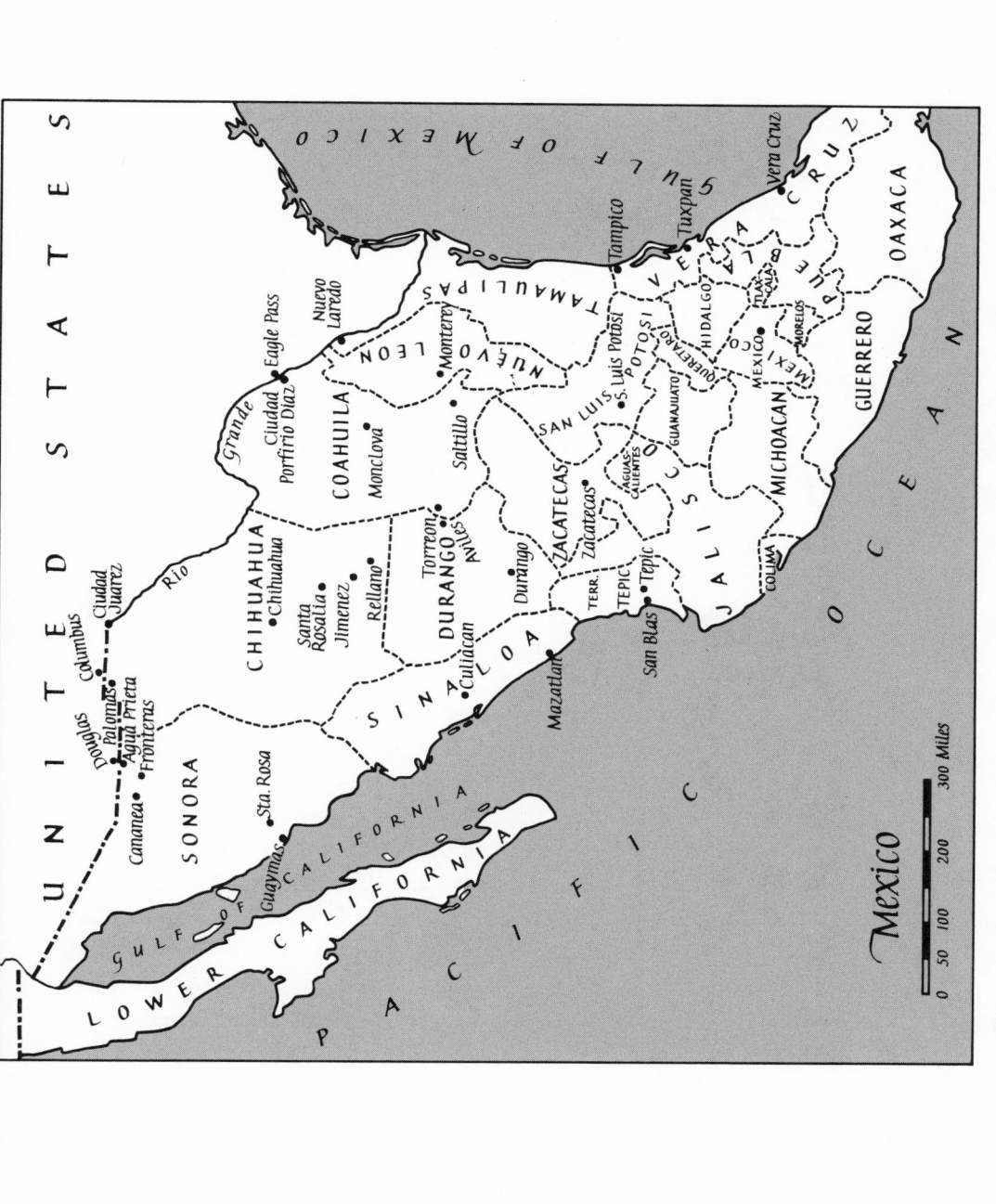

UNITED STATES

GULF OF MEXICO

Vera Cruz

VERA CRUZ

Tampico

Tuxpan

TAMAULIPAS

Eagle Pass

Nuevo Laredo

Ciudad Porfirio Diaz

NUEVO LEON

Monterrey

COAHUILA

Monclova

Saltillo

Grande

Rio

Ciudad Juarez

Columbus

Douglas

Palomas

Agua Prieta

Fronteras

Cananea

CHIHUAHUA

Chihuahua

Santa Rosalia

Jimenez

Rellano

Torreon

Aviles

DURANGO

Durango

Culiacan

SAN LUIS POTOSI

S. Luis Potosi

POTOSI

QUERETARO

HIDALGO

GUANAJUATO

AGUAS CALIENTES

ZACATECAS

Zacatecas

MEXICO

MORELOS

TLAX.

CO

PUEBLA

OAXACA

GUERRERO

MICHOACAN

JALISCO

COLIMA

TEPIC

Tepic

TERR.

San Blas

Mazatlan

SINALOA

SONORA

Sta. Rosa

Guaymas

GULF OF CALIFORNIA

LOWER CALIFORNIA

PACIFIC OCEAN

Mexico

0   50 100   200   300 Miles

shown by an ordinary barbed-wire fence such as farmers and ranchers use between their fields and pastures. In still other places there is not even a wire fence—nothing but the somewhat inconspicuous stone monuments, two or three miles apart.[2] As is so along the Rio Grande, the Mexican and American communities tend to be social and economic units, twin towns lying athwart the boundary—Douglas, Arizona, and Agua Prieta, Sonora; Naco, Arizona, and Naco, Sonora; Nogales, Arizona, and Nogales, Sonora; Calexico, California, and Mexicali, Baja California.

From El Paso westward the borderland is largely desert, or semidesert, but it includes areas of rich agricultural land and enormous stretches of grazing country. It is mineral rich, and its mines and smelters have been important ever since the first Spanish explorers and conquistadores penetrated the region.

It was in the Lower Rio Grande Valley, however, that the first clashes between Americans and Mexicans occurred after the Mexican War and the Treaty of Guadalupe Hidalgo. Before the Mexican War, Mexico had consistently refused to recognize the independence of Texas, and after the annexation of Texas by the United States, the broad strip of territory between the Rio Grande and the Nueces was disputed land—a no man's land with neither government exercising any effective jurisdiction. But when the outcome of the Mexican War gave the United States (and the state of Texas) a clear title to the region, it still remained for many years a region in which there was little effective enforcement of the law. The area, however, began to attract settlers; commerce with Mexico became profitable, and a number of small towns sprang into existence on the United States side of the river. Brownsville, Edinburg, Rio Grande City, Eagle Pass and a dozen or so other hamlets, dignified by the title of city or town, were founded and began to prosper from the traffic to and from Mexico. In addition to the native Mexican inhabitants of the region (who became United States citizens as a result of the Mexican War), the population was augmented during the 1850s by numbers of Mexicans of all classes, from the elite to the humble *pelado*, who sought refuge from the almost continuous civil war that wracked their country at the time.[3] Considerable numbers of Americans also established ranches, built homes, branded the wild cattle and constructed corrals and fences.

It should not be supposed that annexation by the United States and the establishment of jurisdiction by the state of Texas made the Lower Rio Grande Valley a region of law and order. Officers of the law were few and far between on both sides of the boundary. The sparseness of the population and the almost impenetrable jungle of chaparral made the Lower Valley a natural haven for scoundrels and desperadoes of both nations. The character of a considerable part of the American population was recorded by a young French missionary priest, Abbé Emanuel Domenech, in the early 1850s, as he made his pastoral way along the river: "The Americans of the Texian frontiers are, for the most part, the very scum of society—bankrupts, escaped criminals, old volunteers, who after the Treaty of Guadulupe [sic] Hidalgo, came into a country protected by nothing that could be called judicial authority, to seek adventure and illicit gains."[4] The Abbé was strongly prejudiced against Americans, but even so, his unflattering description contains grains of truth. He added: "On the frontiers of Texas, where human life is valued little, the inhabitants have little personal protection except in their arms. Hence, they always go armed."[5] The Abbé was also impressed (not too favorably) by the sheriff of Brownsville, who sometimes returned to Brownsville and reported that the culprit he had pursued had resisted arrest, or attempted to escape.

Abbé Domenech visited all the towns and settlements on both sides of the Lower Rio Grande during his sojourn in America. He described the new settlement at Rio Grande City as a "vast assemblage of American stores and Mexican huts, where smuggling progresses on an extensive scale."[6] He believed that unscrupulous American merchants were amassing immense fortunes from the inability of the Mexican government to enforce its own revenue laws, and he was particularly incensed at the severity with which the Irish Catholic soldiers of the nearby United States garrison (Ringgold Barracks) were treated. He ascribed this severity to anti-Catholic prejudice of the Protestant officers, not realizing that what he saw and heard were the disciplinary practices of all armies at that time.

In addition to outlaws, blood feuds and similar features of life on the Border in the 1850s, there was another major complication. The thick chaparral gave cover and concealment to Indians, some of them native to the region, others traveling great distances, intent upon loot and scalps. The isolated ranches and farms, the tiny settlements, the lonely roads and trails, all made Indian attacks easy and defense and retaliation difficult, especially when the Indians discovered that American soldiers would not pursue them south of the river, or Mexican soldiers to the north of it.

Throughout the nineteenth century the protection of the frontier was the major and most important mission of the United States Army, except for rare major emergencies, such as the Mexican War and the Civil War. The annexation of Texas and the acquisition of enormous additional territories as a result of the Mexican War added immeasurably to the Army's duties and difficulties. Predatory tribes with which Americans were previously unacquainted, inhabiting country that was largely unexplored, suddenly became the responsibility of the United States. Thousands and thousands of square miles of new territory had to be explored; emigrants swarming into the new west, especially after the discovery of gold in California, needed protection.

Before the Mexican War the United States Army never exceeded 10,000 men and was usually below that figure. In 1842, for example, it consisted of 9,847 soldiers and 781 officers. Although the Regular Army was expanded during the Mexican War, Congress made haste to reduce it to its prewar strength as soon as peace was proclaimed in 1848. "Economy" was the watchword of the day, and Representative Robert Toombs, of Georgia, even went so far as to say the the country neither needed nor wanted a Regular Army. "When we shut the doors of the temple of Janus," he thundered with the classical allusion so dear to the orators of the time, "we ought to strip off the epaulets from every man in the Republic, to put the soldiers to work, and let the officers return to their other employments."[7] Toombs hoped that the House of Representatives would vote to disband the Regular Army; freemen, he said, do not want to be defended by mercenaries; they would rather defend themselves—a dogma that would have surprised the freemen of the frontiers, who much preferred tending their herds and tilling their fields to spending their days fighting Indians or outlaws.

Congress was intent upon reducing the army to its former strength but was not ready to do away with soldiers altogether, in spite of Toombs and others who regarded a permanent force as unnecessary. To save on the purchase of forage and animals, some mounted troops were dismounted, and others were disbanded. The new regiments that had been formed during the war were abolished, and in the old units that were retained, an executive order limited the number of men authorized in each company. By the end of 1848 the United States Army was a bit below its prewar strength, with 9,106 soldiers. The number of officers remained about the same, between seven and eight hundred.[8]

For some time, after "gold fever" struck the country, it was difficult to maintain the army even at the modest figure fixed by Congress. Among the troops stationed in California, the percentage of desertions reached staggering figures. In spite of such handicaps and difficulties, the army nevertheless continued conscientiously to endeavor to perform its duties, covering the frontiers (nearly a hundred posts and stations), escorting exploring and mapping parties of the Corps of Topographical Engineers, and fighting Indians. Fights with Indians were almost a daily occurrence, so commonplace that it is probable that many small skirmishes were never reported. As an illustration of those that were recorded, on May 10, 1854, Brigadier General Persifor F. Smith, then commanding the Department of Texas, reported an attack on a government wagon train twelve miles from Fort Ewell. Sergeant Byrne, "a gallant and good soldier," was killed, pierced by several arrows. Two men were missing, probably killed in the chaparral, and Lieutenant Blake Cosby was badly wounded in the "sword arm." At almost the same time, in a fight near Fort Inge, Texas, Captain Michael E. Van Buren was so dangerously wounded that the surgeon doubted that he could recover.[9]

These two instances are typical, not only of the Texas frontier, but of the entire vast area of the West where white men were impinging upon the Indians' hunting grounds. As an example of other duties the United States Army was called upon to perform, there was an exploration carried out by Brevet Second Lieutenant William Holding Echols, of the Topographical Engineers. In June, 1860, he was ordered to make a survey of the "Camanche [*sic*] Trail" in western Texas, select a site for a military post commanding the trail, and mark a route for a road by which the post could be supplied. He left San Antonio on June 11 with a small escort. At Camp Hudson his escort and party were increased to thirty-one men, including soldiers, herders and camel drivers. For transportation, in addition to saddle animals, he had twenty camels and fifteen packmules. Two months later, in August, the party staggered into Fort Davis, the men drawn and haggard from hardship and thirst, barefooted, in rags, and even the camels suffering from lack of water. One man was missing; he had strayed out of the bivouac one evening and was never seen again. But Lieutenant Echols had accomplished his mission.[10]

In its efforts to cover the entire frontier in the early 1850s, the army frequently resembled a man who is trying to be in two or three places at once. Some of the marches and other troop movements were astonishing. The Regiment of Mounted Rifles, reorganized at Fort Leavenworth after the Mexican War, marched at once to Oregon, and within a few months from Oregon to Texas. Four companies of the 1st and 2d Dragoons marched from the Lower Rio Grande Valley to California. These marches were not made over roads; they were through country that was largely unexplored. There were no supply depots, and no one knew in advance where the next water would be found. A military organization on the march in the Far West had to carry the bulk of its necessities and depend upon the country, the ingenuity of officers and men and pure luck for everything else.

Aside from unavoidable hardship and the ever-present danger from Indians, troop movements often entailed other perils. More than two hundred men and officers of the 3d Artillery, en route to California via the long voyage around Cape Horn, were drowned when their ship was wrecked on Cape Hatteras. The 4th Infantry, going to California by way of Panama, lost more than a hundred men from cholera before reaching San Francisco.[11]

The frontier posts where the bulk of the army was stationed were often primitive in the extreme. Frederick Law Olmsted (or Olmstead), visiting briefly at Fort Inge, Texas, in 1855 or 1856, noted that the buildings were all very rough and temporary; many of the officers' quarters were mere *jacales*, built of sticks and mud. But in spite of the nature of the post the amenities were as carefully observed as though the "commander-in-chief" were looking on, and the conversation in the officers' mess showed that the officers had a "cultivation belonging to a more brilliant position."[12]

It soon became apparent to Congress that the government was demanding the impossible of an army of fewer than 10,000 men. In 1850 Congress authorized the President to increase the number of men in each company, at his discretion. This would result in a strength of approximately 13,000 men; however, the actual increase was slow. There is always a lag between authorized strength and effective strength, and California gold was attractive to everyone who could go there. Even a year or so later, when something approaching 13,000 men had been enlisted, the force was still inadequate for its tasks. In 1855, spurred by the Secretary of War, Jefferson Davis, and undoubtedly, also, by frontier constituents (who did not know that they did not want to be defended by "mercenaries"), Congress authorized two regiments of cavalry and two new regiments of infantry. This brought the theoretical strength of the army to some 17,000 men.[13]

Throughout the period between the Mexican and Civil wars, an almost disproportionate part of the army was stationed in Texas and the adjacent parts of New Mexico. The disposition of troops in Texas, however, bore no relation to Mexico. Most of the Texas garrisons were north and west of the settled parts of the state, an argument that requires a brief explanation for the sake of clarifying later events.

The introduction of the horse into the regions of the Great Plains produced a revolution in the habits and ways of life of the Plains tribes. Becoming superb horsemen of almost unbelievable mobility, they found an easy and fertile source of loot, scalps, prisoners and glory in the scantily defended settlements and towns of northern Mexico. There are abundant indications that such raids were frequent in Colonial times, before the Plains Indians had any contact with Americans. As the nineteenth century progressed, the westward expansion of the American people, including the settlement of Texas, began to restrict the range in which the Plains Indians could move and hunt buffalo—their staff of life. The colonization of the eastern tribes in what became the Indian Territory further narrowed the domain in which the nomads could move freely, and caused them more and more to extend their operations southward. All of the Plains tribes were affected, but the most numerous and warlike, who led the way in raiding, were the Comanches. In 1873, when relations between the United States and Mexico were critical, the Mexican government appointed a Committee of Investigation, which found that "the Comanches and Apaches never showed so much energy in evil-doing as was observable from 1836 onwards. . . ."[14] In 1840 "thousands of savages" irrupted into the state of Zacatecas, supposedly killing hundreds of victims and destroying *haciendas* and villages. In sixteen years the little city of Miers was raided no less than twenty times. In fact, the Mexican Commission attributed *all* Indian raids to tribes and bands from the United States and ascribed the increase in such incursions to the Indians' being able to dispose of horses and other loot at Bent's Fort and other frontier trading posts.

This was the Mexican side of the picture. On the other hand, the Americans claimed that great bands of Comanches and other warriors established themselves in Mexico, with the full knowledge of Mexican officials, and from Mexican bases raided into Texas and New Mexico, murdering, burning, and gathering loot, which they sold readily to the *hacendados* and merchants of Mexico. It is not unlikely that both versions are true. The Indians were quite impartial about where they obtained their loot and equally impartial about where they disposed of it—wherever they could get the greatest return for it.

But regardless of conflicting American and Mexican claims,

the fact is clear that the movement of bands of savages from the north and west of the settled portions of Texas, all of them bent on scalps and plunder, made Texas an extremely critical military zone. Under the Treaty of Guadalupe Hidalgo the United States was bound to prevent incursions of Indians from north of the Rio Grande into Mexico—a provision that was abrogated in 1852 because of the complete impossibility of carrying it out. At the same time it was the recognized duty of the army to protect the ranches and settlements that were multiplying on the Texas frontier. Thus, in 1852, when the army's effective strength was less than 10,000, 2,300 were in the Department of Texas. Of these, however, less than 600 were at the border posts on the Rio Grande. The remainder, almost 2,000, were scattered in stations on a perimeter covering the northern and western frontiers of the state.[15] After the army was augmented in 1855, the same proportion was maintained. In that year there were 3,449 officers and soldiers in Texas, of which only 1,364 were at the border stations.[16]

It is obvious that the "high command" of the Department of Texas did not anticipate any serious trouble from the direction of Mexico. The danger that caused real concern was from the north and west. The troops were deployed facing in the direction from which trouble was anticipated.

Because such a large fraction of the United States Army was in Texas, and Texas was a danger area, it was the policy of the War Department to assign that command to an officer of high rank and demonstrated ability. For several years the department commander was Brevet Brigadier General Persifor F. Smith. He was succeeded in the late 1850s by Brevet Major General David E. Twiggs. Twiggs was a veteran of the War of 1812 and had been in every war waged by the United States since that time. In the Mexican War he had commanded a division with conspicuous success and had been noted for his undeviating loyalty to General Winfield Scott in the conspiracies and political cabals that threatened the success of the expedition. He was rewarded with the brevet rank of major general and was made one of the two substantive brigadier generals the army was authorized to have.[17] Although Twiggs was almost seventy years old (there were no retirement laws before the Civil War), he was widely known as a tough, determined and fearless commander who was also something of a martinet. Among the soldiers he was known by two distinctive and descriptive nicknames, "The Old Horse" and "The Bengal Tiger." Despite his record and his unquestionable abilities, when he became the commanding general of the Department of Texas, his age was a handicap. He no longer had the physical vigor to take the field personally or exercise personal supervision over the execution of his orders; he was compelled to view affairs through the eyes of his subordinates and consequently did not always get a clear picture of a situation.[18]

Throughout 1858 and the early part of 1859, all indications seemed to point toward increased aggressiveness by the Comanches and other Plains tribes. There was a report of a large band of Comanches who had established themselves in Chihuahua, but if the report was true, it could be no more than a small fraction of the tribe. Twiggs obviously did not anticipate any serious danger from that direction. Mexico, moreover, was torn asunder by the Three Years' War between the clerical and anticlerical factions—a rift that was to result in French intervention and Maximilian's empire. The real problem for Texas, it seemed clear, was from the Plains Indians, and the solution of that problem lay in a succession of heavy blows struck into the very heart of their home country, in the region of the Llano Estacado and to the north. But to strike such blows effectively required more troops than Twiggs had available in his northern and western garrisons.

To assemble enough troops to bring the hostile tribes to terms without leaving other parts of the frontier exposed and helpless was impossible. In 1858 the General-in-Chief, Winfield Scott, stated to the Secretary of War: "The want of troops to give reasonable security to our citizens in distant settlements . . . can scarcely be too strongly stated; but I will only add, that as often as we have been obliged to withdraw troops from one frontier in order to reinforce another, the weakened points have been instantly attacked or threatened with formidable invasion."[19] In 1859 the entire United States Army was committed. A large force was immobilized in Utah, where the Mormons had threatened revolt; troops were required in Kansas to keep Abolitionists and pro-slavery men from killing each other, and in the Northwest the tribes were restless and uneasy. In all the United States there were no troops available to reinforce the Department of Texas, although General Scott promised Twiggs to try to get two additional squadrons of cavalry for him. To gain the troops necessary for an invasion of the Indian country, Twiggs would have to "rob Peter to pay Paul." The only troops with which he could reinforce his frontier forces were those in the relatively quiet region of the Lower Rio Grande.

In January, 1859, Twiggs and Scott conferred together at New Orleans, and on the thirteenth Twiggs submitted a formal proposal requesting permission to abandon Fort Brown, Ringgold Barracks and Fort McIntosh. With the troops thus gained, he would increase the garrison at Fort Duncan (at Eagle Pass) and establish several small infantry posts along the mail route to El Paso. He would concentrate the greater part of his infantry at Camp Cooper, a central point from which forces could be moved readily to any threatened point on the frontier. He would concentrate his mounted troops at Camp Radziminski, in the Indian Territory, where they would be the striking force.[20]

Scott approved everything that Twiggs suggested. As soon as Twiggs returned to his headquarters at San Antonio, he issued his orders, and within a few days the troops were on the march. Not only were the posts on the Lower Rio Grande abandoned, but he also removed the garrisons of Forts Belknap, Mason and McKavett, on the western frontier, to gain more power for his striking forces.[21]

Of course, these posts were not abandoned without most vehement protests from local inhabitants, who immediately bombarded Washington with petitions in which they related, with grim detail, some of the incidents that had recently occurred. But Twiggs, having made his dispositions, could not make any eleventh hour changes; moreover, from his long experience, he was inclined to attribute local protests to merchants, liquor dealers and brothel keepers, who were anxious to retain the soldiers' pay, rather than from any real fear of danger. Twiggs remained adamant, and the summer of 1859 found the entire Lower Rio Grande denuded of United States soldiers.

NOTES

1. See John S. Galbraith, *Reluctant Empire. British Policy on the South African Frontier, 1834–1854* (Berkeley and Los Angeles, 1963), *passim*.

2. In the nineteenth century there was probably not a single piece of fencing to indicate the boundary. Although from each monument the two adjacent are supposed to be visible, many of them are hard to locate and see. As recently as the 1920s, when the writer, as a new second lieutenant on border duty, marched from one station to another, the road over which troops of both nations marched zigzagged from one side of the line to the other, so that United States troops spent much of their marching time on Mexican soil, and vice versa. No one gave the matter a thought, although there was considerable tension between the two countries at the time.

3. One of the favorite charges made by embittered Texans was that Mexico gave refuge to runaway slaves and refused to return them; Mexican *hacendados* asserted vehemently that their *peons* fled to Texas and Texas officials refused to return them.

4. Abbé Emanuel Domenech, *Missionary Adventures in Texas and Mexico. A Personal Narrative of Six Years' Sojourn in Those Regions* (London, 1858), p. 228.

5. *Ibid.*, p. 231.

6. *Ibid.*, pp. 267–68.

7. *Congressional Globe*, 30th Cong., 1st sess., Aug. 4, 1849, p. 1035.

8. Annual Report of the Secretary of War, Nov. 30, 1848, 30th Cong., 2nd sess., H.R. Exec. Doc. No. 1, p. 184b, Serial No. 537.

9. Report of Bvt. Maj. Gen. Persifor F. Smith, May 10, 1854, Annual Report of the Secretary of War, Dec. 4, 1854, 33rd Cong., 2nd sess., H.R. Exec. Doc. No. 1, p. 28. Lt. George Blake Cosby was later chief of staff to General Buckner at Fort Donelson. Captain Michael Van Buren was said to be a relative of President Van Buren. He died at Corpus Christi a few days later.

10. Annual Report of the Secretary of War, Dec. 3, 1860, 36th Cong., 2nd sess., Exec. Doc. [no number], pp. 34–50.

11. William Addleman Ganoe, *The History of the United States Army* (New York and London, 1924), pp. 234–35.

12. Frederick Law Olmsted, *A Journey Through Texas; or a Saddle-Trip on the Southwestern Frontier: with a Statistical Appendix* (New York, 1857), pp. 285–86.

13. This is the first appearance of "cavalry" in the United States Army since the War of 1812. Of the three existing mounted regiments, two were designated as "dragoons" and one as "mounted rifles." They were not regarded as cavalry, even though they were "horse soldiers."

14. *Reports of the Committee of Investigation Sent in 1873 by the Mexican Government to the Frontier of Texas* (New York, 1875), pp. 250, 260. See also Ernest Wallace and E. Adamson Hoebel, *The Comanches, Lords of the South Plains* (Norman, Okla., 1952), p. 13.

15. Annual Report of the Secretary of War, Dec. 2, 1852, 32nd Cong., 1st sess., Senate Exec. Doc. No. 1, pp. 200–203. The posts covering the Lower Rio Grande were Fort Brown, Ringgold Barracks, Fort McIntosh, Fort Duncan and Fort Inge. Fort Clark was added in the middle of the decade, and Fort Inge was abandoned shortly before the Civil War. Forts Brown, Ringgold, McIntosh and Clark were maintained and garrisoned until the end of World War II.

16. Annual Report of the Secretary of War, Dec. 3, 1855, 34th Cong., 1st sess., Senate Exec. Doc. No. 1, pp. 131, 136–37.

17. See the *Dictionary of American Biography*. In the days when medals and decorations were regarded as out of place in a republic, brevet rank was customarily awarded for military distinction. Brevet rank was purely honorary and entitled the recipient to wear the insignia of, and be addressed by, the title of the brevet grade, but carried no right of command or increased pay. Brevet rank was abolished several years after the Civil War, because, according to legend, command and authority were thoroughly confused by lieutenants wearing the stars of general officers but under the orders of officers carrying only captain's bars or major's leaves.

18. General Twiggs's reputation has suffered because of his unresisting surrender of his department to the Secessionists in 1861. He became at once the senior major general in the Confederate Army but, because of his age, took no active part in the war.

19. Annual Report of the Secretary of War, 1858, 35th Cong., 2nd sess., H.R. Exec. Doc. No. 2, p. 761.

20. Message of the President of the United States, communicating information on "Difficulties on Southwestern Frontier," 36th Cong., 1st sess., H.R. Exec. Doc. No. 2, p. 761.

21. *Ibid.*, pp. 7–8.

CHAPTER 2

"Robin Hood" on the Rio Grande

FOLLOWING THE WAR between Mexico and the United States, Mexico was in a more or less constant state of internal turmoil. Changes in government were accomplished by force; "elections" merely confirmed and added a touch of legality to the results of revolutions. Many military commanders were, in actual fact, independent *caudillos*, giving allegiance to the central government in Mexico City only when it suited them to do so, and obeying only those laws and decrees that promised them personal advantages. The farther from the capital, the more likely this was to be true; hence in the border states governors were overthrown or established themselves in office without any regard to the national government. To complicate matters, in the 1850s efforts to reform the national constitution and break the death grip of the church on Mexican politics resulted in a deep cleavage that split the Mexican people into two bitterly hostile factions and developed into a savagely fought civil war that eventually brought European intervention.

In the borderlands, even though there were innumerable instances in which Mexicans and Americans formed warm personal friendships, there was, in general, a deep hostility between the two peoples. This was a natural outcome of the Texas revolt and the Mexican War, in which Mexico lost vast areas of her national territory. The mass of the Mexican people regarded Americans with dislike and suspicion, believing that the gringos were only biding their time to seize more of the Mexican patrimony. On the

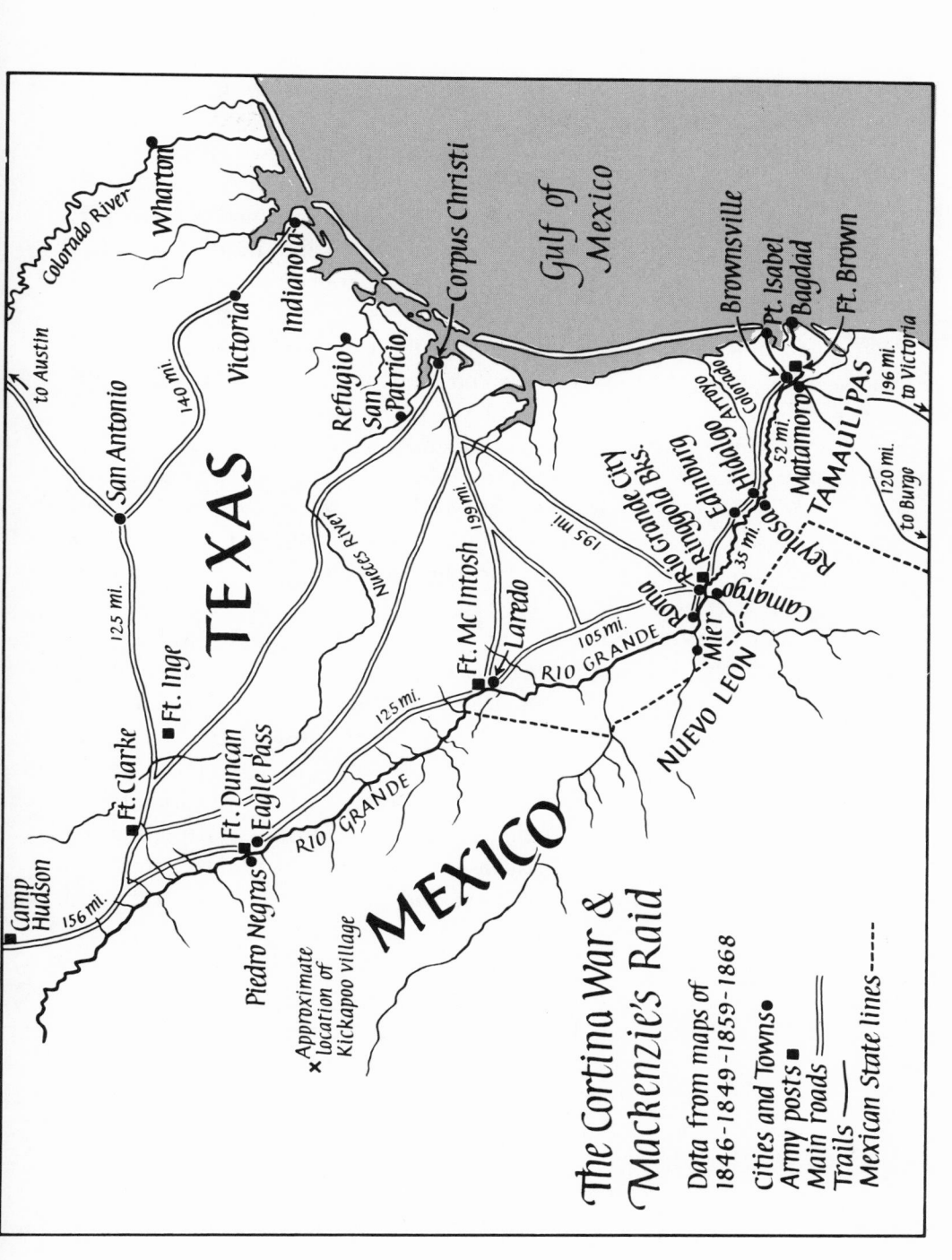

The Cortina War & Mackenzie's Raid

Data from maps of
1846-1849-1859-1868

Cities and Towns ●
Army posts ■
Main roads ——
Trails ——
Mexican State lines -----

other side, many Americans, with their point of view warped by the memories and myths of the recent war and the Texas rebellion, were fully convinced that all Mexicans were treacherous, undependable and cruel.

Given such attitudes and feelings on both sides of the boundary, with the lack of adequate and dependable law enforcement agencies, it is not at all surprising that from time to time there were troubles that became international and military matters. And it is not surprising, in view of the internal condition of Mexico and the inclusion of numerous drifters and soldiers of fortune in the population of the American side of the borderland, that Americans were often conspicuous among the troubles that beset the neighboring country.

While participation of individual Americans in Mexican affairs cannot be considered as intervention by the United States, or as American military expeditions into Mexico, it definitely constituted international meddling and sharpened the suspicion of the United States on the part of Mexicans. The first really noteworthy incident occurred in 1851, in the so-called Merchants' War. Some American merchants doing business in northern Mexico believed that they were being unduly discriminated against by the Mexican border officials. At the same time a visionary Mexican, José María Jesús Carbajal (or Carvajal), who had been educated in the United States, planned for the establishment of a new country, the Republic of Sierra Madre, which would be free of the abuses prevalent in Mexico. Financed by the aggrieved American merchants, Carbajal recruited his revolutionary force in Texas, and crossed the Rio Grande in September, 1851. A month later his motley army advanced upon Matamoras, but after twelve days of street fighting in the little city, Carbajal was defeated and driven across the river to Texas. But a considerable fraction of his force was composed of Americans, probably costing him much popular support among the Mexican population. And the thoroughly undisciplined conduct of many of his American adventurers added nothing to the regard held for Americans.[1]

Mexican feelings were exacerbated by Americans in Carbajal's army of liberation, but people on the American side were en-

raged by the execution of a number of the prisoners captured by
the government troops. The people of Brownsville promptly
hanged an effigy of General Guadalupe Avalos, who commanded
the government forces, and left it swinging on a gallows on the
river bank, where the general could see it. According to Abbé
Domenech, who was decidedly not prejudiced in favor of the
Americans, General Avalos took his revenge for the insult by
permitting a number of Indian raids into Texas from tribes
under his control—raids that continued until Avalos received a
sharp warning and a threat from American authorities (presumably military authorities).[2]

Border Americans were firmly convinced that Indian raids
from Mexico had the tacit consent, if not the open support, of
Mexican officials. The American point of view received support
in 1855, when Captain James H. Callahan, of the Texas Rangers,
followed a band of raiding Indians across the river near Eagle
Pass. Before crossing the river Callahan's force was joined by
a volunteer company commanded by one W. R. Henry—a company of professional soldiers of fortune who had been trying, un-
successfully, to peddle their services to the governor of Chihuahua. On October 3, 1855, Callahan caught up with his quarry,
but in the meantime the Indians had been reinforced by large
numbers of Mexicans. After losing several men in the fight,
Callahan retreated to Piedras Negras. The Mexican militia was
assembling in large numbers, and to cover his further retreat
across the river, Callahan set fire to the whole town, and he and
his rangers and Henry's freebooters returned ingloriously to the
United States.[3]

Callahan's foray into Mexico added fuel to the smoldering
resentment of Mexicans for Americans and increased the distrust
of Border Americans for Mexicans. Americans charged that
treacherous Mexicans deliberately led the rangers into an ambush; many Mexicans believed that the expedition had other
objectives than the punishment of raiding Indians. There were,
however, no immediate or noteworthy repercussions from Callahan's action. There were numerous small Indian raids in the
Rio Grande Valley, usually with murder and other atrocities,
but the greatest threat to the borderlands of both countries, and

to the Texas frontiers, seemed to be from the north and north-west. It was from those directions that bands of Kiowas, Mes-caleros, Lipans and, above all, Comanches, burst onto the fron-tiers or made their way into Mexico to loot, slaughter, ravish and burn. And it was warrior bands of those same tribes that estab-lished themselves in Mexico at places from which they could lunge into the United States. This was the situation, as noted in the preceding chapter, that caused General Twiggs to reinforce the troops on the northern and western frontiers of Texas, at the expense of the river frontier.

On the evening of September 28, 1859, a large segment of the population of Brownsville went across the river to Matamoras to a *fiesta* and *baile* in celebration of Mexican independence. The inhabitants of Brownsville at this time numbered about two thousand, of whom not more than a hundred were Anglo-Ameri-can. The majority of the citizens of the town were of Mexican stock, although most of them were United States citizens. In spite of the resentment between the two nationalities, personal relations were friendly and cordial. But there was friction never-theless. A prominent Mexican-American was Juan Nepomuceno Cortina (or Cortinas), whose mother, of aristocratic lineage, owned a ranch a few miles above Brownsville, lying on both sides of the river. During the summer Cortina had rescued, by force, one of his followers who had been arrested by the town marshal, Robert Shears, for being drunk and disorderly. Cortina also had had an almost perpetual feud with one Adolphus Glarucke, for reasons which are no longer clear.

At three o'clock in the morning the fiesta in Matamoras was still going strong. There was music and laughter; *aguardiente* and *mescal* flowed freely; there was probably an occasional burst of fireworks. But in Brownsville, everything was quiet and dark. People who had not gone to Matamoras were asleep in their homes; the streets were deserted.[4]

Suddenly there was a terrifying thunder of galloping horses, pistol shots and wild shouts: *"Viva México! Viva Cortina! Mueran los gringos!"* Cortina and his followers charged for the jail. There was a crash of gunfire. The jailer, Robert Johnson, ran to his door to see what was the matter. The raiders demanded that he open the jail. He refused; someone shot him, but wounded as he was, he fought his way to the home of a Mexican-American neighbor, Viviano García. García threw open his door and stood between Johnson and the raiders. The maddened intruders killed García, then dragged Johnson into the open and fired several shots into him, but before he died he managed to draw his own pistol and kill one of them. Then the raiders took the keys from Johnson's body, opened the jail, and released the prisoners, most of whom were Mexicans, and included highwaymen, cattle rustlers and horse thieves, along with several murderers, all of whom gleefully joined the band. The invaders next tried to open the powder magazine at Fort Brown but did not succeed. After that they spent several hours hunting for Shears and Glarucke, both of whom, fortunately for themselves, were absent that night.[5]

Thus, explosively and dramatically, Juan Nepomuceno Cortina burst onto the historical stage and assumed the role of a Mexican patriot fighting against the power and arrogance of the gringo—the first of the flamboyant characters who have been equated by romancers and a few historians with the legendary Robin Hood, who "took from the rich and gave to the poor." Cortina was born in 1824, but unlike the later "Robin Hood" of the Mexican border, Pancho Villa, he was neither of peasant nor *peon* stock. His father was wealthy; his mother was related to the bluest-blooded families of New Spain. Thus, Cortina himself was related to many of the most prominent citizens of Mexico. From his earliest childhood he was willful and headstrong. He stubbornly refused to go to school, and as an adolescent he preferred the company of *vaqueros* and *pelados* to association with members of his own class. During and just after the Mexican War he is supposed to have worked for the United States forces as a muleteer, and he was also suspected of being implicated in the murder of an American who was purchasing mules and who was known to be carrying a considerable sum of money. By the time Cortina became famous (or infamous) there were some twenty indictments against him in Texas, for offenses ranging all the way from petty theft to murder, but for some unknown reason no peace officer ever molested him or attempted to arrest him. According to all accounts, Cortina was a man with an engaging personality and impressive appearance, with gray eyes and a red beard, features that are unusual in a Mexican. His activities as a *vaquero* and his friendliness toward the *pelados* built up for him a considerable following among the Mexicans of the borderland, many of whom had genuine grievances against the Americans.[6]

In 1859, it appears, Cortina was commissioned as a captain in the Mexican Army and directed to enroll a company for service at Tampico. On July 19 of that year, he rode into Brownsville with a few followers, from a ranch belonging to his mother, located about eight miles above Brownsville on the United States side of the Rio Grande. As to what happened on that July day, various accounts differ in details, but all agree that the marshal, Robert Shears, arrested one of Cortina's men. Cortina came to the rescue, fired at and wounded Shears, took his followers, and galloped out of the town.[7]

Vanishing in a cloud of dust, Cortina dropped from sight until that eventful night of September 28, 1859. Within a few minutes after killing the jailer and opening the jail, Cortina had the whole town of Brownsville firmly in his possession. He continued his occupation of the place through the whole of the next day. Americans dared not appear on the streets in groups or with weapons. He threatened to slaughter all Americans and burn the town. Indeed, there was nothing to stop him. His band, of eighty to a hundred men, probably outnumbered the Anglo-Americans of Brownsville, who could not get together to concert some sort of common action. At some time in the afternoon General Carbajal and Don Miguel Tijerinas (who was Cortina's cousin), came over from Matamoras, and after a lengthy discussion the freebooter was persuaded to evacuate the town without carrying out his bloodcurdling threats. In the meantime, the militia company of Matamoras was drawn up on the riverbank where Cortina and his followers could see them. Late in the afternoon Cortina assembled his men and marched out of Brownsville, up the river. As they left, the Mexican militia crossed to Brownsville and encamped on the Fort Brown parade ground, to the immeasurable relief of the citizens of the town.[8]

As soon as the people of Brownsville could breathe freely

again, they organized themselves into two volunteer companies
and began looking for help. Francis W. Latham, the Collector
of Customs, wrote a lengthy letter to General Twiggs. Twiggs,
of course, did not receive the letter for several days—the time it
took a messenger to cover the miles to San Antonio—and upon
receiving it, apparently believed either that the account was exaggerated or that the raid was made by a small band of Indians.
On October 7 (probably the day on which he received the first
reports), he forwarded Latham's letter to The Adjutant General,
in Washington, without other comment than, "There are at
present, it is said, small parties of marauding Indians supposed
to be from across the Rio Grande. . . . There are no parties of
hostile Indians within the limits of Texas." Twiggs added that
he was ordering a company of infantry to the junction of the
Leona and Frio rivers, and another one to some point on the
Rio Grande below Fort Duncan. Scouting parties would cover
the ground between Fort Clark and Fort Duncan, and Captain
Stoneman's cavalry company would scout from Camp Hudson.[9]

But if Twiggs was unmoved by the news, other people took it
very seriously. Senator John Hemphill, who happened to be in
Austin when the news was received, wrote to President Buch-
anan, demanding the reoccupation of the posts in the Lower
Valley. 2d Lieutenant Loomis L. Langdon, of the 1st Artillery,
who had been left behind at the time of the evacuation to take
charge of the government property, took his courage in hand,
and ignoring customary military channels, also wrote to the
President.[10] The merchants of New Orleans, fearing the ruin
of their profitable business with northern Mexico and the Lower
Rio Grande Valley, added their voices to the clamor. The result
was a somewhat peremptory order from the Secretary of War
to General Twiggs, directing the reoccupation of Fort Brown at
once.[11] As sometimes happens, even in the twentieth century,
Twiggs first learned of the order through the newspapers. He issued his warning orders at once, and upon the arrival of the
official notice, two companies marched from Fort Clark to Fort
Brown.

It would take the troops from Fort Clark at least two weeks to
reach Fort Brown, and in the meantime wild rumors snowballed

until "eye witnesses" stated positively that Cortina had made a second descent upon Brownsville, had massacred all who were unable to escape, and had totally destroyed the town. In fact, one plausible "escapee" was absolutely sure that he himself was the only American to escape from the general massacre.[12]

A trained military intelligence interrogator would soon have detected the fallacies and lies in these rumors, but in 1859 no army in the world had such a specialist. Every commanding officer was his own intelligence officer, without benefit of such an assistant on his staff. General Twiggs, as has been shown, was skeptical at first, but the volume of chilling detail was so convincingly presented that he changed his mind. On November 12, 1859, he sent a telegram to the Secretary of War:

> Express from Rio Grande City just in. Brownsville burnt. One hundred Americans murdered. Cortinas on the march for the Nueces with eight hundred men. A gentleman of intelligence says there is no doubt it is the priest party of Mexico, as Cortinas has plenty of money. Seven companies of foot and two of horses ordered in the field, under Major Heintzelman. I am not able to take the field.[13]

Convinced now that the deviltry on the Lower Rio Grande was more serious than that of a few prowling Indians, Twiggs took energetic measures. On November 12, the day on which he sent the telegram just quoted, he ordered all the troops available to march at once to a rendezvous at old Fort Merrill, on the Nueces. The troops he could send included a strongly reinforced company of the 2d Cavalry, commanded by Captain George Stoneman, four companies of infantry and the two companies of artillery that were already on the way to Fort Brown. The artillery also included a gun section. The whole force was to be commanded by Major Samuel P. Heintzelman, of the 1st Infantry, who was ordered to report to department headquarters without delay, to receive instructions.[14]

The reports of horrors on the Rio Grande stirred Twiggs; they caused a tornado in Washington. Telegraphic orders from the Secretary of War went to Baton Rouge, Louisiana, Fort Monroe, Virginia, and Fort Leavenworth, Kansas, for the troops at those stations to prepare for immediate field service in Texas.

Colonel Edwin V. Sumner, who was in command of the Department of the West, at Fort Leavenworth, was also directed to obtain steamboats to transport his troops down the Mississippi to New Orleans. Of course, orders for these emergency troop movements were canceled as soon as it was ascertained that the reports from Texas were exaggerated, and there were probably some red faces in the War Department.[15]

Heintzelman arrived at San Antonio within a few days. The orders he received from Twiggs were for him to go to old Fort Merrill at once, assume command of the troops assembling there, and as soon as he had a sufficient force in his judgment, to march to Fort Brown. He would spare no effort to bring Cortina to battle and use every means at his disposal to destroy Cortina's band. Marauders would be pursued to the Rio Grande, but the United States troops would not cross the river unless in "hot pursuit."[16]

In the interim between Cortina's raid of September 28 and the assembling of United States forces to suppress him, the events in the vicinity of Brownsville, while not as disastrous as rumor had said, were still depressing and humiliating for the Americans. On leaving Brownsville, Cortina and his brigands rode rapidly to his mother's ranch, which, as has been mentioned, was about eight miles above the town, on the American side of the river. There, on September 30, 1859, he issued a flaming proclamation that was simultaneously a declaration of war against Americans and his self-announced position as champion and protector of all Mexicans who had any grievance against the gringos.[17]

At the ranch, which he fortified, and over which he hoisted the Mexican flag, Cortina welcomed and enrolled recruits, and assembled arms, ammunition and such supplies as his somewhat primitive followers needed. At first, but not for long, he kept an exact account of the cattle he "requisitioned" from American ranchers to feed his men. He maintained strict discipline, a measure that was necessary in a force that included an organized gang of bandits from the interior of Tamaulipas and a group of convicts who had escaped from the Tamaulipas prison, armed themselves somehow, and hastened to cross the river to join him. He spent much time in Matamoras, where the authorities made no effort to molest him, and he undoubtedly had spies among the Mexican population of Brownsville. His men captured a United States mail rider, and because Cortina himself was completely illiterate, he captured an American rancher, whom he held as a prisoner for ten days, reading and translating the contents of the mail pouch.

In Brownsville the citizens lived in daily expectation of another raid. They organized two volunteer companies, barricaded the streets, and established a twenty-four-hour guard. Proof that by no means all of the Mexican population of Brownsville favored Cortina was furnished by one of the volunteer companies: it was composed exclusively of Mexicans. Tense with apprehension and tired from long periods on guard without rest, the people of Brownsville considered themselves to be in a state of siege. They dared not go outside the protected limits of the town, and they saw a Cortinista lurking behind every bush. It is quite likely that small parties of Mexicans seen from time to time were Cortina's men, reconnoitering and keeping the place under observation.

On October 12, 1859, the sheriff of Brownsville, with a small posse, rode up the river toward Cortina's lair. Just what the sheriff expected to accomplish is uncertain, but on the way, a Mexican named Tomás Cabrera (or Cabura) rode into their arms and was seized. He was identified as a member of Cortina's force and was said to have been second in command the night of the raid. Triumphantly the posse returned to Brownsville and lodged the prisoner in jail. Cortina, on learning of the capture, threatened to "lay the town in ashes" unless Cabrera were released. This, the people of Brownsville refused to do.

On October 21, 1859, the sheriff with a small posse again approached Cortina's position. The posse's personnel were mostly Mexicans, and the posse was strengthened by a small field gun, or howitzer. But when they were still some two miles distant from Cortina's fort, the sheriff, very sensibly, decided to return to Brownsville.

In Brownsville the committee of safety decided that the time had come for offensive action. A force of eighty men was organized, and on the evening of October 23 the Brownsville company was joined by a militia company from Matamoras, also with a small field gun. Early next morning the joint American-Mexican expeditionary force marched bravely forth. Although the distance was only eight miles, the force did not reach the neighborhood of their objective until late in the afternoon. An outpost, well hidden in the chaparral, opened fire on them. After a few minutes' delay, the advance was resumed. Suddenly, without warning, a heavy fire was opened by riflemen well hidden in the thickets. The volunteers, considering their lack of training and the absence of real discipline, did not do badly at first. They returned the enemy fire vigorously. The Mexican field gun fired three rounds but was then thrown off its carriage. Meanwhile the mounted members of the expedition were retiring, at the gallop. The men with the field guns, finding themselves unsupported and unable either to save the guns or roll them into the river, also retreated. The Brownsville *American Flag* frankly admitted that "the rout became general," and Heintzelman, in his later report to Colonel Robert E. Lee, remarked dryly that all the volunteers were "anxious to be the first to reach Brownsville." And what may have caused some mortification among the Americans: the Mexican company from Matamoras maintained its cohesion and continued firing at the enemy until they were out of ammunition, thus covering the retreat of the Americans.[18]

The first succor from the outside to arrive at the "besieged" town was a company of Texas Rangers, hastily raised at San Antonio by Captain William G. Tobin. They arrived at Brownsville late at night, October 10, 1859. Cortina had full and complete information and had planned an ambush, but Glarucke, Cortina's particular enemy, met the company and guided it over indirect trials. Even so, Tobin's Rangers had a taste of adventure. Lieutenant Langdon had managed to get a heavy, 24-pounder howitzer, with ammunition, from the depot at Brazos Santiago. The Brownsville volunteers, hearing unidentified horsemen approaching in the dark, opened fire. Fortunately the volunteers' gunnery was strictly amateur, and nobody was touched by the shower of grapeshot that plastered the road and the mesquite.[19]

Tobin's Ranger company bolstered the morale of Brownsville by its presence, but otherwise it proved to be more of a liability than an asset. Tobin was no disciplinarian, and it appears that his company included a considerable number of the less desirable citizens of San Antonio. Within a short time after their arrival, the prisoner, Tomás Cabrera, was taken out of the jail at night and hanged—and there can be little doubt that Tobin's men were responsible. Regardless of moral or legal aspects, the lynching of Cabrera was an act of pure stupidity, for it would seem obvious, even to the thickest witted, that he was of infinitely greater value as a hostage than as a corpse. Walter Prescott Webb, who cannot be accused of any prejudice against the Texas Rangers, remarked that "on the whole these men were a sorry lot, and their conduct for the remainder of the war reflects no credit on the organization."[20] F. M. Campbell, the rancher whom Cortina kidnaped to read the contents of the mail pouches, complained of Tobin's company that they burnt his pens and fences for firewood; they stole a number of hogs and goats and fifty barrels of sweet potatoes, and refused to pay for anything. "I estimate the value of the property taken by Cortinas at . . . two hundred dollars, and the value of the property destroyed by Tobin's command at fully one thousand dollars. . . ."[21]

Eight days after Tobin's arrival at Brownsville, a detachment of thirty men, under command of Lieutenant John Littleton, was sent toward Arroyo Colorado to meet and guide a company from Indianola. The Rangers never found the Indianola company; instead they ran headlong into a trap set by Cortina on the plain of Palo Alto, where Zachary Taylor had fought a battle during the Mexican War. Completely surprised, they lost three men killed, one wounded and one taken prisoner. A strong force sent the next day to recover the dead found that the prisoner had also been killed.[22]

Late in November, 1859, the decision was made (by whom is not recorded) to take the offensive and attack Cortina in his stronghold. On the morning of the twenty-third, the force, numbering about 250 men, including Tobin's company, the Indianola company and the Brownsville volunteers, advanced up the river. To add weight to the attack, the heavy howitzer that Langdon had brought from Brazos Santiago was dragged along. The march was slow; next day, November 24, the column was still only about seven miles from Brownsville and at least a mile short of its objective. Up to this point, there had been neither sight nor sound of a Cortinista. Tobin ordered a guard of sixty men to remain with the howitzer, while with the bulk of the force, he pushed forward to reconnoiter. They had not gone far when they were greeted by the sharp reports of Cortina's artillery (the two guns abandoned by the previous expedition) and the rattle of musketry from the chaparral, with bullets whining unpleasantly close about their ears. There seem to have been no casualties. Tobin ordered the force to fall back a short distance, to remain until the howitzer could be brought up. But a rearward movement with green troops, though easy to start, is often impossible to stop. Most of the men did not stop until they had the comforting howitzer between them and the enemy —and some of them did not stop there but kept right on. The force bivouacked that night where they were. Next morning, November 25, Tobin ordered another advance, but some sixty of the heroes raced to Brownsville instead. With the few firm spirits remaining, Tobin advanced toward Cortina's position; another consultation was held, and the general opinion was that any further advance would be most imprudent. The force marched ingloriously back to the safety of Brownsville.

Cortina's reputation now reached the skies among his countrymen. He had defeated the gringos in battle, and now they were afraid of him. They skulked in their fortified position at Brownsville, afraid to move out. Recruits flocked to Cortina's camp to enroll themselves under the leader who would soon drive the gringos out of Texas and again place the Mexican flag over the whole state.

This was the general situation when Major Heintzelman arrived at Brownsville late on the night of December 5. Captain Tobin reported immediately and placed his company of Rangers under Heintzelman's command. Heintzelman brought with him Captain Stoneman's company of cavalry, two companies of artillery and a few odd lots; he found at Fort Brown the artillery company that had just arrived from Fort Clark. Thus he had a force totaling about 220 officers and men.

Heintzelman found that his first great difficulty was to obtain information upon which to base plans. Local estimates of the strength of Cortina's band ran as high as 1,500 men. Heintzelman knew that this figure was much too high, but he found it impossible to obtain anything more accurate. Local Mexicans, some of whom had probably been in Cortina's camp, were close-mouthed and vague. A careful reconnaissance of Cortina's position would reveal much, but Tobin's Rangers and the local volunteers were so demoralized that none of them could be induced, by any means, to undertake the mission.

Nevertheless, concluding from such scraps of information as he could glean that Cortina could not possibly have more than 350 men, Heintzelman decided upon an attack. At one o'clock in the morning, December 14, 1859, the column marched from Brownsville. The first expedition had taken all day to cover the distance from the town to Cortina's ranch, and Tobin's force had taken two days, but this time, with the example set by the Regulars, and probably under the lash of Heintzelman's tongue, the force was within a few hundred yards of the objective half an hour before daybreak. Heintzelman tried to get Tobin's Rangers to reconnoiter, but they "were so thoroughly stampeded by their previous expedition" (in Heintzelman's words) that it was only after a well-known and trusted citizen, a Judge Edmund J. Davis, volunteered to accompany them, that they consented.[23]

Their fears were groundless: the quarry had fled. Cortina's position was deserted. Heintzelman ordered the advance continued, after breaking a way through the entrenchments so that the artillery could follow. Three miles farther along, where a long, straight stretch of road ran through the jungle-like chaparral thicket, there was a flag fluttering in the breeze, with a group of men about it. There was a puff of smoke, and a round shot came hurtling down the road. Under Heintzelman's orders the artillery moved forward, and completely ignoring the enemy's fire, which continued, the gunners unlimbered and prepared to fire. The Rangers were nervous, but seeing the calm way of the Regulars, they stood their ground. Several rounds from Heintzelman's guns were fired, and he ordered his two foot companies of artillery to move forward. He ordered the Rangers to go also; this time he did not ask them, he *ordered* them, and they responded. Cortina's men had lost a great deal of their spirit and élan from the fire of the heavy 24-pounders, and seeing a disciplined attack coming, they lost no time in getting away. In a few minutes the Rangers and Regulars arrived and were in undisputed possession of the enemy's position. There was not a Cortinista in sight, except for six or eight who were sprawled grotesquely on the ground. On the American side one Ranger had been killed and two artillerymen wounded.

By this time the day was well advanced. Men and horses were tired, but Heintzelman pushed them forward relentlessly in pursuit. To give the enemy time to rally would be folly. It was apparent after two or three miles that the enemy had scattered in small groups that could not be pursued. A few mounted men were seen to plunge their horses into the river and swim across the channel to Mexico; the dismounted men, by twos and threes, had vanished into the chaparral. Consequently, Heintzelman ordered a halt to give men and horses a chance to rest.

A little while later, when most of the men were stretched out on the ground, many of them asleep, and the horses were nibbling at the scanty grass, there was a sudden sound of horsemen approaching at speed—Major John Salmon Ford, with a new company of fifty-five Texas Rangers. Ford had heard the sound of distant firing earlier in the day and had driven his men hard for forty miles in an effort to arrive before the fighting was over.[24]

Unlike Tobin, Ford was known as a strict disciplinarian, who demanded and got the same order and obedience from Rangers as was expected of Regulars. He was an experienced frontiersman and Indian fighter, although he was a physician by profession. He was in Austin when the exaggerated rumors of Cortina's activities reached there. Rumor had Cortina burning Corpus Christi and butchering the inhabitants. Governor Runnels said to him, "Ford, you must go, you must start tonight, and move swiftly."[25] Ford left Austin early the next morning with a few men whom he had been able to enroll in a few hours. On the road he collected more men, many of whom had previously served with him on the Indian frontier. For expenses he borrowed money from anybody who could lend him any, until such time as state funds became available. Believing it likely that Cortina's sympathizers were keeping his growing force under observation, Ford conducted his march toward Brownsville exactly as though an attack could be expected at any minute. By the time the company arrived at Brownsville, it was thoroughly "shaken down," and the men who had not known him previously had discovered that it was extremely unwise to argue with him or to disregard his decrees.

Heintzelman's soldiers and the two Ranger companies camped that night near the battlefield. During the night a violent, drenching rainstorm made everyone miserable, and even more important, ruined most of the gunpowder, leaving the command without enough serviceable ammunition for sustained combat. The rain continued through the next day; consequently Heintzelman decided to return to Brownsville. On reaching Brownsville, he found a new flock of rumors flying; Cortina was on his way to Point Isabel (the port of Brownsville, at the mouth of the river), where the United States customs house was filled with valuable goods. Heintzelman at once ordered his mounted troops (Stoneman's cavalry company and the two Ranger companies) to intercept and destroy the bandits, but no enemy was discovered for the simple reason that there were no Cortinistas threatening Point Isabel.

Within a few days scraps of information that filtered into Heintzelman's headquarters indicated that Cortina had reassembled his forces and was moving up the river, away from the town. Finally, positive and reliable information was received that Cortina was fortifying a ranch known as the Baston, belonging to a William Neale, and located some thirty-five miles from Brownsville. On December 21, 1859, Heintzelman again marched from the town, with a column including 150 Regulars, two heavy field howitzers and the two Ranger companies, totaling some 200 men. The force arrived at the Baston at noon, December 23, but Cortina, fully informed of its approach, had not waited. The once prosperous ranch was a scene of destruction and desolation. Fences and outbuildings had been burned, the brick ranch house thoroughly plundered, and cattle and horses slaughtered or driven off.

During the approach march, Ford's company, covering the

right flank, was led by a local Mexican guide. It became apparent during the morning that the guide either was lost or was deliberately misleading them. Ford finally called a halt and took the guide aside for a few quiet words: unless the Mexican's memory was quickly restored, the Rangers would hang him on the nearest tree. His memory came back to him miraculously, and Ford's company continued on its march without further difficulty.

It was Christmas Day. One can imagine the remarks among the soldiers and Rangers about spending the day ploughing through the chaparral instead of celebrating properly in barracks or town. Neverthless, on finding the Baston abandoned, Heintzelman continued the march. Information came in from an unrecorded source that Cortina had taken position in a canebrake above Edinburg. The report was true, but on arrival at the canebrake, the expedition found that Cortina had vanished. During the march there was plenty of evidence that Cortina had passed that way—destroyed fences, burned ranch houses, slaughtered animals.

Ford's company had all the aggressiveness usually attributed to Texas Rangers. While the command bivouacked for the night near Edinburg, Ford pushed out scouts and reconnoitering patrols. Next morning, December 26, he was able to inform Heintzelman positively that Cortina was at Rio Grande City, his men occupying both the little town and the abandoned post of Ringgold Barracks. Heintzelman at once decided upon a halt, and the force ostentatiously went into camp. After dark, with orders strictly enjoining a complete blackout and silence, the march was resumed. The plan was for Ford's Rangers to work past the Mexican position and cut across the road up the river to insure that the enemy did not escape in that direction. Tobin's company was to assault Cortina's right, half an hour in advance of the Regulars, who would attack directly along the road against Cortina's center.

Excellent plans often break down in actual execution, but aggressive and intelligent action by subordinates can save the situation. That is what happened in the little and forgotten battle of Rio Grande City. Ford found it impossible to get past Cortina's outposts without discovery; he moved in for an immediate attack. To complicate matters, a heavy fog suddenly descended, muffled sounds, and made it difficult to distinguish friend from foe. The firing became sharp, with Cortina's two guns (the ones he had captured) firing rapidly but, fortunately for the Rangers, without any skill. A sudden mounted charge by a dozen or more Cortinistas failed to move Ford's men, and most of the horses vanished, riderless, in the mist. Actually, the battle was over; the charge was evidently made to give Cortina's gunners time to drag the artillery to safety. The Rangers pursued on foot for a short distance, and Ford then ordered them back to their horses so that they could pursue more effectively.

About this time Heintzelman came up. The strange atmospheric effect of the fog had prevented any sound of firing from reaching him, and Ford's messengers had been unable to find him. Heintzelman quickly took in the situation, approved everything Ford had done, and ordered the pursuit pressed hard. The fog suddenly lifted. Cortina and a considerable part of his band, with the two guns, were seen moving up the river road toward Roma, the next little town. Numbers of fugitives were running toward the river and plunging in. There was a small crowd on the Mexican shore. Stoneman's cavalry company galloped to the riverbank, cutting down a few fugitives on the way. The cavalry dismounted and opened fire on the Mexicans in the water and on the group gathered on the Mexican side. Stoneman's men were armed with the new Sharps carbines; the far shore was within easy range; most of the Mexicans were killed before they could scramble up the steep bank to cover and safety.

Meanwhile, Ford was pressing ahead on the Roma road. Four or five miles above Rio Grande City, where the road crossed a deep ravine, Cortina tried to rally his men and make a stand. The Rangers, flushed with victory, did not even pause; at the gallop they smashed into Cortina's escort, capturing one of the guns. An unidentified Ranger dismounted, swung the gun around by main force, and fired a "salute" at the retreating enemy. Panic-stricken, the fragments of Cortina's force broke and fled, disappearing into the thick chaparral and abandoning the other gun.

During the morning sixteen Rangers were wounded, none seriously. On the other hand, at least sixty Cortinistas were killed and an unknown number wounded. Sixty was the official estimate; unofficial estimates, which could easily be as accurate as the official ones, place the Cortinista dead at nearly two hundred.[26]

Cortina himself had escaped, and he still had an unknown number of followers, but after the battle of Rio Grande City, there was a lull, and the Americans had a few days of much needed rest. During the lull, orders arrived from Austin which vitally affected the Rangers. For some reason the Texas authorities canceled all existing Ranger commissions and required the election of all officers. Ford, as has been mentioned, was a strict disciplinarian; in the ensuing election the affable, friendly, easygoing Tobin was elected by a small majority. Heintzelman regarded the whole business with deep disfavor, but of course, as a Federal officer, he could do nothing about a purely state matter.[27]

But in the end the affair worked out so that Ford remained. Early in January, 1860, Governor Sam Houston, who had been elected in Governor Runnels' place, sent two commissioners to Brownsville to investigate the situation, with full authority to take any action necessary to improve and increase the effectiveness of the Rangers. One of their first steps was to order the immediate discharge of all Rangers then in the service, a measure that got rid of Tobin, and to direct Ford to raise two new companies. The other company was to be commanded by Lieutenant John Littleton, who had shown high qualities of leadership during the campaign, despite his earlier surprise and defeat at Palo Alto. After inquiring of Heintzelman if two Ranger companies would be sufficient, the commissioners next sent an order to Ford:

> Sir: From and after this date [February 2, 1860] your movements and the troops under your command will be directed by Major Heintzelman, or other commanding officer of the United States army on this frontier. You will therefore obey all orders emanating from such officer.[28]

It might be remarked that up to this point the submission of the Rangers to Heintzelman's orders had been purely voluntary.

They were not under his authority in any legal sense whatever.

Meanwhile, the Cortina War was again becoming "hot." During the lull there had been numerous small incursions by Cortinistas to steal cattle, and there had been several skirmishes. Cortina, seemingly, had lost none of his prestige with his own people, who ascribed his defeat to pure hard luck and believed that he would soon regain all his losses. He appeared openly in Matamoras and was known to be gathering men and supplies. He established and fortified a camp on the Mexican side of the river, about thirty miles above Brownsville, at a sharp bend in the river known as La Bolsa. Here he could watch the road on the United States side, and watch the river for the steamboat *Ranchero*, which was due on its downward voyage from Laredo and was known to be carrying a valuable cargo and a large sum in specie (said to have been sixty thousand dollars). Cortinistas once again captured the United States mail riders and opened and riffled the mail pouches.

Late at night, February 4, 1860, a messenger galloped into Brownsville with an urgent message to Heintzelman from Ford. During the afternoon a Ranger had been mortally wounded by a shot fired from the Mexican side at La Bolsa. At almost the same time, the *Ranchero*, slowing her speed to make the dangerous turn in the river, had been fired upon. There was a large force, Ford stated, hidden on the Mexican side at La Bolsa, to capture the boat. Ford further informed Heintzelman that he intended to pass his men across the river and "beat the bush in the neighborhood." He would then pass his horses across and would march down the Mexican side, keeping abreast of the *Ranchero*. Captain Stoneman, who had intercepted Ford's messenger, added a pencil note saying that he was marching at once for La Bolsa but would not cross the river with his Regulars except to repel an attack. Lieutenant Langdon, who was a passenger on the *Ranchero* and had with him the two guns that had been recovered from Cortina, added a note confirming what Ford had reported and saying that the firing was continuing while he was writing. Langdon did not report something that came out later: he had fired the recovered guns from the *Ranchero*'s deck, causing the bandits to retire into the brush.[29]

Late in the afternoon, Tobin (who had fortuitously arrived on his way to Brownsville to be discharged) volunteered to cross the river to reconnoiter. A short time later, Ford himself, with thirty or forty men, followed. As it was dark, or nearly dark by this time, the crossing was unobserved by the Cortinistas, who were massed opposite where the *Ranchero* was anchored in deep water. Moving cautiously and quietly, the Rangers were able to get within thirty or forty yards of the Cortinista position before they were discovered. Ford's men were sheltered by the river-bank, and Ford cautioned them to fire slowly and carefully, to make every shot count. An attempted mounted charge by a few Cortinistas was beaten back. As the enemy fire slackened, Ford shouted, "Charge!" Yelling like Indians (the "rebel yell" of a few years later), the Rangers surged forward; the enemy broke and fled—all except Cortina himself. With magnificient courage he tried to stem the rout, then turned, faced the Rangers, and emptied his revolver at them. Several Rangers fired at him at close range, but he seemed to be invulnerable. Shouting defiance, he galloped away, uninjured.[30]

The fight at La Bolsa was significant in one respect. It was the first time in the Cortina War in which troops under the command of a United States Army officer crossed into Mexico. It is true that the Rangers were state troops, but the orders that the commissioners had given Ford made the Rangers, for the time being, an integral part of the United States forces. The fight was an indication, too, that it was necessary to carry the war into Mexico to prevent effectively such incursions as the Cortinistas had made.

Heintzelman, on receiving the report of the action late at night, February 4, approved what Ford proposed to do. The fight was actually over before Heintzelman received Ford's report but, of course, he had no means of knowing that. He directed Ford to confine himself strictly to protecting the *Ranchero* and not allow himself to be drawn away from the Rio Grande. Next day, February 5, 1860, he sent information to both Ford and Stoneman that General Guadalupe García, the commandant at Matamoras, was sending a force to disperse Cortina's band. Stoneman soon found, however, that the troops from Matamoras had orders only to protect the steamboat. They were not authorized to take any sort of action against Cortina.[31]

Cortina vanished after the fight at La Bolsa and was not heard from again for some time. But there were immediate repercussions from Ford's action in crossing the river. Heintzelman received a lengthy letter from a Mexican official protesting against the violation of Mexican sovereignty and complaining bitterly that Ford had burned the buildings at La Bolsa. Heintzelman replied sharply, pointing out that Cortina had been allowed to organize and maintain his forces on Mexican soil and from there raid into the United States without the slightest interference by Mexican authorities. As for the burning of La Bolsa, Ford did not order it, but if he had, the act was perfectly justified under international law. "We are entitled," said Heintzelman, "to make reclamations for our devastated frontier and for our murdered citizens.[32]

Early in February, 1860, almost simultaneously with the election of new officers by the Rangers, General Twiggs was authorized to go on leave, as he had been requesting for some time. Brevet Colonel Robert E. Lee, of the 2d Cavalry, was assigned to command the Department of Texas in Twigg's absence. It would be several weeks, however, before Lee could arrive and assume his new duties. He was on leave of absence himself—a leave that was interrupted by John Brown's raid on Harpers Ferry.[33] Lee arrived at San Antonio on February 18 but found it necessary to remain at his headquarters for some time, attending to multitudinous administrative details and familiarizing himself with the Department's problems. Like Twiggs, he found that in spite of the Cortina war his most serious problems were on the northern and western Indian frontiers; like Twiggs, too, he found that he did not have enough troops to handle both situations simultaneously.

In solving the Cortina problem, Lee had one great advantage that had been denied to Twiggs. When Twiggs asked for authority to send troops across the border, he was refused. Heintzelman doubtless wondered if he would receive a sharp reprimand or perhaps even a court-martial for approving Ford's invasion of a "friendly" country. Lee brought with him two letters signed by the Secretary of War, one directing that enemy raiders should be pursued, if necessary, "beyond the limits of the United States." The second was even stronger: if the Mexican authorities refuse or fail to break up the "banditti" on the Mexican side of the river, "you will cause this to be done by the force under your command."[34]

On March 15, 1860, Lee at last was able to get away from his headquarters. Escorted by a company of his own regiment, the 2d Cavalry, he marched first to Eagle Pass, because of a rumor that Cortina was assembling a force near that place. Finding that the rumor was entirely false, Lee moved down the river to the scene of recent operations.

While Lee was on the road, the Cortina War took another turn. General García informed Heintzelman that Cortina, with a large band, was at a ranch named La Mesa, about midway between Matamoras and Reynosa and three or four miles back from the river. Heintzelman forwarded the information to Ford, who was inclined to be skeptical and suspicious. But the next day Stoneman, with his company, rode into Ford's camp with positive orders to cross the river and capture or kill Cortina. Ford was partially disabled because a horse had fallen upon him a few days previously, but since Stoneman was in command, he obeyed promptly. Stoneman promptly took charge of getting all the horses across the river—a technical problem that was solved by cutting a ramp down the bank just wide enough for a single horse. The first horses were led down, and when the ramp was crowded with animals, a whip was cracked sharply. The horses in the rear pushed the foremost animals into the water, and then all swam for the opposite shore. By three o'clock in the morning all three companies, one of Regulars and two of Rangers, with all their horses, were safely across. Scouts sent forward by Ford discovered that the direct road to La Mesa was covered by an outpost. The Americans approached their objective by a roundabout trail that Ford knew, but half a mile short of the place, a hidden Mexican picket opened fire on them. A moment later they could hear drums beating the long roll—the alarm signal and call to arms. Since surprise was now impossible and there was just enough daylight to see, Stoneman signaled for deployment and the charge. Riding over scattered opposition, the Americans swarmed into the ranch. There was sharp firing for some ten minutes, the Mexicans gave way—and it was suddenly discovered that an unbelievable mistake had occurred. These Mexicans at the ranch were not Cortinistas; they were the local Guardia Nacional and were, presumably, guarding the place against Cortina. There were hasty apologies; arms were returned to their owners, and the Americans withdrew to a nearby well to make coffee and eat their hardtack.

The Americans, however, did not let down their guard, and it was well that they did not, for soon a large mounted Mexican force rode in. The Mexican colonel angrily demanded to know why the Americans had invaded Mexico and attacked part of his command. Ford, acting as spokesman, replied by demanding to know why the colonel's men had sounded the alarm and opened fire on the Americans. By this time the soldiers and Rangers were visibly reloading their weapons, and the colonel decided to accept the Amercans' explanation and apology. The affair at La Mesa was unfortunate, but ended without serious harm. Both Ford and Stoneman were convinced that Cortina had actually been at the ranch, probably among those who vanished when the American attack developed. They were both convinced, too, that the unnamed Mexican colonel intended to attack them but found them too strong and too ready.[35]

Orders from Heintzelman brought the Americans back to their own side of the river, but within a few days they were in Mexico again. Having received information that Cortina was again at La Bolsa, and without waiting for orders or authority from Heintzelman, Stoneman and Ford crossed and searched the area. There was no sign of Cortina, but Ford's men captured an Indian known as Faustino, who was known to have killed several Americans. He was shot on the spot. Meanwhile, an order from Heintzelman arrived directing Stoneman and Ford to return to the United States immediately.

At this point the available records are confused and confusing. It appears, however, that Stoneman and Ford disregarded the order, for they had learned that Cortina was supposed to be at Maguey, twenty-four miles south of Matamoras, and sixty miles by road and trail from La Bolsa. Instead of returning to the American shore, they marched for Maguey. When they were a few miles from Maguey, a mounted Mexican was seen to leave the brush and gallop ahead of them. All efforts to overtake him failed; the tired American horses simply could not get up enough speed. As the force approached Maguey, there was a rattle of shots. Supposing that the patrol that had tried to catch the Mexican horseman had run into trouble, the Americans spurred their tired horses into a gallop. One lone Mexican fired a shot at them as they came into the plaza; he was instantly knocked over. As for the rest of the assembled crowd of Mexicans: they were firing into the air in celebration of St. Joseph's Day, and a fiesta in honor of the occasion was taking place. And if Cortina had been there, he had had ample time to get away. Ford believed that Cortina had been there, especially since Cortina's wife and one of his daughters were recognized in the crowd.

Troopers and horses were tired and hungry. Stoneman decided upon a few hours' rest. The horses found good grass; an ox was purchased and roasted whole. Meanwhile, someone whispered that Cortina had gone toward Monterrey. Hours later, in the dead of the night, when the last fiesta merrymaker had staggered home, the men were quietly aroused, horses saddled, and the force again "hit the road." At daybreak, several hours later, the column arrived at Rancho Cayetano, forty miles distant, but found that Cortina had not lingered there. The pursuit was becoming too hot.

Stoneman decided then to return to the United States. The command was not over two hundred men, in the midst of a hostile country; they were short of rations, without forage, and their ammunition was low. And it happened that when Cortina disappeared up the road toward Monterrey, and the Americans turned their horses toward the Rio Grande, the Cortina War was virtually over. Cortina had been given an ample demonstration that the Rio Grande was no more of a barrier for his enemies than for himself.[36]

When Colonel Robert E. Lee arrived at the scene of the trouble a few days later, he quickly quenched the lingering embers of the Cortina trouble and, by two or three scrupulously polite but stinging letters, quelled any disposition on the part of local Mexican officials to make trouble because of the Stoneman-Ford "invasion." In response to a protest by General Guadalupe García, Lee said, "I have been directed by the honorable Secretary of War . . . to notify the Mexican authorities that they must break up and disperse the bands of banditti concerned in the outrages. . . . I shall, therefore consider it my duty to hold them [the Mexican officials] responsible for its faithful performance. . . ."[37]

The Cortina War cannot be considered an important military episode, and yet it has considerable significance in the history of American and Mexican border relations. The parallels between it and the Punitive Expedition of 1916 are so obvious they scarcely need mention. Moreover, it seemed to fix the pattern of borderland affairs for a long time to come—lawless raids into the United States from Mexico, with Mexican officials either unwilling or unable to prevent them or punish raiders, and with the United States finally stirred to direct action, at the same time arousing the liveliest indignation and resentment on the part of the Mexicans.

As for Juan Nepomuceno Cortina himself, he was a man who unquestionably had elements of greatness. He was intelligent, forceful and courageous. In his violent and ignorant way he was probably devoted patriotically to Mexico. His entire life and career, however, belie the idea suggested by some writers that he was a "Robin Hood." From all evidence he seems never to have had an ideal beyond advancing himself, despite the high sentiments expressed in his proclamation. Throughout his life he betrayed, changed sides without hesitation, murdered and stole whenever he saw the slightest advantage to himself. Regardless of his innate capabilities, his lack of any moral foundation made it impossible for him ever to be more than a glorified bandit.

NOTES

1. Domenech, *op. cit.*, pp. 334–46; John Salmon Ford, *Rip Ford's Texas*, Stephen B. Oates, ed. (Austin, Tex., 1963), pp. 195–202. Ford, who was in the Carbajal affair, had abandoned the practice of medicine for the more exciting life of a ranger and a frontier newspaper editor

and publisher. His nickname came from the Mexican War, when, as a regimental surgeon, he entered the letters RIP, after the name of each man who died. The work cited here, although written in the third person, is autobiographical, the lacunae being skillfully filled in by the editor from Ford's voluminous papers.

2. Domenech, *op. cit.*, pp. 347–48. The writer has been unable to confirm either that there was any marked increase in raids or that any special warning was sent to Avalos. Either or both of these alternatives are quite probable.

3. Ford, *op. cit.*, pp. 215–16; Walter Prescott Webb, *The Texas Rangers. A Century of Frontier Defense*, Foreword by Lyndon B. Johnson (Austin, Tex., 2nd ed., 1965), pp. 146–47. Mexicans asserted that the Fort Duncan garrison emplaced artillery, prepared to fire, to cover Callahan's retirement across the river. Frederick Law Olmsted, who visited Texas shortly after the incident, said that Callahan's expedition was actually a reconnaissance, preparatory to another attempt to establish the "Republic of Sierra Madre." See Olmsted, *A Journey Through Texas; or a Saddle-Trip on the Southwestern Frontier: with a Statistical Appendix* (New York, 1857), pp. 333, 506.

4. Ford, *op. cit.*, p. 264.

5. *Ibid.;* Webb, *op. cit.*, pp. 178–79; Petition of the People of Brownsville to the President, Oct. 2, 1859, H.R. Exec. Doc. No. 52, 36th Cong., 1st sess., "Difficulties on Southwestern Frontier," Francis W. Latham, Senator John Hemphill, Mayor Stephen Powers to the President, pp. 31–35; correspondent, New Orleans *Picayune*, pp. 39–40. The basic document is hereafter cited as *Difficulties on Southwestern Frontier.*

6. Ford, *op. cit.*, pp. 175–77; Webb, *op. cit.*, pp. 262–63; Ruel McDaniel, "Juan Cortina—Hero or Bandit?" *The Best of True West*, Joe Austell Small, ed. (New York, 1964), pp. 305–7.

7. Webb, *op. cit.*, pp. 175–76.

8. Latham and Hemphill to the President, *Difficulties on Southwestern Frontier*, pp. 31–34.

9. It will be noted that these are "anti-Indian" rather than "anti-Mexican" measures. Before the Civil War and for many years after, only one or two companies of each artillery regiment were equipped to act as artillery. The other companies habitually functioned as infantry.

10. Langdon to the President, *Difficulties on Southwestern Frontier*, p. 35.

11. The Adjutant General to Twiggs, Oct. 25, 1859, *Difficulties on Southwestern Frontier*, p. 36.

12. Statement by H. A. Miller, *Difficulties on Southwestern Frontier*, p. 53.

13. Twiggs to The Adjutant General, Nov. 12, 1859, *Difficulties on Southwestern Frontier*, p. 56. Official communications intended for the Secretary of War were (and still are) addressed to The Adjutant General.

14. Heintzelman graduated from West Point in the class of 1826. He

had a distinguished record in the Mexican War and several Indian wars; he was also noted as an explorer. In the Civil War he was wounded at Bull Run and later commanded a corps in the Army of the Potomac.

15. Telegrams from The Adjutant General to commanding officers, Baton Rouge, Fort Monroe, Fort Leavenworth, *Difficulties on Southwestern Frontier*, pp. 54, 59, 60–61.

16. Special orders No. 105, Department of Texas, *Difficulties on Southwestern Frontier*, pp. 55–56.

17. Cortina's proclamation, *Difficulties on Southwestern Frontier*, pp. 70–72.

18. Heintzelman to Col. Robert E. Lee, H.R. Exec. Doc. No. 81, 36th Cong., 1st sess., "Troubles on Texas Frontier," p. 5. The basic document is hereafter referred to as *Troubles on Texas Frontier*.

19. *Ibid.*, p. 6.

20. Webb, *op. cit.*, p. 181.

21. Campbell to Heintzelman, Jan. 28, 1860, *Troubles on Texas Frontier*, p. 19.

22. Heintzelman to Lee, *Troubles on Texas Frontier*, p. 6.

23. *Ibid.*, pp. 7–8; Ford, *op. cit.*, p. 267.

24. Ford, *op. cit.*, pp. 266–67.

25. *Ibid.*, p. 265.

26. The foregoing outline of the "Battle of Rio Grande City," and the subsequent pursuit is synthesized from Ford's own narrative (*Rip Ford's Texas*, pp. 270–75) and Heintzelman's official report to Colonel Lee (*Troubles in Texas Frontier*, pp. 9–10). The two accounts differ only in minor details.

27. Heintzelman's report to Lee, *Troubles on Texas Frontier*, p. 10; Ford, *op. cit.*, pp. 276–77.

28. Heintzelman to Texas Commissioners, and Commissioners to Ford, Feb. 2, 1860, *Troubles on Texas Frontier*, pp. 62–63.

29. Ford and Langdon to Heintzelman, Feb. 4, 1860, *Troubles on Texas Frontier*, pp. 63–64.

30. Ford, *op. cit.*, pp. 282–87.

31. Heintzelman to Ford, Stoneman to Heintzelman, *Troubles on Texas Frontier*, pp. 65–66, 70.

32. Heintzelman to General Guadaloupe [*sic*] García, Feb. 9, 1860, *Troubles on Texas Frontier*, p. 70.

33. Douglas Southall Freeman, *R. E. Lee. A Biography* (New York and London, 1934), I, 405.

34. The Adjutant General to Lee, *Difficulties on Southwestern Frontier*, pp. 134–35.

35. Stoneman and Ford to Heintzelman, Mar. 18, 1860, *Troubles on Texas Frontier*, pp. 80–81; Ford, *Rip Ford's Texas*, pp. 292–95.

36. Ford, *op. cit.*, pp. 295–98; W. J. Hughes, *Rebellious Ranger. Rip Ford and the Old Southwest* (Norman, Okla., 1964), pp. 175–76.

37. Lee to General Garcia, Apr. 12, 1860, *Troubles on Texas Frontier*, pp. 102–3.

CHAPTER 3

Civil War on the Rio Grande

THE ACRID POWDER smoke of the Cortina War had scarcely drifted away when the borderlands were again enveloped in the confusion and horror of war being waged on both sides of the river. In the United States, only a few months after Cortina had vanished up the road to Monterrey, the long and bitter controversy between the slave states and the free states blazed into open conflict as the slave states seceded from the Union and formed themselves into the Confederate States of America.

Upon the secession of Texas, General Twiggs, who had resumed command, promptly and meekly surrendered all the troops, posts and government property in his department to the Texas Secessionists, in spite of his half-century of service in the United States uniform. Captain George Stoneman, at Fort Brown, flatly refused to obey the order to surrender and managed, with part of his command, to get to Union territory. Colonel Robert E. Lee was hurriedly summoned to Washington for a conference with the President, in which he was probably offered the supreme command of the Union armies. If so, he declined to accept the position; he resigned from the army and joined the forces of his native state. In Texas, John Salmon Ford became Colonel Ford, Confederate States Army, charged with the primary mission of keeping the border open for the importation of the necessities that the South could not produce for itself.

In Mexico, as the Civil War in the United States progressed, the long war between clericals and liberals blazed with renewed fury. The liberal government of President Benito Juárez found itself unable to pay the interest on Mexican bonds held by European investors and speculators. The result was an allied French, British and Spanish expeditionary force to enforce payment. The British and Spanish soon left; the French remained. Napoleon III saw a marvelous opportunity to fish in troubled waters. The almost defeated clerical-conservative party of Mexico saw an opportunity to gain French support for itself. The outcome was that the clericals proclaimed themselves to be the lawful and legitimate government of Mexico, announced that Mexico was a constitutional monarchy, and invited Napoleon III to nominate a suitable emperor for the country. Napoleon responded with alacrity; the French forces in Mexico were expanded to an army strong enough for conquest, and the Archduke Maximilian, a younger brother of the Emperor of Austria, was seated on the "throne" of Mexico, supported by French bayonets.

As the Union blockade tightened its grip on the seacoasts of the Confederacy, the little towns along the Rio Grande became increasingly important. Cotton could be shipped from Texas into Mexico, eventually finding its way to the mills and factories of Europe, and producing credit and specie for the Confederacy; arms, clothing, blankets, medicines and even occasional luxury articles could be brought to Texas via Mexico, even though Mexico was in a condition of virtual anarchy. It is true that such indirect import and export were awkward and expensive, but under the circumstances, they were well worth while. On January 30, 1863, Brigadier General Hamilton P. Bee, who commanded the Confederate forces on the Lower Rio Grande, reported that no less than sixty vessels were anchored off the mouth of the river, awaiting lighterage to unload. The Confederate quartermaster at Fort Brown stated that he had been able to contract with reliable and reputable mercantile firms in Brownsville for a six months' supply of the articles for which he was responsible. All these commodities were shipped from Europe with bills of lading that specified Mexico as their destination. Landed at Bagdad, on the Mexican side of the river's mouth, they were hauled by wagon to Matamoras and thence into the Confederacy.[1] The traffic was unhindered as long as the Confederates held the river line, and for a long time the United States was unable to dispute their control. As a theater of operations the Rio Grande frontier remained almost dormant until late in 1863.

Almost dormant, but not entirely so. A series of pinpricks kept the situation from becoming stagnant. On February 8, 1863, General Bee sent an indignant letter to Governor Lopez, of Tamaulipas, saying that on December 26, just past, a party of Mexican citizens had crossed into Texas and attacked a Confederate Government wagon train. They had killed the teamsters, plundered the train, and "found shelter and protection on the soil of Mexico." On the same day, Bee declared, another party from Mexico had murdered Don Isidro Vela, the highly respected and esteemed justice of Zapata County. Captain Refugio Benavides, of the Confederate Army, had pursued the latter band across the river into Mexico and had inflicted severe losses upon them. These outrages, Bee asserted, were not the work of ordinary bandits, robbing for gain, but were committed by a pro-Union organization formed on the soil of Mexico by a renegade Texas citizen, one Antonio (or Octaviano) Zapata. Members carried the United States flag and called themselves the "First Regiment of Union Troops."[2] Governor Lopez, in reply, was extremely noncommittal; he actually gave Bee a polite "brush-off," intimating that Zapata's men were outlaws who claimed Mexican or United States citizenship according to their needs at the moment.

In February, 1863, Bee quietly began correspondence with Lopez for an agreement whereby the bandits and Unionists (he equated them) might be brought under control by concerted efforts of Confederate and Mexican troops, and the movement of individuals across the boundary could be regulated by the issue of passports. At this time Bee was perturbed because of the number of his men (unwilling "volunteers," mostly of Mexican stock) who were deserting and taking refuge in Mexico. Bee asserted that the United States consul at Matamoras, Leonard Pierce, was enlisting these men in the Union Army. Governor Lopez courteously refused to take any action on this issue. The consul, he said, was not enlisting men and hence was not violating Mexico's neutrality; he was caring for indigent citizens of the

United States who appealed to him for assistance, as was his consular duty. As for mutual action against outlaws, Lopez consented to an agreement whereby troops of either country might cross the boundary to assist the forces of the other country and when in direct pursuit of malefactors or hostile Indians.[3]

Affairs on the Lower Rio Grande remained quiet for a short time, but on March 15, 1863, it was Governor Lopez' turn to protest. A soldier of Captain Santos Benavides' company had got into trouble in the village of Nuevo Laredo. He resisted arrest and was killed in the fracas, whereupon Captain Benavides at once crossed into Mexico with his company, "trampling on the civil and military authorities and committing other outrages."[4] And even more serious, in the early morning hours of March 15, some soldiers of Bee's command crossed the Rio Grande near its mouth and seized Colonel Edmund J. Davis, of the Union Army, and several other Union officers, who had just arrived in Mexico on official business. This was a distinct violation of Mexican sovereignty and neutrality, and Lopez sharply demanded the immediate release and return to Mexico of the prisoners.

Since Davis was a pro-Union and anti-Confederate Texan, other Texans regarded him as a combination of Judas Iscariot and Benedict Arnold, and the popularity he once had with the people of the Lower Valley was forgotten. Nevertheless, under the circumstances, Bee had no choice but to yield as gracefully as possible, but he took occasion again to complain of the scandalous conduct of the consul of the United States in "openly enlisting soldiers in Mexico." Lopez again skillfully side-stepped the issue. He denied that the United States consul was permitted to violate Mexican neutrality, adding, "What appears to you indisputable is not clear to me, and what the authorities of Texas conceive to be an imposition on the part of the North is represented by others as the protection which a consul extends to his fellow-citizens, and the fulfillment of his duty in facilitating their passage to their country.[5]

The agreement between Bee and Lopez bore fruit from the Confederate point of view on the first of September, 1863. On that day Santos Benavides, now a major, Confederate States Army, received an urgent call for help from the *alcalde* of the

Mexican town of Guerrero. A detachment of the town's militia had been attacked and routed by a band of outlaws. Benavides, with such soldiers of his regiment as he could assemble quickly (the 33d Texas Cavalry), crossed into Mexico at once. He followed the trail of the marauders to the vicinity of the town of Mier. On overtaking them, Benavides attacked; in the ensuing fight ten of the band were killed. One of the corpses was identified as Zapata. In forwarding Benavides' report to the department commander, Bee exulted: "We shall no more be troubled with this emissary of the Lincoln Government, who has so long disturbed the peace of this frontier."[6]

Bee had only slender forces in the Lower Rio Grande Valley, and even those were weakened in the summer and early autumn of 1863, when the department commander, alarmed by the movements of General Bank's Federal forces in Louisiana, strengthened the troops in East Texas by withdrawing units from the border. The Federals seemed to threaten East Texas and those parts of Louisiana that were still held by the Confederates; there were no indications of any Federal movement toward the Rio Grande. Not only were the regular Confederate troops withdrawn from the Rio Grande frontier, but all along the Texas coast the regulars were replaced by state troops as rapidly as the latter could be organized.

This was the situation when an express brought a startling message to department headquarters. At 7 P.M., November 1, 1863, seven enemy steamers suddenly appeared at the mouth of the Rio Grande. The next afternoon Bee sent another message: there were now fifteen enemy vessels off Brazos Santiago, and the houses at the mouth of the river had been heavily shelled. Bee proposed to retreat up the Rio Grande slowly, delaying the enemy as much as possible.[7]

Bee's defensive problem was complicated because only a few days before the unexpected appearance of the Union armada, one of his companies—a company of "six months volunteers"—composed entirely of Mexican-Americans, commanded by a Captain Adrian I. Vidal, and stationed at the mouth of the river as an outguard—had mutinied. Preparing for the transfer of forces to East Texas, the regimental commander had sent an order to

Vidal to move his company to Brownsville. Instead of complying, Vidal's men had killed one of the messengers and badly wounded the other, who managed to escape. The mutiny seemed to involve the whole company, including the captain himself. Upon receiving the news, Bee made immediate preparations to defend Brownsville, but instead of moving up the river, Vidal led his company across into Mexico, after committing all sorts of horrible atrocities, according to Bee. Bee sent an urgent request to the governor of Tamaulipas (then General Manuel Ruiz), asking him to apprehend the dangerous culprits. Ruiz replied the same day that twenty of the mutineers had been captured by General Cortina, acting under his orders. (This was the same Juan Nepomuceno Cortina who was last heard of fleeing toward Monterrey.) Captain Vidal, however, had escaped.

All this transpired only a few days before the appearance of the United States vessels at the mouth of the Rio Grande. The mutiny and desertion of a whole company was an indication of something that Confederates hated to admit, and only reluctantly took into account: a large part of the people of the Lower Rio Grande Valley, and especially the Mexican-Americans, were only lukewarm at best in their loyalty to the Confederacy. Further proof was furnished in a short time by the enrollment of Vidal's company into the Federal service, for the duration of the war, and by the ease with which Colonel Edmund Davis recruited his 1st Texas Cavalry Regiment (Federal). (Incidentally, Davis was the respected judge who had persuaded Tobin's Rangers to reconnoiter toward Cortina's lair, as noted earlier.[8])

The Federal expedition to seize the Lower Rio Grande had been carefully and secretly planned and prepared for some time. The assembly of troops had taken place in mid-October. Second Lieutenant Benjamin E. McIntyre, of the 19th Iowa Infantry (a veteran regiment) noted in his diary, "at Champ d' Mars" [sic], Louisiana, that there were rumors that the regiment was going to Texas. He noted, too, that orders were issued for every man to "make known his wants in the way of clothing &c."[9] A few days later all men who were not physically fit were sent to a convalescent camp. Rumors boiled, but nobody really knew anything, except a few senior officers who would not talk. The

French vice consul at New Orleans protested that some French citizens on board a schooner regularly cleared for departure for Matamoras on October 21 had been grievously inconvenienced because the provost marshal had not allowed the vessel to sail. The French official also inquired why the local military authorities were refusing passes from New Orleans to Vera Cruz and Tampico. Brigadier General Charles R. Stone, the department chief of staff, replied courteously but briefly that for sufficient military reasons, and for a limited period of time, there could be no communication between New Orleans and any Mexican port.[10]

On Friday, October 23, 1863, the troops embarked in the midst of a heavy downpour; the next day the already loaded transports dropped downstream to the Southwest Pass of the Mississippi and anchored there. McIntyre noted that there were vessels anchored as far as the eye could reach. On the night of October 27 the convoy weighed anchor and stood out into the Gulf, the soldiers and junior officers still wondering and speculating about where they were going. The voyage was rough and stormy; apparently the convoy was caught in the tail of a Gulf hurricane. For two days and nights the vessels, many of which were really unseaworthy, were in grave danger. On McIntyre's ship (the *General Banks*) it was necessary to jettison caissons and some unfortunate horses and mules to lighten the load. But finally, after ten uncomfortable and peril-filled days, the convoy dropped anchor off the mouth of the Rio Grande. At 1:30 P.M., November 2, 1863, the 19th Iowa landed at Brazos Santiago, and the United States flag flew over that bit of Texas for the first time since the state had seceded from the Union.[11]

The Federal disembarkation was unopposed. The Federal threat to East Texas had stripped the border of troops, and Bee's remaining force was so utterly inadequate that he made no effort to resist. Unknown to the Federals, however, their landing was closely observed by small Confederate patrols that took care to keep themselves out of sight.[12] Athough unopposed by the Confederates, the disembarkation was attended by danger. The sea was still running high from the recent storm, and the surf made handling small boats extremely perilous. At least one boat cap-

sized, and an unknown number of soldiers were drowned. Most of
the vessels were unable to cross the bar into the sheltered lagoon
behind the island. Few of the horses and mules that were pushed
overboard to swim ashore ever made the land. One small ship
sprang a leak and had to be run ashore and abandoned, a total
loss. Another, the *Nassau*, sank in the channel at Brazos Pass
and was lost.[13] To facilitate communication between the small
islands on which the expedition had landed, several ponton
bridges were constructed, one of which anticipated the equipment of World War II. It consisted of "two long huge india
rubber bladders on which cross timbers are placed. . . ." It was
an item of Civil War equipment which has escaped the attention
of historians.[14]

Once ashore in sufficient force, the Federals moved quickly.
A detachment occupied Point Isabel, and the main force marched
directly for Brownsville, arriving there on November 5 in the
afternoon. They found Fort Brown and a considerable part of the
little town in smoldering ruins. Since he was unable to resist,
Bee had set fire to the post and all the government property and
supplies he could not move, and the flames had spread to the
town. Before the arrival of the Union troops the townspeople had
endeavored to extinguish the fires and to salvage (or loot) whatever they could from the stores and supplies. Very soon a wagon
train loaded with cotton rolled unexpectedly into the town; the
teamsters were startled to find themselves impressed into the
Federal service, while their wagons, teams and cargoes were
confiscated for the benefit of the United States Government.

The Federals found themselves entangled at once in the meshes
and intricacies of Mexican politics. Among the foremost in endeavoring to extinguish the fires and salvage articles from the
flames after the departure of the Confederates was a well-known
Mexican general and political figure, General José Cobos, who
had been residing in Brownsville for some time as an exile. Cobos
was an officer of the Mexican Regular Army, and in the turmoil
that had split Mexico into two bitterly hostile factions, he was
a strong supporter of the ultraconservative party that was in
revolt against the government and party of President Benito
Juárez. Within a few hours (almost within a few minutes)

after the Federals reached Brownsville, and long before they had any opportunity to become familiar with the local situation, Cobos assembled his followers in Brownsville and crossed the river to Matamoras. He surprised and captured the Juarista governor of Tamaulipas, General Manuel Ruiz, and then issued the proclamation without which no Mexican revolution is complete.

Cobos did not actually designate himself governor, although that was the general purport of his proclamation, and he clearly indicated his complete sympathy with the Imperialists and the French intervention. But Cobos reckoned without that sterling Mexican patriot, General Juan Nepomuceno Cortina. On November 7, 1863, Cortina captured Cobos, and within a few hours Cobos fell before a firing squad. General Ruiz, supposing himself to be restored to office, issued a proclamation and tried to pick up the reins of government, but upon receiving an offer from Cortina of a bodyguard for his personal protection, he decided to seek the safety of the United States. Cortina was then the supreme power in Matamoras and very soon became the self-elected governor of Tamaulipas.

General Banks was inclined to regard Cortina's accession to power as a development favorable to the United States, in spite of Cortina's previous record. Cortina had, so far, been consistently hostile to the Imperialists and the French, who were believed to favor the Confederacy, and Banks noted in his report to Washington that Cortina, as soon as he was in power, had placed three river steamers at the disposal of the Union forces.[15] During the disorder that attended the successive "revolutions" in Matamoras, all within a few hours, The United States consul, Leonard Pierce, sent a note to Banks asking for military protection for the consulate. Banks declined to send any troops across the river, but he did place a battery of artillery on the riverbank, in a position to fire into Matamoras.

The situation remained static (at least on the surface) for several weeks, but late at night, January 12, 1864, the consul sent a frantic note to Major General J. F. Herron, who had succeeded to the immediate command of the Federal forces on the Lower Rio Grande. Pierce said that heavy fighting had broken out in Matamoras between the partisans of Cortina and the followers of Ruiz. The consulate was in grave danger, and Pierce had almost a million dollars in specie in his possession, as well as valuable property of other sorts. Pierce did not trust Cortina and his followers.

Herron at once sent an officer to the consulate to reconnoiter and report on the situation. At the same time he ordered the seizure of the ferry across the river and notified both Cortina and Ruiz that he was dispatching United States troops into Mexico to guard the consulate and remove the consul and his family and belongings as soon as possible. Colonel Henry Bertram, of the 20th Wisconsin Infantry, was then ordered to take four companies of his regiment to the consulate. Under no circumstances was Bertram to open fire, or take any part in the fighting, unless actually fired upon. Stray shots were to be ignored even if they caused casualties. By 11:30 P.M. the same night Bertram's force was at the consulate; he reported that all firing stopped as soon as the American troops appeared, and was not resumed for some time. At daybreak Herron sent a small wagon train to the consulate, and by seven o'clock the consul, his family, the consular records and the specie, United States government funds, were all safely in Brownsville. The fighting in Matamoras continued until noon, when Ruiz and his faction fled to the United States. Cortina had won a complete and decisive victory; he issued a proclamation formally announcing himself to be the governor of Tamaulipas, a position he had held *de facto* for some time.[16]

For reasons that are not recorded, the strength of the Union forces in the Rio Grande Valley was sharply reduced during the summer of 1864. Consequently, when Colonel John Salmon Ford organized an "Expeditionary Force" to expel the Yankee invaders, he encountered small resistance. The Federals withdrew to a fortified position at Brazos Santiago from which the Confederates never attempted to dislodge them but which effectively blocked the Rio Grande. Ford easily reoccupied Brownsville, and small Confederate detachments again held the principal river crossings.

In Mexico it seemed that the Republic was doomed. President

Juárez and his government were fugitives. Powerful French forces and their Imperialist puppets ranged almost unresisted throughout most of the country. The state of Tamaulipas, now presided over by Cortina, was one of the few regions still nominally under control of the Republic. But late in August even this last stronghold was threatened when French and Imperialist columns began converging upon the state from the interior, and a French naval force landed troops at Bagdad (at the mouth of the Rio Grande) that began immediate and obvious preparations to advance up the river. Cortina abandoned his state capital and about the first of September, 1864, arrived at Matamoras with some fifteen hundred men and several pieces of artillery. The troops he had were too few in number to offer any hope of defending Matamoras successfully against the forces converging upon the city. After a council of war (at which the American consul may have been present) he decided to pass his troops across the river and surrender them to the Union commander. On the sixth or seventh of September, 1864, a part of Cortina's men, with an unrecorded number of artillery pieces, actually crossed the Rio Grande, broke through the thin Confederate cordon along the river (Ford had advance information that this was likely to occur), and surrendered themselves to Major E. R. Noyes, of the Federal 1st Texas Cavalry. But, both before and after their surrender, they fought against Ford's Confederates— conduct that aroused extreme indignation on the part of the commander of the French force advancing up the river and resulted in an icy exchange of correspondence between Ford and the Union commander at Brazos Santiago, Colonel Henry M. Day. Especially indignant was Brigadier General Thomas F. Drayton, C.S.A., who arrived at Brownsville a few days later and reported that Cortina "has most treacherously and unexpectedly allied himself with the Yankees. . . ."[17]

Although it was fully expected that Cortina himself, with his staff and entire force, would cross the river, he evidently changed his mind. Cortina was no believer in standing for a lost cause, and the Republic of Mexico seemed doomed. Instead, he hoisted the Imperialist flag and changed sides.

During the time when the two neighboring countries were

simultaneously fighting desperate civil wars, the Lower Rio Grande was the most critical part of the borderlands simply because it was the most populous region, and one of the few channels through which the Confederacy and the Mexican Republic could obtain essential supplies from the outside world. The Confederate coast was blockaded by the Union Navy, and the French held tight control over most of the Mexican gulf ports. To say, however, that the Lower Valley was the most critical region is not to imply that the turmoil and bloodshed did not extend to other border regions. From the Gulf of Mexico to the Colorado River, Indians were on the prowl, outlaws raided, and occasionally Union and Confederate troops met in combat.[18]

In the western tip of Texas, a thousand miles from the mouth of the Rio Grande, a band of outlaws led by one Edward Hall established itself at the abandoned post of old Fort Leaton. Using the fort as a base, they raided ranches and settlements in Chihuahua. Apparently they confined their activities to Mexico; in western Texas there was very little to loot, and the presence of a formidable force of Federal troops acted as a deterrent. In February, 1863, Brigadier General James H. Carleton, in command of the Department of New Mexico, cordially invited General Luis Terrazas, the governor of Chihuahua, to send Mexican troops into the United States to clean out the band. Whether or not Terrazas availed himself of the invitation is not recorded.[19]

After four years of fraternal bloodshed, the Civil War in the United States came to its end, but in Mexico the war raged on. The end of the war in the United States made one great difference to the opposing sides in Mexico; the Confederates favored the Imperialists and their French sponsors. The Unionists, now in complete control of the border, had always favored President Juárez and the Republic and had consistently refused to recognize Maximilian's government. Immediately after Lee's surrender, Major General Philip H. Sheridan was assigned to command the Department of the Gulf and the Military Division of the Southwest and Gulf. His assignment was so important that General Grant refused to allow him to delay long enough to lead his wartime command in the great victory parade in Washington. For troops he was given the IVth, XIIIth and XXVth

Corps and two cavalry divisions, all under experienced and battle-tried commanders. The strength of the force amounted to some 52,000 men. Moving such a force to Texas, and a large part of it to the Rio Grande, entailed tremendous transportation and supply problems, but they were overcome. There was some dissatisfaction among the troops, especially in Custer's cavalry division ("I wanna go home!"), but discipline was sternly and quickly restored, and in a few weeks a tough, war-hardened army of veterans and commanders faced the Rio Grande. It was a force that Napoleon III dared not overlook.

Secretary of State Seward was opposed to active intervention in Mexico except as a desperate last resort. Consequently, Sheridan's orders required him, to his own intense disgust, to observe the strictest neutrality. Nevertheless, he had his own interpretation of strict neutrality and saw no reason why he should not give the Republicans all the moral and material support possible. He (and General Grant also) regarded the war in Mexico as an extension of the Civil War in the United States, especially as large numbers of Confederates had entered the service of Maximilian. Sheridan at once opened a "cold war" against the French and Imperialist commander at Matamoras for the immediate surrender of arms and munitions that had been turned over to him by Confederates entering Mexico. He ordered large-scale demonstrations and maneuvers at places and times that were sure to be reported to Mexico City and the French high command. He ostentatiously reviewed the IVth Corps and Merritt's cavalry division at San Antonio, inspecting them for their readiness for an immediate campaign. Escorted by a whole cavalry regiment, he rode to Fort Duncan and from there sent messengers to President Juárez with instructions to inquire openly about routes into Mexico, the availability of forage for large numbers of horses and arrangements for its purchase.[20]

Not quite so ostentatious were some of the other measures Sheridan took to support and bolster the Republican cause in Mexico. His authority as a department commander enabled him legally to declare surplus or to condemn large numbers of weapons and great quantities of ammunition. Such items were "destroyed" by being deposited at various points on the Rio

Grande, after word had been conveyed to the Republicans. There is an apocryphal story that on one occasion a lieutenant in command of a wagon train loaded with arms, munitions, medicines and other supplies was instructed: "If you are attacked by Indians, you will, of course, defend the train to the last man. If you encounter Mexicans, you will immediately abandon the train and return to the nearest post with your men."[21]

A curious incident, which has never been fully or satisfactorily explained, occurred shortly before the final collapse of Maximilian's empire. In November, 1866, Matamoras was occupied by a small Imperial force (all Mexican) commanded by a General Canales. Republicans, under General Escobedo, surrounded the city on three sides and were preparing to assault. On November 24 the commander of the United States troops at Brownsville, for some unknown reason, sent a formal demand to Canales that he surrender the city to United States forces. Canales submitted; a ponton bridge was thrown across the river, and Matamoras was occupied by United States troops. But oddly enough, the demand had been for the surrender of the city and not for the surrender of Canales' troops. Thus, since Canales was not obliged to leave any guards or security elements in Matamoras, his whole force was available to man the fortifications, and his combat strength was greatly increased. In the ensuing attack by Escobedo, the Republicans were sharply repulsed, with heavy losses. Too late the actual effect of the unauthorized and injudicious demand of the American commander became apparent; the Americans were quickly withdrawn and the bridge dismantled.

Meanwhile the Americans of Brownsville became seriously alarmed. It was rumored that Cortina, who had switched sides again and was now a staunch Republican, was about to raid Brownsville in retaliation. (There were citizens in Brownsville who remembered Cortina's last raid only six years earlier.) To augment the United States forces, a volunteer force was raised with John Salmon Ford as colonel. Ford was described by the New York *Tribune*, in reporting the matter, as a "notorious fillibuster and confederate." Cortina's anticipated attack did not occur, but an inevitable result of the American commander's ill-considered act was a high degree of resentment among the Mexicans for all gringos. In apologizing to the Mexican minister at Washington for the incident, Secretary Seward said that there was reason to believe that the American officer who ordered the invasion of Mexico was acting in response to urgent requests from leading Republicans of Matamoras and that he had believed that he was actually aiding the Republican cause. In any event, the responsible officer had been disciplined and relieved of his command; the United States government completely disavowed his act.[22]

Whether or not Seward's determination not to intervene actively in Mexico prolonged the life of Maximilian's empire, that empire was doomed. Napoleon III saw clearly the handwriting on the wall. The French armies were withdrawn and the tinsel empire collapsed. Maximilian, with his two principal Mexican supporters, Mejía and Miramon, died before a Republican firing squad, and the government of President Benito Juárez again became the recognized government of Mexico. In the United States the ways of peace were resumed. In Mexico, although disorder was rife for several years to come, the same was largely true. But the borderlands remained much the same as they had always been—the haunt of desperadoes and freebooters and the hunting grounds for roving Indians.

NOTES

1. For examples illustrating the importance of this traffic to the Confederacy, see *O.R.*, Ser. 1, Vol. XXVI, Pt. 2, 137–39, 153–54, 157–58, 169, 421.
2. *Ibid.*, Ser. 1, Vol. XV, 966–67. Bee's identification of Zapata as "Antonio" seems to have been erroneous, since all other references to him show that his given name was Octaviano. He is said to have been an American citizen who, like many other Mexican-Americans, was bitterly anti-Confederate.
3. *Ibid.*, pp. 991–98, 1006–8.
4. *Ibid.*, p. 1129.
5. *Ibid.*, pp. 1130–35.
6. *Ibid.*, Pt. , pp. 284–85.
7. *Ibid.*, pp. 432–33.

8. *Ibid.*, pp. 447–51, 439–40, 830.

9. *Federals on the Frontier. The Diary of Benjamin F. McIntyre, 1862–1864,* Nannie M. Tilley, ed. (Austin, Tex., 1963), pp. 234–35. Hereafter referred to as *Diary.*

10. *O.R.,* Ser. 1, Vol. XXVI, Pt. 1, 792.

11. *Diary,* pp. 240–49.

12. *O.R.,* Ser. 1, Vol. XXVI, Pt. 1, 443–45.

13. *Diary,* 251–53; *O.R.,* Ser. 1, Vol. XXVI, Pt. 1, 787.

14. *Diary,* p. 253.

15. *Ibid.,* p. 257; *O.R.,* Ser. 1, Vol. XXVI, Pt. 1, 399–409.

16. *O.R.,* Ser. 1, Vol. XXXIV, 81–84.

17. *O.R.,* Ser. 1, Vol. XLI, Pt. 2, 931. See also Clarence C. Clendenen, "Mexican Unionists: A Forgotten Incident of the War Between States," *New Mexico Historical Review,* XXXIX (1964), 32–39.

18. The reader who may be interested in a more detailed study of Indian affairs in the border regions is referred to Robert M. Utley, *Frontiersmen in Blue. The United States Army and the Indian, 1848–1865* (New York, 1967), chaps. 8 and 12.

19. *O.R.,* Ser. 1, Vol. XV, 687.

20. Philip Henry Sheridan, *Personal Memoirs* (New York, 1888), II, 208–16; "Report of Operations of the United States Forces and General Information of the Condition of Affairs in the Military Division of the Southwest and Gulf and Department of the Gulf, Major General P. H. Sheridan, U.S.A., Commanding, from May 29, 1865 to November 4, 1866" (New Orleans, 1866), *passim.*

21. Carl Coke Rister, *Border Command. General Phil Sheridan in the West* (Norman, Okla., 1944), pp. 17–18. As for the legendary incident related, the writer has heard several versions and does not recall when, or from whom, he first heard it.

22. "Diplomatic Correspondence," 40th Cong., 2nd sess., H. R. Exec. Doc. No. 1, Pt. 2, pp. 494–500. See also John Salmon Ford, *Rip Ford's Texas,* Stephen B. Oates, ed. (Austin, Tex., 1963), p. 409. The name of the responsible officer is given in "Diplomatic Correspondence" as General John Sedgwick. None of the army lists of the time, however, show any officer of that name. The only John Sedgwick shown on any list was the commander of the Sixth Corps, who was killed at Spottsylvania in May, 1864.

CHAPTER 4

Kickapoos, Mescaleros and Mexico

THE ECHOES OF the Civil War in the United States had not yet completely died away, and Mexico was still in a turmoil from internal war and the French invasion, when a new and deadly peril for the Americans of the borderland appeared—the Kickapoos.

To recount in detail how the Kickapoos, originally a forest tribe inhabiting Wisconsin and northern Illinois, became a border tribe living in and raiding from Mexico, is beyond the scope of this narrative. Suffice it to say that the Kickapoos, from their first contacts with white men (the French missionaries and traders of the seventeenth century) had consistently and stubbornly refused to be friendly. Occasionally they allied themselves with one group of white men or another, but they always refused to submit in the slightest degree to the white man's rule. Thus they aided Clark in the capture of Vincennes in 1779; they fought against the Americans in the War of 1812. As a result of that war swarms of Americans began moving into the Mississippi Valley; the Kickapoos fought savagely, but there was only one possible outcome. By 1830 the whole tribe migrated to the Great Plains, where it quickly became one of the foremost of the horse-riding tribes.

War parties of Kickapoos were active in terror-inspiring raids on the Texas frontier in the 1830s and 1840s—activities in which they were encouraged by the agents and officials of the Mexican government, then at war with Texas. Gradually, however, the

Kickapoos, along with other Plains tribes, began to feel the pressure of the steadily advancing white settlements and to be restricted by the cordon troops and military posts that General Twiggs was establishing on the northern and western frontiers of Texas in the late 1850s. During the Civil War, large bands of Kickapoos, taking advantage of the white men's so busily shooting at each other that they had almost no time to devote to Indians, migrated from Kansas and the Indian Territory to Mexico. Small groups of Kickapoos had previously settled in Mexico, where they met with much favor from Mexican officials and the general population. A village of Kickapoos near a Mexican town was insurance against raids by other tribes. In January, 1865, a large band of Kickapoos, moving toward Mexico, encamped for a few days' rest on Dove Creek, in western Texas. The Indians had purposely gone far to the west of the usual trails into Mexico in order to avoid any encounter with Texans. Nevertheless, a company of Rangers discovered them and attacked on January 8. The Texans, badly mauled in their indiscreet attack, retired during the night; the Kickapoos, anticipating further attacks, broke camp and resumed their march for the Rio Grande, in spite of zero weather.

Burning with hatred for Americans, and especially for Texans, the Indians arrived in Mexico in the middle of January and found themselves welcomed by the Mexicans. They were immediately granted wide lands for their exclusive use and were furnished with seed, implements and oxen. In return they were expected to protect the Mexican settlements from incursions by plundering Comanches and Apaches. Any loot they gathered was to be theirs, with no questions asked. The Kickapoos interpreted the attack made on them during their hegira as a declaration of war. With real enthusiasm they accepted the challenge and within a short time proved to be the worst scourge the Rio Grande frontier had ever known.

The Kickapoos were out for more than revenge against the Americans; they quickly discovered a new and easy way to make themselves rich, according to their ideas of wealth. Cattle, horses, mules and all sorts of saleable articles, along with captives for ransom, were easily picked up in raids across the Rio

Grande. Through a Mexican business agent they were provided with proper documents needed to legalize the sale of their loot to Mexican buyers. The same business agent conducted a store or trading post where the Kickapoos could buy or barter for sugar, tobacco, liquor, weapons, powder and everything else they wanted or needed.[1]

Very soon after the Civil War the United States government began efforts to bring the Kickapoos back from Mexico to the reservation that had been selected for them in the Indian Territory. In 1871, John D. Miles, an Indian agent who had had wide experience in dealing with the nation's troublesome wards, was sent to Mexico to persuade the Kickapoos to return to the United States. Miles was a Quaker and sincerely believed that peaceful persuasion could be successful. After weeks of effort and continual frustration by local Mexican officials and merchants, Miles had to admit defeat. The Indians were indifferent, and Miles found that the officials and merchants who were profiting immensely from Kickapoo plunder had convinced them that the Americans were trying to lure them across the Rio Grande only to massacre them—a not unreasonable fear, in view of the things that had happened in the past. Miles found, too, that the people of Santa Rosa, the town near which the Kickapoos were located, feared that if the Kickapoos were removed, the Comanches would resume their raids. In short, Miles found that every effort and argument on his part was quickly and skillfully sabotaged by the local Mexicans.[2]

While Miles was en route for Mexico, the State Department called upon William Schuchardt, the United States Commercial Agent (or consul) at Piedras Negras for a report upon Indian and Mexican depredations against Texas. His answer was that the depredations were largely committed by the Kickapoos, with some assistance from bands of Lipans and Mescaleros (subdivisions of the Apache tribe) living in Mexico a short distance from the Rio Grande. Schuchardt mentioned a merchant (presumably in Piedras Negras) who had advanced twenty dollars' worth of ammunition and other items to a Lipan, to be paid for later. The merchant was paid with a new Spencer carbine of the latest model, property of the United States government, which the

Indian had taken from a soldier whom the Indian had killed, "the Mexicans listening to the Lipan's story all through as though it had been a very funny trick."[3]

Indian raids across the Rio Grande devastated whole districts, and the Governor of Texas wrote to the President that the entire region was being depopulated. The well-intentioned philanthropists in Washington planned another peaceful mission similar to the abortive one by Miles. Through diplomatic channels efforts were made to insure the cooperation of the central Mexican government—efforts that failed to take into account the weaknesses that made the Mexican government unable to enforce its authority upon local officials.

The Americans of the borderland, meanwhile, continued to suffer. In the early spring of 1873, Colonel (Brevet Major General) Ranald S. Mackenzie, of the 4th Cavalry, who had just completed a decisive campaign against the Comanches and had brought that warlike tribe to terms for the first time, was ordered to transfer his regiment to Fort Clark, Texas. Mackenzie can justly be described as a military leader of almost Napoleonic genius. He had graduated from West Point at the head of the class of 1862, when the Civil War had been raging for over a year; three years later, at the end of the war, he was a major general in command of a corps. During his rapid ascent up the promotion ladder he had been wounded no less than five times and had acquired a reputation as an unbending martinet who would brook no slackness.

Frontier regiments were frequently moved from one station to another, and the transfer of the 4th Cavalry to Fort Clark appeared to be another routine change of station. A change of station was much more than a mere matter of saddling horses and riding down the road. Most of the officers and many of the noncommissioned officers and soldiers were married men with families. They had household effects, things that they needed and cherished, all the way from ancestral silver to children's toys. Consequently, when a regiment changed station in the days before railroads, it more closely resembled a caravan than a military formation. Wagons were piled high with all sorts of nonmilitary articles. Ambulances, buckboards and "mountain wagons" were crowded with women and children. Dogs rode high on loaded wagons or trotted alongside.

Five companies, with their wagon train, moved out from Fort Richardson, Texas, on March 5, 1873. In spite of the "family" atmosphere, they were moving through Indian country, and all precautions were taken. The soldiers' ammunition belts were full, advance guards rode ahead, all suspicious hills were covered by flank guards. At night, the wagons were circled, horses were "side-lined" and hobbled, and outguards were posted. At one point on the march the reason for care was apparent—the debris of a burned wagon train, with human bones still scattered on the ground, where a war party of Kiowas, led by a famous and dreaded chief named Satanta, had surprised the unfortunate teamsters only two years before. In addition to the danger from Indians, it was an uncomfortable march. Water was scarce, and the overloaded wagons needed frequent repairs, causing lengthy delays. But after what seemed to be an interminable number of days on the road, the column finally arrived at Fort Clark on April 1, 1873. Fort Clark was merely a frontier post, but after days in the seemingly endless plains of western Texas, the solidly built structures of stone, adobe and logs, with trees and gardens watered from an enormous spring that gushes forth there, it looked good to the arriving people.

A few days after the 4th Cavalry arrived at Fort Clark, Colonel Mackenzie arrived (he had not marched with the caravan), accompanied by no less personages than the Secretary of War, the Honorable William Belknap, and General Sheridan. Sheridan was in command of the whole frontier, from Canada to the Gulf of Mexico. He inspected the troops closely and found them fit and ready for field service. A few hours later the Secretary of War, General Sheridan and Colonel Mackenzie held a conference behind closed doors. Mackenzie, later and with explicit orders for absolute secrecy, told his adjutant what had transpired. Sheridan had "taken the floor," and the Secretary of War remained silent, but indicated tacitly that he approved fully of what Sheridan had to say:

Mackenzie, you have been ordered down here . . . because I want something done to stop these conditions of banditry, killing, etc., by these people across the river. I want you to *control* and *hold down* the situation, and to *do it in your own way*. I want you to be bold, enterprising, and at all times *full of energy*, when you begin, let it be a campaign of *annihilation, obliteration and complete destruction.* . . .

Mackenzie asked, "Under whose orders and upon what authority am I to act? . . . Will you issue me the necessary orders for my action?" Sheridan replied brusquely, "Damn the *orders!* Damn the *authority.* . . . Your authority and backing shall be Gen. Grant and myself."[4]

Mackenzie devoted the next month to carefully planned preparation. Given his reputation as a martinet, the officers and men saw nothing extraordinary in the rigor with which they were drilled and trained. The soldiers were drilled in dismounting and fighting on foot, in any direction; they were drilled in the mounted attack; they fired their carbines on improvised ranges. The men grumbled, as soldiers always do, and the officers kept out of the colonel's way as much as possible. (Mackenzie was noted for his somewhat explosive temper.) To take the fullest advantage of the grazing in the vicinity of Fort Clark, the companies were scattered out of the post, each one in a different place. This not only guaranteed ample grass to bring the animals into condition but also prevented the prying eyes of possible spies among the Mexican population of Brackettville from seeing what was going on. Everybody in the regiment knew that there was something in the wind. Curiosity became keen when orders were issued to grind all sabers to a razor edge; sabers were not usually carried in an Indian campaign. The regimental quartermaster, Captain Henry Lawton, insisted that he had to know in order to make necessary supply arrangements, but even he was brushed off. All efforts to pump the colonel and the adjutant failed. Mackenzie quietly established an intelligence system that gave him knowledge of the terrain south of the river, and accurate information on what was taking place in the Indian villages.

In the small hours after midnight, May 17, 1873, messengers

hurried from headquarters at Fort Clark to the scattered companies: "Saddle up and march at once" to a designated rendezvous. No one was allowed to return to the post; no one had an opportunity to say good-bye to his family. The first companies arrived at the rendezvous at eight thirty the following morning. They unsaddled and awaited the arrival of troops from outlying stations and places. At two o'clock in the afternoon the whole force was assembled. There were six companies of the 4th Cavalry and a large detachment of Seminole-Negro Scouts, commanded by Lieutenant John L. Bullis, who had already achieved a reputation as an Indian fighter with this almost forgotten organization. The entire force—officers, soldiers, scouts and civilian guides—numbered about four hundred men.

Marching slowly down Las Moras Creek, so as not to reach the Rio Grande before dark, the column moved out. At the last halt, just before dark, Mackenzie assembled the officers and briefly explained his plans and intentions. He spoke bluntly, stressing that the Mexicans would probably regard the expedition as an invasion of their country—an act of war—and that any man who was captured or wounded ran the risk of execution as a filibuster or outlaw.

Immediately after dark the column marched to the river and plunged in. There was a short delay while the first elements cut a ramp in the almost vertical bank on the Mexican side. That done, the crossing took only a few minutes. The troops were in territory that was unknown to all but the guides, and not too well known to them. About ten o'clock they emerged from the timber and canebrakes of the river bottom and came out onto rolling, semidesert plains. Mackenzie was a commander who cared for his horses, but on this occasion he pushed them to the limits of their strength and endurance. Moving alternately at the the walk and trot, the usual cavalry marching gaits, he ordered occasional periods of galloping, thus adding considerably to the speed of the march. It soon became apparent to the officers at the rear of the column that the pack mules, heavily laden with ammunition and rations, could not keep up. They were too heavily loaded, and a mule cannot travel as fast as a horse even without a load. Carter, who was a lieutenant in a company as well as adjutant, rode forward and risked Mackenzie's temper to tell him. Mackenzie ordered a five-minute halt. "Cut the packs loose. Tell the men to fill their pockets with hard bread." In five minutes the column moved again.

By daybreak men were visibly tiring, and the pace was beginning to tell on the horses. Mackenzie had hoped and planned to strike the Kickapoos at dawn, but the guides miscalculated the distance, and the delay caused by the pack mules had cost precious minutes. A rocky streambed in which there were pools of clear cold water gave the tired animals and troopers a new lease on life. They were close to their target, but just how close, none of them knew. While the horses buried their muzzles in the water, the soldiers tightened girths and checked their equipment. The column emerged from the ravine, rode around a small hill, and not far distant, at the foot of a long slope, they saw the huts of an Indian village. There was a signal from the head of the column: "Form platoons, prepare to charge."

The tired horses were spurred into a gallop. There was a burst of firing, scattered and uncertain, as the surprised Kickapoos grabbed such weapons as they could reach. The leading companies raced through the village, revolvers in hand, shooting any Indian who had not reached shelter; the companies in the rear dismounted at the village edge and ploughed through on foot, with carbine and revolver. The month of intense training at Fort Clark paid rich dividends; the operation proceeded as smoothly as a parade ground maneuver. The dismounted troopers, killing an occasional Indian who had not escaped into the brush, capturing others (mostly women and children), quickly set fire to the huts, which, being made of thatch, practically exploded.

The casualties among the Americans totaled only three wounded; officially, the dead among the Indians came to nineteen or twenty, with between forty and fifty prisoners. Actually, there were probably more enemy dead and an unknown number wounded, for Mackenzie refused to consider those who had probably crawled off to die in the brush; he counted only those who could be seen.

Leaving the horses saddled, but staked and strongly guarded, the troopers were allowed a few hours for rest. The wounded were bandaged by the surgeon; horse litters were improvised for those who could not ride. Indian horses (many bearing Texas brands) were herded in for the captives to ride. Late in the afternoon Mackenzie gave the order to mount, and the long march back to the Rio Grande started. To delay any longer would have been suicidal. The Mexican militia was undoubtedly beginning to assemble; escaped Kickapoos and their Mescalero and Lipan allies were probably hurrying to intercept the Americans.

The guides had urged Mackenzie to strike the Kickapoo and Lipan villages simultaneously: the main Lipan village was only a few miles distant. Mackenzie refused to divide his force. It was so small that defeat for one portion would spell disaster for the whole. Wisely, it seems, he decided to confine his attack to the Kickapoo village, the largest Indian village in the region. He had accomplished his main mission—to teach the Kickapoos that they were not safe from American vengeance, even in Mexico.

The night march back to the river was sheer agony and was attended with danger that was absent from the swift and unexpected thrust into Mexico. With the column hampered by its wounded and the prisoners, most of whom were women and children, the march was necessarily slower than the advance had been. Villages of Mescaleros and Lipans could easily send out swarms of fast-moving, hate-filled warriors to intercept the column before it could reach the river. The militia of the nearby Mexican towns could assemble quickly in numbers large enough to be formidable. Men and horses were ready to drop from sheer fatigue and lack of sleep. The Indian children at first caused delays by dropping asleep and falling from the ponies on which they rode with their mothers. This difficulty was solved by lashing them to the saddles so that they could not fall off. The officers, as tired as anybody else, had to ride continually up and down the column, keeping the soldiers awake and making sure that everything was ready for instant battle. Several times during the night the Seminole-Negro scouts reported the enemy approaching, but none appeared. Just as dawn was breaking, the weary troopers could see trees ahead, in the distance. Everybody's spirits rose, for the timber marked the Rio Grande. Some time later, possibly an hour, the horses plunged their muzzles deep into cool water and drank their fill. Recrossing the river was slow work because of the care necessary for the wounded men on their litters. One man died in midstream, before he could be carried to the safety of the United States.

Once across the stream, the horses were unsaddled for the first time in more than forty-eight hours, fires were lighted, strong black coffee brewed, and breakfast was a veritable feast of coffee and hard bread. Very shortly, however, there was a rumble of approaching wagons, and the quartermaster, Captain Henry Lawton, appeared with an ample supply of food for the men and grain and hay for the animals. One of the guides, who owned a ranch near the crossing place, brought several buckets of freshly distilled *mescal*, but before his good intentions could result in any harm, Mackenzie ordered the liquor poured onto the ground. There was probably many a muttered curse among the soldiers, but tired and hungry as they were, the potent liquor could have done nothing but bring trouble.

In a little while, an hour or so later, shots were heard from across the river. On the far shore there was a mixed crowd of Mexicans and Indians, shouting that they would take their revenge that night. A few carbine shots dispersed them quickly, and nobody worried about their boasts and threats. Before dark Mackenzie drew the entire force back from the river a short distance and organized a defensive position, where the tired men and animals enjoyed a night of uninterrupted rest. No enemy appeared, The next day, May 27, 1873, the expedition arrived back at Fort Clark, having made one of the most grueling marches in the long history of the cavalry arm, 159 miles in thirty-two hours, fighting a battle, and returning encumbered with wounded men and a large number of prisoners.

In a campfire discussion after the raid, one of the officers declared that if he had known that the operation was not specifically sanctioned by higher authority, he would have refused to cross the Rio Grande. Mackenzie replied quietly, "Any officer or man who refused to follow me across the river, I would have shot."[5] There can be no doubt that he meant what he said.

Patriotic Mexicans were indignant at the invasion of their country, which, they asserted, was entirely unjustified. They charged that Mackenzie has attacked a peaceful agricultural village while the men were away, tilling their fields; it was claimed that most of the raids into Texas were actually perpetrated by Texans disguised as Indians. The Mexican press demanded that Mackenzie be severely punished. President Grant, however, took no such action, thereby fulfilling Sheridan's promise to Mackenzie: "Your authority and backing shall be Gen. Grant and myself." A few months later the majority of the Kickapoos were induced to return to the United States, in spite of strenuous efforts by local Mexican officials and merchants to discourage the move. The prisoners taken by Mackenzie constituted a strong argument in themselves. The few Kickapoos who remained in Mexico lost their taste for raids into the United States, and the Kickapoo peril was abated. General Sheridan, in his report for 1873, said, "I am happy to state that these depredations have diminished very materially since the punishment administered by Col. Ranald Mackenzie, Fourth Cavalry. . . ."[6]

While Mackenzie's drastic action had been decisive against the Kickapoos, it had little effect upon other tribes, such as the Lipans and Mescaleros, bands of which had moved into Mexico, and no apparent effect at all upon lawless Mexicans who regarded the ranches and farms of Texas as fair prey and easy sources of loot. The perennial Cortina reappeared on the border as mayor of Matamoras and commander of the Mexican government forces on the Lower Rio Grande. It was widely believed that he was responsible for most of the cattle "rustling" that occurred in the next few years, or that if he was not a key figure in the "racket," he still profited hugely by it, and that other forms of robbery and violence took place with his knowledge, if not his blessing.[7]

In March, 1875, one of the boldest, most brazen raids in border history occurred. With plans carefully laid in advance, four widely separated bands of Mexican outlaws crossed the river. Three of the groups were intercepted, and turned back, but the fourth, of about fifty men, rode swiftly over little frequented trails to the vicinity of Corpus Christi, 150 miles from the boundary. They arrived without having been detected on the way. They looted a crossroad store and post office near the town, killing a Mexican employee who refused to join them. A number of Americans who were on the road, unsuspicious of any danger, were seized and maltreated in various ways. Herding their prisoners before them, the band stopped at another wayside store, where they killed an American but lost one of their own number in the brief gun play. Then they looted the store and set fire to it.

The alarm was given in Corpus Christi, and women and children were hastily put aboard a coastwise liner and a lumber schooner; the two vessels stood out to sea and anchored at a safe distance from the shore. The men of the town quickly organized themselves into two volunteer companies and set out to repel the invaders, who released their prisoners and fled. The pursuers caught up but were outnumbered. There were a few casualties on both sides. Fortunately for the Texans, the raiders were intent on getting back to Mexico; they reached the river without any further difficulty, and vanished, with their loot, into the fastnesses of their own country.[8]

While the raid on Corpus Christi was spectacular, and illustrative of conditions in the borderlands in the 1870s, it was not nearly as destructive as the seemingly endless raids by smaller gangs of brigands and small bands of Indians. Life in the hamlets and on the isolated ranches and farms was hazardous; travelers were murdered daily on the roads and trails; herds of cattle, bearing Texas brands, were sold openly in Mexico. Any attempt by Americans to recover stolen animals or property was brushed off by the local Mexican officials, and such attempts were frequently attended by personal danger. In March, 1875, the governor of Texas wrote to President Grant that bandit depredations threatened to depopulate the whole Lower Rio Grande Valley. A few days after the Corpus Christi raid, he wrote to Brigadier General Edward O. C. Ord, who now commanded the Department of Texas: "The country between the Rio Grande and Nueces has been invaded and plundered, and many of the citizens killed, by organized bands of marauders from Mexico."[9]

The turbulence of the borderland region was intensified by the internal state of Mexico. Ever since the attainment of independence, disorder and civil war had been usual rather than extraordinary. Mexico had just come through the long agony of the War of the Reform and the French intervention. After the departure of the French the country was thronged with men who had known nothing in their lives but violence and warfare— discharged soldiers from both the Republican and Imperialist forces. In 1871, shortly after the reelection of President Juárez, General Porfirio Díaz, one of the young and vigorous heroes of the resistance against the French, "pronounced" and started a revolution. Díaz's first revolution was easily suppressed, but in 1876, when he revolted against the government of President Lerdo de Tejada, he threw all Mexico into turmoil again, and eventually, in 1877, he seated himself in the Presidential chair.

Because Díaz launched his attack upon the Lerdo government from the United States, much of the early fighting was in the border regions of Mexico. This gave banditry a powerful stimulus (if one were needed), especially after the success of the revolution, and discharged soldiers without occupations started to drift homeward. In fact, it is hardly an exaggeration to say that at this period, cattle stealing and other forms of banditry became established industries in parts of Mexico. In the Upper Rio Grande Valley, above Laredo, incursions from Mexico continued, although none of them attained the grand scale of the Kickapoo raids before Mackenzie's descent upon their settlement.

Raiders, both Mexican and Indian, usually crossed the Rio Grande in small parties of three or four men, then met at a designated rendezvous to form a stronger band. Thus they escaped detection while crossing, and it was impossible either to prevent their crossing or to trail them through the chaparral. As soon as they had herded some cattle and horses together, often killing the owners, they hurried back to the river and into Mexico, often before their presence was known to anyone but their victims. Occasionally they grew bold and openly defied any attempt to bring them to terms. In 1872 a band supposed to have been composed of both Mexicans and Indians attacked and destroyed a wagon train near Howard's Wells, Texas, slaughtering the Mexican teamsters as callously as if they were gringos. Early

in 1872 a small Mexican raiding party attacked a picket near
Ringgold Barracks, killing two of the soldiers and losing one of
their own number before disappearing into Mexico.[10]

The American commanders on the southern frontier were
more than willing to take the same drastic action that Mackenzie
had taken, but there was always doubt about how far the high
authorities in Washington would back them. Mexico was a
"friendly" country, and Mexicans always chose to regard any
movement of armed Americans into their country as an unjustified "invasion." Except in extreme emergency, or under
the greatest provocations, few Regular Army officers were willing
to risk the displeasure of the President or wanted to take a
chance on a court-martial that would ruin a professional career.

An illustrative episode was the so-called Las Cuevas War, in
November, 1875. Captain James F. Randlett, of the 8th Cavalry,
received reliable information that a gang of raiders already in
the United States would very shortly pass their stolen cattle
across the Rio Grande at Las Cuevas ranch. Las Cuevas was on
the Mexican side of the river, a few miles from Edinburg, Texas,
and was a notorious haven for bandits and cattle thieves. Randlett telegraphed the information to the district commander at
Fort Brown and in reply received instructions that if he caught
up with the robbers while they were crossing the river, he would
follow them into Mexico. Randlett reached the river crossing
late in the afternoon, November 17, just as the brigands were
herding the last of the stolen animals up the bank on the Mexican
side. The Americans opened fire, killing two of the raiders and
wounding a third. Because it was nearly dark, and Randlett did
not know the country, he decided not to cross until the next day.
Early the next morning Captain L. H. McNelly (or McNally),
of the Texas Rangers, arrived with his company of about thirty
men. Meanwhile, also, Major David R. Clendenin, of the 8th
Cavalry, had arrived, and as senior officer present, had assumed
command. McNelly crossed the river; Major Clendenin positively
forbade any crossing by the soldiers. To make a complex story
short, McNelly and his Rangers ran into trouble. They were
outnumbered heavily and were forced back to the riverbank.
Believing that they were in danger of being massacred (Major

Clendenin having departed, for some reason), Randlett crossed with part of his company. Shortly after, a Major J. R. Alexander, also of the 8th Cavalry, arrived at the scene. His first act was to order Randlett to return to the American shore at once. McNelly and his Rangers were left to extricate themselves as best they could, although Alexander posted a Gatling gun to cover their retreat across the river if necessary.[11]

Within a few months after his accession to power, General Porfirio Díaz was induced to order Cortiná to Mexico City and to keep him there. It was noticed that there was an immediate lessening of bandit and cattle-stealing raids in the Lower Rio Grande Valley.

In the region then known as the Upper Rio Grande, extending roughly from Fort Duncan, through what is now Big Bend National Park, to old Fort Leaton, there were few bandit raids because the adjacent parts of Mexco were almost uninhabited and virtually unexplored. Thus the region was a natural highway and haunt for small bands of Mescaleros and Lipans, slipping across the Rio Grande at any one of dozens of crossing places, slinking on foot through the chaparral until they reached a place where there were cattle and horses. Then, mounted at the expense of some hapless rancher, often after killing the rancher and his family, they raced to the river and vanished, often before any news of their raid could become known.

After Mackenzie and his 4th Cavalry were transferred to other areas, soon after the destruction of the Kickapoo village, the United States military commander on this sector of the frontier was Lieutenant Colonel William R. Shafter, of the 24th Infantry. (Later he was the commander of the American expedition to Cuba, in 1898.) His headquarters and most of his regiment were at Fort Clark. Like all the senior officers of his era, Shafter was a Civil War veteran. He was energetic, determined, and most important of all in his particular sphere, he was utterly unafraid of responsibility.

Closely teamed with Shafter was a relatively junior officer, 1st Lieutenant John L. Bullis, also of the 24th Infantry. Bullis, like his commander, was a Civil War veteran. He found civilian life distasteful after the war and had elected to become a career soldier. It fell to his lot to organize, train and command a remarkable organization mentioned before, which today is virtually forgotten, the detachment of Seminole-Negro scouts. These were Seminoles who were removed from Florida during and after the long Indian war in that state. Several bands of them had wound up in Mexico, and for several years they were among the most determined and most feared of the raiders into the United States. The story of their repatriation is too long and too complicated to be repeated here, but it is sufficient to say that by 1870 most of them had recrossed the Rio Grande and were perfectly willing to serve as scouts with the United States Army. Racially, they were much more Negroid than Indian, and Lieutenant Bullis, whose Civil War service had been largely with Negro troops, was a logical choice to command them.[12]

Bullis and his odd organization were prominent in Mackenzie's raid against the Kickapoos. This was their first notable service as a unit, although they were already known as skillful trailers and scouts. And Bullis, even before he took command of them, was already known as a bold and daring officer. In November, 1871, for example, with a patrol of only four Negro soldiers of the 9th Cavalry, he attacked a band of Indians, some thirty warriors, who were driving a large herd of stolen horses toward Mexico. The disparity in numbers made it impossible for him to destroy, or even seriously injure the band, but the boldness and dash of his attack caused the Indians to flee, and he recovered all the stolen animals. This and several similar exploits brought Bullis to the highly favorable attention of his military superiors, and especially the lieutenant colonel of his own regiment, Shafter.[13] Bullis and his Seminole-Negro scouts quickly became the spearhead of Shafter's efforts to bring the Mescaleros and Lipans to terms and protect the Texas frontier from their incursions.

In 1875, shortly after the Corpus Christi raid, the department commander, Brigadier General Ord, took the responsibility of ordering that troops on a "hot trail" would pursue marauders wherever they might go, even into Mexico. In December, 1877, General Ord testified before the Military Affairs Committee of the House of Representatives: "I gave orders nearly two years ago to cross over on a fresh trail. I stated my reasons for giving the order and communicated these orders to the administration, and I received no instructions in regard to the matter. The order was not disapproved and consequently it was tacitly approved."[14]

Believing that the murderous incursions of the Lipans and Mescaleros could be stopped only by striking them when they believed themselves safe in the Mexican mountains, Shafter lost little time in availing himself of this authority. At the same time, he gave a very broad interpretation to the term "fresh trail." Early in June, 1876, he encamped, with five companies of cavalry, on the Rio Grande, about sixty miles above the mouth of the Pecos. From this point he dispatched Bullis, with a Mexican guide and three of his Seminoles, to locate the Indian villages that were supposed to be in the mountains to the south. Bullis penetrated sixty to eighty miles into the unexplored Mexican region without finding any villages but finding plenty of other Indian signs. Soon after his return, Shafter crossed the river into Mexico with the entire force, to search for a large band of Indians reported to be in another area. No Indians were found, and the command returned to the American side in four or five days.

A month later, near the end of July, 1876, Shafter again crossed into Mexico, twenty-five miles above the mouth of the Pecos, and marched southward for several days. On July 29 he halted the force but directed Bullis, with his Seminole scouts, reinforced with an officer and twenty soldiers of the 10th Cavalry, to march rapidly to the San Antonio River, where an Indian camp had been reported. Bullis left late in the afternoon and marched until three o'clock in the morning, when he ordered a halt to give the men and animals a short rest. At daybreak they discovered that they were within a mile of an Indian encampment. Quietly leading the horses into the cover of some trees, the force saddled and mounted, in absolute silence. Silently the troopers and scouts formed a line, and with a sudden yell, dashed from their cover and charged into the surprised Indians—an attack that, on a smaller scale, reproduced Mackenzie's attack on the Kickapoos. Fourteen Lipan warriors were killed; four women and ninety-six horses and mules were captured. Bullis allowed a few hours for further rest and then marched to rejoin Shafter. The entire force returned to United States soil on July 31, 1876.[15] There was no protest from Mexico.

On the first of November, 1877, Bullis' scouts had a sharp fight with a band of Indians at an unnamed spot near the Rio Grande. Attached to an expedition commanded by Captain S. B. M. Young (later a lieutenant general), they pursued the Indians (who were described in official reports as "Apaches and other Indians") deep into Mexico. Nearly a month later, on November 29, when the Indians probably thought they were safe, Young's column surprised them in the Carmen Mountains. A sudden charge scattered the Indians, who ran for safety wherever they could. An unreported number were killed; their camp and belongings were destroyed; seventeen horses, six mules and a number of firearms were taken.

As for the hardships and privations of officers and soldiers on such extended excursions into the wilderness, they are probably best illustrated by the experience of one of the officers upon returning to his post. His own description was:

> I had lost my blouse, the back of my blue shirt (the only one I had left) was missing, my long hair reached almost to my shoulders, my beard untrimmed for three months, fell on my breast, and I had on a soft wool hat, the crown of which was missing entirely and the brim had been torn off at various times to help kindle a fire. . . . I trotted up to my quarters and found Mary [his wife] standing on the porch. I dismounted and said to her, "Hello, old lady." She looked me up and down and then, turning to the orderly . . . she cooly said, "Orderly, is that my husband?" The grinning orderly touched his cap and said, "Yes, mam." "Take him down to the creek and wash him," was her unexpected reply.[16]

American entries into Mexico, whenever they came to the attention of Mexican authorities, always aroused excited indignation. Every crossing of the Rio Grande by United States troops, no matter how fresh the trail or great the provocation, brought protests from Mexico City and cries of "invasion" from the Mexican press. For several years requests by the United States for formal permission to pursue Indians or bandits across the boundary were rejected by Mexico, and still the raids into the United States continued. The diplomatic situation was complicated because the new dictator, Porfirio Díaz, was not yet firmly seated in the Presidential chair; he was still opposed and bitterly hated by large numbers of his people. One of the surest ways of assuring support at home is to adopt a strong line in foreign affairs, and the attitude of Mexican officials became increasingly truculent. Newspapers in both countries began speaking ominously of war.

At this juncture, in April, 1877, information came to General Ord's headquarters that two Mexican guides who had led one of Shafter's expeditions against the Lipans had been arrested at Piedras Negras and imprisoned, charged with treason. They were in danger of being summarily executed. The *alcalde* of Piedras Negras, in reply to a demand for the release of the two men, stated that his orders were to arrest any person who guided American troops into Mexico. General Ord addressed a strong protest to the governor of Tamaulipas, and even more significant, he telegraphed orders to Shafter to rescue the two men at once. Shafter moved quickly. He and the Adjutant General of the Department of Texas arrived at Fort Duncan late at night, April 2, 1877. At two o'clock in the morning he crossed the river a short distance above the town, with three companies of cavalry. At dawn, two companies of infantry crossed directly from Fort Duncan. Both forces converged upon the jail, but the two unfortunate guides had been removed; the jail was open and empty. The Americans returned immediately to their own side of the river; most of the population of Piedras Negras did not even know that another "invasion" of their country had occurred.[17]

At last, on June 1, 1877, finally convinced that Mexican officials would not, or could not, prevent bandit and Indian raids into the United States, President Hayes authorized his Secretary of War to send a formal directive to General Ord:

General Ord will at once notify the Mexican authorities along the Texas border, of the great desire of the President to unite with them in efforts to suppress this long-continued lawlessness. At the same time he will inform those authorities that if the Government of Mexico shall continue to neglect the duty of suppressing these outrages, that duty will devolve upon this government, and will be performed, even if its performance should render necessary the occasional crossing of the border by our troops.[18]

As may be supposed, when this order became known in Mexico, it evoked a cyclone of indignation and protest. General Treviño, who was in command of the Díaz forces on the border, received orders from Díaz to exert himself to the utmost to prevent any criminals from either side of the boundary from taking refuge by crossing it. He was directed to cooperate fully with General Ord in apprehending offenders, but under no circumstances was he to permit United States troops to enter Mexico. "You will repel force by force should the invasion take place."[19]

Many Mexicans (possibly the majority) regarded the orders to General Ord as an entering wedge for a serious invasion of Mexico and as a preliminary to further conquest of Mexican territory. It was asserted that there was no reason for such orders, and it was even charged that President Hayes was endeavoring to overthrow the new regime in Mexico and reestablish Lerdo de Tejada in the Mexican presidency. Statements published in the official *Diario* were so violent that the American minister, John W. Foster, lodged a vigorous protest, which resulted in a weak apology.[20]

It is safe to say that the last thing the new President of Mexico wanted was a war with the United States, and in spite of hints by a few writers that the Hayes Administration would have welcomed a Mexican war to unite the country and obscure its own questionable title to office, no evidence of such a plot has ever come to light. President Hayes was not a man to court war as a means of keeping himself in office. But despite the undeniable international friction and ranting by irresponsible men, the situation along the Rio Grande became quieter with the passage of time. American troops crossed the boundary a number of times on "hot" trails, as evidenced by the testimony of Colonel Shafter and Lieutenant Bullis. On the Mexican side of the border General Anacleto R. Falcon succeeded to the command of the Mexican forces, to which was added a considerable number of Mexican Regulars. Falcon was cooperative; very quickly he and Shafter established a warm personal relationship, which greatly facilitated their mutual mission. In fact, Shafter testified before the House Committee on Military Affairs that on only one occasion had Mexican troops made a gesture toward repelling the Americans. On the other hand, "fifteen or twenty days ago" (*i.e.*, about December 15, 1877), detachments from Falcon's and Shafter's commands had joined together in the pursuit of cattle thieves.[21]

As has been noted before, the Mexicans claimed, almost violently, that American allegations about depredations from Mexico were untrue or exaggerated, and that Mexico suffered as much under attacks from Texas as Texas did from Mexico. Responsible American authorities rejected the Mexican assertions flatly and held that there could be no peace or safety on the border unless American troops pursued raiders across the boundary.

As a matter of fact, "invasions" of the United States by Mexican armed forces, quite comparable to the American expeditions into Mexico, were not unknown, but they attracted little attention because they evoked no resentment on the part of Americans. On an unspecified date before the Civil War, a Mexican military force attacked an Apache camp near old Fort Cummings, New Mexico. Most of the warriors were absent; women and children were slaughtered or carried off into slavery.[22] In March, 1872, shortly after the Mexican Government had refused permission for American troops to cross the boundary, a company numbering about sixty officers and soldiers crossed into the United States from Chihuahua, in pursuit of Indians who had stolen horses near the city of Chihuahua. Colonel Shafter, who was then at Fort Davis, reported that this was the second of such incursions from Mexico within six months. A short time later, Shafter was ordered to capture and imprison Mexican armed forces entering the United States, even though they were authorized by the governor of Chihuahua, as the one reported on claimed to be.[23] In his testimony before the House Committee on Military Affairs, previously mentioned, Shafter testified that Mexican troops, often local militia, had crossed the Rio Grande whenever they had occasion to do so. "I can give you numerous instances," he told the committee, "in which they crossed to this side during the past twenty years, and up to as late as September of this year." In one instance a Mexican force had remained in the United States as much as forty-five days; General Falcon, he added, had recently crossed twice in pursuit of Mexican thieves who had committed robberies in Mexico.[24]

General Ord testified that several years before, when he was in command of the Department of California (which then included the District of Arizona), he had furnished rations for two weeks to a detail of Mexican troops that had entered the United States in pursuit of Cochise and his Apache marauders; he said, further, that as commander of the Department of Texas, he had no objection at all to Mexican troop's crossing the Rio Grande in pursuit of Indians. On the contrary, he would welcome their assistance.[25]

But complications resulted occasionally when Mexican troops entered the United States and Indians were not involved. In June, 1877, during the Díaz revolution, a government force (Lerdistas), defeated on their own side of the boundary, fled to the United States, not far from the mouth of Devil's River. They were pursued and attacked on United States soil by Díaz forces, with heavy casualties. While American authorities could look with approval on the pursuit of Indians or outlaws, a battle on United States soil by two opposing Mexican political factions was something that could not be overlooked or condoned. Shafter moved quickly from Fort Clark and within a few days had captured and interned a force of several officers and some forty-five soldiers. In response to his inquiries about what to do with them, he was directed to feed them and keep them under guard until further orders. Apparently, they were eventually repatriated to their own country.[26]

Gradually and almost imperceptibly the Indian and bandit troubles on the Rio Grande died away, although it was many years before they ceased altogether. By contrast with the bloody 1870s, the succeeding decades were eras of peace and quiet. In spite of friction from many causes, the new dictator of Mexico was anxious for American recognition and support, and his ruthless suppression of banditry helped bring peace to the border.

General Juan Nepomuceno Cortina was kept in honorable, but helpless, confinement in Mexico City until his death at a ripe old age. But the bloodshed on the borderland was by no means ended; it was transferred to another region, and the recountal of what occurred is another chapter of borderland history.

NOTES

1. For a full discussion of the Kickapoos' war against Americans, see A. M. Gibson, *The Kickapoos: Lords of the Middle Border* (Norman, Okla., 1963), pp. 208–21, for a scholarly and authoritative study by a writer who is sympathetic toward the Indians but makes no attempt to condone their activities.

2. *Ibid.*, pp. 222–35; see also *Foreign Relations, 1871*, pp. 649–50.

3. *Foreign Relations, 1871*, pp. 643–44.

4. Robert Goldthwaite Carter, *On the Border with Mackenzie, or Winning West Texas from the Comanche* (New York, 1961, reprint from the 1935 ed.), pp. 399–406. The italics are Carter's. He was the adjutant to whom Mackenzie confided the mission. See also Colonel Eugene B. Beaumont, "Over the Border with Mackenzie," *United Service Magazine*, XII (1885), 281.

5. This summary of Mackenzie's raid is based upon the eyewitness accounts of Carter and Beaumont.

6. Gibson, *op. cit.*, pp. 245–52; Annual Report of the Secretary of War, 1873, I, 41.

7. Lyman L. Woodman, *Cortina, the Rogue of the Rio Grande* (San Antonio, Tex., 1950), pp. 99–100.

8. Leopold Morris, "The Mexican Raid of 1875 on Corpus Christi," *Texas Historical Association Quarterly*, IV (1900–1901), 128–39; "Report and Accompanying Documents of the Committee on Foreign Affairs on the Relations of the United States with Mexico," 45th Cong., 2nd sess., Report No. 701, pp. 190–92.

9. Special Committee of the House of Representatives to investigate Texas Frontier Troubles, H.R. Report No. 343, 44th Cong., 1st sess., pp. 73–74.

10. "Testimony Taken by the Committee on Military Affairs in Relation to the Texas Border Troubles," Testimony of Capt. Lewis Johnson, 24th Infantry, Dec. 4, 1877, 45th Cong., 2nd sess., Misc. Doc. No. 64, pp. 137–38.

11. Special Committee of the House of Representatives to Investigate Texas Frontier Troubles, H.R. Report No. 343, 44th Cong., 1st sess., pp. 85–96; Walter Prescott Webb, *The Texas Rangers. A Century of Frontier Defense*, Foreword by Lyndon B. Johnson (Austin, Tex., 2nd ed., 1965), pp. 255–79. There was a change of face by the district commander, Col. Potter, or he may have received unrecorded orders from higher authority. Initially he authorized Randlett

to follow the raiders into Mexico, then subsequently forbade any crossing by American troops. Majors Clendenin and Alexander were merely following the orders they had received.

12. Edgar S. Wallace, "General John Lapham Bullis, Thunderbolt of the Texas Frontier," Part II, *Southwestern Historical Quarterly*, LV (1951–52), 77–78; see also Kenneth Wiggins Porter, in the same volume, "The Seminole-Negro Indian Scouts," pp. 358–63. Bullis later served as an Indian agent and in the campaigns in Cuba and in the Philippines. He was made a brigadier general in 1904. Camp Bullis, Texas, a subpost of Fort Sam Houston, is named for him.

13. Wallace, *op. cit.*, pp. 77–78.

14. "Testimony Taken by the Committee on Military Affairs in Relation to the Texas Border Troubles," Testimony of Brig. Gen. Edward O. C. Ord, Dec. 6, 1877, 45th Cong., 2nd sess., Misc. Doc. No. 64., p. 103.

15. *Ibid.*, testimony of 1st Lt. John L. Bullis, 24th Infantry, Jan. 8, 1878, pp. 187–204.

16. Frederick E. Phelps, "A Soldier's Memoirs," Frank D. Reeve, ed., *New Mexico Historical Review*, XXV (1950), 206–21.

17. "Message of the President of the United States . . . transmitting reports in reference to Mexican Border Troubles," H.R. Exec. Doc. No. 13, 45th Cong., 1st sess., pp. 9–12.

18. *Ibid.*, pp. 14–15.

19. *Ibid.*, pp. 19–20.

20. *Ibid.*, pp. 21–35.

21. "Testimony Taken by the Committee on Military Affairs, . . ." Testimony of Lt. Col. William R. Shafter, 24th Infantry, Jan. 7, 1878, H.R. Misc. Doc. No. 64, 45th Cong., 2nd sess., pp. 160, 186.

22. Jason Betzinez and Wilbur Sturtevant Nye, *I Fought with Geronimo* (Harrisburg, Pa., 1959), pp. 19–20.

23. *Foreign Relations, 1872*, pp. 398–99.

24. Testimony of Lt. Col. William R. Shafter, *op. cit.*, p. 186.

25. "Testimony Taken Before the Committee on Foreign Affairs," Statement of Brig. Gen. Edward O. C. Ord, Dec. 2, 1877, H.R. Report No. 701, 45th Cong., 2nd sess., pp. 8–9.

26. *Foreign Relations, 1877*, pp. 414–15.

CHAPTER 5

Apaches in the Sierra Madre

A<small>S THE IRON FIST</small> of President Porfirio Díaz began to be felt in Mexico, the disturbances on the Lower Rio Grande gradually died down. All over Mexico bandits were either shot out of hand or were persuaded to join the Corps of Rurales, enforcing order, whether legally or not, upon a people who had never known order. The decimated bands of Kickapoos and Lipans were returned to the jurisdiction of the United States, and the few who remained in Mexico ceased to look to raids across the Rio Grande for horses and other loot. But simultaneously with the decline of tension on the Rio Grande frontier, the problem of the Apaches on the western borderland became acute. Because the international boundary west of El Paso was nothing but a surveyor's imaginary line on the ground which the Apaches knew nothing about, the tribes of Arizona and New Mexico became an international problem of the first magnitude in the 1870s and 1880s and a military problem that was difficult to solve.

A word of explanation is necessary at this point—the term "Apache." The Apaches were (and are) a linguistic and cultural group, composed, during the period under discussion, of independent, nomadic bands, ranging over a vast expanse of territory. The Lipans and Mescaleros who featured so prominently in the troubles on the Rio Grande were actually Apaches but are usually referred to by the names just mentioned. In the present context the word "Apache" will refer to the tribes, usually from Arizona, who carried terror and devastation from the White Mountains of Arizona deep into the unexplored recesses of the Sierra Madres in Mexico. There were several main groups of these Indians, the White Mountain, Warm Springs, Coyotero and Chiricahua tribes being the ones most deeply involved in the wars of the late nineteenth century. The Apaches were probably late migrants into the country in which Americans first encountered them, a probability that accounts for their warlike proclivities. They had to fight to enter; they had to fight to survive. Under these circumstances they developed a hardihood and an aptitude for war and aggression that has seldom been equaled by any people in the world.[1]

Physically, the Apache's height was usually a little below that of the average white man, although there were, of course, many exceptions. The famous war chief, Cochise, is said to have been over six feet tall. The Apache's lung and chest development gave him a "top-heavy" appearance. Captain John G. Bourke, General Crook's aide-de-camp, who, in addition to being a most efficient officer, was an anthropologist of recognized standing, said, "Physically, the Apache is perfect; he might be a trifle taller for artistic effect, but his apparent 'squattiness' is due more to great girth of chest than to diminutive stature. His muscles are as hard as bone, and I have seen one light a match on the sole of his naked foot."[2]

Although the Apache was perfectly at home in the desert, he preferred the mountains. By his standards, life was relatively easy there. There was plenty of game to supply meat, there were berries and edible plants, water was abundant, and above all, the mountains made the ambush of an enemy easy and afforded a ready refuge for quick escape. Because of his endurance and "toughness," there were few enemies who could even follow, let alone catch up with, the Apache in the mountains. Hence, the Apache bands that made life in the western borderlands an absolute hell for American setlers and Mexican villagers were, in general, mountain Indians.

From the perspective of nearly a century after the last of the Apache wars, it is easy to see that the Apaches suffered almost unbelievable wrongs at the hands of both Americans and Mexi-

Campaigns Against the Apaches

From Dan L. Thrapp, The Conquest of Apacheriá, by permission of the University of Oklahoma Press

Map labels:

TEXAS
El Paso
Ft. Quitman
CANDELARIA MTNS.
TRES CASTILLOS (Victorio killed)
Chihuahua
NEW MEXICO
CHIHUAHUA
CASAS Grandes River
Lake Guzman
Lake Santa Maria
Santa Maria RIVER
Janos
Corralitos
Casas Grandes
SIERRA EN MEDIO
Garcia Fight
Janos RIVER
Crook meets hostiles about here in 1883
Cumbre
SIERRA MADRE MOUNTAINS
Crawford killed about here
Bacerac
Huachinera
Nacori
HAROS RIVER
Ft. Bowie
SKELETON CANYON
CANYON DE EMBUDOS
Bavispe R.
San Bernardino River
Bavispe
Fronteras
TERES MTNS. Geronimo contacted about here by Gatewood
Oputo
Huasabas
Bacadehuachi
Ft. Crittenden
Douglas
ARIZONA
Santa Cruz
Nogales
SONORA
Santa Cruz River
Loco Fight
Ures
Hermosillo
Yaqui RIVER

0 10 20 30 40 50 Miles

cans, but the Americans and Mexicans of the time did not see it that way. In order to understand the events of the Apache wars and the resultant American military movements into Mexico, it is necessary to endeavor to see the Apache through the eyes of the people of the time. Americans and Mexicans were one in regarding the Apache as hardly a human being. They saw only the tortured bodies of men, women and children, burned and devastated farms and ranches, and an enemy from whom no mercy could be expected. From the earliest days of contact between the white man and the red, there was war between the Apache and the newcomer. There were, nevertheless, periods of peace, and the various Apache tribes did not make war simultaneously. This led to endless trouble and bloodshed when Americans and Mexicans failed to distinguish between the different kinds of Apaches.

In the early 1850s a large band of Warm Springs Apaches, believing themselves to be at peace with Mexicans, were treacherously slaughtered at Ramos, in Chihuahua. Months later a band of Apache warriors lunged out of the morning mist at Ramos and exacted revenge; no prisoners were taken.[3] A few years later a band of Apaches encamped near Janos, in Chihuahua. They were at war in Sonora but believed themselves to be safe in Chihuahua. The warriors were plied with *aguardiente* in the town, and when they staggered back to their camp, hours later, they found the corpses of their women and children sprawling on the ground. One Indian who found his wife, children and mother murdered was a man known later as Geronimo.[4]

When the governor of Chihuahua offered a liberal bounty for Apache scalps, a number of unsavory Americans were among those who embarked on the lucrative business of scalp hunting. A character named Johnson carefully wormed his way into the confidence of an Apache band; the chief befriended him on a number of occasions. Offering a special treat for the women and children, Johnson gathered a crowd of Indians into a small space, then fired a heavy blunderbuss loaded with scraps of metal, nails and other missiles into the group. Johnson himself killed the friendly chief, when his henchmen balked at such treachery.

Johnson collected a very considerable sum as a bounty, and the Apaches learned that Americans were untrustworthy.[5]

But regardless of the wrongs that justified the hatred of the Apache for Americans and Mexicans, he responded with a vindictiveness and ferocity that left almost no recourse but to fight. And when the outbreak of the Civil War in the United States caused the withdrawal of the slender military forces in the Southwest, the Apaches' primitive ignorance of the white man's real power caused them to believe that they had driven the soldiers from their country. The immediate result was increased aggressiveness against the white men who remained in the Apache country. Fugitive miners, traders and settlers hurried to Tucson or to California, but many of them never reached safety.

Actually, the war between Americans and Apaches started a few months before the Civil War, brought about by the lack of sound judgment shown by a young lieutenant, only a short time out of West Point. The most powerful of the Apache tribes, the Chiricahuas, led and dominated by Cochise, had never been notably unfriendly toward Americans. In the summer of 1860, however, Apaches kidnaped the small son of an Irish father and Mexican mother, and Lieutenant George N. Bascom invited (or ordered) Chief Cochise to a conference at the Butterfield stage station at the top of Apache Pass, in the Chiricahua Mountains. Bascom imperiously ordered Cochise to return the child, but Cochise asserted that he knew nothing about the kidnaping. Bascom then attempted to put the chief and his party under arrest. Cochise himself escaped, but some of his warriors were held. Upon Bascom's refusal to release the prisoners, Cochise started the war by killing the employees of the stage company. From that moment on, the Americans had no more vindictive enemy in the world than Cochise.[6]

In the spring of 1862 Brigadier General James H. Carleton's Column from California marched through Arizona on its way to the Rio Grande. For some time there had been little trouble with the Apaches or other Indians, and Carleton, who was a veteran Indian fighter, hoped to be able to keep them at peace so that he could devote his whole time and strength to his major mission, the destruction of the Confederates in New Mexico. The first echelon of the California force, a battalion of cavalry, paused at the stage station (now abandoned) where the Bascom affair occurred, to water the horses, fill the men's canteens, and rest. A party of Apaches approached, making peace signs, but an hour later, when the parley was over, three soldiers were missing. What was left of them was found after an hour of search.

A few days later the second element of the California force, a company of infantry with two howitzers, toiled up the steep slope toward the old stage station, the men looking forward to a long, cooling drink from the spring. But when they were within a few hundred yards of their goal the barren and apparently empty hillsides erupted with musketry and showers of arrows, while the cañon resounded with war whoops. Although surprised, the Californians did not panic. Months of rigid training under Carleton, who was as strict a martinet as Mackenzie, paid rich dividends at that moment. The company fell back coolly to a place where there was room for deployment, unlimbered the howitzers, which opened fire while the soldiers moved forward to the attack. The Indians incontinently took off, demoralized by the howitzer fire, which exacted a heavy toll and which they had never encountered before.[7]

For the next several years there was unending war on the Apache frontier. The discharge of the volunteers at the end of the Civil War increased Apache raids and depredations because the number of troops available to protect the region was sharply decreased. The harassed people of the land—Americans, Mexicans agricultural Indians—were all threatened with extinction. Nobody was safe outside the few towns and military posts, and they were not always safe there. Ranchers who tried to cultivate a patch of corn or a small field of barley plowed with loaded revolvers on their hips and rifles slung on the plow handles.[8]

The situation was desperate when, in May, 1871, President Grant personally ordered Lieutenant Colonel George Crook to take command of the Department of Arizona immediately. Crook was described as "about six feet in his stocking, was straight as an arrow, broad-shouldered, lithe, sinewy as a cat, and able to bear any amount of fatigue."[9] He had graduated from West Point in the class of 1852, and as a lieutenant before the Civil War served in several Indian campaigns in California. In one of these campaigns he was badly wounded, and for the rest of his life he carried an arrowhead that was never extracted. Crook rose to high command during the Civil War but really reached his stride after the war as an Indian fighter. He came to the conclusion, partly as a result of his experiences as a lieutenant, that Indians could be subdued only by fighting in the Indian way. Soldiers could almost invariably defeat Indians in open battle, but the problem was to bring them to battle. This could be done only by small, fast-moving bodies of men, not by heavy columns that outnumbered the enemy. Crook had learned also that the Indian is a human being who responds to honesty and fair treatment, but that there could be no peace on the frontier until the tribes were thoroughly defeated.[10]

Crook arrived at Tucson in June, 1871, after a trying and monotonous trip by rail from the Midwest, by coastwise ship from San Francisco to San Diego, and across the desert from San Diego by an army ambulance. The monotony of the trip was broken and possibly the journey enlivened a bit by the antics of a remarkable character, Archie McIntosh, whom Crook had learned to trust as a scout. Archie was the half-breed son of a Hudson Bay Company official. He was educated at the University of Edinburgh but nevertheless returned to the frontier and took up the adventurous life of a scout. Archie had one major weakness, the bottle. In San Francisco, Archie traded his clothes for cheaper ones and spent the difference on liquor. He was carried aboard the ship by the guard. At Yuma, evidently fearing a long, dry trip across the desert, he repeated the performance. The clothes he obtained in exchange for his San Francisco clothes (plus a bottle or two of "red-eye") made him look like a caricature from a "comic almanac" (Crook's own description), but Crook refused to leave him behind. He was bundled into the ambulance in which Crook was traveling, and taken along.[11]

A few weeks before Crook's arrival at Tucson, Lieutenant

Howard Cushing, of the 3d Cavalry, with a detail of about twenty soldiers and a number of civilians, was ambushed at Bear Spring, in the Whetstone Mountains, southeast of Tucson. Cushing and several soldiers were killed. A small force from Camp Crittenden pursued the Indians across the international boundary and followed them for several days but was finally forced to give up because of the sorry state of its horses.[12]

This is the first recorded crossing of the boundary on the Apache frontier after the Civil War, but it was not, by any means, the first time that American troops had crossed the line in pursuit of Apaches. In May, 1857, for example, a small American force penetrated Chihuahua as far as Carrizal, returning to the United States on May 7, "after a march marked by heat and thirst, devoid of incident except killing of a few rattlesnakes . . . ," according to one of the officers.[13]

There is no indication that any Mexican official protested the pursuit of Apaches across the boundary. Herein lies a major difference in the situation in the Apache country from that on the Lower Rio Grande. The people of Sonora and Chihuahua did not regard the Americans as invaders; rather, they frequently hailed the American troopers as saviors and cooperated to the fullest extent of their limited resources.

Crook was not familiar with Arizona or with the Apaches, but he lost no time in informing himself as fully as possible. On the very day on which he arrived at Tucson, every officer within reach was ordered to report to him. He questioned each one closely and minutely. He asked about terrain and topography (large parts of Arizona were still unexplored), streams, springs, roads, trails, timber, grass, pack animals and a score of other items. He asked personal questions, in order to get to know his officers. Above all, he asked questions about Indians. But not an inkling of what he intended to do escaped from his lips.[14]

Within a few days he assembled about four hundred troops and started on an inspection trip. Included in his escort was a company of Mexicans enrolled as scouts on the recommendation of the territorial governor. After watching them for a few days, Crook decided that the Mexicans would not do. On arriving at Fort Apache, he ordered their immediate discharge.[15]

To replace the unsatisfactory Mexican scouts, Crook decided upon a bold experiment. In interrogating his officers, he found that there was little unity, and often there was distinct hostility, among the various Apache tribes. Without any difficulty a large number of White Mountain and Coyotero Apaches were persuaded to enroll as scouts. This was the first time that Indian scouts were employed on the Apache frontier.

Crook's initial inspection trip had an additional and important objective. It was a training march in which officers and men of different organizations learned to know one another, to learn Crook's methods, to observe the country, and what proved to be extremely important in the near future, to know how to pack animals and handle packtrains. Crook's aide-de-camp, Bourke, said, "We learned to know a great deal about packers, pack-mules and packing, which to my surprise I found to be a science. . . ."[16]

Crook had hoped to be able to strike the hostiles at once, but found, on his return from the inspection, that operations were suspended. Well-meaning people in Washington who had never heard a war whoop were convinced that the Apaches could be persuaded by peaceful means to abandon the war trail and adopt the white man's ways. Vincent Colyer, a sincere Quaker, arrived from Washington with full authority from the President to make peace treaties with the Indians. Escorted by soldiers furnished by Crook, Colyer made a series of treaties, only to learn, when he arrived at San Francisco, that the whole Apache frontier was aflame, with the chiefs with whom he had just concluded treaties among the foremost of the raiders. Shortly after Colyer's departure, Major General Oliver O. Howard arrived from Washington on the same mission, and also with authority to supplant Crook if he deemed it advisable. Howard was widely acclaimed as "the Christian soldier" because of his sincere piety. Almost alone among the senior officers of the army at that time, he had had no experience on the western frontier or with western Indians. He was convinced, nevertheless, that the Apaches could be brought to reason and peace by purely peaceful means. Like Colyer, General Howard made numerous treaties; he even penetrated daringly into the depths of Cochise's stronghold in the

Dragoon Mountains, accompanied only by his aide and an interpreter. In a lengthy conference, Howard granted Cochise and his Chiricahaus a reservation in the southeast corner of Arizona, abutting on Mexico, in return for Cochise's promise that his warriors would not molest Americans in the future. This treaty took the Chiricahuas completely out of Crook's jurisdiction, as long as they observed its provisions, but Cochise had given no promise to stay out of Mexico or to leave Mexicans alone. And within a very short time after Howard departed for Washington, bands of Chiricahua warriors were again on the prowl.[17]

Feeling sure that the Indians would be on the warpath soon in spite of their treaties with General Howard, Crook used the period of enforced idleness to prepare for eventualities. Ammunition, blankets, rations and forage were purchased and stored at convenient points. He quietly increased the number of his Apache scouts and gathered probably the finest group of American scouts the frontier ever saw. He organized several packtrains and made a contract with the manager of a noted civilian packtrain. Crook was prepared, as soon as the Indians took the war trail, to strike and strike hard.[18]

Crook's campaigns in Arizona in the early 1870s lie outside the field of American military ventures in Mexico, and yet they dovetail into the later campaigns in Sonora and Chihuahua. The achievements of Crook's soldiers and Apache scouts are thrilling enough to satisfy any addict of "western" stories or motion pictures. For the first time in their memory or tradition the hostiles could find no safety or refuge. They were hunted down and killed while hiding in caves; they were surprised in the dead of night on almost impregnable mountaintops. Within a few months they began surrendering in droves—all except Cochise and his bands, who were beyond Crook's reach because of Howard's treaty. Of course, there were occasional incidents, usually when some Indian got hold of whiskey, or some band brewed a supply of "tizwin." Some teamsters of a wagon train were killed by drunken Apaches—a fitting reward for the teamsters, who had sold the Indians the liquor. Crook curtly told the tribal chiefs to bring in the guilty warriors. A few days later the chiefs came to him with grisly evidence of their good faith—the severed heads of the outlaws.[19]

Peace brought new settlers, new miners and hundreds of other immigrants into Arizona. The Southern Pacific Railroad through the territory was completed, but the altered conditions brought only trouble for the Indians. Land-hungry people noted that the land occupied by the Apaches was good land—much too good for Indians, they thought. And worst of all, many of the officials and agents of the Indian Bureau were small politicians who were appointed as a reward for party services in eastern states. There was ample evidence that agents were often grafters; materials and supplies purchased for the Indians wound up in some merchant's warehouse. Short quantities of food for issue, "rigged" scales for weighing cattle intended for issue to the Indians, all combined to bring the reservation Apaches to the verge of starvation. Naturally, the Apaches became restless, but most of them continued grimly to bear their lot. In 1877, two years after Crook was transferred from the Department of Arizona, his successor, Colonel August V. Kautz, said in his annual report, "I am in constant apprehension of an outbreak . . . on the San Carlos reservation. . . . I charge this to the corrupt management."[20]

In 1879 the New Mexico kinsmen of the Arizona tribes, the Mescaleros, revolted and broke away from their reservation, led by their chief, Victorio. Raiding ranches and settlements as they went, they hurried into Mexico, killing, looting and burning on their way. Late in the summer, arrangements were made between the Department Commander and the governor of Chihuahua, General Luis Terrazas, for a joint expedition against Victorio's band. Two American columns were to march southward, while Terrazas advanced to the north, the three forces converging toward the place where the Mescaleros were believed to be. The American forces, commanded by Colonel George P. Buell, of the 15th Infantry, included a large detachment of Chiricahua scouts from Fort Apache, while a company of Texas Rangers served with Terrazas. But international cooperation did not last long. On October 9, Terrazas politely but firmly told the Americans to return to their own country. One or two days later he brought Victorio's band to bay, and in the fight the gallant (and dangerous) old chief was killed, and most of his people were slaughtered. A remnant, however, survived, and in hot pursuit of these Lieutenant John Guilfoyle, of the 9th Cavalry, crossed the border the following summer and fought on at least two occasions.[21]

In Arizona the outbreak that Colonel Kautz feared occurred late in August, 1881, detonated by the arrest of an Apache mystic who declared that his incantations would bring the dead back to life and render Apache warriors immune to the white man's bullets. The arresting force, commanded by Colonel Eugene A. Carr, of the 6th Cavalry, was attacked, and for the first and last time some of the Apache scouts were disloyal. While Carr's detachment was absent on its mission, other Apaches attacked the post at Fort Apache but were quickly repulsed.

Wild rumors spread that the Indians had captured the post and massacred everyone there. Telegraph keys clattered all over the United States; Mackenzie was ordered to concentrate his regiment at Fort Wingate, preparatory to marching into Arizona. Colonel Hatch, who commanded the Department of New Mexico, was directed to assemble all the troops he could spare from his department at Fort Craig, for the same purpose.[22] Actually, the uprising in Arizona involved only a few Apaches. Most of them had nothing to do with it, and wanted no part of it, but became alarmed by the movements and concentration of troops. In October, 1881, two well-known Apache desperadoes, Juh and Natchez (as the names are usually rendered), bolted from the reservation with a small band of followers and vanished in the direction of Mexico. The malcontents failed utterly to persuade a large village of Warm Springs Apaches, presided over by an elderly chief known as Loco, to join them. The "broncos," hurrying toward Mexico, attacked a wagon train near Cedar Springs, Arizona, but it happened that two troops of the 1st Cavalry were within hearing distance. They sped toward the sound of the firing and were joined shortly by two troops of the 6th Cavalry who had been trailing the fugitives. The fight lasted until dark, when the Indians vanished. Two or three days later Captain Reuben Bernard, of the 1st Cavalry, followed an Indian trail, probably that of the same band, for a long distance into Mexico, without being able to force the Indians into a fight.[23]

After the dissatisfied Chiricahuas fled to Mexico, the situation in Arizona remained almost static for several months, but at daybreak on a morning in April, 1882, the people of Loco's band found themselves staring down the muzzles of guns held in the hands of their kinsmen who had gone to Mexico. There was some disorder in the village, but Loco's people were helpless against the intruders. Without being given a chance to do a thing, or even eat the breakfasts that were on the fires, they were ordered to leave. One of the invading chiefs was heard to say, "Shoot anyone who refuses to go with us."[24] Albert Sterling, the chief of the recently established Indian police, who rode into the village to see what the commotion was about, was shot and killed instantly. Within a few minutes, Loco's band—men, women and children—was herded on foot on the long trail to Mexico. The outlaws in the Sierra Madres needed more men; the only way to get them was to "draft" the Warm Springs people. The raid was led by Geronimo, who inspired it and planned it. It was skillfully executed, and one must admit that Geronimo proved his qualities as a war chief in this episode.

Loco's reluctant people were hustled along on foot until they reached the ranches along the Gila River and in the San Simon Valley, where a series of raids, accompanied by the usual outrages, produced enough horses to mount everyone. And Loco and his followers, knowing that they would be blamed for the thefts and atrocities, became full-fledged members of the outlaws.[25]

Within a few hours troops were on the move all over Arizona. A traveler, one of the first to visit Arizona purely as a tourist, described the scene at Fort Apache:

Orderlies flying around, horses being saddled, ammunition distributed, rations packed up . . . in less than three hours . . . the command is drawn upon the parade ground for inspection.

Everything looked meant for service. Two-thirds of the men wear large white sombreros; buckskin pants and shirts are frequent; hardly an officer wears anything to show his rank. . . .

The men are drawn up in a long line. At the right are a dozen Indian scouts squatting around, each armed with a long rifle. . . . In their midst stands the guide and interpreter, a tall, weather-beaten man, a typical frontiersman, who has been on such duty for years and years. [Note: possibly Al Sieber.]

Back of all, the packers vainly try to keep the pack-train of about fifty mules in some sort of order.[26]

The first troops to catch up with the fugitives were the Apache scouts with Colonel George A. Forsyth and a strong force of the 6th Cavalry. There was a sharp fight in a deep cañon in the side of Stein's Peak; as soon as night descended, the hostiles slipped away.[27] Once in Mexico they felt safe. By this time all Apaches knew that there was an imaginary line on the ground, across which the troops were not supposed to follow them. A few miles northeast of Janos, Chihuahua, they selected a camp-site on a mesa from which they could see for miles across an almost treeless plain. The band felt so secure that the usual Apache watchfulness was relaxed. For two days the Indians gave themselves up to feasting and dancing. But at dawn on the third day there was a sudden burst of gunfire and the roar of galloping hooves. Because of their own carelessness, something the Apache was seldom guilty of, they had been surprised.

After the fight at Stein's Peak, Colonel Forsyth ordered Captain Tupper, of his regiment, to take two troops of cavalry, two companies of Indian Scouts, and move hard after the runaways. Forsyth himself, with the remainder of the force, would follow. The Apache scouts were led by Al Sieber, whom they knew and trusted and who was reputed to be as good at trailing as the Indians themselves. Unknown to the hostiles, Sieber and three of his scouts wormed their way around the camp during the night, April 29, 1882. Tupper's soldiers and the scouts attacked at daybreak, surging into the camp, and shooting into the brush shelters and at anything that moved. At the same time, previously designated men, scouts or soldiers, rounded up the Indians' horses and drove them away. In the camp six warriors were killed in the first rush and an unknown number of people were wounded. But in spite of the surprise, the warriors soon managed to rally. They entrenched themselves among the rocks of the mesa and fought back. After several hours Tupper held a quick conference with his officers and Al Sieber. The troops were actually outnumbered, although the Apaches on the mesa did not know that. Ammunition was running low, and Tupper's men had been without food, water or rest for many hours. Feeling certain that his little force had accomplished everything it could do and that further effort might result in disaster, Tupper gave orders for a quiet withdrawal.[28]

If the outlaw Indians detected the withdrawal, they did nothing about it. They were only too glad to see the soldiers go. Their losses in dead and wounded were heavy; Chief Loco himself had been badly wounded, and their horses had been run off.

Tupper halted a few miles away to rest and to feed the animals. While the men were eating, Colonel Forsyth suddenly arrived with seven troops of the regiment and two companies of scouts. Forsyth's orders postively forbade him to enter Mexico; he had deliberately disobeyed, and now he decided to continue the pursuit. The troops found the Apache position empty, but there was a plain trail leading south from it. During the day the soldiers captured an old Apache woman who had been unable to keep up with the band. She was questioned, given some food and water, and left where they found her. The column passed the body of a warrior, evidently somebody of importance, lying beside the trail. Since it was very unusual for the Apaches to abandon their dead, the corpse was visual proof of the desperation of the fugitives. By nightfall Forsyth's force was near the upper part of a tributary of the Janos River. Early the next morning the sound of Mexican bugles could be heard in the distance, and a little while later Colonel Forsyth and Colonel Lorenzo García, of the Mexican 6th Infantry, met. García was courteous but firmly demanded that the Americans return to their own country. Forsyth, equally firm, replied that he would pursue the Apaches until he had captured or exterminated them, whereupon García sprang a surprise. He had destroyed the band the day before. The bodies of seventy-eight Apaches, along with many Mexican soldiers, lay scattered through the brush. Finding that there were numerous wounded men without a surgeon's care in García's command, and that the Mexicans were hungry, Forsyth sent over his surgeons and a supply of food. The two forces parted with mutual expressions of esteem. García apparently forgot to report the incident to Mexico City, and when Forsyth submitted his report to Mackenzie, who was then the Department Commander in New Mexico, Mackenzie handed it back, saying, "The less said about it, the better."[29]

From their hideout in the high Sierra Madres, the Apaches now began a series of devastating raids into Chihuahua and Sonora. The villages and ranches of the two states became their

major source of supply—cattle, horses, liquor, clothing and occasional weapons and ammunition. The continual danger from
the Indians caused the total abandonment of hundreds of miles
of productive country; it was feared that the region would be
completely depopulated.

President Díaz, now firmly in power, finally consented to an
agreement for a reciprocal right to cross the boundary in pursuit
of marauders. To save the dignity and sovereignty of Mexico
he insisted on certain restrictions, which, if applied literally,
would have vitiated the agreement, but fortunately for the unhappy people of northern Chihuahua and Sonora, the local officials of both nations saw eye to eye on the Apache problem. They
reached agreements easily.[30]

Only a few days before the agreement was signed (July 29,
1882), Crook, who was now a brigadier general, was ordered
to resume command of the Department of Arizona. He arrived
in Arizona early in September and at once set about familiarizing
himself with the situation. At Fort Apache he had a tent set up
for himself about a mile from the post. He ignored the post, not
even returning the courtesy calls the officers made on him, as required both by regulation and custom. Apparently he spent his
time hunting. After some time, when the post commander and his
officers were beginning to fear that they had, somehow, incurred
Crook's disapproval, several of them were ordered to report to
him. Lieutenant Cruse, whose Apache scouts had mutinied and
joined the attackers at the arrest of the medicine man, related in
his memoirs: "When one by one we were ushered into his tent,
to face his statue-like face and utter silence, while Captain Bourke
cross-examined like a prosecuting attorney, our uneasiness increased. General Crook had campaigned against the red man for
so many years that his manner and method were similar to the
Indian's. . . ."[31]

During the time when he was apparently "sulking in his tent"
Crook had been far from idle. He had visited most of the disaffected bands and listened to their grievances; he had regained
control of the Apache reservation from the Indian Bureau and
placed two trusted officers in charge, Lieutenant Charles Gatewood at Fort Apache and Lieutenant Britton Davis at San Car-

los. Both officers were directed to enroll additional Apache scouts at once.[32]

It was apparent that there could be no peace as long as the Apache outlaws held out in the Sierra Madres. Sooner or later they would raid into the United States for recruits, and for ammunition and other supplies they could not find in Mexico. In fact, this is exactly what happened in March, 1883, when a small war party led by a chief named Chatto swooped across the boundary after ammunition. They covered some eight hundred miles on the raid, killed twenty-five persons, and lost but two.[33]

The government forces realized an unexpected gain from Chatto's raid. One of the war party who did not want to be an outlaw deserted and made his way to San Carlos, where Lieutenant Britton Davis quickly picked him up. "Peaches," as the soldiers nicknamed him because of his youthful appearance and relatively fair skin, was not a Chiricahua; he disliked the Chiricahuas because they had mistreated him and compelled him to be a raider when he did not want to be one. He knew exactly where the Apache hideout in the Sierra Madres was located and was perfectly willing to guide the soldiers to it.[34]

General Crook, after laying his plans and making all necessary arrangements in his own department, made a hasty trip to Mexico to confer with the governors and the chief military commanders in Chihuahua and Sonora, the two Mexican states that were suffering most from the Apache blight. He found them cooperative and willing to welcome any American force he might lead into Mexico to rid them of the horror they were suffering.

While Crook was in Mexico the scanty forces he had available for an expedition were assembling at Willcox, Arizona, on the railroad. Willcox was in a fairly central location from which troops could be moved quickly to any threatened locality. Forage, ammunition, clothing, rations and other equipment and supplies came into Willcox on every train, turning the place into a depot or base for the coming campaign. The troops assembled at Willcox were six troops from the 3d and 6th Cavalry regiments. Lieutenant Gatewood, at Fort Apache, was directed to enroll seventy additional Apache scouts and march them to Willcox at once. Gatewood was delayed several days, however, in enrolling the

additional men. A self-appointed company of volunteers known
as the Tombstone Rangers was moving toward the reservation
with the avowed purpose of killing all the Indians there. The
warriors were naturally reluctant to leave their women and children to the mercy of these hoodlums, and the chiefs held up all
enlistments until the situation was clarified. Fortunately, the
Tombstone Rangers ran out of whiskey before long, and their
enthusiasm evaporated. The organization (if it can be called that)
broke up and disappeared, to the relief of everyone concerned
with the campaign.[35]

Crook had agreed with the Mexican officials that he would
not move until May 1, 1883. The delay would throw the Apaches
off guard and, it was hoped, cause them to believe that they were
not being pursued. But to be able to move promptly, on April
23, the troops, scouts and packtrains moved from Willcox to San
Bernardino Springs (Slaughter's Ranch), only a few hundred
yards from the boundary, where the force was joined by Captain
Emmett Crawford with nearly a hundred scouts with whom he
had been patrolling the border.

Several busy days were spent at San Bernardino. Crook saw
to it personally that baggage was reduced to the irreducible minimum. No one, regardless of his rank, was allowed more than the
clothes he wore and one blanket. Everyone carried forty rounds
of ammunition; there were reserve supplies in the packtrains.
Five packtrains, totaling more than 350 animals, had been assembled. The packers were issued carbines and revolvers, although they were not expected to fight except in self-defense. The
Apache scouts, as a highly necessary part of their preparation for
the campaign, staged a nightly war dance.[36]

At daybreak, May 1, the force crossed the line into Mexico.
It was almost laughably small, consisting of Captain Adna R.
Chaffee's troop of the 6th Cavalry, and about two hundred scouts,
under Crawford. There was one surgeon, attached to Chaffee's
troop, and for his staff Crook had his two aides, Captain Bourke
and Lieutenant Gustav J. Fiebeger, of the Corps of Engineers.
In addition to the Apache scouts there was a small group of
highly competent civilian scouts, which included Al Sieber, Sam
Bowman and Crook's old friend Archie McIntosh. As interpreters

there were two frontier characters known as Severiano and Mickey Free. By a strange coincidence, Mickey Free was the individual whose kidnaping by Apaches over twenty years before had precipitated the Apache war when Lieutenant Bascom charged Cochise with the guilt. He had been raised as an Apache, and it was some time before anybody realized that he was not an Indian. Sieber, who disliked him, described him as "half Irish, half Mexican, and whole son-of-a-bitch."[37] Despite Sieber's dislike, there is no evidence that Mickey Free ever betrayed a trust or failed to interpret according to the best of his illiterate ability.

For several days the marches were easy and pleasant. The front and flanks of the force were covered by the Apache scouts, who straggled along in a most unmilitary manner but missed nothing, "with vision keen as a hawk's, and ears so sensitive that nothing escapes them."[38] But in a few days the going became rough. The trail led up and down steep hills where loose gravel and small boulders made poor footing for men and animals. One unfortunate mule lost its footing, fell, and was impaled on a mesquite branch. The animal was destroyed and its load distributed among the others. Not a human being was seen, but there was abundant evidence of war as the force passed abandoned ranches and deserted villages and fields that were grown into jungles of brush and weeds.

In five days the Americans reached the little towns of Bávispe and Basaraca. They were too large for the Apaches to attack directly, but they were in a state of virtual siege. The people welcomed the Americans joyously. The *alcalde* offered the services of the local militia company, an offer that Crook declined tactfully. Attempts by officers and soldiers to buy food revealed that the community was on the brink of starvation. Nothing but a few eggs and some chile could be found. Crook was able, after a while, to buy four small steers for the scouts, who did not like the army's field ration. The packers, to their great happiness, found several gallons of freshly distilled *mescal*.

Inspired by the *mescal*, they decided to have a street dance. To their chagrin, none of the *señoritas* would accept, but the packers were determined to have a dance anyway. They found some musicians, and for partners they drafted every male Mexican they could catch. The *baile* was strictly stag, and the draftees seemed to have as much fun as their hosts. The dance finally broke up when the *mescal* was exhausted and somebody fell into the bass drum.[39]

With the packers probably somewhat the worse for wear, the column marched the next day to Tesorababi, an abandoned ranch at the foot of the towering Sierra Madres. There was shade and plenty of water. Here, Crook ordered a day of rest for men and animals to put them in condition for the grueling ordeal ahead. The next march would be at night, so that eagle-eyed enemies in the mountains ahead would not see the telltale column of dust raised by the force. After dark on May 7, 1883, the troopers broke camp and marched eastward. There was no moon; the night was pitch black. Word was passed from the head of the column to dismount and lead. Captain Chaffee was riding a horse he had selected because of the animal's strength and power. Suddenly, in the inky blackness, the horse slipped on some loose gravel and rolled down a steep hillside that could easily have been a sheer cliff (it was not visible). Chaffee, with his arm entangled in the reins, was carried downward with the horse. Fortunately, after man and horse had been carried for a few yards, their descent was checked by a clump of bushes, and they were able to scramble back to the trail, but it was a narrow escape for a future Chief of Staff, United States Army.[40]

The next day, May 8, 1883, the column continued to climb. Several packmules lost their footing, but almost by a miracle, none were killed. There were abundant evidences of the Apaches —slaughtered cattle, odds and ends of loot that had been discarded—but not a sign of a warrior. That night the medicine men among the scouts performed the incantations necessary to enable them to foresee the immediate future and guarantee success. The scouts carefully picketed every possible approach. The next morning, the trail continued up and up and up. It became so steep and narrow that five packmules fell off and were dashed to death, hundreds of feet below. Shortly before noon the column, led by Peaches, passed through a narrow ravine and emerged into a natural amphitheater. This was Geronimo's hideout where the outlaws had camped for months, but there was not an Indian in sight. The place had been abandoned since Peaches had last been there.

Late in the afternoon a committee of scouts went to Crook with suggestions. The packtrains, they said, could not keep up with the column. Already, five mules had been killed and their cargoes lost. Let the packtrains and the white soldiers camp here, they said, while the scouts pushed ahead. They could destroy any small groups of the enemy; larger parties they could pin down until the General and the white soldiers could arrive. Crook found the suggestion good. On May 11, 150 scouts, under Crawford's command, accompanied by five white scouts, moved out. Each scout carried food for four days, a canteen of water, a hundred rounds of ammunition and his blanket.

For the next four days Crook and the main body moved ahead slowly. Another Apache camp was passed, but not a single hostile warrior was seen. About noon, on May 15, a squad of scouts brought a message from Crawford that the enemy was close at hand; an hour later there was another message saying that his scouts had fired on a small party of the enemy. As the messenger was delivering his message, the faint sound of firing could be heard in the distance. Cinchs were tightened, carbines loaded and inspected, but the sound of firing died out, and no other message arrived. After dark Crawford himself rode into the bivouac. His scouts had run into Chatto's camp. He had not intended to attack at that moment, but one of the scouts had fired impetuously. Otherwise there would have been a complete surprise, for the hostiles had not even suspected the approach of Crook's force. Nine of the enemy were killed and five prisoners were captured, without any casualties among the scouts.

One of the women who had been captured volunteered to carry word to her people that they must surrender. The hostiles were tired of war; for the next week Warm Springs Apaches and Chiricahuas straggled in by twos and threes to surrender. Among the first to give himself up was a noted chief, Chihuahua, who confessed that he was tired of the warpath and its uncertainties. He sent runners to all his bands, telling them that they must surrender, regardless of what other bands might do. The climax occurred when Geronimo himself, with thirty-six warriors, came in, just returned from a raid into Chihuahua. Geronimo wanted to talk to Crook, who coldly refused to see him, sending word through an interpreter that complete and unconditional surrender was all that he would offer. On May 21 the great chief was convinced; he and his warriors surrendered.

Several days elapsed before the return march to the United States could start. It was necessary to allow the prisoners time to collect and roast *mescal* root (a staple article of diet with the Apaches), hunt deer, slaughter and dress cattle for provisions for the long march. Meanwhile, small groups of Apaches continued to come in. The march started on May 24, and the column was undoubtedly one of the most motley military sights ever to be seen under the United States flag. The column consisted of soldiers, dressed more or less as they pleased, Apache scouts, dressed mostly in nothing at all, women, children, horses, packmules, burros and dogs. At the Bávispe River, Crook ordered a halt to give stragglers a chance to catch up, and to await Geronimo, who, after giving his pledge to return, had gone back to the Sierra Madre to collect the rest of his people. True to his word, he arrived on the night of May 28, with more than a hundred Indians, making a total of over three hundred who had surrendered. The remainder of the march was uneventful, except for a prairie fire that threatened the whole force. Soldiers, officiers, scouts, packers and all the recently hostile warriors with their women and children labored side by side, beating at the encroaching flames. Finally, on June 15, 1883, the column crossed the international boundary, marking the end of a small campaign in which there was little actual fighting but which was, nevertheless, one of the most difficult ever waged by the United States Army.[41]

For the next two years the Apache frontier enjoyed an unaccustomed peace. Under Crook's stern but fair administration, exercised largely through Lieutenants Davis and Gatewood, most of the Apaches tried to adapt themselves to the new way of life. There was some discontent when Davis took sharp action against the time-honored Apache custom of slitting off the nose of an unfaithful wife, and there was grumbling when he tried to suppress the manufacture of tizwin, but Apache good faith was demonstrated when the Indians themselves "liquidated" a notorious troublemaker.

But the peace was too good at last. Davis interfered in a tizwin bout. Fearing that General Crook would come with soldiers to punish them. Geronimo, Chihuahua, Natchez and thirty-five or forty warriors, with eighty or ninety women and children, vanished from the reservation and headed for their old refuge in the Sierra Madre. The remainder of the Chiricahuas, dominated by Chatto, who had developed a deep hatred for Geronimo, remained quietly on the reservation. And more than that, when orders came to augment the numbers of scouts, Chatto himself with most of his band promptly enlisted.[42]

As soon as it became known that Apaches were again on the warpath, all available troops were ordered in pursuit. Davis, with his scouts from San Carlos, caught up with the fugitives once. It was early in the morning. The fugitives were cooking breakfast; there was a long-range exchange of fire, and Geronimo's band fled. Davis and his scouts ate the breakfast. Except for one more brief skirmish at long range, this was the last seen of the hostiles for a long time.

Meanwhile, the telegraph lines were busy over the whole Southwest. Captain Emmett Crawford, who had been relieved of Indian scout duty at his own request and returned to his regiment, was hastily recalled. Immediate preparations were made to follow the runaways into Mexico. Lieutenant Robert Hanna, of the 6th Cavalry, wrote a vivid word picture of the assembly:

> The command to which I belonged was ordered to go to Deming [New Mexico] and report to Captain Crawford awaiting us with a train of stock cars, all ready to pull out as soon as some Indian scouts should arrive on the train from the east. . . . We were soon loaded [after the arrival of the scouts] . . . and after dark disembarked at Separ. . . .
> The darkness was intense, and unloading the animals on an open freight platform difficult in the extreme. The cries of the scouts, the trampling of loose animals, and the efforts of the men to find their belongings in the darkness created an indescribable confusion; while the resemblance to pandemonium was, if anything, increased by the little fires the scouts had

lighted, and showed the savage faces and almost naked forms of the Indian scouts gathered around them.[43]

Simultaneously with Crawford's expedition another one commanded by Captain Wirt Davis was launched into Mexico farther west. Each force was composed almost exactly like the one Crook led personally in 1883—a troop of cavalry, a large number of Apache scouts, and packtrains. Because the operations and experiences of these small forces were so similar to those of Crook's force, which have been discussed, there is no need to go into detail, except for one or two instances. Mexicans, to whom all Apaches were alike, killed a scout and wounded another near a Mexican village. Crawford, Al Sieber and Britton Davis had to exert all their authority and influence to prevent the scouts from visiting a summary vengeance on the village, but they succeeded. Near Oputo, Chihuahua, the trail of three Indians was discovered. Chief Chatto, now a sergeant, was sent, with thirty scouts, to follow it. Chatto returned a few days later with thirty prisoners, the women and children of Chihuahua's band—a heavy blow to Chihuahua. Near the end of the summer the two American forces made contact with each other, by pure chance, and Crawford learned that Wirt Davis had had a skirmish with Geronimo only the day before, in which most of Geronimo's horses and several women and children were captured.[44]

One incident is worth repeating as illustrating the dependability and loyalty of the Apache scouts, regardless of what they might have done in the past. An American interpreter and several civilian packers were arrested by the Mexicans in a town a few miles from where the force was encamped. On learning this, Britton Davis, after giving strict orders for the scouts to remain in camp, set out alone for the town. On the way he met two Mexican officers and two soldiers. There was a flash of lightning, and the Mexicans sat "as though turned to stone." The group was "surrounded by ten or a dozen naked men, their black eyes flashing in their set, determined faces, upturned inquiringly. . . ." Unbeknown to Davis until this instant, Chatto and his warrior-scouts had escorted him all the way, fearing that he might run into danger.[45]

Late in September, 1885, after another skirmish with Wirt Davis, Geronimo's band slipped across into Arizona, remounted at the expense of Arizona ranchers, obtained ammunition and other supplies, and hurried back into Mexico without having been caught. Crook decided to withdraw the troops from Mexico temporarily. The animals were worn to skin and bone, the men were tired, and the terms of service of most of the scouts had expired. Late in November, 1885, Davis again entered Mexico, followed two weeks later by Crawford, who had been delayed by a fruitless pursuit after a minor chief named Josanie, whose band, in four weeks' time, covered nearly a thousand miles, killed thirty-eight people, and lost only one warrior.

Crawford's force in this expedition differed from all previous forces. It included no soldiers; he had four officers (one of whom was the surgeon), an interpreter, and nearly two hundred scouts. Crawford had become convinced that regular American cavalry, supposed to be a backbone and rallying point for the scouts, was merely a handicap to mobility in the Sierra Madre. Predictions of treachery were freely made, but Crawford had discovered that the Apache's word was good. Before leaving Arizona, Crawford was threatened with trouble when a United States marshal from Tombstone came into camp with a warrant for the arrest of one of the scouts, charged with murder. Crawford firmly refused to honor the warrant, and when the marshal became threatening, hinted broadly that the official was not safe in camp. He left hurriedly.[46]

On January 9, 1886, Crawford learned that the renegades' main camp was within striking distance. The command was so worn out that even the iron scouts were exhausted, but nevertheless, a grueling night march was made somehow. An attack at dawn surprised and completely demoralized the enemy. There were few casualties, but Crawford's men captured all the horses, food and camp equipment. Geronimo sent an old woman as an emissary, asking Crawford for a talk; Crawford replied that Geronimo and the chiefs must come to him, that he would talk to them the next day.

At daybreak the next morning, there was a sudden burst of rifle fire. The first thought of everyone was that Geronimo was attacking, but instead, it was a Mexican force. Crawford and Lieutenant Marion P. Maus ran out waving white handkerchiefs, shouting that they were Americans and friends. Crawford sharply ordered his scouts to cease fire, then walked forward to talk to the Mexican commander. A moment later a single shot cracked on the Mexican side, and Crawford slumped to the ground, with a bullet in his skull. The scouts fired again, the Mexican officer fell with a dozen bullets in him; a Mexican lieutenant was shot no less than thirteen times, and an unknown number of Mexican soldiers dropped under the scouts' fire.

Lieutenant Maus, who succeeded to the command, finally got the scouts to stop their fire; then he went forward with a flag of truce, and at the express invitation of the Mexicans. Once in their lines however, they refused to let him return until a chorus of war cries from the scouts indicated that they were about to come to Maus's rescue. The Mexicans released him but demanded six packmules and *aparejos* (packsaddles). To save further possible trouble, Maus agreed.

Meanwhile, Geronimo, who, with his braves, was an interested spectator, sent a messenger to Maus offering to help in exterminating the Mexicans, an offer that Maus could not accept. The next day, carrying Crawford on an improvised litter (he was still living, but never recovered consciousness), Maus started the march for the United States. Crawford died several days later.

Geronimo and his band had disappeared after the fight but overtook Maus's column after a few days. Maus, entirely alone, except for the interpreter, Tom Horn, faced the chief and a scowling circle of Apaches. He took a bold line, saying that he had come into Mexico to destroy them, and he intended to do it. Their only hope was to surrender. Geronimo refused to surrender but finally said that he would talk to General Crook.[47]

Crook met Geronimo at a point twenty-five miles south of the border, on March 25, 1886. Crook was alone except for his aide and an interpreter. The Apaches were wary and kept their weapons close at hand. After several days of talk, Geronimo agreed to surrender, and the war seemed to be over. But hopes were dashed very quickly: a patriotic American rancher-boot-legger plied Geronimo and his warriors with whiskey and assured them that Crook was only taking them to the reservation to kill them. Fearful of Crook's wrath at their drunkenness, and fearing that Tribolet (the rancher) was telling the truth, Geronimo and several of his warriors and their families, vanished back into Mexico. The war was on again.[48]

There was a sharp interchange of telegrams between Crook and General Sheridan, who was now the Commanding General, United States Army. Sheridan believed that Geronimo's escape was due to treachery on the part of the scouts. Crook knew that it was not. Crook interpreted Sheridan's messages as a reprimand and asked to be relieved, whereupon Sheridan assigned him to another department and ordered Brigadier General Nelson A. Miles to take command of the Department of Arizona. Crook's relief was greeted with cheers by a certain segment of Arizona's population, who wanted the Apaches exterminated and also wanted the mineral and agricultural lands in the Apache reservations.

Miles had a distinguished record in the Civil War and a wide experience in the Indian wars in the Northern Plains regions, but he had never been in Arizona, and had no knowledge whatever of the Apache. As a result, he arrived with certain preconceptions. Sheridan, who also had never served in the Southwest or even seen an Apache, believed firmly that American cavalrymen could do anything the Indians could do and that the only Indian scouts needed were a few to nose out a trail.

Miles soon found that his preconceptions were wrong, that American cavalrymen could *not* overtake or keep up with Geronimo's warrior's, each of whom had several horses, which they rode in relays. As a partial offset, Miles ordered that in each troop of cavalry, the heavier men should be dismounted so that the lighter men would have two horses apiece, and he adopted Crooks's method of having a hard core of soldiers to support the scouts and provide a rallying point. Probably most decisive of all was his establishment of a network of heliograph stations at the posts and on the high peaks of Arizona, so that messages and information could be transmitted in minutes, whereas it had taken hours, or even days, before.[49]

The American operations in Mexico that brought about

Geronimo's final surrender were under the direct command of Captain Henry W. Lawton, the same individual whose timely arrival with food and forage was so welcome to Mackenzie's troopers after the raid on the Kickapoo villages. Lawton had as his surgeon a young man who had recently graduated from Harvard Medical School, named Leonard Wood, who was thus introduced to the army and to military life.[50] Lawton's operations in Mexico followed so closely the pattern set by Crook and his officers that to relate them in detail would be repetitious. Geronimo's band was pressed day and night; his warriors and people could find no safety and no rest.

The real hero of the campaign was Lieutenant Charles Gatewood, who has been almost forgotten. The Apaches knew him and trusted him. Under orders from Miles he rode, accompanied only by an interpreter, to Geronimo's band, which he located after days of search. There were several days of arguing with the chief. Geronimo demanded terms; Gatewood had only one reply, unconditional surrender. At last Geronimo agreed to meet General Miles at San Bernardino Spring, and there he finally surrendered. As for Gatewood, he had taken his life into his hands when he rode into Geronimo's camp. Medals of Honor have been awarded for acts far less daring, but he was barely mentioned in the final report.

Any discussion of the unfortunate controversy that developed between Miles and Crook over the treatment and disposition of the Apache prisoners is beyond the scope of this discussion. Geronimo had tired of the warpath and was ready to surrender when a villainous profiteer changed his mind. The foundations for the surrender had been laid by Crook; Miles achieved the final victory.

NOTES

1. John Gregory Bourke, *On the Border with Crook* (New York, 1892), pp. 36–37. Bourke was Crook's aide-de-camp.
2. John Gregory Bourke, "General Crook in the Indian Country," *Century Magazine*, XLI (Mar., 1891), 652.

3. Jason Betzinez and Wilbur Sturtevant Nye, *I Fought with Geronimo* (Harrisburg, Pa., 1959), p. 309. Betzinez was a relative of Geronimo and when he was a child knew many of the warriors who were in this revenge raid. See also John C. Cremony, *Life Among the Apaches* (San Francisco, 1868), p. 39.

4. Betzinez and Nye, *op. cit.*, pp. 16–17.

5. Ralph A. Smith, "The Scalp Hunter in the Borderlands, 1835–1850," *Arizona and the West*, VI (1964), 5–22, and "The Scalp Hunt in Chihuahua, 1849," *New Mexico Historical Review*, XL (1965), 117–40.

6. Robert M. Utley, *Frontiersmen in Blue. The United States Army and the Indian*, 1848–1865 (New York, 1967), pp. 162–63; "The Bascom Affair: A Reconstruction," *Arizona and the West*, III (1961), 59–68; Benjamin H. Sacks, ed., "New Evidence on the Bascom Affair," *Ibid.*, IV (1962), 261–78.

7. Cremony, *op. cit.* pp. 155–67.

8. Bourke, "General Crook in the Indian Country," *op. cit.*, p. 650.

9. *Ibid.*, pp. 652–53.

10. Martin F. Schmitt, ed., *General Crook: His Autobiography*, 2d ed. (Norman, Okla., 1960), p. 38. Hereafter referred to as Crook, *Autobiography*.

11. *Ibid.*, pp. 162–63. See also Dan L. Thrapp, *Al Sieber, Chief of Scouts* (Norman, Okla., 1964), fn, pp. 88–89.

12. Bourke, *On the Border with Crook*, pp. 105–6. See also James M. Barney, *Tales of Apache Warfare. True Stories of Massacres, Fights and Raids in Arizona and New Mexico* (1933), pp. 25–27. Lt. Cushing was a brother of the famous daredevil who sank the Confederate ram *Albemarle* in the Civil War.

13. Lt. Henry M. Lazelle, "Puritan and Apache: a Diary," Frank D. Reeves, ed., *New Mexico Historical Review*, XXIII (Oct., 1948), 297.

14. Bourke, *On the Border with Crook*, p. 108.

15. Crook, *Autobiography*, pp. 163–65.

16. Bourke, *On the Border with Crook*, pp. 138–39.

17. Crook, *Autobiography*, pp. 167–73; Oliver O. Howard, *My Life and Experiences Among Our Hostile Indians* (Hartford, Conn., 1907), pp. 187–225. There can be no question about Howard's sincerity or his personal courage. A few years later, when an Indian outbreak occurred in the department he was then commanding, the measures he employed were not those of gentleness and persuasion.

18. Thrapp, *op. cit.*, p. 96.

19. Bourke, *On the Border with Crook*, p. 220. Unlike the forest and Plains Indians, the Apaches seldom took scalps but often cut off the head of a dead enemy as a temporary trophy. For a similar incident, see Martha Summerhayes, *Vanished Arizona. Recollections of My Army Life*, Milton Quaife, ed. (Chicago, 1939), pp. 111–12.

20. *Annual Report of the Secretary of War, 1877*, p. 143.

21. Martin L. Crimmins, "Colonel Buell's Expedition into Mexico in

1880," *New Mexico Historical Review*, X (1935), 133–42; James B. Gillett, *Six Years with the Texas Rangers, 1875 to 1881* (Chicago, 1943), pp. 261–64; *Annual Report of the Secretary of War, 1881–1882*, pp. 126–27.

22. *Annual Report of the Secretary of War, 1881–1882*, pp. 138–43. It was about this time that cavalry companies were redesignated as "troops," the term that will be used hereafter.

23. *Ibid.*, pp. 146–47.

24. Betzinez and Nye, *op. cit.*, pp. 55–56.

25. *Ibid.*

26. W. C. Barnes, "In the Apache Country," *Overland Monthly*, IX, Ser. 2 (Feb., 1887), 172–80.

27. Thrapp, *op. cit.*, pp. 229–37; Betzinez and Nye, *op. cit.*, pp. 68–70.

28. Thrapp, *op. cit.*, pp. 236–40; Betzinez and Nye, *op. cit.*, pp. 70–74.

29. George A. Forsyth, *Thrilling Days in Army Life* (New York and London, 1900), pp. 104–21.

30. *Foreign Relations, 1882*, pp. 396–97.

31. Thomas Cruse, *Apache Days and After* (Caldwell, Id., 1941), p. 179.

32. Britton Davis, *The Truth About Geronimo* (Chicago, 1951), pp. 45–50: Thrapp, *op. cit.*, pp. 258–62; Crook, *Autobiography*, pp. 243–45. Lt. Davis was the son of the Judge Edmund Davis who urged Tobin's Rangers into action in the Cortina War and who later aroused Texan resentment by raising and commanding the 1st Texas Cavalry (Federal) during the Civil War.

33. Crook, *Autobiography*, pp. 245–46; John Gregory Bourke, *An Apache Campaign in the Sierra Madre. An Account of the Expedition in Pursuit of the Hostile Chiricahuas in the Spring of 1883* (New York, 1886), p. 11.

34. Bourke, *An Apache Campaign*, pp. 14–17; Thrapp, *op. cit.*, pp. 269–72. Peaches' real name, as recorded by Bourke, was Pa-nayo-tishn. He proved to be reliable and truthworthy.

35. *Ibid.*, pp. 13–14.

36. "Report of Gen. Crook to Hq., Military Division of the Pacific, July 23, 1883," *48th Cong., 1st sess., H.R. Exec. Doc. No. 1*, pp. 173–78; Bourke, *An Apache Campaign*. pp. 54–56; William H. Carter, *The Life of Lieutenant General Chaffee* (Chicago, 1917), pp. 101–2.

37. Thrapp, *op. cit.*, p. 262.

38. Bourke, *An Apache Campaign*, p. 22.

39. *Ibid.*, pp. 70–72.

40. *Ibid.*, pp. 65–75; Carter, *op. cit.*, pp. 102–3.

41. Bourke, *An Apache Campaign*, pp. 74–127; Betzinez and Nye, *op. cit.*, pp. 116–22; "Report of Gen. Crook . . . July 23, 1883," pp. 173, 178. Betzinez was one of the warriors who surrendered on May 20. Incidentally, he sheds the first light on the fate of little Charles McComas, whose parents were killed by Chatto's band. According to Betzinez, the child was killed by an Indian known as Speedy, whose mother was killed in Crawford's attack.

42. Davis, *op. cit.*, pp. 208–16; Bourke, *On the Border with Crook*, pp. 463–65; Betzinez and Nye, *op. cit.*, pp. 129–30.

43. Robert Hanna, "With Crawford in Mexico," *Overland Monthly*, VIII (July, 1886), 56–57.

44. "Report of Gen. Crook to Hq., Military Division of the Pacific, April 10, 1886," 49th Cong., 2nd sess., H. R. Exec. Doc. No. 1, p. 147. Britton Davis said that there were 130 scouts (Davis, *op. cit.*, p. 222). As the force crossed the border the scouts killed two bears. This gave Al Sieber a chance for a bit of rough frontier humor. Pulling a mule out of a packtrain and lashing the fresh bearskins on the animal was but the work of a moment. One of the things a mule fears most is a bear, or the scent of a bear. The mule, bawling with terror, galloped back to its accustomed place near the bell mare, but as it passed the other mules and they caught a whiff of the terrible odor, they put their legs under them and got away as fast and as far as possible. Many of them bucked their packs off, strewing the contents all over the country. It took several hours to gather up the frightened animals and repack them. Crawford was noted as a man with a very even temper, but after a private interview with him, Sieber was a much chastened person.

45. Davis, *op. cit.*, pp. 266–67.

46. Report of Lt. Marion P. Maus, quoted in Gen. Miles, *Personal Recollections and Observations of General Nelson A. Miles, Embracing a Brief View of the Civil War, or From New England to the Golden Gate, and the Story of His Indian Campaigns with Comments on the Exploration, Development and Progress of Our Great Western Empire* (Chicago and New York, 1896), p. 453.

47. *Ibid.*, pp. 458–63; also Bernard C. Nalty and Truman R. Strobridge, "Captain Emmett Crawford, Commander of Apache Scouts," *Arizona and the West*, VI (spring, 1964), 30–40.

48. Charles R. Lummis, *General Crook and the Apache Wars* (Flagstaff, Ariz., 1966) pp. 136–37. See also Bourke, *On the Border with Crook*, pp. 480–81. The rancher, Tribolet, was quoted by various sources as saying that the longer the Apaches stayed out, the better for him; he was selling them arms and ammunition, as well as whiskey.

49. General Miles is usually credited with having introduced the heliograph in the Apache wars, but Tom Horn, who was the interpreter with Crawford, said that the device was used by Crook before Miles's arrival. See *Life of Tom Horn, Government Scout and Interpreter, Written by Himself, Together with His Letters and Statements by His Friends. A Vindication*, (Norman, Okla., 1964), p. 128. By what seems to have been a gross miscarriage of justice, Horn was hanged for murder in Wyoming in 1903.

50. Joseph Hamblen Sears, *The Career of Leonard Wood* (New York and London, 1919), pp. 44–47.

CHAPTER 6

Porfirian Mexico and the Dictator's Fall

ALTHOUGH, strictly speaking, the causes and initial progress of the revolution in Mexico are outside the scope of this narrative, it is desirable to devote some time and attention to these subjects in order to show the reasons for the bitterness of the upheaval and account for the hatred of Mexicans toward the United States. The basic causes of the Mexican Revolution lay in the deep past, and for a century had been slowly gathering force, unnoticed by the rest of the world, and ignored by Mexican aristocrats and American and other foreign investors in Mexico's natural resources.

On September 16, 1810, Father Miguel Hidalgo y Costilla, parish priest of Dolores, rang his church bell early in the morning, as though to summon his flock to mass. This morning, however, instead of uttering the solemn words of the mass, in a fiery speech, Father Hidalgo called upon his people to rise in revolt against the Spanish oppressors. Seizing a picture of the patron saint of Mexico, and displaying it as a banner, Father Hidalgo led his parishioners forth to battle. For years he had labored, endeavoring to better the lives and condition of his people. At his own expense he had introduced the vine and the olive tree, only to have Spanish officials cut down the trees and grub up the vines. No colonial could be allowed to produce wine or oil; these products must be imported from Spain. No colonial, even of pure Spanish blood, could be allowed to hold any but the lowest offices in either state or church. The higher offices were reserved for peninsular Spaniards, *gachupines.*

But in spite of the rigid wall of isolation with which the royal Spanish government tried to surround its colonies, the ideas and thoughts that ignited, and were in turn stimulated by the French Revolution, infiltrated into Mexico. Already the Inquisition had noted that Father Hidalgo was a reader of forbidden French philosophy, but no action had been taken against him. He was also a member of a literary and discussion club in Querétaro in which the forbidden topics were discussed. Gradually, over a period of time, the literary club became a revolutionary organization, a front for a conspiracy to free Mexico from the intolerable oppression of Spanish rule. A rising was planned for December 10, 1810, but the authorities received full information and moved to arrest the conspirators. Warned of the danger in time, Father Hidalgo decided to strike at once. The *Grito de Dolores, "Viva México! Viva la Independencia! Viva Nuestra Señora de Guadalupe!"* stirred the downtrodden Indian peasantry to action. Armed with any sort of weapon they could obtain or improvise, they followed Hidalgo in droves. The suddenness of the uprising gave it an initial period of success, and the hopeless and oppressed hordes that followed the banner of the Virgin of Guadalupe turned the movement into a social revolution. They were untrained, unorganized and undisciplined. Their excesses, which Hidalgo could not control, threw nearly all but the humblest classes of Mexican society into the arms of the Royalists. Within a year after Hidalgo had tolled his church bell, the relatively well-equipped and well-trained soldiers of the viceregal government slaughtered the rebels in masses. Hidalgo himself was captured (by treachery), unfrocked and executed at the city of Chihuahua.[1] But even though the Hidalgo rebellion was suppressed, the parish priest of Dolores had ignited a fire that could not be entirely extinguished. Future generations of Mexicans would regard the *Grito de Dolores* as the beginning of Mexican independence.

On September 16, 1910, a full century had passed since Hidalgo rang his church bell. All Mexico, and particularly the capital, was celebrating the centennial of Mexican independence. At midnight, General Don Porfirio Díaz, President of Mexico, stepped onto the balcony of the National Palace in Mexico City. The vast crowd that was assembled in the plaza before the palace became silent. Slowly and impressively the President reached up and sounded three strokes on the same bell that Father Hidalgo had rung just a century before. Then, in a resonant voice that belied his eighty years of age, he shouted the words of the *Grito de Dolores*. The crowd broke into a pandemonium of cheers; sixteen bands simultaneously played the solemn and impressive tones of the "Himno Nacional"; the bells of the cathedral and every parish church in the city began to ring; fireworks reddened the sky. The President and his guests then retired inside the palace and toasted the Republic of Mexico with vintage champagne. The party inside the palace were all clothed in immaculate evening clothes, or glittering uniforms, with the ladies wearing the latest modes from Paris.[2]

For a full month, the celebrations continued. Monuments were dedicated, cornerstones for new public buildings were laid with appropriate ceremonies; there were banquets, parades, bullfights and innumerable other events, all indicating that under the wise and paternal rule of Porfirio Díaz, Mexico had attained political and economic maturity. The officials, the diplomatic corps and the special missions were entertained with an elegance that could not have been surpassed in any regal court of Europe. At the state dinner given in honor of the special ambassadors, the first eight courses were served on plates of sterling silver, the last two upon plates of pure gold.[3]

The erect, distinguished and soldierly-looking man who rang Hidalgo's bell had been President of Mexico for a third of a century, except for four years in which he relinquished office to a trusted follower. He had just been reelected to a further term of six years, by "unanimous vote" of the electors. In the course of his long tenure, his inaugurations had become as colorful as a royal coronation. In 1910, when he entered upon his new term (his seventh), the streets were lined with troops in full uniform. The Austro-Hungarian chargé d'affaires appeared in the uniform of an officer of Hungarian hussars, of plum-colored velvet, with fur pelisse and plumed shako. The Austrian Secretary of Legation wore the uniform of an officer of the Duke of Lorraine's Dragoons. These were typical. En route to the National Palace, the President was escorted by a detachement of the Blue Horse

Guards, in full dress uniform. There was little of the traditional "republican simplicity" in evidence.

Porfirio Díaz had first become prominent as a loyal and dependable supporter of President Benito Juárez during the War of the Reform in the late 1850s, when the President endeavored to curb the power of the church and render the church amenable to the laws of the country. Clerical conservatives fought bitterly, and the civil war thus unleashed led directly to French intervention in the affairs of Mexico and the attempt by Napoleon III to impose a European monarchy upon the people of Mexico. During the bloody years that followed the French invasion, Díaz proved himself to be an unusually capable field commander whose loyalty to the Mexican Republic never wavered; he turned a deaf ear to various attempts by Marshal Bazaine, the French commander, and by the "Emperor" Maximilian, to persuade him to change sides.

After the French evacuated Mexico and the puppet "emperor" had been executed, Díaz and Juárez gradually became estranged. In the early 1870s Díaz attempted a revolution but was quickly defeated and forced into exile for a time. Juárez died suddenly and unexpectedly in 1872 and was succeeded in office by Sebastian Lerdo de Tejada. Lerdo de Tepada lacked tact and succeeded in offending many of the generals and colonels who comprised the majority of the Mexican Congress and who had scant sympathy with any civilian president. Because of this, Díaz, in his next attempt at revolution, commanded stronger backing than before, and he was successful in seizing the presidency in 1876. By the end of 1877 his authority over most of Mexico was complete.

The Mexico in which Porfirio Díaz seized supreme power was little more than a travesty of a country and a nation. Mexico had not known a year of internal peace since attaining independence. The enormous province of Texas, after a bitter war, broke away and gained independence. War with the United States resulted in the loss, not only of Mexico's unsurrendered claim to Texas, but to the loss of nearly a third of the remaining national territory. The French invasion brought further devastation and bloodshed, and even more serious for the welfare of the country were the endless civil wars, revolts by ambitious *caudillos* anxious for power and utterly unscrupulous as to how they might achieve it. The most noteworthy of these gentry was General Antonio Lopez de Santa Ana, the self-styled "Napoleon of the West," who held supreme power several times, always with disastrous results for Mexico.

In all Mexico there were less than four hundred miles of railroad; most of the country's rich mines were inoperative; schools were almost nonexistent, and the public debt was so tremendous that there seemed to be no possibility of ever re-establishing the nation's credit. And as a result of the endless wars and the absence of anything resembling law and order, banditry was so widespread that it was almost a recognized and respectable occupation.

The new President's first care was, understandably, to insure that no ambitious politician unseated him by the same means that he himself had employed. To this end, would-be revolutionists were dealt with promptly and ruthlessly. In the state of Vera Cruz nine young men of prominent families, accused of plotting against the President, were summarily executed, without even the shadow of a trial. This was done by the local commander, General Mier y Teran, apparently on orders from Díaz himself. The example was not lost upon other potential plotters, especially because Díaz, in the early years of his power, was careful to see that the army was paid promptly and regularly, regardless of other financial obligations.[4]

Concurrently with insuring his own continuance in office, the new dictator dealt with the problem of banditry. The solution was the old one of "set a thief to catch a thief." When the government police, the Corps of Rurales, was formed, captured bandits were given their choice between the firing squad or enrolling in the force. Naturally, most of them opted for the latter. Their loyalty to the regime was assured by regular pay; their efficiency was guaranteed by training and strict discipline, and their egos were expanded by the provision of a handsome gray uniform, trimmed with silver, modeled upon the traditional Mexican *charro* costume. Their predatory instincts were satisfied by allowing them free play as long as they did not molest the

upper classes or a foreigner. Díaz offered no objection to anything the Rurales might do in enforcing the law or his orders.
It was usually much less trouble to shoot a suspect than to take
him to a magistrate for formal examination and trial. The Rurales
held human life very cheaply and never hesitated to kill, whether
the victim was a murderer, a runaway *peon* from some *hacienda*,
or a personal enemy of the local *jefe político*. The *ley fuga*
covered all such cases: "The prisoner attempted to escape."[5]

With a semblance of order established in Mexico, and even
before, the new executive turned his attention to establishing
the country's credit abroad. There was no capital in Mexico for
the economic development of the country; it would be necessary
to borrow in New York, London and Paris. But with Mexico's
past record of failure to pay debts, American and European
bankers and capitalists were hesitant about investing in Mexico
without all sorts of guarantees and concessions to insure the
safety of their funds. Within a few years Díaz succeeded in
building confidence in the Mexican government's willingness and
ability to safeguard foreign investments and to pay its own obligations, even though some of those obligations were highly
questionable. His methods and measures lie outside the scope
of this narrative. It is enough to say that Díaz and his government became highly regarded in Wall Street, the City of London,
and in Paris and Berlin. Railroads, mines, smelters, factories,
haciendas and cattle ranches sent a golden stream of profits to
proprietors in the United States and Europe—profits that were
enormous because of the cheapness and docility of Mexican
labor. By the time the centennial of Mexican independence approached, Mexican bonds, formerly regarded as little better than
so many highly decorated bits of paper, had become gilt-edged
investments. Mexico was being opened up to the rest of the
world and was progressing at an amazing rate under the wise
and beneficent dictatorship of General Porfirio Díaz.

Of course, the world that gauged "progress" in terms of
dividends and profits (as much of the Western World did),
made a hero of the man who was considered to be responsible
for the happy state of affairs in Mexico. In fact, Díaz was ac-
corded praise and adulation far in excess of what was extended

to any of his contemporaries in any country. In 1910, shortly
before the centennial celebration, a special correspondent for an
American magazine said, "I do not hesitate in saying that only
three great men have existed on this earth in the last two hundred years—and I measure their greatness in the order in which
I name them: Napoleon, Washington, Díaz, and I am not sure
that there are moments when I would change the order, and
say, 'Napoleon, Díaz, and Washington.' "[6]

Senator Henry Cabot Lodge referred to Díaz as "one of the
most remarkable men of our time," and James Bryce, who was
British Ambassador to the United States and one of the most
acute political observers of his era, said, "President Díaz stands
out to-day as one of the foremost men of this age in the world."[7]

Scores of other statesmen, industrialists, journalists and
travelers joined in the paeans of praise for the aged dictator of
Mexico. But there was one interview that he granted to an American journalist which was destined to have far-reaching effects.
During the course of a conversation with James Creelman, representing *Pearson's Magazine*, Díaz gave Creelman to understand
that he would not be a candidate for reelection in 1910 and that
he believed that Mexico was now ready for the formation of an
opposition party. (It must be emphasized that hitherto an opposition party was not tolerated, and was positively dangerous for
its proponents. Opposition leaders in past years had sometimes
vanished without a trace or had been arrested on some sort of
charge and thereafter had "attempted to escape.") Three years
after the interview, Creelman published a book beside which all
earlier praises of Porfirio Díaz were colorless. And, as journalists
often try to do, Creelman pontificated about the future: "With
the old specter of armed ecclesiasticism laid in its grave, it is
preposterous to talk about a reversion of the Mexican people to
the old revolutionary habit. Díaz has done his work well. . . . The
Mexican people are too busy to fight each other now. . . ."[8]

Creelman was far from alone in his estimate of the dictator's
work and in his belief that Díaz's accomplishments would prove
permanent. An English geographer, Percy F. Martin, in a massive work not intended especially to be a work of praise for Díaz,
said, "So thoroughly has this great Soldier-Statesman done his

work, so well has he laid the foundations, built up the walls, and roofed over the whole structure, that the fabric stands to-day self-supporting and indestructable. . . ."⁹ It remained for an English woman, Mrs. Ethel Brilliana Tweedy, who wrote travel books, to express unknowingly and unconsciously the fallacies that were universally overlooked in the adulation of Díaz by people and classes who benefited by his rule:

> That terrible poverty which sapped the life's blood from the country during three-fourths of the last century has turned to affluence. . . . The Mexicans are better governed, they can afford to pay the taxes for the benefits they receive, and yet are more wealthy. Instead of money pouring out to repay old debts, foreign capital is pouring into the country. . . . Manufactures are building up new sources of internal revenue, and agriculture . . . is so admirably encouraged by the State, that agriculture must ensure the nation's prosperity. . . .[10]

Oddly enough, Mrs. Tweedy spoke of poverty in the past tense, and yet she was horrified by the evidence of current poverty that she saw about her. To her, Mexican officials were models of honesty and integrity in their management of government funds, and she had an aristocratic contempt for the *peon*: "The politican is beyond bribery and corruption; the *peon* gladly accedes to both, and is at heart a thief withal."[11]

Like Mrs. Tweedy, none of the observers and commentators who were so impressed with the dictator's government, and with the prosperity of the people with whom they were brought into contact, seem to have realized for an instant that that prosperity was limited to a small class of people—that in Mexico the old saw about "the rich get richer and the poor get poorer" was true. The American and European visitors to Mexico were entertained, with all the gracious hospitality for which Mexicans are famous, at great country mansions. They saw the good life of their hosts, their obvious wealth, the luxury in which they lived, but never saw or became conscious of the humble and subservient laborers who made this wealth and luxury possible.

In fact, although most of the mines, smelters, railroads and other industrial installations that were beginning to dot Mexico were owned by foreigners, by far the greater part of the agricultural and grazing land of the country was owned by a small, tight caste of landowners whose estates, or *haciendas*, were fantastic, exceeding anything known in Europe or the United States. Under the royal rule of Spain, and later under the Republic, various laws were enacted intended to protect the communal holdings of the Indians, but under Díaz such laws were so interpreted and so twisted in meaning that most of the communal holdings were added to the estates of neighboring *hacendados*. The evicted Indians had no choice but to labor for the landholder or starve. The seizure of the lands of the Indian peasantry under the Díaz regime finally became such a scandal that the church, by this time strongly devoted to Díaz, protested, but was ignored.[12] It has been estimated that 3 per cent of the population owned 95 per cent of the arable or grazing lands in the Republic. In the state of Durango, for example, ten persons owned almost 7.5 million acres of land. In the same state, 97 per cent of the population did not possess land at all; in short, to survive, they had to work for the great landowners on terms fixed by the landowners. There were other states in which the proportion of landless peasants was even greater.[13]

Not only were the poverty-stricken peasants without land under the Díaz regime, they were held to a system of servitude that differed from chattel slavery only in name. Slavery, as it existed in the United States before the Civil War, had never flourished in Mexico. It was not necessary; cheap labor existed in the thousands of docile Indians who had behind them the unhappy tradition of centuries of enforced labor. Peonage was a form of slavery cheaper than the purchase of Africans. A debtor could be required to work out his debt to his creditor; his wife and children could be compelled also to work to discharge the debt. If the debt was never satisfied, the entire family remained in servitude. Debts were heritable; a person's children were responsible if he died before making full payment. Given the illiteracy and improvidence of the Indian peasant, it was easy to assure a permanent labor force on a *hacienda*, especially as the peons were forbidden to leave and were required to purchase their necessities and occasional luxuries at the *hacienda* store.

It was easy to keep them permanently in debt. Debts were trans-
ferable from one creditor to another; in other words, *peons* were
bought and sold as though there were a regular slave market.[14]

Under Díaz, even more medieval than the lot of the *peons*
was the fate of the Yaqui Indians of northwestern Sonora. They
occupied a fertile region in the Yaqui River Valley, which had
been coveted by Spaniards and Creoles for centuries, and for
centuries the war between them and the Caucasians had flared
sporadically. Under Díaz a serious attempt, lasting for several
years, was made to evict the Yaquis and preempt their lands.
The Indians fought vigorously, but large numbers of them—men,
women and children—were taken prisoner and shipped to Yucatán
and the territory of Quintana Roo, where almost all of them
soon died. One of the officials who profited from the confiscation
of Yaqui lands and the open sale of Yaqui prisoners was Don
Ramón Corral, at that time the governor of Sonora and subsequently the Vice President of the Republic.[15]

From the foregoing, it is apparent that the conclusions drawn
by people who were impressed by the apparent solidity of the
Díaz regime and the accomplishments of the old dictator were
mistaken. Creelman's estimate that "no numerous or important"
segment of the Mexican population wanted any revolutionary
change was one of the greatest errors in the history of journalism
and illustrates the perils of predictions based upon superficial
knowledge. And Creelman himself was unknowingly and un-
intentionally responsible, in a way, for detonating the explosion
that tore Mexico asunder. After his interview with Díaz in 1908,
which was widely publicized, the latent opposition to Díaz in
the upper and intellectual classes began to appear in the open.
Clubs were formed to promote the candidacy of General Bernardo Reyes, who was widely believed to be a liberal. The most
decisive effect of the Creelman interview, however, was the pub-
lication of a small book written by a young man named Francisco
I. Madero. The title of the book was *La sucesión presidencial en
1910 (The Presidential Succession in 1910)*. The effect of the
book was to make the almost unknown Madero the chief of
opposition to the Díaz government, especially as Bernardo Reyes

denied any Presidential ambitions and was shortly sent by Díaz
to Europe on a quasi-diplomatic mission that kept him out of
Mexico until after the election.

Despite his statement to Creelman that he would not be a
candidate for reelection in 1910, Don Porfirio quickly changed
his mind. He had no intention of yielding the power that he had
exercised for over thirty years. Opposition political clubs were
suppressed, often violently; newspapers that criticized Díaz or
his regime were also suppressed, the doors of the editorial offices
padlocked and often, too, the editor and all the reporters and
the press crew were jailed, charged with subversive activities.
When the election took place, on July 10, 1910, it was announced that by universal demand of the Mexican people, President Díaz and Vice President Corral had been unanimously reelected for a further term of six years.

Meanwhile, and before it became apparent that Díaz intended
to keep himself and his henchmen in power, Francisco Madero
had started an active campaign as the candidate of the liberal
elements of Mexican society. Because he seemed so obviously
a person of no force or importance, he was ignored at first, but
when it became apparent that he had a large measure of popular
backing, the dictator decided upon action. In June, 1910, Madero
was seized at Monterrey and clapped into jail, charged with
subversion, slandering the President, defying the authorities and
various other crimes. After the election returns had been verified,
in July, he was transferred to the penitentiary at San Luis Potosí.
Probably because of his wealth and the prominence of his family,
he was not executed or subjected to the *ley fuga*. With the help
of friends, on October 5, 1910, he escaped and fled to the United
States, disguised as a railway worker.

Discontent among Mexicans of all classes and conditions was
deep and dangerous. On June 4, 1910, there had been an open
outbreak at Valladolid, Yucatán, which was suppressed with
heavy casualties. In the state of Sinaloa, on June 8, the antire-
electionistas revolted, led by Gabriel Leyva. They were defeated
a few days later. Leyva was captured and a few days later "attempted to escape" while being transferred from one prison to
another.[16] At Monterrey, Madero's followers and supporters

planned an uprising for July 14 (the anniversary of the fall of the Bastille), but Madero, still in his prison cell, ordered it postponed until a more opportune time.

As soon as he was safely in the United States, beyond the reach of Díaz's police and Rurales, Madero issued the "Plan of San Luis Potosí," calling upon all Mexicans to rise against the dictator's tyranny. To avoid possible complications with the United States, the proclamation was backdated to October 5, while he was still in Mexico. The proclamation called for the rebellion to start on November 20, but it actually started several days before. There was sporadic fighting in the state of Vera Cruz, and at Puebla, on November 18, the local chief of police, Colonel Miguel Cabrera, together with several of his policemen, was killed while attempting to search the house of Aquiles Serdan, an adherent of Madero. A pitched battle followed, in which Serdan, his brother and several other partisans were killed.[17]

The major opening acts of the Revolution, however, occurred in the northern part of the Republic. At the little town of Cuchillo Parado, Chihuahua, a week before the revolt was scheduled to start, the enraged villagers, led by Toribio Ortega (destined to become a Villista general), defeated a detachment of Rurales. On November 19, in Chihuahua City, a tradesman named Pascual Orozco shut his shop and assembled a band that had been previously organized and prepared, and proclaimed himself in rebellion against the government of Porfirio Díaz.

A movement that proved to be one of the most significant of all had occurred several days before, without fanfare or open proclamation. On November 15, 1910, a man known locally as Francisco Villa slipped quietly out of the city of Chihuahua at night, with fifteen men, and made for the mountains. For years the Díaz authorities of the states of Chihuahua and Durango had been trying to capture this man, who had every reason to hate "Porfirismo" and everything connected with it. His baptismal name was Doroteo Arango; he was born on a *hacienda* in the state of Durango belonging to the immensely rich Negrete family. His father had died when Doroteo was a mere boy, leaving him the responsibility of caring for his mother and several younger brothers and sisters. He soon gained the reputation of being a hard worker, steady and dependable. But, according to legend which he confirmed himself, a scion of the Negrete family ravished or seduced a much adored younger sister. Doroteo shot the young aristocrat. In Porfirian Mexico there was only one fate for a *peon* who molested a member of the wealthy classes. Doroteo Arango had to flee for his life. He went to the Sierra Madre, where the Apaches had defied pursuit for many years. There he fell in with a gang of bandits, which he joined. He provided himself with a good horse and set of saddle equipment by simply riding the animal away while the owner was in a nearby *cantina*, and became a full-fledged member of the band. His forceful character and intelligence soon made him the acknowledged leader, in spite of his youth. From then until the outbreak of the Revolution he was a bandit, although, according to legend, he made several attempts to live honestly. Regardless of whether or not there is truth in the stories of Francisco Villa's early life, he had years of experience in guerrilla activities and developed qualities of leadership during those years which quickly became apparent in the Revolution.

At some time, while the Revolution was being planned, Villa was recruited to the cause by Don Abrán González, who was candidate for the vice presidency on the ticket with Madero. Don Abrán was bitter against the dictator. When Madero came to Chihuahua on his electoral campaign, before his arrest, he and Villa had a quiet and discreet conference, during which Madero confirmed promises that González had previously made. It may be surmised that Don Abrán had noted Francisco Villa as a man who would be useful when the fighting started.[18]

At first no one but the rebels themselves took seriously the revolt against Díaz. Only three days after Villa and his army of fifteen men vanished into the mountains, Henry Lane Wilson, the United States Ambassador at Mexico City, reported that although the revolutionary movement was widespread (he called it a "conspiracy"), "it lacks coherence, and the Government will easily suppress it." A week later he referred to the "recent revolutionary outbreaks" and to the "lack of intelligent leadership and organization [which has] enabled the Government to suppress the rebellion."[19] The *Literary Digest*, in the issue for December 3, 1910, had on its first page a photograph of Madero, with the statement, "He dared defy Díaz, and now is a fugitive, his estates confiscated, and his army dispersed. Francesco [sic] Madero tried to vault into the saddle of the Mexican dictator, but found it still pretty firmly occupied." In the same issue it was noted that most American editors believed that Madero's rebellion was foredoomed to failure very quickly.[20]

The first few weeks of the insurrection seemed to confirm the opinion that Madero could not possibly prevail against Díaz. The rebels had a few petty successes but were more often defeated by the Federals. Nevertheless, Ambassador Henry Lane Wilson was premature in using the past tense, for weeks later the rebels were still active, and the dictator was becoming more and more worried. The revolution was so widespread over the whole country that it was impossible for the government to concentrate an adequate number of troops in any one place, especially as it was necessary for Díaz to maintain a force in Mexico City strong enough to forestall riot and rebellion there.

The war dragged along, past the New Year of 1911, without any decisive event. Pascual Orozco was named as commander of the revolutionary forces in the north, which, according to Don Enrique Creel, the Minister of Foreign Relations (and former governor of Chihuahua), did not exceed twelve hundred men. Orozco systematically damaged the railroads, in order to make the reinforcement and supply of the Federal troops as difficult as possible. Bridges were dynamited or burned, trains were wrecked, but in almost every encounter between Federal troops and rebels, the latter were defeated. In March, 1911, when the Revolution had been under way for more than three months, the bored correspondent of the New York *Herald* wrote: "Nothing has been accomplished by the insurgent forces outside the columns of the El Paso press. . . . It is now possible to view the future of the revolution in Chihuahua in the light of what has passed, and it can be taken for granted that there will be no insurgent victories of any importance to chronicle."[21]

In the first weeks of 1911, it seemed that the reporter's prophecy was true. Two rebel attacks on Ciudad Juarez, across the Rio Grande from El Paso, were repulsed easily. The small Federal garrison of the city was reinforced by the arrival of General Navarro with several hundred men. Shortly after, the garrison was further strengthened by Colonel Rábago, who broke through the thin rebel lines with a strong cavalry force.

In February, Madero slipped across the border from the United States and placed himself at the head of the Revolution. Early in March, on learning that the Federal garrison of Casas Grandes, Chihuahua, was small, and being anxious for a victory that would raise the morale of the insurrectionists and add prestige to the revolutionary movement, Madero ordered an attack. Both Orozco and Villa were absent at the time, on other missions. The attack was launched on the morning of March 5. The battle went on from early in the morning until late in the afternoon, with the advantage resting first with one side, then the other. When the day was almost over, the Federals were suddenly and un-expectedly reinforced. Panic struck the rebels, and in spite of Madero's herculean efforts to stay the rout, most of them fled in disorder. The insurgent losses were heavy, nearly sixty killed, forty-one taken prisoner, and an unspecified number were wounded, including Madero himself. Yet, oddly enough, the crushing defeat at Casas Grandes actually strengthened Madero. After the fair-weather soldiers had run for home, the men re-maining were a hard core of dependable troops. Within a few days Villa rejoined with some eight hundred men, and Orozco with an unknown number. Madero's force was stronger than before the defeat, and Madero himself had aroused admiration by his coolness in danger and crisis.[22]

The revolution was actually gaining ground and spreading, despite defeats and pessimistic predictions by diplomats and correspondents. Durango, Sinaloa, Sonora and other northern states were in a turmoil. In the south, revolutionary outbreaks occurred in Guerrero, Morelos and as far as Yucatán. At the same time, it was becoming apparent that the government's military power was far less than had been supposed. For years the Díaz government had appropriated funds for an army of 35,000 men, but there proved to be little more than half of that number available for service. The funds had gone to line the pockets of a number of senior officers. The personnel of the

Federal army was, broadly speaking, inferior to that of the rebels. The Federal army was largely a "penal" army. Numbers of its soldiers were criminals, sentenced to serve in the army instead of being confined in a prison; others were unfortunate peasants who had aroused the ire of some petty official, or *jefe político*. Thus the Díaz army was an army of highly unwilling conscripts, whose slavery was disguised by the pay of about seventeen cents a day. After the revolution started, in a burst of generosity occasioned by alarm, the government increased the pay to fifty cents a day, but it is still a matter of wonder that the Federals fought at all, let alone that they fought loyally and bravely.[23]

Besides the inherent weaknesses of the Federal forces, it seems beyond doubt that the field commanders were handicapped and interfered with by detailed orders from Mexico City—orders that often were based upon a complete misunderstanding of the situation in the zone of operations. In Mexico City it was assumed that the main insurgent effort would be directed against the city of Chihuahua. On orders from the capital, General Navarro, at Juarez, was required to reduce the garrison of the border city to about seven hundred men, and sent the rest to the state capital. Troops from other border points were transferred to strengthen the forces at Chihuahua, leaving only small and scattered detachments to guard the frontier. Early in April, 1911, the insurgents began moving northward from Bustillos, where they had been reorganizing since the defeat at Casas Grandes. Moving both by rail and by marching, the main rebel force arrived on April 14 at a point a few miles south of Juarez, between that city and the Federal forces concentrated to cover the city of Chihuahua. Attacking a Federal outpost on the railroad, the rebels displayed a discipline and vigor that they had not shown before. A few days later Juarez was completely invested on three sides; only the side facing the United States remained open. Madero hesitated to order an attack. A short time before, when rebel forces in Sonora had attacked Agua Prieta, opposite Douglas, Arizona, a number of Americans had been killed and wounded by wild shots from Mexico. The United States government had protested vigorously, and Madero wanted to take no chances on arousing American resentment or provoking American intervention.

There seemed to be a possibility that peace could be brought about by negotiation. Madero agreed to an armistice of six days, to begin on April 22. At the end of the period, nothing had been accomplished; the armistice was extended for five days and again for three additional days. On May 7, with no peace in sight because of Díaz' intransigence, Madero announced that the campaign against Juarez was to be broken off, because of danger of complications with the United States. But Madero reckoned without his military chiefs, General Pascual Orozco and Colonel Francisco Villa.

What followed is obscure to this day. While negotiations for a further armistice were under way, firing began between the outposts. Within a brief time, in spite of Madero's efforts to stop the fighting, the battle became general. Unable to control events, Madero notified General Navarro that the truce was at an end and confirmed what was already happening—a large-scale attack. On May 10, losing all hope, with ammunition almost exhausted, the men tired and thirsty, the Federals surrendered.[24]

The capture of Ciudad Juarez was the straw that broke the camel's back. Díaz and his emissaries to the revolutionary forces had been agreeable to all sorts of compromises as long as the dictator was allowed to remain in office. Upon his determination to retain power, all efforts to bring peace had broken down. The capture of an important city on the international boundary changed the balance and marked the end. From that moment on, the rebels would be able to import freely anything that was not contraband of war and would be able to smuggle in arms and ammunition with much greater ease than before. Finally convinced that there could be no peace in Mexico as long as he held office, Porfirio Díaz resigned on May 25, 1911. He was escorted to Vera Cruz and aboard the German ship *Ypiranga* by a grim-faced, taciturn Indian general named Victoriano Huerta.

At his temporary capital at Juarez, Madero announced the names of his provisional cabinet. Pascual Orozco was deeply offended because he was not named Minister of War but instead was relegated to the relatively unimportant position of commanding general in the state of Chihuahua. Both Orozco and Villa were disgusted with Madero's humanity. They both demanded the immediate execution of General Navarro, since he had executed, without mercy, all insurgents who fell into his hands. Madero refused and personally saw to it that Navarro reached the safety of the United States. Three days after the capture of Juarez, a file of Villa's soldiers, but commanded by Orozco, attempted to arrest Madero. Madero's coolness and personal courage defeated the attempt, and Villa conceived an admiration for Madero that made him, thenceforth, a devoted disciple. At the same time, Villa came to believe that Orozco had used him as a cat's paw, and as a result he conceived a hatred for Orozco that was matched only by his later hatred for Huerta and Carranza. Anyone who incurred Pancho Villa's hatred was likely to have ample reason, sooner or later, to regret it.[25]

Even though the revolution of 1911 was mild as compared with what was to follow, it split the country asunder. With Madero installed in the National Palace as constitutional President a few months later, it appeared on the surface that Mexico was on the road to recovery and peace. Nevertheless, under the surface, all sorts of disruptive elements were busy. In the south, the Zapatistas refused to accept the new regime and continued in arms. In Chihuahua, General Pascual Orozco was carefully cultivated by the social elements that hated Madero and everything that Madero stood for—elements that hoped for a return of the golden age of the Díaz dictatorship. He was admitted to the best clubs; aristocratic *hacendados* accepted him as a social equal; he was wined and dined; mine owners and landlords listened to him and nodded their heads in agreement. When the time seemed to be ripe, they dug into their pockets for huge sums to buy munitions and supplies. Orozco suppressed a mutiny in the Juarez garrison in February, 1912, but at the end of the month, when adherents of Emilio Vázquez Gómez, a perennial aspirant for the Presidency, "pronounced," Orozco threw off any pretenses to loyalty to Madero and joined the rebels.[26] It was not long until Vázquez Gómez was relegated to the background, and Pascual Orozco was the acknowledged head of the new revolution.

After the fiasco of the attempt to arrest Madero, Villa left the army, with Madero's consent, and returned to Chihuahua. For several months he was engaged in the meat business—one of the few peaceful interludes in his stormy life, although it has been alleged that most of the cattle that he butchered and sold cost him very little and bore the Terrazas brand. Meanwhile, he unobtrusively kept a close watch on Orozco and the situation as it was developing. On three occasions he was summoned to Mexico City to confer with the President and give information. Upon the announcement of Orozco's defection, Villa again slipped quietly out of the city late at night, with eleven followers, and vanished into the Sierra. Within a few days his force had grown to five hundred men, most of them members of his former command.[27]

For several weeks Villa conducted a lone campaign against Orozco, with varying degrees of success. The Government, meanwhile, was mobilizing its forces and resources for a serious campaign against the rebels. On March 23, 1912, the Federal forces were sharply defeated at Relleno, in southern Chihuahua. The Federal commander, General González Sala, who had resigned from the Ministry of War to command the expedition, was so humiliated that he committed suicide. In the crisis Madero turned to Victoriano Huerta, the tough old Indian who had escorted Díaz to Vera Cruz. Huerta, regardless of what his private character might have been, was an able field commander. He arrived at Torreón, where he established his headquarters, on April 11 and spent a month in careful preparation. Among the troops that were placed under his command were Villa's irregulars; they kept him supplied with information on the enemy's location and activities and made it unsafe for any small groups of Orozquistas to stray far afield. On May 23 Huerta struck the rebels in a second battle of Relleno and smashed them so thoroughly that from then on, the campaign consisted merely of herding the rebels northward, preventing their reassembly, and "mopping up."

When Villa's force came under Huerta's command, relations between the two men were outwardly cordial at first, but there was, nevertheless, a clash of personalities from the start. Villa would have been a difficult subordinate for the most tactful commander in the world, and Huerta was anything but tactful. He made little effort to conceal his contempt for the uncouth barbarian serving under his command. Villa's rank was "honorary general," and he must have boiled inwardly when addressed, with unconcealed irony, as "*Mi general honorario*," or "*Su señoria.*" His unprepossessing appearance, his crude manners, his rough clothes, all made him the butt of sarcasm that deeply hurt and offended him. The climax came on June 12, 1912, when, after a disagreement about a horse that Villa had confiscated during the campaign, Huerta ordered Villa to return the horse to its owner. Villa declined. Huerta at once ordered his confinement and after a "trial" by court-martial, decreed his immediate execution. Pancho Villa came close to death; he was actually standing in front of the firing squad when telegraphic orders arrived from the President to send him to Mexico City. In Mexico City he was confined in the military prison of Tlaltelolco, where Generals Bernardo Reyes and Felix Díaz were already confined.[28]

Villa's imprisonment was not long. In the following December, in broad daylight, disguised only by a pair of dark glasses, he walked boldly out of the prison. A few days later, "Don Jesús José Martínez" walked across the international boundary at Nogales, Arizona, and bought a railway ticket to El Paso, where he spent the next few months. Villa's escape from prison was effected so easily that it seems probable that the authorities were not loath to see him go.

As mentioned above, General Bernardo Reyes and General Felix Díaz were in the same prison as Villa. Reyes had been regarded by many people as a logical successor to Porfirio Díaz; he had been sent to Europe before the election of 1910 but soon returned to Mexico. From the safety of the United States, he plotted a revolution against Madero but was apprehended by American authorities. He soon "jumped bail," crossed the Rio Grande, and announced a revolt—but no one joined him, and on Christmas Day, 1912, he was picked up alone, by a patrol of Rurales. General Felix Díaz, a nephew of the dictator, attempted a revolution in the state of Vera Cruz in October. He, like Reyes a little later, found no support. Before many days he was taken prisoner by the Mexican Regular Army, which he had expected to join him. One of Madero's greatest weaknesses as a revolutionary leader was his humanity and lack of ruthlessness. Felix Díaz and Bernardo Reyes, instead of being shot at once, as Porfirio Díaz would have done, were placed where they could plot at their leisure and without any great danger of detection.[29]

Villa was approached, while in prison, by an emissary of the plotters. Villa gave a noncommittal reply to the proposition tendered him, and vanished before a categorical answer was expected. As soon as he was safely in the United States, he informed Don Abrán González of the plot against the President, but no action was taken, or possibly the information came too late to be of use. While Villa was in El Paso, the revolt exploded in Mexico City. A disaffected battalion released Reyes and Felix Díaz from prison and attacked the National Palace—the beginning of the terrible Decena Trágica. Reyes was killed almost at once. General Lauro Villar, commanding the government defense, was seriously wounded. Madero turned to General Victoriano Huerta, the victor over Orozco. For more than a week the battle seesawed through the capital. Unburied bodies lay in the streets; artillery and machine guns turned the city into a shambles. On February 18, General Huerta announced that President Madero and Vice President Pino Suárez had been arrested and that he himself was assuming the presidency of Mexico. He addressed a personal message to President Taft: "I have the honor to inform you that I have overthrown this Government. The forces are with me, and from now on peace and prosperity will reign."[30] Within a week Madero and Pino Suárez were murdered, under circumstances that seemed to make Victoriano Huerta directly and personally responsible.

The world was shocked and horrified. In El Paso, Pancho Villa was grieved and enraged, especially when he learned that his old friend Abrán González had been brutally murdered by Huertistas; he was bound hand and foot and thrust between the cars of a speeding railway train. Cautiously, and with some difficulty, Villa collected modest funds (partly from Governor Maytorena, of Sonora, who avoided a fate similar to that of Don Abrán by flight to the United States). He purchased arms and ammunition and by highly irregular means acquired some horses. On a dark night in April, 1912, with only eight followers, he quietly crossed the Rio Grande. The real Mexican Revolution was just starting. Decades under the iron rule of Porfirio Díaz —during which a tiny minority lived in luxury and the vast majority lived in conditions of poverty and oppression that almost defy description, when foreigners reaped profits while Mexicans were barely able to subsist—laid the foundations for a bitterness among Mexicans and a hatred for foreigners, particularly Americans, that would produce years of agony and blood. And Huerta, far from bringing peace and prosperity to his country, had initiated the longest era of strife and horror that Mexico had known in its turbulent history.

NOTES

1. Henry Bamford Parkes, *A History of Mexico*, 3rd ed. (Boston, 1960), pp. 144–54.
2. Ellen Maury Slayden, "The Grace and Gaiety of the Mexican Centennial," *Independent*, LXX (May 25, 1911), 1091–98. Mrs. Slayden's husband was a member of the Special Commission representing the United States at the centennial celebration.
3. *Ibid.*, p. 1097.
4. Ethel Brilliana Tweedy, *The Maker of Modern Mexico, Porfirio Diaz* (London, 1906), pp. 384–87.
5. Carlo de Fornaro, *Diaz, Czar of Mexico*, 2nd ed. (New York, 1909), pp. 35, 41–45. Carlo de Fornaro was so bitterly anti-Díaz that his statements must be regarded with reserve, but basically his accusations are undoubtedly true.

    The *ley fuga* (flight law) was the custom whereby guards had not merely the right, but the duty, to shoot a prisoner to prevent his escape. The only proof required was an oral statement by the guard. The *ley fuga* was an easy and convenient way of getting rid of anyone who was considered undesirable by the authorities. Instances of cold-blooded murder by Díaz's Rurales are so numerous and so well authenticated as not to require documentation.
6. Pierre N. Beninger, "The Awakening of a Nation," *Overland Monthly*, LVI (1910), 4.
7. Quoted in José F. Godoy, *Porfirio Díaz, President of Mexico. The Master Builder of a Great Commonwealth* (New York and London, 1910), p. 135.
8. James Creelman, *Diaz, Master of Mexico* (New York and London,

1911), pp. 416–17. It is ironical that this book appeared from the press *after* the revolution in Mexico was well under way.

9. Percy F. Martin, *Mexico of the Twentieth Century*, 2 vols. (London, 907), I, vii.

10. Tweedy, *op. cit.*, p. 390.

11. *Ibid.*, p. 382.

12. Ernest Gruening, *Mexico and Its Heritage* (New York and London, 1928), pp. 124–30.

13. *Ibid.*, pp. 130–34.

14. John Kenneth Turner, *Barbarous Mexico* (Chicago, 1911), pp. 67–119. Turner was so thoroughly hostile to the Díaz government that his statements may be exaggerated. For a moderate, and far more damning for being moderate, estimate of peonage, see *U.S. Department of Labor Bulletin No. 38, 1902*, "Labor Conditions in Mexico," pp. 27–34. Also see Edward Alsworth Ross, *The Social Revolution in Mexico* (New York, 1923), pp. 68–79.

15. Turner, *op. cit.*, pp. 37–66; Casasola, *História Gráfica*, I, 49–50; Creelman, *op. cit.*, pp. 403–7. Creelman was sympathetic toward the dictator's Yaqui policies. The small Filipino tribe known as the Macabebes, which joined the Americans en masse in 1898, are reputed to be descendants of Yaquis exiled to the Philippines when the islands were ruled as a distant province of Mexico.

16. Casasola, *op. cit.*, I, 159–60.

17. *Ibid.*, pp. 202–8.

18. Martín Luis Guzmán, *Memorias de Pancho Villa* (Mexico City, 1934), I, 64–65; Ramón Puente, *Vida de Francisco Villa, Contada por Él Mismo* (Los Angeles, 1919), pp. 30–32; Puente, *Hombres de la Revolución: Villa* (Los Angeles, 1931), pp. 68–69.

19. *Foreign Relations, 1911*, pp. 363, 367–68.

20. *Literary Digest*, XLI (Dec. 3, 1910), 1019.

21. *Literary Digest*, XLII (1911), 489–491.

22. Stanley Ross, *Francisco I. Madero, Apostle of Mexican Democracy* (New York, 1955), pp. 146–49; Casasola, *op. cit.*, I, 229–33.

23. William Archer, "The Collapse of the Diaz Legend," *McClure's Magazine*, XXXVII (May–Oct., 1911), 397.

24. There is disagreement about the details of the capture of Juarez, but it appears that the attack was started by Villa's men, quite likely with his full knowledge and approval. For a scholarly discussion of the event, see Charles Curtis Cumberland, *Mexican Revolution: Genesis under Madero* (Austin, Texas, 1952), pp. 138–41.

25. Ross, *op. cit.*, pp. 167–68.

26. Cumberland, *op. cit.*, pp. 191–95; Casasola, *op. cit.*, I, 422–25.

27. Guzman, *op. cit.*, I, 179–89.

28. *Ibid.*, pp. 245–63; Edward S. O'Reilly, *Roving and Fighting: Adventures under Four Flags* (London, 1918), pp. 289–290.

29. Cumberland, *op. cit.*, pp. 202–5.

30. *Foreign Relations, 1913*, pp. 720–21.

CHAPTER 7

Transition from the Old Army to the New — 1900–1916

T HE YEARS FROM the Spanish-American War to the Mexican Punitive Expedition of 1916 marked a transition that amounted almost to a revolution within the United States Army. During this era the "Old Army" gave place gradually to the new, without any break or convulsion. It was a change that was almost unnoticeable while it was taking place.[1] In the incredible confusion of the Spanish-American War the anachronistic command system of the "Old Army" broke down—the system whereby the Commanding General, United States Army, had no authority over the entrenched bureau chiefs, and the actual administrative authority, under the Secretary of War, was not the Commanding General but was The Adjutant General.[2]

In 1881, when the major Indian wars were settled and the army had a breathing spell in which it could take stock of ieself, General Sherman, then the Commanding General, ordered the establishment of a "School of Application" for cavalry and infantry, at Fort Leavenworth, Kansas. There was indifference, and even some passive opposition, among the military conservatives, who scoffed at the idea that war could be learned any place but on the battlefield. Nevertheless, the school survived and over a period of time came to have a degree of influence on American military thought. This was due largely to one particularly inspiring instructor in military art, Lieutenant Arthur L. Wagner. Wagner, a close student of military history, was impressed by the supposed smoothness and efficiency with which the Prussian armies had operated in the wars of 1864 and 1870 and had come to believe that their success was due largely to their command system, with a general staff planning and controlling training and operations. Hence, Wagner became an ardent advocate of the establishment of a general staff for the United States Army. He was a persuasive lecturer who converted many doubters and skeptics to his own ideas.

The confusion and mismanagement attendant upon the Spanish-American War are too well known to need more than passing comment. The command system did not so much fail as simply cease to exist. The Adjutant General, administrative head of the army, was so swamped by the overnight expansion from 25,000 men to 250,000 men that his department was almost unable to function. The Commanding General, Lieutenant General Nelson A. Miles, was designated to command the expeditionary force to Puerto Rico. When he departed on this mission, the army was left without a head in Washington; there was no one below the President himself to exercise command. (The Secretary of War seems hardly to have entered into the chain of command, except to transmit the President's orders.)

There was no office or agency in Washington charged with prior planning or the assembly of information upon which to base plans. The expedition for the invasion of Cuba gathered at a port that was inadequate for the purpose. It had occurred to no one—and it was no one's responsibility—to look into camping areas, water supply, sidings, warehouses or ship-loading facilities. The troops arrived and embarked chaotically and landed on a hostile shore that had not been reconnoitered and in a country that, from a military point of view, was completely unknown. The troops were clothed in heavy wool in a tropical country; rations were inadequate and of poor quality. To add to the troubles, epidemics that took a toll of hundreds of lives broke out both in Cuba and in the assembly camps in the United States —malaria and yellow fever in Cuba, typhoid in the United States. Although the epidemics were caused largely by the medical ignorance of the time, they were also due to the rudimentary discipline of the hastily recruited volunteers, and they were not helped by the "red tape" by which the bureaus had protected themselves against adverse decisions by the Treasury. The issue of needed medical supplies was less important than that requisitions be made out correctly to the last comma.[3]

Before discussing the changes in organization and ideas that affected the army in the opening years of the twentieth century, mention must be made of the conquest of the major diseases that had played havoc with armies since before the dawn of history. This was a revolutionary development in itself and made possible the two expeditions into Mexico which will be discussed later. The three great camp killers were typhoid, yellow fever and malaria. At the time of the Spanish-American War the exact nature of typhoid was still unknown to the medical profession; the cause of yellow fever was unknown (it was generally believed to be highly contagious), and malaria was still generally believed to be transmitted by noxious air, or by "miasmas." It was known, however, that quinine was a specific for malaria. Within a few short years at the turn of the century the researches of Dr. Walter Reed, of the United States Army Medical Corps, disclosed the causes of yellow fever, and that it could be eliminated by mosquito control. This automatically reduced malaria, which is also transmitted by mosquitos. And in a very few years a vaccine was developed that renders a person immune to the threat of typhoid.

After the Spanish-American War Congress realized that the new commitments the United States had taken on required a much larger military force than before. After a certain amount of backing and filling, the strength of the army was fixed at about 80,000 men, a figure that remained fairly constant until 1917, when the country entered the war against Germany. The necessary increase in the number of officers was effected by giving Regular Army commissions to volunteer officers of the Spanish and Philippine wars. This had been done after the Civil War, when volunteer officers were commissioned in all grades from second lieutenant to colonel. In 1900, however, all the new officers, except for four brigadier generals, were commissioned as lieutenant, including many who had held higher rank during the war.

An event of great importance to the army was the appointment of Elihu Root as Secretary of War by President McKinley, after the wartime Secretary of War had resigned. Root was one of the most eminent lawyers of the country, and upon being offered the appointment had objected mildly, on the ground that he knew nothing at all about the War Department or military affairs. Root's qualifications, however, were exactly what the President wanted. Because the government of the newly acquired territories devolved upon the War Department, he wanted a man in the office of Secretary of War who was capable of handling the complex legal problems that were already arising. Root soon concluded, nevertheless, that his major problem was not the government of the new possessions but the preparation of the army for war.

Quite naturally, he turned at first for advice and assistance to his senior officers, who were the various bureau chiefs in Washington. Root, unlike some of his predecessors, was not a man to sign on the dotted line without asking questions. He quickly saw that the army's command system was an anachronism and that it needed drastic changes. In arriving at this conclusion Secretary Root was aided by Major William Harding Carter, who was one of the assistants to The Adjutant General and whose duties brought him into almost daily contact with the Secretary of War. Along with others, Carter had been urging the establishment of a general staff for the army for several years. In a magazine article in which he reviewed the military lessons of the war with Spain, Carter said, "The one crying need of the army during the past half century has been the want of a General Staff Corps, or a body of officers whose duty it is to do the preliminary planning for the army to make its various elements a more harmonious working machine. In this connection a 'Chief of Staff' must be substituted for the 'Commanding General of the Army,' or the General Staff will fall short of its real value."[4]

Secretary Root was easily convinced, but knowing that there would be strong opposition and that Congress would have to be persuaded, he moved cautiously. His first step, under his own legal authority as Secretary of War, was the formation of a "War College Board," in November, 1901. Several months later he was sufficiently sure of his ground to sponsor a bill in Congress authorizing the establishment of a general staff. The bill radically abolished both the offices and the titles of Commanding General and The Adjutant General. For the Commanding General, a Chief of Staff, holding office for four years, and directly subject to the Secretary of War, was substituted. The Adjutant General was replaced by the Military Secretary, whose duties were those of correspondence and records and who was without administrative authority. The previously independent bureau chiefs were made directly subordinate to the Chief of Staff.

There was bitter and determined opposition from the bureau chiefs, who rallied unitedly to the defense of their special positions; the Commanding General, Lieutenant General Nelson A. Miles, was vehemently opposed, and his position and his long and distinguished career gave his opinions great weight. Some newspaper editors feared that a general staff might be an entering wedge for German militarism. But other senior officers, such as Lieutenant General John M. Schofield, who had been, himself, Commanding General, and also Acting Secretary of War for an extended period, favored the innovation, and the bill became a law on February 14, 1903.

The first three Chiefs of Staff were the three senior general officers of the army, in their order of rank. They were all nearing the retirement age, and none held the office more than a few months; hence none of them made any considerable impression upon the new system. The first one to leave the mark of his ideas and personality was Major General J. Franklin Bell, who became Chief of Staff on April 14, 1906, the first man to hold the highest military office in the nation since the Civil War who was not a veteran of that war. Bell was an enthusiastic supporter of the army's expanding school system, and when appointed Chief of Staff, was the Commandant of the General Service School (as it was then named) at Fort Leavenworth.

Within a few days after Bell took up his new duties in Washington, the General Staff was subjected to its first test. A revolution had broken out in Cuba; under the Platt Amendment, the United States decided to intervene. The operation in 1906 was far different from that of 1898, only eight years before. It is highly doubtful that any advance planning had been done for such an operation, but the troops arrived at the port of embarkation in an orderly succession, instead of in swarms. Transports were loaded, and troops embarked according to a schedule. There was none of the hectic confusion of 1898, simply because there was a coordinating agency with authority to enforce its decisions. The smoothness and economy of the operation fully justified the new General Staff.

There was still among the military conservatives, however, a great deal of latent hostility to the General Staff. In 1907 Congress was induced to revive the office and title of The Adjutant General. The incumbent was Major General Fred C. Ainsworth, a former medical officer who had shown a remarkable flair for administration—and politics as well. In 1910 Major General Leonard Wood became Chief of Staff, in succession to Bell, whose term had expired. In a short time Wood and Ainsworth were at loggerheads about who was the head of the army. Without going into the details of the dispute, the Secretary of War, Henry L. Stimson, and President Taft backed Wood. Ainsworth applied for retirement, to avoid a trial by court-martial for insubordination; the authority of the Chief of Staff over the bureau chiefs was confirmed and strengthened and was never again seriously questioned.[5]

Shortly after Wood became Chief of Staff, but before the duel with Ainsworth, the Madero revolution broke out in Mexico and slowly gained headway. The regime of Porfirio Díaz had seemed to be so firmly founded that few people in the United States anticipated a revolt against him, and in Washington the information about conditions in Mexico and the revolution was too scanty for evaluation. Since gathering and evaluating military and pertinent political information is a recognized function of any general staff, the United States embarked upon one of the first (if not the very first) of its efforts to gain such information. Captains Charles D. Rhodes and Paul B. Malone (both of whom later rose to high command) were selected personally by Secretary Stimson for this duty. They were ostensibly accredited as newspaper correspondents for the Washington *Post* and traveled under assumed names; Rhodes was Charles R. Ross, and Malone became Paul B. Maitland. In addition to their press credentials, they carried secret letters of identification to show to the American ambassador in Mexico City and to the various American consuls in Mexico. They were instructed to converse with Americans of all classes and occupations and conclude whether or not American intervention would be necessary, and if so, when. They parted at San Antonio, in order to arrive in Mexico by different routes and at different times. Rhodes, alias Ross, went first to Chihuahua, then to Torreón. He found that Americans in Mexico were very reluctant to talk to a newspaper correspondent. From Torreón he went to Durango, where he was eyewitness to a clash in the streets between two Mexican factions. At Aguascalientes he was joined by Malone, and from there they went together to Mexico City and to other principal cities of the country, quietly interviewing numerous American and British residents. Their mission completed, they returned to the United States, via Laredo, Texas, on October 13, 1911. Both of them had felt sure that their identities and mission were unsuspected, but as the train crossed the Rio Grande, a fellow passenger remarked, "I'm certainly glad to see you boys safely across in God's country again!"[6]

Several months before Rhodes and Malone went on their unpublicized tour of Mexico, and before the showdown between Wood and Ainsworth, the General Staff was subjected to a severe and unexpected test. As noted already, it seemed in the winter of 1910–11 that the Madero revolution was doomed. In January, 1911, the *Independent* remarked in an editorial that the revolutionists in Mexico were carrying on a sort of guerrilla warfare but that their power was broken. Madero's funds were exhausted, it said, and it quoted an unnamed "prominent alienist" who said that Madero was quite insane and believed himself to be a reincarnation of Father Hidalgo.[7]

Most Americans were not deeply interested in Mexico and regarded the turmoil in that country as more a gaudy spectacle than anything else. There were few who saw in the revolution anything more significant than a struggle between rival politicians, and one that was almost quelled. Consequently, the American people were somewhat startled by the announcement, on March 8, 1911, that President Taft had ordered the concentration of some 30,000 troops near the border for large-scale maneuvers. In spite of the statement that the concentration was for maneuvers, most people, including many in the army, assumed, or took for granted, that the real purpose was to form an army poised to strike into Mexico. In fact, Brigadier General Frederick H. Smith, commanding the Department of the Missouri, with headquarters at Omaha, was quoted in the press as saying that he was sure that more than maneuvers was intended.[8]

The troops were to be assembled in three locations: on the Pacific Coast there would be an infantry brigade near San Diego; thirty-six companies of Coast Artillery from various coast defense installations would be formed into three provisional regiments at Galveston, and the bulk of the troops would be formed into a provisional division near San Antonio. Orders for the troop movements were sent from Washington by telegraph on the night of March 6–7, 1911. There is no indication of how much advance information the still new General Staff might have had of the President's decision, although it is quite likely that the plan originated within the General Staff.

The movement toward the border proceeded smoothly and rapidly. There was delay in a few places because the railroads could not furnish enough cars on such short notice, but such instances were not general. Within a few hours after the orders were sent out from Washington, at practically every military post in the United States soldiers were loading equipment and supplies into railroad cars. Trains were soon rolling toward the border from such widely separated places as Fort Mackenzie, Wyoming; Fort Oglethorpe, Georgia; Fort Myer, Virginia; Fort Snelling, Minnesota; and Fort Wingate, New Mexico. The first troops to arrive at San Antonio detrained on March 10, a few hours less than four days after the orders were issued in Washington; the last units arrived ten days later.

One of the first organizations to arrive was Colonel James Parker's 11th Cavalry, from Fort Oglethorpe, Georgia. Parker was promptly informed by an unnamed general staff officer that "conditions were such that we would be probably on the other

side of the Mexican border within a week. . . ."⁹ This opinion
was fortified when the 11th Cavalry immediately received 429
recruits and more than 400 remounts, bringing the regiment
virtually to war strength.

In 1911 the departure or arrival of troops was still a spectacle
and a novelty to the public. At New York City a reporter for
the *Tribune* watched, with keen interest, the embarkation aboard
a chartered transport of the Coast Artillery companies from the
defenses of New York, who were being sent to Galveston. Shortly
before the ship was scheduled to sail, he noted, the provost
guard (forerunners of the military police) made the rounds of
the waterfront saloons and gathered up a dozen or so of the
stragglers in those places. Every man was searched at the gang-
plank, and several who had a forbidden flask of liquor watched
glumly as it splashed into the waters of the harbor. Private
Joseph Mulcahey, overlooked somehow by the provost guard,
tried to get aboard undetected, but missed his footing and somer-
saulted into the cold water between the ship and the pier. Someone tossed him a rope; he was hauled aboard, and the S.S.
Jamestown sailed on time, with not a man missing.¹⁰

No provision had ever been made in the United States Army
for any permanent tactical organization above the regiment. Thus,
the Maneuver Division (as it was designated) was an improvised
organization, and its staff and the staffs of the brigades were
equally improvised. William Harding Carter, who had convinced Secretary Root of the need for a general staff and who
was now a major general on duty in Washington, was designated
to command. His division staff came from far and wide, but it
included such men as Captain Malin Craig, who would one day
be the Chief of Staff himself, and Major Blanton Winship, who
was destined for distinction as a soldier-diplomat and governor
of Puerto Rico.

While on the train en route to San Antonio, Carter organized
his staff and held his first staff conferences; the first directives,
to be issued as soon as division headquarters was established,
were drawn up. Probably one of the most important of these first
directives was that in which Carter made antityphoid inoculation
compulsory for the entire command—officers, soldiers, and civ-

ilian employees alike. Antityphoid vaccine had been available for several years, but taking it was optional; large numbers of officers and men were not immunized. But that was now changed. The results were so obvious and striking that in a short time the requirement was made army-wide, and never since has an American military force been endangered by typhoid, which had been so devastating only a few years before.

Carter further required that all water for drinking or cooking be boiled, even though the water supply for the camp was supposed to be potable. And amazing and somewhat shocking to a generation many of whose members still believed that water applied to the skin was somehow weakening, or at least unhealthy, Carter ordered that every soldier must bathe at least twice a week, and that company commanders were responsible to see that the order was carried out.

Carter opened his headquarters and formally "activated" the Maneuver Division on March 12, 1911. For the next several months a succession of field exercises hardened the troops and accustomed them to the conditions of war, as far as such conditions can be simulated in peace. Staff officers and senior officers became accustomed to the problems of handling large bodies of men in the field. With twelve regiments of infantry, a brigade of cavalry, a large amount of artillery and numbers of the necessary auxiliary troops, it was possible to develop situations and present problems that previously had been impracticable in the United States. And it is noteworthy that although Carter was an elderly man, he was no military conservative. His command included the new and highly experimental airplanes—three or four airplanes, four or five pilots and a handful of mechanics and technicians.[12] He made full use of them for reconnaissance and as fast messengers and predicted that their importance would increase. He made full use, too, of the equally new wireless telegraph and was deeply impressed with its potential for the future.

Probably even more important in the long run than the training the division received, was the revelation of military weakness. Many weaknesses in the American military structure and practices were well known to the army, but others were revealed

by the mobilization and maneuvers that were previously unsuspected. Some weaknesses could be corrected only by congressional action. The motor age was dawning; the army was fully
aware of the possibilities of motor transportation. Almost unanimously, observers and inspectors urged that motor transportation be given a trial to determine its suitability, either to sup-
plement, or possibly to replace, animal transportation. Many
units arrived in the maneuver area short of organic transportation—wagons, ambulances, horses, mules, harness, etc. Instances
occurred in which the railroads were unable or unwilling to
satisfy the army's needs. These were all deficiencies that required action by Congress, to make the necessary appropriations
or enact the necessary laws.

There were, however, weaknesses and deficiencies revealed
that could be remedied by the army itself. Inspectors found, for
example, that there was a wide variation between the equipment of companies of the same arm, and sometimes of the same
regiment. This was caused, not so much by the issue of different kinds of equipment, as by the failure to prescribe a single
standard. Commanding officers took into the field what each
thought was necessary, and no two opinions were exactly alike.
It was found, too, that the infantry needed more training in
marching and stricter enforcement of march discipline.[13]

Nearly all American officers were well aware that their
army was far from perfect, and nobody was more anxious than
they to correct all weaknesses and deficiencies. But with all of
its faults, the United States Army of 1911 was not as negligible
as the superficial and supercilious military critic of the *Berliner
Tageblatt*, a certain Colonel Gaedke, who pontificated scornfully
that the United States did not really have an army, seemed to
believe. All that the Washington government could put into the
field, he said, was a disjointed aggregation of fragments of
various arms. The United States Army, he continued, had no
reserves [he was right about that], no commissariat, no means
of transport, and practically no officers. It was deficient in training and in everything that made a fighting force.[14]

Early in August, 1911, the Maneuver Division was disbanded,
and most of the troops returned to their home stations. It is im-

possible to say whether or not the Maneuver Division had any effects upon the course of events in Mexico, but it undoubtedly made many United States officers conscious of Mexico and the Border country. Likewise, there can be little doubt that the division staff gave considerable thought to just what action would be taken if the division was suddenly ordered to cross the Rio Grande. The mobilization of the troops in the Border regions gave the General Staff and the administrative services actual experience in the rail movement of large bodies of troops, experience that would prove invaluable in the next few years, when other troop movements converged toward Mexico. If there had not been a revolution in progress in Mexico in 1911, it is extremely likely that there would have been no Maneuver Division. Thus, although the Maneuver Division of 1911 did not fire a single shot in combat, its briefly told story is a part of the history of American military relationships with Mexico.

NOTES

1. For a wider discussion of the transition from the "Old Army" to the new than would be appropriate here, the reader is referred to Russell F. Weigley, *History of the United States Army* (New York, 1967), Chaps. XII, XIII and XIV.
2. In present practice and regulations, this official is always referred to as The Adjutant General, with the article capitalized (abbreviated TAG). The other bureau chiefs in the Department of the Army are referred to similarly, such as The Quartermaster General (TQMG), The Surgeon General (TSG), etc. An officer of The Adjutant General's Department, or the adjutant general of a command echelon high enough to have such an officer on its staff, is referred to without capitalizing the article. The current practice will be followed in this discussion, so that when the writer refers to The Adjutant General, he means only one particular official.
3. Major General James Parker, *The Old Army: Memories, 1872–1918* (Philadelphia, 1929), pp. 211–13.
4. William Harding Carter, "Will America Profit by Its Recent Military Lessons?" *North American Review*, CLXXIV (May, 1902), 671.
5. Henry L. Stimson, *On Active Duty in Peace and War* (New York, 1947), pp. 33–37.
6. "Diary of a Special Mission to Mexico," in the unpublished memoirs of Major General Charles D. Rhodes, U.S. Army, Ret., in the library of the United States Military Academy, West Point, New York.

7. *Independent*, LXX (Jan. 12, 1911), 122.

8. Washington *Post*, Mar. 8, 1911, from newspaper clippings on Mexico, Vol. I, Manuscript Division, Library of Congress.

9. Parker, *op. cit.*, p. 411.

10. New York *Tribune*, Mar. 9, 1911, from newspaper clippings on Mexico, Vol. I, Manuscript Division, Library of Congress.

11. "With the Army in Texas," *Outlook*, XCVII (Apr. 1, 1911), 726–29. See also William Harding Carter, "The Border Patrol," *Outlook*, XCIX (Dec. 23, 1911), 974–75.

12. The writer has been unable to ascertain exactly how many pilots and airplanes were in the maneuvers of 1911. The total air power of the United States Army at the time consisted of five airplanes, three small captive balloons and six qualified officer-pilots. See "Report of The Chief Signal Officer," *War Department Annual Reports, 1911*, I, 739.

13. "Report of The Inspector General," *War Department Annual Reports, 1911*, I, 268.

14. "German Scorn for Our Army," *Literary Digest*, XLII (Apr. 1, 1911), 617–18.

CHAPTER 8

Americans at Vera Cruz

THE YEAR 1913 CLOSED without any sign of fulfillment of the promise made by Huerta to President Taft in an extraordinary message at the end of the Decena Trágica: "The forces are with me, and from now on peace and prosperity will reign."[1] On the contrary, the revolution broke with a fury that astounded and horrified a generation that had come to believe that the days of war on earth were almost over—that the dawn of universal peace was at hand. With the news of Huerta's usurpation and the assassination of President Madero and Vice President Pino Suárez, opposition to Huerta quickly developed, especially in the north. Within a few days Governor Venustiano Carranza, of the State of Coahuila, announced the refusal of his state to accept Huerta. Francisco Villa, in exile in El Paso, Texas, gathered seven followers, purchased a small amount of arms and ammunition, crossed the Rio Grande secretly at night (riding horses acquired by highly unconventional means), and in a short time was at the head of a formidable force. In the State of Sonora the anti-Huerta forces, led by Álvaro Obregón and Plutarco Calles, were soon making war against the Huertista garrisons.

Within a few months a semblance of unity was given all these northern forces by their nominal acceptance of Carranza as their head and their adherence to his Plan of Guadalupe. In Mexican history and politics a "plan" is not a scheme of action; it is a political platform. The Plan of Guadalupe announced the refusal of its adherents to recognize any part of Huerta's government, the legislative and judicial as well as the executive. The army was designated as the "Constitutionalist Army," with Carranza as "First Chief in Charge of the Executive Power." Upon the occupation of the capital by the Constitutionalists, he would become President *ad interim* and would call for a general election as soon as possible after peace was established.[2] While the Plan of Guadalupe gave the Constitutionalists an outward show of unity, it is probable that the only real unity came from their mutual hatred of Huerta and all that he stood for.

Originally, Huerta was strongly supported by the American ambassador in Mexico City, Henry Lane Wilson, who had been appointed by President Taft and who was a conservative of the most extreme kind. He lost no opportunity to urge Washington to recognize the Huerta government immediately. But shortly after Huerta's *coup d'état*, there was a change in administration at Washington. The new President, Woodrow Wilson, whose social and political philosophy was as far apart as the poles from that of Ambassador Wilson, was shocked at the murder of Madero and Pino Suárez and by the way that Huerta had gained power. He determinedly refused to recognize Huerta and made it clear that he would never do so; Huerta must go before the United States would consider the recognition of any regime in Mexico.

Late in January, 1913, President Wilson lifted the embargo upon exports of arms and munitions from the United States, to enable the Constitutionalists to arm and equip themselves and maintain their resistance to the usurper.[3] In February, a few days later, the Maneuver Division of 1911 was reconstituted and designated as the 2d Division. It was assembled at Galveston and Texas City, where it could be trained, and was close enough to the border and a port of embarkation to be quickly available in case of emergency. By this time, too, an appreciable fraction of the United States Army, approximately seven thousand officers and men (mostly cavalry), was patroling the border from the Gulf of Mexico to Sasabe, Arizona, a distance of some sixteen hundred miles.[4]

By the spring of 1914, a year later, Huerta's hold on Mexico was weakening, especially in the militant north, although he enjoyed the recognition of Great Britain, Germany and other powers of Europe. But in spite of diplomatic pressure and strong representations from Americans who had business and financial interests in Mexico, President Wilson was adamant; he would not recognize a regime that came into power by revolution and murder. In Sonora, General Obregón had cleaned out the Huertista garrisons and centers of resistance. In Chihuahua and Durango, Villa's original seven followers had multiplied to something like twenty thousand men, fairly well armed and equipped, sternly disciplined and strongly led by a man who can be described accurately as a natural military genius, regardless of his ignorance and faults. On April 3, 1914, after days of savage fighting, Villa's troops entered the key city of Torreón, a major rail center, the possession of which gave the holder the freedom of movement.

With Torreón in their hands, the Constitutionalists began moving toward the port of Tampico. Tampico was an especially critical point, for a number of reasons. Its capture would give the revolutionists a seaport, which they needed badly. It was an oil center of world importance, with refineries, immense oil storage tanks and producing oil fields clustered closely about. Large numbers of Americans and other foreigners were employed there as managers and skilled technicians. Very few Mexicans were employed except as unskilled laborers, a condition that aroused deep resentment among Mexicans. In early April of 1914, because of the danger for foreigners, a strong American naval force was assembled at Tampico, along with naval forces from other countries.

This was the general situation when two separate incidents, occurring almost simultaneously, became blurred and merged into a single crisis in the relations between Mexico and the United States. On April 9, 1914, the U.S.S. *Dolphin* lay at anchor in the Panuco River at Tampico. The *Dolphin* was actually a lightly armed "dispatch boat," normally assigned for the personal use of the Secretary of the Navy. Secretary of the Navy Josephus Daniels had released her for duty with the fleet, and so she was in Mexican waters, instead of at her usual berth in the Potomac. On the morning of April 9, Paymaster Conn went ashore with a boat and boat's crew to pick up some supplies that had been purchased locally. The boat flew the United States flag, both fore and aft, but nevertheless, while loading the supplies, the party was arrested by a squad of Huertista soldiers, commanded by a Colonel Hinojosa. Hinojosa's men boarded the boat to seize two of the sailors. The arrested officer and men were released soon, but not before they had been paraded through the streets, in full view of the people. General Zaragoza, the local Huertista commander, sent a prompt apology to Admiral Henry C. Mayo, who was in command of the American ships at Tampico, using one of his subordinates as a messenger. Admiral Mayo was not satisfied. He saw, in the incident, a deliberate affront to the United States, especially as the Mexicans had boarded the boat, thus violating United States territory. Mayo at once sent a sharp note to General Zaragoza, demanding a formal apology, prompt punishment of the responsible officer and, most important of all, the public hoisting of an American flag in a prominent place, to be saluted with twenty-one guns. The salute would be returned by Mayo's flagship, and he demanded a reply within twenty-four hours.

Reported promptly to both Washington and Mexico City, the affair passed from the control of the local commanders and became a grave international issue. The pacifistic Secretary of State, William Jennings Bryan, was not at all pacifistic on this occasion. He told President Wilson (who was absent from Washington at the moment), "I do not know how Admiral Mayo could have done anything else." With the President's full approval, Bryan insisted that the Huerta government comply with Mayo's demands, but he extended the time limit to April 13. The Secretary of the Navy, meanwhile, ordered all available ships at Hampton Roads (the greater part of the Atlantic Fleet), together with a regiment of Marines, to sail for Mexican waters at once. It seemed apparent within a few days that Huerta had no intention of yielding to the American demands but was stalling for time, hoping to "save face." President Wilson then issued his own ultimatum; unless Huerta complied with American demands by 6:00 P.M., April 16, 1914, the whole matter would be laid before Congress. It is unlikely that either Huerta or any member of his government understood the seriousness of this threat, for no reply was received before the expiration time. President Wilson appeared before a joint session of the two houses of Congress on April 20; early on April 22, a joint resolution was passed by overwhelming majorities:

> RESOLVED, by the Senate and House of Representatives in Congress assembled, that the President of the United States is justified in the employment of the armed forces of the United States to enforce demands made upon Victoriano Huerta for unequivocal amends to the Government of the United States for affronts and indignities committed against this government by General Huerta and his representatives.[5]

Long before this, members of the armed forces were acutely aware that they might be used in Mexico, but information about the Mexican armed forces, the terrain between the coast and the capital, and a thousand and one other items of military importance, was lacking. It is no exaggeration to say that most of the military information about the interior of Mexico was no more recent than the war of 1846–48. On an unrecorded date in early 1914, a thin-lipped Marine major who had acquired a reputation as a reckless daredevil, Major Smedley D. Butler, reported to Admiral Frank F. Fletcher, at Vera Cruz, for duty as the Marine Corps member of his staff. Admiral Fletcher was curt and almost rude in his reception of the new officer, until Butler sensed that the admiral was "pulling his leg" and was actually very glad to have him aboard. A few days later the admiral invited Butler to go ashore with him. They took a ride on the railroad, part way to Mexico City, in the private car of the superintendent of the railroad. After several hours of viewing the scenery, and casual conversation, Admiral Fletcher suddenly suggested that he would like to have Butler go to Mexico City. "For various reasons of state," he said, "our officers have been requested not to go outside Vera Cruz, but I'd like an accurate description of conditions in Mexico City. I want to know how many soldiers the Mexicans have up there. The statements have been conflicting." Fletcher added that Butler must go without formal orders, and if he were caught, "I can't help you."[6]

For two weeks Butler, masquerading under the name of Johnson, inspected the railroad from the port to the capital, looked at power plants and water systems, and, posing as a secret service man looking for a fugitive criminal, even obtained a pass from Huerta that enabled him to search in the ranks of Huerta's soldiers. Butler finally decided that the Mexicans were becoming suspicious. He boarded a train for Vera Cruz, dodged off at a wayside station, and while waiting for a boat from the flagship, was pounced upon by a gang of Mexican hoodlums. He was rescued by the boat's crew, who were much chagrined that he refused to allow them to drop the Mexicans into the harbor.[7]

Before the Tampico crisis could be resolved, and even a few hours before President Wilson's address to Congress, a far more serious crisis arose. In the small hours of the morning of April 21, 1914, a cablegram arrived at Washington from Consul William W. Canada, at Vera Cruz, saying that the German ship *Ypiranga* (also spelled *Iparanga* in some accounts) was nearing Vera Cruz with a cargo that included two hundred machine guns and fifteen million rounds of ammunition for the Huerta forces. The ship was scheduled to dock at ten o'clock the next morning and would unload at once. Locomotives and cars were already in the port area to receive the cargo. General Gustavo Maas, the local Huertista commander, had stated that if the Americans interfered, he could not resist; he would leave Vera Cruz with all his troops and all the rolling stock, destroying the railroad as he left.[8]

In Washington there was a hasty telephone conference between the President, the Secretary of State and the Secretary of the Navy. The conference ended when the President said, "Daniels, give the order to Fletcher to take the customs house at Vera Cruz." Within minutes, radio orders to Admiral Fletcher directed him to seize the customs house, prevent the landing of the *Ypiranga*'s cargo, and prevent its delivery to Huerta or any other Mexican faction leader.[9]

The *Ypiranga* approached the port early the next morning, but, under orders from an American ship, stopped and anchored outside the harbor. At eleven thirty, Marines and landing parties of sailors began moving ashore. The customs house was seized and occupied without any resistance. It seemed, for a while, that the whole operation would be accomplished peacefully, but before evacuating, General Maas had released and armed the prisoners in the jail. They roamed the streets, doing some plain and fancy looting, and some of them opened fire on the Americans. Large numbers of patriotic Mexicans, excited by the sound of the firing and believing that it was their duty to defend their country against the Americans, loaded their weapons and began shooting from rooftops and second-story windows. They inflicted a number of casualties, especially among the sailors of the landing parties, who were not trained for land warfare, and were marched in what was practically a parade formation.

On the first day (April 21, 1914) the objectives of the landing force were strictly limited; they were the customs house, the postoffice and certain streets that gave control over the railroads. By early afternoon all these objectives were in American possession. Snipers were cleared from the area, including a few who had occupied the ancient Benito Juárez lighthouse, from which they were dislodged by a few well-placed shells from an American ship. Through the American consul, William W. Canada, Admiral Fletcher tried to get in touch with Mexican civil officials but was unsuccessful; they had all fled. Shortly after noon a column of mounted troops was seen in the sand hills beyond the city; quick fire from the guns of the transport *Prairie* sent the horsemen skittering for safety.[10]

At Tampico the American naval forces fully expected orders to seize and occupy that city, but on April 21 a radiogram directed them to sail at once for Vera Cruz. Without waiting for a signal from the flagship, Commander William A. Moffett, of the U.S.S. *Chester*, a light cruiser, turned his ship's prow southward and ordered full steam. Moffett drove his ship through the darkness at a speed that she had never made before, and to give greater power, had oil poured over the coal that the "black gang" shoveled continuously into the furnaces. The ship creaked and groaned, and it seemed at times that her plates might spring apart from the mighty effort she was making. The *Chester* arrived at Vera Cruz at eleven o'clock at night. The lighthouse was dark, and there were no harbor lights; the only light came from an occasional burst of gunfire ashore. There was no pilot and no way to get one, but Moffett conned his ship into the harbor himself and came to anchor near the *Prairie*, a feat of seamanship that brought congratulations from Sir Christopher Craddock, the commander of the small British squadron at Vera Cruz. Although the *Chester*'s arrival was unannounced and un- expected, she was more than welcome. Signals flashed at once for her Marines and landing party to go ashore. Her Marine detachment was commanded by the same Major Smedley D. Butler who had prowled about Mexico City on an espionage mission; one of his subordinates was 1st Lieutenant A. A. Vande- grift, who, years later, commanded the Marines at Guadalcanal when for months they "hung on by their teeth" against Japanese assaults.[11]

The forces from Tampico arrived at Vera Cruz early in the morning of April 22, and the powerful fleet from Hampton Roads, under command of Rear Admiral Charles J. Badger, dropped anchor at about the same time. Watching from the bridge of the flagship the fleet's Marine officer, Colonel John A. Lejeune, saw a scene that he later described as stirring him to the depths of his soul. A regiment of landing-force sailors de- bouched from a street into a large plaza fronting on the Mexican naval academy. The young naval cadets (apparently abandoned by their officers), enraged at the insult offered their country by the American landing, had placed flimsy barricades of mat- tresses, or anything else they could find, and opened fire on the Americans from a second-story window of their school. They inflicted several casualties, but it was a tragic and futile gesture on their part. Within a few seconds the guns of the *Chester* and *Prairie*, both ships anchored close inshore, turned the interior of the building into a shambles, with a number of the heroic boys killed and wounded.[12]

At an unrecorded time during the day the *Chester* (which had been hit more than a hundred times by small-arms fire) encountered another problem. Boats loaded with sailors and Marines headed for the shore were fired upon repeatedly from a Norwegian freighter anchored in the inner harbor. Commander Moffett swung his ship's guns to bear on the Norwegian and sent a signal that if the fire continued, he would sink the ship. He then sent a boarding party, and seized five crew members, three Chileans, one Venezuelan and one Peruvian. With not a Mexican in the group, they were apparently motivated by nothing but the traditional Latin American dislike for and suspicion of the United States.[13]

It soon became apparent to Admiral Fletcher (who remained in command, although Admiral Badger was senior to him) that he would have to occupy the whole city. Sniping from rooftops continued; the Americans suffered numerous casualties, and the Mexicans suffered more. A correspondent for *Collier's Magazine*, who was on board Admiral Badger's flagship, recorded his first impressions:

> Decks and awnings were black with cinders [all of the ships burned coal], stokers throwing in their last ounce of strength, the whole great steel fabric quivering with speed, the dreadnaught plowed through the warm Gulf water and raised land at breakfast time. Across the still sea now came an occasional thud of shell fire and the rattle of machine guns. As we slowed down to our anchorage a large open launch put-putted close under our quarter. The young bluejacket at her tiller looked up as if what he was doing were the most natural thing in the world—bringing the fleet its first dead. On a few boards amidships, four bodies, with faces covered, lay stiffly, side by side, in the bright sunshine. . . .[14]

On shore the landing forces were now reinforced by the regiment of tough, experienced and war-hardened Marines who were accustomed to this kind of fighting from recent campaigns in Nicaragua, Haiti and other places. They began a house to house search for snipers and weapons, but unlike the inexperienced sailors, who swarmed down streets without any reconnaissance or preparation, they stationed a machine gun and some riflemen at each intersection, with orders to shoot snipers on sight. Instead of exposing themselves in the street after searching a house, they took pickaxes and broke through the adobe walls into the next house. On one occasion two Marines were shot in the stomach as they forced the door of a house. The angle showed that the shot was fired from below. A volley was fired through the floor, and then the Marines ripped it up. They found two dead Mexicans, with weapons in their hands.[15]

By the end of the day, April 22, 1914, resistance had ceased. Nineteen Americans and some three hundred Mexicans had been killed, and now the Americans were in complete control of the whole city. A strong force was dispatched to seize the pumping plant at El Tejar, about nine miles south of the city, and upon which the city's water supply depended. At the other end of the American line, Lieutenant Vandegrift was ordered to establish an entrenched outpost. The shifting sands of the dunes made entrenching difficult, and there was no brushwood or other material for revetments. A veteran sergeant pointed out to him an obviously abandoned house nearby. The house was quickly dismantled by the willing hands of the Marines, but before the job of revetting was complete, an extremely irate Mexican appeared; the Americans had destroyed his house. Vandegrift gave him a note explaining the situation and circumstances; several months later the Marine received a stiffly worded letter from the Claims Commission, demanding an immediate explanation of the vandalism and the payment of five thousand pesos. Hurrying as fast as his feet could carry him, Vandegrift went to Colonel Lejeune. Lejeune's reply was brief, and in substance was, "Young man, let this be a lesson to you. Never sign a paper you don't have to sign. Since you were carrying out my orders, I am responsible."[16]

As for the *Ypiranga*, after she had been detained for several days, it was decided by the State Department that there was no legal basis for holding her. Accordingly, she was released and sailed a few miles to the south to Puerto Mexico and discharged her cargo there. She was joined, or followed within a short time, by another German ship, the *Bavaria*, also carrying a cargo of arms and munitions for Huerta.

In the United States, on April 19, 1914, the 5th Infantry Brigade, part of the 2d Division, marched into Houston, Texas, and went into camp. The brigade was combining training with participation in exercises in commemoration of the Battle of San Jacinto. At eleven thirty that night the division commander telephoned from his headquarters at Texas City, to inform the brigade commander that Huerta had refused to fire the salute demanded by the Americans. Fifty minutes later the division commander again telephoned, ordering the 5th Brigade to return at once to Galveston and prepare for embarkation. The return trip would be by rail, and the brigade would be strongly reinforced. A telegram to Washington asking what the reinforcements would include brought a reply on April 21. The 5th Brigade would be strengthened by one or two troops of the 6th Cavalry, by the 3d Field Artillery (less one battalion), the 4th Field Artillery, the 2d Engineer Battalion (less one company), Field Company D, of the Signal Corps, Ambulance Company No. 3, Field Hospital No. 2 and an aviation detachment. The next day a field bakery of the Quartermaster Corps was added to the troop list. On April 23 orders arrived for the brigade to embark at daybreak on the twenty-fourth and to sail as soon as the transports were loaded. Five days' rations were to be taken; tentage was to be left standing. Regimental combat trains were also to be left at Galveston. Twenty-two mules were authorized for each regiment—a number far below what would be needed for active campaigning, but there was not enough space on the transports for the full number of animals. As it was, each regiment had enough mules for the machine guns, for three wagons and for the medical pack and the ambulance.

From the moment the warning order was received until a few hours before embarking, there was a question about who was to command. The brigade commander was in poor health; with approval from Washington, the division commander relieved him at once. On April 23 a telegram from the Secretary of War ordered Brigadier General Frederick Funston to accompany the force; late in the day another telegram directed him to assume command. Because the small staff of a combat brigade would be totally inadequate for the complex duties of an occupational force that actually amounted to a small division, the staff of the 2d Division was transferred to the expedition, almost in a body.[17]

At Galveston, as soon as the brigade arrived from Houston, the officers and men set to work; they worked round the clock, preparing for embarkation. 2d Lieutenant Charles C. Drake recorded in his personal diary that he was up all night. His young wife (he was out of West Point only two years) accompanied him through the night, bravely concealing the fear and grief she must have felt. After all, she was an "army wife" and had to live up to the traditions. Drake's regiment left camp at seven o'clock in the morning, marched to the dock, and boarded the transport *Sumner*, with everyone, officers and soldiers alike, almost exhausted. Drake noticed the next day that everybody felt better for a night's rest and relief from the strain of the day before.[18]

The transports, convoyed by four destroyers, and joined a day or so later by the battleship *Louisiana*, arrived off Vera Cruz at eleven o'clock at night, April 28, and docked at seven the next morning. Nobody was allowed to go ashore until afternoon, but meanwhile a crowd of Mexicans gathered on the dock, "mostly barefooted and selling cigars and candies," and affording most of the Americans their first view of the "enemy." There was a rumor (unverified) that some sniping had occurred the night before, in the red-light district.

The troops were held aboard the transports until Wednesday, April 30, when they disembarked early in the morning and marched directly to their assigned stations in the city and on the outpost line. The force landed consisted of 183 officers, 3,147 soldiers, 11 civilian employees, 155 mules, 27 wagons, 4 ambulances, 3 buckboards and 4 newspaper correspondents. General Funston would have dispensed with the correspondents gladly, but his orders required him to allow them to accompany the expedition, and he had no choice.[19] After conferring at some length with Admiral Fletcher, Funston formally assumed command of all United States forces ashore at Vera Cruz. The sailors reembarked, but the Marines remained behind with the army. Behind the scenes, in Washington, there had been some tugging and hauling over the disposition of the Marines. Funston wanted to keep them, especially as his total strength from the army would never exceed 4,000 men—a force entirely inadequate to

control and safeguard a city the size of Vera Cruz if trouble
occurred. The Navy Department wanted to return the Marines
to their ships and normal stations. Unable to agree between
themselves, the two Secretaries referred the matter to President
Wilson for decision, and he decided in favor of the army. The
Marines became an organic part of Funston's command for the
duration of the expedition.[20]

On April 28, the day in which the army transports arrived
at Vera Cruz, Admiral Fletcher took the final step for the complete occupation of the port. The ancient Spanish castle of San
Juan de Ulloa, guarding the entrance to the harbor, still flew
the Mexican flag. During the fighting in the city the commandant
of the fort was notified that if he fired a single shot, the heavy
guns of the fleet would be turned on him at point-blank range.
The castle was known to be a prison, and it was known also
that some of the workshops of the small Mexican navy were
within its walls. A small occupying force moved in; the Mexican
flag was lowered and the American flag hoisted in its place. The
dungeons were opened, and the prisoners (most of them political prisoners) were brought out, some of them seeing sunlight
for the first time in years. It was with difficulty that many of
them were convinced that they were not being led forth to
execution. In fact, the world, not yet accustomed to the barbari-
ties of the Nazi and Russian concentration camps, could hardly
believe the horrors revealed in San Juan de Ulloa. The Americans immediately examined the prison records; political prisoners
were released, and prisoners with genuine criminal charges
against them were transferred to more humane confinement in
the jail.

After the brief ceremonies of formally taking over the command of the city and the American forces, General Funston
addressed himself to the herculean task of organizing an administration. The Mexican officials almost unanimously refused
to have anything to do with the occupation government. To do
so would be a violation of Mexican law and subject them to
penalties and retaliation when the Americans withdrew. A brief
attempt to have a civilian American military governor was a
failure, and Funston himself assumed the title and functions of

military governor. Before leaving the United States he had been empowered by the War Department to appoint provost courts, at his own discretion, for the trial of Mexican offenders against the expedition. Since the Mexican courts had ceased to function, one of his first official acts was to appoint such courts. On May 2, 1914, two days after he became military governor, he issued a general order outlining the form and functions of the military government of the city. Authority over all departments of the city government, except for a few, was vested in a Provost Marshal General, who was directly responsible to the commanding general. Exempted from the Provost Marshal General's authority were the General Treasury, the Customs and Lighthouse services, the civil courts, the General Post Office and the United States Mail Agency, all of which remained under Funston's personal control.[21]

Although fighting had stopped before the army arrived at Vera Cruz, it was taken for granted that, sooner or later, the Mexicans would attack. On May 3 an American physician who lived and practiced in Mexico City got through the Mexican lines into Vera Cruz by representing himself as a German. He told Funston that while on the way from the capital he had seen five troop trains, crowded with troops; he had also seen fifteen flatcars loaded with artillery and machine guns. He had heard a rumor, too, that General Rubio Navarette had arrived at a point near Paso del Nache with eight thousand men, sixteen field guns and nineteen machine guns. Funston relayed this information to Washington, saying that he could hold the city against any force the Mexicans could send against him but that the isolated pumping plant at El Tejar, nine miles from the city, presented a serious problem. The pipeline from the plant to the city could not be guarded along its entire length and could easily be damaged at some unguarded point.[22]

On May 2 there was a brief flare of excitement. A Mexican force estimated at five hundred men suddenly appeared at El Tejar. An officer with a white flag came forward and demanded that the Americans surrender within ten minutes. The outpost commander sent a hurried message to Funston (the Signal Company had established wire communication) and was told that under no circumstances would he fire the first shot. Within minutes a battalion was on its way from the city—and was deeply disappointed that the Mexicans had vanished. After a futile night spent fighting mosquitos, the battalion returned to Vera Cruz.[23]

Vera Cruz was traditionally one of the unhealthiest and most disease-ridden cities of the world. Although considerable progress had been made under the Díaz regime, it was still swept more or less regularly by yellow fever, malaria, dysentery and a dozen other ailments. The water supply was polluted, clouds of mosquitoes swarmed from the stagnant and undrained pools. At the public market offal was dropped to the floor or tossed into the street to be fought over by packs of mangy dogs or by the vultures that habitually roosted on nearby rooftops. There was not a screen in the market, and meat was piled on tables that were never cleaned.

With the primary object of safeguarding the health of his own command, Funston ordered an immediate cleanup of the whole city and its environs within the American lines. Stagnant pools of water were drained or sprayed with oil; new concrete floors were laid in the market, food stalls were screened, and vendors were made to clean up themselves and their wares. Heavy fines were levied upon those who disobeyed the unaccustomed sanitary regulations. An editorial comment in an American weekly review said:

> According to the latest reports Funston is already fighting in Vera Cruz. But he is fighting, not the Mexicans, but the enemies of the Mexicans and all mankind, the microbes. He has turned his soldiers into scavengers, which is even better than turning swords into plowshares. He has sent squads of men scouting up the back alley, not so much to route out snipers with revolvers as mosquitoes loaded with malaria. He has ordered his skirmishers to search the cellars, not for concealed weapons but for forbidden filth. . . .[24]

Before many days had passed, the people of Vera Cruz learned that their lives and property were safe. The invaders did not loot, and nobody was stood before a firing squad for having resisted. Requisitioned property was paid for promptly. Criminals were not released from jail to rob and murder, but instead the gringos added to their number by confining all sorts of petty offenders, whose labor added materially to the sanitary squads. When the Americans started to clean up the wrecked Naval School to use it as a barracks, crowds of poor Mexicans had a wonderful time, salvaging articles that the Americans threw away. "Thousands of poor Mexicans—men, women, and children —surrounded the Building and battled over the old shoes, shattered furniture, and discarded clothes. It was the women who fought fiercest and most vociferously, and, to the accompaniment of much hair-pulling, many a pair of linen trousers had its legs irrevocably separated."[25]

With the rigid discipline that Funston imposed on his troops, and the innate tendency of the American soldier to be friendly, even with recent enemies, it was not necessary to give many public demonstrations that the city was actually under martial law. There were a few occasions, however, in which the steel under the velvet glove was displayed. On May 9, 1914, Funston ordered the seizure of the ice plant. The manager favored his best customers, the *cantinas* (saloons). The saloons had all the ice they wanted, while the American hospital, the numerous officers' and troop messes and Mexican private customers were without ice. A local anti-Huerta newspaper editor tried to stir up a riot to kill a former Huerta cabinet minister who had taken refuge in Vera Cruz with his family. The newsman, one Heriberto Jara, was promptly jailed but released after a few days. Upon his release, and somewhat stupidly, it would seem, Jara made another attempt; this time he was jailed for an extended period.

Although administration and sanitation seemed to occupy most of the time of the commanding general and his staff, they dared not lose sight for a second that the Americans were an invading force in a thoroughly hostile country. If trouble were to occur, they had the necessary physical power to cope with it and could bring it to bear very quickly. Jack London wrote: "Beneath my window, with a great clattering of hoofs, is passing a long column of [United States] mountain batteries, all carried on the backs of our big Government mules."[26] Target ranges

were improvised and were in daily use. Combat exercises and
daily drills kept the men in condition. Daily parades enabled
the staff to estimate the discipline and training of the command
and also gave the Mexicans (including, beyond doubt, a considerable number of spies) an opportunity to see American military
power.

During the first month of the occupation the situation was
critical; a spark would have set off an explosion. Mexicans of
all classes and factions resented the invasion bitterly. Huerta
made strong efforts to rally the Mexican people behind himself
as the defender of the *patria*. From the state of Sinaloa, where
he was operating at the time, General Álvaro Obregón, who was,
next to Villa, the most prominent revolutionary general, urged
Carranza to join Huerta and declare war against the United
States. Carranza himself said to the State Department's representative with him, George C. Carothers, "The invasion of our
territory . . . violating the rights that constitute our existence
as a free and independent sovereign entity, may indeed drag us
into an unequal war . . . which until today we have desired to
avoid."[27]

The almost unanimous voice with which the revolutionary
generals denounced the action of the United States did not include the voice of General Francisco Villa. Just before the landing at Vera Cruz, and while the Tampico incident was causing
excitement, he stilled criticism in his own followers by remarking curtly, "It is Huerta's bull that is being gored."[28] He took
prompt measures to guarantee that there would be no anti-
American demonstrations in the territory that he controlled. He
turned a deaf ear to invitations that he join the Federals to expel
the invaders. He made it bluntly clear to Carranza that he and
his forces would not support any action against the United
States; there is evidence that a Villa emissary persuaded Zapata
to take a similar stand. Villa addressed a personal letter to
President Wilson, in which he expressly disavowed Carranza's
bitter note of protest. Unable to gain allies among the Mexican
factions because of Villa's position, Huerta was powerless against
the Americans at Vera Cruz. In the middle of July he submitted
his resignation to his puppet Senate and like other unsuccessful
Latin-American dictators, betook himself to Europe.

Without an enemy to fight and with the passage of time, increasing improbability that one would materialize, the expeditionary force marked time during the summer of 1914. Outposts were fully manned at all times and ready to repel the attack that never came. Duty hours were filled with drills, target firing, routine military duties and other training. In off-duty hours there was little to do; officers, soldiers, Marines, all were thoroughly bored. They went to the bullfights, attended second-rate motion pictures, drank beer in the *cantinas*, all the time hoping for something to happen. It was a healthy army because of the sanitary measures that Funston enforced, and because of plenty of hard exercise, ample food and the watchful care of the medical officers. The Mexicans of the city, who had always regarded disease and death fatalistically as acts of God from which there was no escape, were amazed at the sudden drop in the death rate among themselves.

As mentioned before, one of Funston's first acts was to establish provost courts, because of the refusal of Mexican judges to serve under the military government. Provost courts, it should be explained, are for the trial of civilian offenders under the rule of martial law. An unnamed correspondent, visiting one of the courts at Vera Cruz, commented on some of the cases he heard being tried. A man had been jailed for a month, and just after he had paid a month's advance rent for the apartment he occupied with his *querida* (mistress). While he was in jail, his friend took up with another man; the complainant wanted his month's rent refunded by his successor in the lady's affections. The court agreed, ordered the third member of the triangle to pay, and when last seen the three were walking down the street together in perfect amity. A drunk who was confined overnight was given his breakfast and released, after being told sharply that another offense would keep him locked up for thirty days. Late that afternoon, he staggered in, with his meager possessions tied in a bundle, all prepared for free meals and a comfortable place to sleep for the next thirty days.[29]

The problems of governing a large city and the possibility of an attack were not the only matters that caused anxiety at the headquarters of the expedition. For good reasons, Funston ordered that nobody was to pass outside the outpost lines, but some of the newspaper correspondents regarded themselves as being above his authority. Three noted correspondents, Richard Harding Davis, Frederick Palmer and Medill McCormick, decided to go to Mexico City. Somehow they got through the outposts without being detected and paused for lunch at a place called Paso del Macho. There, while eating, they found themselves suddenly surrounded by Mexican soldiers and were marched to jail, where they were searched. McCormick carried a letter of introduction to General Maas. Several hours later they were taken to him; Maas treated them with courtesy, and allowed McCormick and Davis to go on to Mexico City, where they were promptly arrested again. The correspondent of the London *Times* interceded for them, and they were released to the custody of the Brazilian minister, who now represented the United States in Mexico. They were finally released upon agreeing not to send dispatches of any sort while they were in the capital and on the condition that they leave within twenty-four hours. The staff of the expedition sighed with relief when they reappeared at Vera Cruz. Funston was understandably irritated; the three never seemed to realize how serious their escapade might have become. They might have been held as hostages; they might have been summarily shot as spies.[30]

Another American, who was then unknown, made an unauthorized sortie from the American lines and reentered hours later. Captain Douglas MacArthur, of the Corps of Engineers, serving then on the General Staff, was attached temporarily to the expedition. He passed surreptitiously outside the American lines to reconnoiter the railroad. Few details of his adventures during the hours he was out have come down to us, but it is known that he was in grave danger several times and that he obtained information that would have been priceless if military operations had extended beyond the outskirts of the city. No official recognition could be given for his exploit because it was unauthorized, but there is no indication that he was ever reproved for it.[31]

As has been mentioned, life at Vera Cruz was boring, monotonous and disagreeable. There was no United Services Organization. Lieutenant Drake recorded in his diary such items as:

"The Old Bengal Tiger," Brevet Major General David Twiggs. *From the National Archives.*

Colonel (Brevet Major General) Ranald S. Mackenzie. Photograph taken during the Civil War, when he was still in his twenties. *Courtesy of the U.S. Artillery and Missile Center Museum, Fort Sill, Oklahoma.*

A posed photograph of Domingo, a Mescalero Apache Indian scout. *Courtesy of the Thomas Gilcrease Institute of American History and Art, Tulsa, Oklahoma.*

Sketch by Frederick Remington of packers with General Crook's force pursuing hostile Apaches. *From Century Magazine*, XLI (*1890–1891*), *654.*

Sketch by Remington of a mounted infantryman in Crook's force while in campaign against Geronimo. *From Century Magazine*, XLI (*1890–1891*), *644.*

Vera Cruz, 1914. General Drake's note says that a Marine, holding a machine gun in his arms, sprayed this building as though with a hose, and that 15 dead Mexicans were taken out of it. *From General Charles C. Drake's collection.*

Vera Cruz, 1914. General Drake's note says, "Machine guns were used like fire hoses. . . ." *From General Charles C. Drake's collection.*

Vera Cruz, 1914. The interior of the Naval School after shelling by the *Chester* and the *Prairie*. *From General Charles C. Drake's collection.*

Headquarters of the 5th Brigade at Vera Cruz. *From General Charles C. Drake's collection.*

Hoisting the U.S. flag over the terminal Hotel, Vera Cruz, 1914. From General Charles C. Drake's collection. This building was used as a signal station to communicate with the fleet, and several signalmen were killed and wounded here by snipers. The Terminal Hotel was also Generel Funston's headquarters. *From General Charles C. Drake's collection.*

Headquarters of the 7th Infantry at Vera Cruz. *From General Charles C. Drake's collection.*

The 19th Infantry marching into Vera Cruz after landing from the transport. *From General Charles C. Drake's collection.*

Searching for concealed weapons and ammunition, 7th Infantry area, Vera Cruz. *From General Charles C. Drake's collection.*

General Francisco Villa, taken probably early in 1914. *From Everybody's Magazine*, XXX (*June, 1914*), *819*.

Insurrecto soldiers in action at Casas Grandes. Probably taken in 1911. *Courtesy of the Thomas Gilcrease Institute of American History and Art, Tulsa, Oklahoma.*

Villista prisoners captured at Columbus. Colonel Hoffman identifies some of them as follows:

Top row, right: "Dad" Archer, the jailer at Deming, New Mexico, in whose custody the prisoners were held.

Top row, left: Antonio Sanchez, a Mexican resident of Columbus, taken with arms in hand during the fight. He was acquitted at the subsequent trial, but was killed on the street in Deming within a few minutes after being released.

Next to him, Juan Sanchez, another local Mexican, who was hanged. In front of Juan Sanchez (wounded): Francisco Alvarez, who killed the Moore baby, and allegedly raped Mrs. Moore. He was hanged. On Alvarez' left, a man known as "Yellow Eyes," reputed to have been Villa's personal orderly. He was hanged.

The man on the left, front row, was supposed to be a Villista general, name unknown. He was sentenced to twenty years imprisonment. Others in the picture are unidentified. *From Colonel Charles W. Hoffman's collection.*

Villista dead at Columbus, gathered up for cremation. *From Colonel Charles W. Hoffman's collection.*

The base camp at Columbus, New Mexico, showing a truck train about to move out. *From Colonel John W. Cotton's collection.*

Infantry on the march in Chilhuahua. *From Colonel John W. Cotton's collection.*

A bivouac at an unidentified place in Chihuahua. *From Colonel John W. Cotton's collection.*

Motor transportation during the rainy season in Chihuahua. *From Colonel John W. Cotton's collection.*

One of the Punitive Expedition's Dodge cars, showing why vehicles often broke down. *Courtesy of Dodge News.*

A Dodge touring car and an improvised armored car, the latter probably brought to the Border by the National Guard in the mobilization of 1916. This picture was apparently taken at Fort Bliss, Texas. *Courtesy of Dodge News.*

A "jackass battery" (mountain, or pack artillery) on the march in Chihuahua. *Courtesy of the Thomas Gilcrease Institute of American History and Art, Tulsa, Oklahoma.*

Lieutenant Colonel Genevevo Rivas Guillén, who took command of the Carranza troops in the Carrizal fight upon General Gomez' death. This picture was taken in 1938, when he was in command of government forces in suppressing an abortive revolution. *From Life,* IV (*June 13, 1938*), *15.*

Captain Charles Trumbull Boyd, 10th Cavalry, killed at Carrizal. *From the archives of the United States Military Academy, through the courtesy of Mr. Egon Weiss, the Librarian of the Academy.*

1st Lieutenant Henry Rodney Adair, 10th Cavalry, killed at Carrizal. *From the archives of the United States Military Academy, through the courtesy of Mr. Egon Weiss, the Librarian of the Academy.*

The National Guard mobilization of 1916. An unidentified field artillery unit in the transition from civil to military life. *From Century Magazine*, xcii (*October, 1916*), *810.*

New Jersey's Essex Troop reporting for duty in the mobilization of the National Guard, 1916. *From Century Magazine*, xcii (*October, 1916*), *805.*

Captain Julien E. Gaujot, 11th Cavalry, the Provost Marshal and command-officer of the women's stockade at Colonia Dublan. *Colonel Geoffrey Galwey's collection, from the original in the National Archives.*

The camp of the 24th Infantry at Colonia Dublan, showing the adobe huts the soldiers constructed throughout the area. *From Colonel John W. Cotton's collection.*

Went to the bull fight this P.M. It's awful, but there is nothing else to amuse one's self.

It rained nearly all the time and the mosquitoes were so thick you could kill a dozen with one blow. [This was at El Tejar.]

The only bright spot in the week is mail day.[32]

To relieve the monotony somewhat and to enable some of the married members of the command to spend a few hours with their families, General Funston devised a plan whereby ten officers and twenty enlisted men or civilian employees could sail to Galveston on the weekly transport and come back on the return voyage of the same ship. The War Department approved but cautiously added that for officers this would be considered as "detached service" and would be added to the number of days of such service debited against each officer.[33]

Huerta's resignation and departure gave the bored officers and soldiers the hope that they would soon be recalled. Everyone in the force, from General Funston down to the newest recruit, was delighted when orders came on September 15 to begin preparations for evacuation. Two days later another message from Washington said that further orders would be issued as soon as necessary arrangements had been made with the Carranza government. Funston cabled an estimate of the shipping that would be needed; the tonnage of equipment and supplies would come to 16,800 ship tons. He concluded his message with the remark: "Although the city was occupied by a foreign army, differing in race and language from its inhabitants, and was governed under martial law in its strictest form, a condition that would naturally be expected to bring about friction, there have been none of the incidents that would ordinarily be expected under the circumstances."[34]

Funston recommended October 10, 1914, as the date for departure, but both he and the State Department were unduly optimistic. Numbers of Mexicans had accepted positions with the occupation government. Clerks in various offices, schoolteachers and many others, relying on the protection of the Americans, had resumed their duties. Hundreds of refugees had swarmed into Vera Cruz, many of them escaping from Huerta, but many, also, fleeing from the Constitutionalists. Businessmen, both Mexican and foreign, had imported goods, paying the customs duties to American officials; property owners had paid their taxes to the American administration. The United States demanded that Carranza guarantee that nobody be punished for cooperating with the occupation forces and that nobody be required to pay any tax or duty a second time.

Carranza stubbornly turned a deaf ear to the American demands. He took the position that the demands were an infringement on Mexican sovereignty and an interference by the United States in purely domestic affairs of Mexico. With a number of transports in Vera Cruz harbor partly loaded already, President Wilson suspended the evacuation order. The Americans would remain until such time as the First Chief might come to reason. Some of the transports had to be unloaded to get equipment and supplies that the troops urgently needed. Since it appeared that the expedition might remain at Vera Cruz indefinitely, Funston requisitioned lumber to build barracks for such soldiers as were still living in tents. The tentage was rotten from months of exposure to tropical rain and sun; the first winter norther would tear the tents to shreds in a few minutes.

The internal situation in Mexico was complicated by this time because Carranza and Villa, who were always suspicious of each other, had finally shed all pretense of friendship or unity and had come to open warfare. An effort to establish a provisional government through a convention of generals, at Aguascalientes, was doomed to failure when Carranza refused to recognize the convention's authority. In spite of increasing danger to his government from Villa, he continued to maintain a stiff attitude toward the United States and maintained as late as October 22, 1914, that it would be inexpedient for him to issue such a decree as the United States demanded. His only action was to designate General Candido Aguilar, his governor of the state of Vera Cruz, to take over the city from the Americans.[35]

Funston found Aguilar cooperative as far as his instructions from Carranza would permit him to be. Aguilar issued a proclamation embodying the desired provisions, but Washington did not regard this as sufficient; Aguilar was a subordinate, and the First Chief could disavow his actions. It was not until November

8 and 9, when Funston's command was making obvious preparations to spend a long winter, that Carranza modified his stand and issued the necessary decrees.[36]

On November 20, 1914, the Acting Secretary of War cabled to Funston: "You will evacuate Vera Cruz on Monday, November 23rd. You will bring with you to the United States all funds in your possession from whatever sources derived, both United States funds and Mexican customs receipts and taxes." Funston was further warned against doing anything that might be construed as recognition of the Carranza government. "It is merely desired that you get out in the best practicable fashion. . . ."[37]

A week earlier Major General Wotherspoon, the Chief of Staff, reached the statutory age for retirement. It was announced in Washington that his successor would be Major General Hugh L. Scott and that the President was nominating Funston for the vacancy in the rank of major general caused by Wotherspoon's retirement, in recognition of the ability and tact with which he had handled the difficult occupation of Vera Cruz.

On November 28 Funston telegraphed to The Adjutant General from Galveston that the expedition had arrived and was disembarking. The last entry was made in the War Diary, and the Vera Cruz Expedition passed into history.

Quite naturally, there have been widely different opinions among historians, scholars and politicians about the seizure and occupation of Vera Cruz. Some have held that it was merely a feeble gesture; others that it was an evidence of imperialism. Among those who held that it was a useless and even worse than futile move was Mrs. Edith O'Shaughnessy, the wife of the First Secretary of the American Embassy in Mexico City, who became chargé d'affaires when Ambassador Henry Lane Wilson resigned. Mrs. O'Shaughnessy was a friend and ardent admirer of Huerta, and in her memoirs she characterized the expedition as a "screaming farce" and stressed that the seizure of Vera Cruz did not prevent the *Ypiranga* from landing her cargo. This, of course, is the major reason for considering the expedition a failure.

Nevertheless, it should be noted that Huerta lasted only ten weeks after the seizure of his principal port. Even with his arsenals filled and his troops armed and equipped by the cargoes of the *Ypiranga* and the *Bavaria*, his position and prestige were immeasurably weakened. From the perspective of half a century later is seems probable that he would have fallen before the heavy concentration of revolutionary force against him. This is probable but by no means certain. Huerta was a capable field commander despite his personal faults, and the outcome of war is often a matter of pure chance. There is no assurance that the insurgents could have prevailed against him without the pressure put on him by the United States at Vera Cruz.

As for the rank and file of the expedition, they left Vera Cruz with no regrets. Years later a veteran sergeant summarized their feelings as they once again set foot in their own land:

> The day the troops came back from Vera Cruz—that was one of the swellest things I ever saw in my life. There was big rows of oleanders—pink and white—on both sides of the street, and it was paved with red bricks—a regular Southern town, yuh know. There'd just been a shower of rain and then all of a sudden the sun came out and shone on the red bricks and those old oleanders were sparkling like diamonds! And the bands were playing *The Stars and Stripes Forever!*[38]

NOTES

1. *Foreign Relations, 1913*, pp. 720–21.
2. The full text of the Plan of Guadalupe is found in Gustavo Casasola, *Historia Gráfica de lo Revolución, 1900–1954* (Mexico City, nd.), II, 534.
3. *Foreign Relations, 1914*, pp. 447–48; Edith O'Shaughnessy, *A Diplomat's Wife in Mexico* (New York and London, 1916), pp. 174–75. Mrs. O'Shaughnessy was the wife of Nelson O'Shaughnessy, the First Secretary of the American Embassy. He became American chargé d'affaires when Ambassador Wilson resigned, and was handed his passports when the Americans seized Vera Cruz. He and his wife were both favorable toward Huerta.
4. "Report of the Secretary of War," *War Department Annual Reports, 1913*, pp. 9–10.
5. *Foreign Relations, 1913*, pp. 449–76; Josephus Daniels, *The Wilson Era. Years of Peace—1910–1917* (Chapel Hill, N.C., 1944), pp.

186–90; "Wilson's Message to Congress," *Outlook*, CVII (May 2, 1914), 107. For a scholarly and exhaustive study of the Vera Cruz incident, see Robert E. Quirk, *An Affair of Honor. Woodrow Wilson and the Occupation of Veracruz* (University of Kentucky Press, 1962), *passim*.

6. Lowell Thomas, *Old Gimlet Eye. The Adventures of Smedley D. Butler* (New York, 1933), p. 171.

7. *Ibid.*, pp. 171–76.

8. *Foreign Relations, 1914*, p. 477.

9. Josephus Daniels, *op. cit.*, p. 193.

10. William H. Goede, *American Occupation, Vera Cruz, 1914* (Galveston, Tex., 1914), pp. 27–28. Goede was the Sergeant Major of the 4th Infantry, which arrived at Vera Cruz a few days later. He obtained his information from participants and eyewitnesses.

11. Thomas, *op. cit.*, p. 178; A. A. Vandegrift, *Once a Marine. The Memoirs of General A. A. Vandegrift, United States Marine Corps, as Told to Robert B. Asprey* (New York, 1964), p. 43.

12. Maj. Gen. John A. Lejeune, *The Reminiscences of a Marine* (Philadelphia, 1930), p. 208. All Americans who witnessed this unfortunate incident are agreed that the conduct of the Mexican midshipmen was indeed *heroic*. Those who were killed were given a military funeral, with full honors.

13. "War Diary, United States Expeditionary Forces, Vera Cruz, 1914," *Records of the War Department, Records of The Adjutant General, Record Group No. 94*, entry for May 9, 1914. Hereafter referred to as *War Diary, Vera Cruz*.

14. Arthur Ruhl, "The Unfinished Drama," *Collier's Magazine*, LIII (May 30, 1914), 7.

15. Thomas, *op. cit.*, p. 179.

16. Vandegrift, *op. cit.*, p. 44.

17. *War Diary, Vera Cruz*, entry for Apr. 23, 1914.

18. Unpublished manuscript diary of Brig. Gen. Charles C. Drake, U.S.A., Ret. Hereafter referred to as Drake, *Diary*. Entries for Apr. 24 and 25, 1914.

19. *Ibid.*, entry, May 2, 1914.

20. In time of war or grave emergency, when the President orders the Army and Marine Corps to serve together, they become completely integrated. The senior officer present, regardless of service, is in command, and officers are interchangeable. In World War I, General Harbord, an army general, commanded a brigade of Marines, and General Lejeune (who has been mentioned in these pages) commanded the Army's 2d Division.

21. *Foreign Relations, 1914*, pp. 495–96. Colonel Plummer, of the 28th Infantry, was designated as Provost Marshal General, Commander Stickney, of the Navy, was appointed Administrator of Customs, and Paymaster Potter, of the Navy, became Treasurer of Customs.

22. *War Diary, Vera Cruz*, entry, May 3, 1914.

23. *Ibid.*

176   BLOOD ON THE BORDER

24. "Warfare Worth While," *Independent*, LXXVIII (June 8, 1914), 441.
25. Jack London, "Mexico's Army and Ours," *Collier's Magazine*, LIII (May 30, 1914), 5–6.
26. *Ibid.*
27. *Foreign Relations, 1914*, p. 484.
28. *New York Times*, Apr. 19, 1914, 1:6.
29. "Vera Cruz; A Crusade for Decency," *Outlook*, CVII (July 4, 1914), 527–28. See also Guy R. Donnell, "The United States Military Government at Vera Cruz, Mexico," in *Essays in Mexican History*, Thomas E. Cotner and Carlos E. Castañeda, eds. (Austin, Tex., 1958), pp. 229–47.
30. Medill McCormick, "Just Out of Jail," *Harper's Weekly*, LVIII (May 30, 1914), 6–7.
31. *The Banners and the Glory. The Story of General Douglas MacArthur*, by the editors of *Army Times* (New York, 1965), p. 24. See also Francis Trevelyan Miller, *General Douglas MacArthur, Fighter for Freedom* (New York, 1942), p. 95.
32. Drake, *Diary*, entries for May 10 and 11, 1914.
33. A recent Act of Congress had prescribed rigidly that an officer could serve away from a "company, troop or battery" of his army only for a specified length of time. The law was probably aimed at the General Staff, the members of which were held to be not serving with troops, but it was interpreted so literally and inelastically that an officer serving with his regiment's machine gun platoon (machine gun companies were not yet authorized) was on "detached service" within the meaning of the law. Such an officer had to return to a company after a certain length of time and thus purge himself before he could again serve with machine guns.
34. *War Diary, Vera Cruz*, entry for Sept. 17, 1914.
35. *Foreign Relations, 1914*, pp. 600–65.
36. *Ibid.*, pp. 618–20.
37. *Ibid.*, p. 625.
38. Edmund Wilson, *A Prelude. Landscapes, Characters and Conversations from the Earlier Years of My Life* (New York, 1967), p. 259. Quoted with Mr. Wilson's permission. He informs the writer that the speaker was a Sergeant Baker, of Base Hospital No. 36, who made the remark on hearing a German girl play "The Stars and Stripes Forever."

CHAPTER 9

The Rise and Fall of Pancho Villa: Critical Events of 1914–1915

IN JULY, 1914, while the Americans were still at Vera Cruz, rumors began to circulate that all was not well between Pancho Villa and his nominal superior, Venustiano Carranza. Both Villa's headquarters and Carranza's government denied the rumors. Without going into details that are not pertinent to the present narrative, it was agreed among the various revolutionary leaders to hold a convention at Mexico City the following September to decide upon a government for their unhappy country. When the convention assembled, it was transferred, largely by Villa's influence, to Aguascalientes, whereupon Carranza refused to recognize it further. Villa and Carranza broke openly, and the convention was thereafter completely dominated by Villa. And when the convention chose Eulalio Gutiérrez, an avowed Villista, as provisional president, all hopes of a peaceful settlement of Mexico's troubles were at an end.

For several weeks after the break the military situation remained static. Both sides were regrouping and preparing for the coming campaign. There was a steady movement of Villa's forces southward. He was reported to be well prepared for eventualities, with 40,000 men, ample arms and ammunition, a train of artillery, 240 carloads of coal for his locomotives, and 300 carloads of provisions and supplies.[1]

Both sides made strenuous efforts to gain American support. Villa initially had a considerable edge over his enemy. There was the fact (or the supposed fact) that he had prevented Carranza from joining with Huerta at the time of the seizure of Vera Cruz. He enjoyed the personal esteem of General Hugh L. Scott, the new Chief of Staff, and he made haste to assure Leon J. Canova, the State Department's representative with Villa, that foreigners' rights would be respected in the parts of Mexico under his control.[2] Villa's personality, moreover, as depicted in the press, was much more appealing to most Americans than that of the cold, aristocratic *hacendado*, Carranza. A special personal envoy of President Wilson, Paul Fuller, who visited Villa in August, 1914, was deeply and favorably impressed by him. The same envoy, visiting Carranza a short time later, was noncommittal about the impression Carranza made on him, but he was most unfavorably impressed by the "spirit of hatred and proscription" among Carranza's officials toward the defeated Huertistas. A favorable opinion by a man who enjoyed the President's confidence added much to Villa's stature in Washington.[3]

When Villa's forces moved southward, the Carranzista resistance was surprisingly ineffective. In fact, it virtually collapsed. Villa made arrangements with Emiliano Zapata, the perennial rebel of the state of Morelos, and on December 6, 1914, the allied armies of Villa and Zapata entered Mexico City. As the "bandit" armies approached, the people of the city, and especially Americans and other foreigners, were terror-stricken. Everyone expected a saturnalia of looting and murder, but instead the two leaders held their troops to the strictest sort of discipline. An American woman living in Mexico City wrote:

> All kinds of rumors were current and most of them were listened to and believed. Then one morning of unbelievable smiling sky and warming sunshine something happened, just what is still a matter of dispute, some say an automobile tire exploded. Whether it was that or the firing of a gun, soon other shots were fired and the city was in a panic.
>
> Mexico shivered and was afraid. Then gradually she crept out into the sunshine and took a long breath of relief.[4]

Zapata's men entered the city first, and to the amazement of everyone, some of them shyly *asked* for food. At least one man who was caught looting was promptly executed.[5] The Villistas, who marched in four days later, were equally under restraint. The Zapatista entry was almost unobtrusive; the Villistas, on the other hand, were impressive. Villa himself rode at the head of the column, a "stern faced, heavy bodied man, dressed in an elaborate suit of dark blue and gold, hardly recognizable as the Villa I had seen on the border," wrote the same American woman. She observed closely, and was struck by the numbers following Villa (the column took four hours to pass) and by the spectacle provided by the men themselves. "Wonderful hats, some gold or silver trimmed, which with the saddles divided the pride of their owners. Soldiers carrying muskets, and soldiers mounted on the ammunition limbers of very modern and effective looking cannons. . . ."[6]

As the insurgents approached Mexico City, First Chief Carranza betook himself and his government to Vera Cruz, which became his capital and remained his capital for several months. In the United States, meanwhile, belief in Villa and Zapata as the probable saviors of Mexico mounted, although President Wilson cautiously refused to commit himself. In northern Mexico, Villa was in full control except for an enclave along the border in Sonora and a narrow strip in the Lower Rio Grande Valley, which included the city of Matamoros. In Sonora and Sinaloa, General Álvaro Obregón was regrouping his forces and preparing for the coming struggle.

Both sides sparred, with numerous small engagements and skirmishes, but the main forces did not confront each other until April, 1915, when they met head on, at Celaya, in the state of Guanajuato. For several days the outcome was in doubt. Carranza's government claimed an overwhelming victory; at Villa's headquarters, on April 12, it was announced that the Carranzistas were surrounded and that their utter annihilation was only a matter of days. But the very next day, April 13, American newspapers carried authentic accounts of a sharp defeat for Villa.[7]

While the forces were assembling for the Battle of Celaya, the Carranzista garrison at the mouth of the Rio Grande became a focus of interest. The area was loosely held by a force commanded by General Emiliano Nafarrete. Villista troops suddenly appeared, drove the outposts and outlying detachments into Matamoros, and encircled the city on three sides. The side facing the United States could not be closed. Since it was useless to attempt a formal investment, because the garrison could obtain practically everything needed, except munitions, from the United States, the Villistas tried to carry the city by a direct assault. They were repulsed with heavy losses. The Villista commander had been warned that his soldiers must not fire toward the United States, a restriction that handicapped his operations but greatly eased the problems of the defenders. During and after the battle large numbers of the wounded of both sides were carried across the river to Brownsville for care and treatment. An unnamed Brownsville physician and an anonymous army surgeon worked for hours, day and night, operating and easing the sufferings of the unfortunate Mexicans.[8]

The Villista defeat at Matamoros, followed in a few days by the reverse at Celaya, started Villa's fortunes on the downgrade, although the fact was not immediately apparent. The whole situation in Mexico was obscure and anarchic, but one thing was clear. Nafarette's Carranzistas now firmly held the Lower Rio Grande Valley, from which the Villistas were completely expelled. With the Mexican side of the river held by the Constitutionalists, a degree of order should have returned to the region, but exactly the opposite occurred. The Lower Rio Grande reverted to the conditions of the days of Cortina. There had been occasional raids from Mexico into Texas ever since the revolution began, but in the summer of 1915, people on the Texas side noticed an increasing tempo of raiding activities. At first the American authorities, including the army, were inclined to believe that the danger was exaggerated and even that most of the raids originated among lawless men on the American side. An investigation by Colonel Frederick W. Sibley led him to the conclusion that the problem was one for the law enforcement authorities rather than for the military. Nevertheless, the governor of Texas and local Texas officials were sure that the bandit raids originated in Mexico and that many members of the raiding gangs were Carranzista soldiers of Nafarette's command. After an appeal by the governor to the President, General Funston, who now commanded the Southern Department, was ordered to cooperate with the state authorities in preserving order.[9]

Before long, however, Americans of the Lower Valley began to feel that there was more to the raids, at least to some of them, than mere bandit deviltry. And when the tale was partly known (the full story is not known to this day), it was so fantastic that sensible, matter-of-fact people could be forgiven for refusing to believe it, or for considering that it was the product of the warped imagination of some "yellow journalist." Late in 1914, or early in 1915, certain of the Mexican-Americans of the Lower Valley, and some of their compatriots across the Rio Grande, incensed by the contempt that many Texans seemed to feel toward them, and completely ignorant of the extent, population and power of the United States, formulated the Plan of San Diego (so called because it was composed at San Diego, Texas). The plan called for a general uprising of the border Mexicans on February 20, 1915, as the initial date, to proclaim their independence. Texas, New Mexico, Arizona, California and Colorado would become an independent Mexican republic that would be annexed to Mexico at some time in the future. After "liberating" the five states named, the revolutionaries would next conquer six additional states (presumably Oklahoma, Kansas, Nebraska, South Dakota, Wyoming and Utah), which would form a buffer between Mexico and "the damned big-footed creatures of the north." The Negroes would be allowed to form a republic of their own, with a flag of their own choice; the Apache Indians would be given back their own lands, in return for supporting the plan. Revolutionaries were forbidden to take prisoners; all American males over the age of sixteen were to be killed.[10]

The scheme was so unbelievable that at first few people could take it seriously. The Federal court at Brownsville dismissed one of the conspirators who was charged with conspiracy against the United States, with the words, "You ought to be tried for lunacy, not for conspiracy against the United States." That the Plan of San Diego was as impossible of fulfillment as a madman's dream was small comfort to isolated ranchers and farmers, or to the people of little hamlets lost in the chaparral, who were exposed to the fury of the increasingly frequent raids. Positive evidence that the Plan of San Diego was real came to light on a hot day in August, 1915, when a patrol of the 12th Cavalry, in a skirmish with a gang who had come across the river, captured a San Diego banner (red, with a white stripe) and several documents that proved, beyond doubt, the existence of the conspiracy and also indicated that the movement was being fanned from Mexico.[11]

To what extent the Plan of San Diego may have stimulated raiders from across the Rio Grande and stirred discontent among the dissatisfied Mexican-Americans is moot. As mentioned earlier, in spite of its utter incredibility, it was a menacing and terrible threat to ranchers, farmers and villagers of the Lower Valley. It was also a double-edged weapon, in that the reaction of the Anglo-Americans against their Latin neighbors was often sharp and brutal. Anyone of Mexican blood became an object of suspicion; all were suspected of treachery and treason. Scores of unhappy and endangered Mexican-Americans abandoned their homes or deserted their employers and took refuge in the larger towns or in the relative safety of revolution-torn Mexico.

To relate in detail the grim events of the summer and autumn of 1915 in the Lower Rio Grande Valley would be redundant. In August of that year there was a week in which Mexicans fired at American troops from across the Rio Grande every day. As for the raids into Texas, one or two examples will suffice. On an unrecorded date, but in the autumn of the year, Deputy Sheriff Mike Monahan, of Cameron County, with three other deputies, guiding a detachment from the 12th Cavalry in pursuit of raiders, approached Los Tulitos Ranch, which was in Texas, some distance back from the river. Los Tulitos belonged to Aniceto Pizana, a well-to-do Mexican-American who was known to be one of the authors of the Plan. Without warning, the party was fired upon from the chaparral; Private McGuire, of the 12th Cavalry, was killed instantly, and Monahan and another deputy were wounded.[12] On August 6, 1915, a band of some fourteen Mexicans raided Sebastian, Texas, an isolated cluster of a few houses and a store. After looting the store, they took two Americans whom they had captured—a father and his young son—out into the brush and shot them. Additional raids were reported on August 8, 9, 10, 15 and 17, 1915. In response to an inquiry from Senator Sheppard, of Texas, in 1925, The Adjutant General listed sixteen raids into Texas in the latter half of 1915. The list is incomplete, as it includes only raids in which the army became involved—and even then, there were numerous encounters and skirmishes that were either not reported to Washington or were overlooked.

While the Lower Rio Grande was the scene of most of the bandit incursions into the United States from Mexico in 1915, such activities were by no means confined to that region. On September 15, 1915, the United States consul at Nogales reported that raids into Arizona and thefts of American cattle and horses by bands of Mexicans were increasing. Both Villistas and Carranzistas were guilty, he said, and also that such raids were increasing. Governor Maytorena, of Sonora, seemed unable to control the situation. On the very day of the report, Maytorenistas (Villistas) had crossed the border only four miles from Nogales and run off twenty American horses. The consul urged vehemently that immediate military action be taken to prevent the rise of a situation similar to that in Texas.[13]

In 1915, American troops on the border were forbidden to cross the international boundary under any circumstances or for any reason. The result was that raiders were safe once they were in Mexico, and there is ample reason to believe that the Mexicans interpreted American failure to follow them as springing from fear. Of course, American officers and soldiers chafed at the restrictions imposed upon them, but they were powerless in the face of the policy dictated by Washington. As far as existing records and evidence show, not an American soldier crossed the line, even when in "hot pursuit" of bands that had looted, raped, burned and murdered on United States soil.

There can be no doubt that raids would have taken place without the stimulus of the Plan of San Diego. The plan, however, probably spurred bandit activities, especially on the Lower Rio Grande, and by its appeal to Mexican irredentism, gave a faint ideological basis for banditry.

At this point it is necessary to survey briefly events in Mexico after the Battle of Celaya and in the autumn months of 1915. After Celaya, the military situation remained static for several weeks. Villa maintained his customary friendliness toward Americans and asserted that his forces were as strong as ever and that Carranza was doomed. He extended every facility to American newspapermen. John W. Roberts, a correspondent of Hearst's International News Service, reported with reference to a battle in which he became involved: "General Villa wants me to write everything I see in the fighting that is to take place tonight. . . ."[14]

In June, 1915, vague reports filtered into the United States that there had been another battle between Obregón and Villa, with both sides, as usual, claiming an overwhelming victory. By June 14 it was definitely known that Obregón had defeated Villa near the city of León. Carranzista reports gloated that Obregón had taken the city, had captured Villa's cavalry commander, and had driver General Felipe Angeles in headlong rout to the mountains. It was rumored, also, that General Obregón had been killed in the battle and that command of the Constitutionalist forces now devolved upon General Benjamin Hill, who had successfully defended Naco, in 1914, in a siege that lasted for several months.[15]

Early in June, and almost simultaneously with Villa's defeat at León, President Wilson attempted a new approach for the solution of Mexico's problems. Employing a method that he was later to use trying to gain the support of the peoples of Europe, he appealed directly to the Mexican people, over the heads of the party and faction leaders. He promised that the United States would give its "moral support to some man or group of men, if such may be found, who can rally the suffering people of Mexico to their support in an effort to return to the constitution of the Republic. . . ." But his final statement carried apparent implications that Mexicans did not like: "I feel it to be my duty to tell them [i.e., the faction leaders] that, if they cannot accommodate their differences and unite for this great purpose within a very short time, this Government will be constrained to decide what means should be employed by the

United States in order to help Mexico save herself and serve her people."[16]

The last sentence of the President's statement seemed to contain a thinly veiled threat of intervention, and it caused some apprehension along the Border. Many people feared that it might arouse Villa's resentment, and that he would attack El Paso in retaliation. Brigadier General John J. Pershing, who commanded the United States troops at El Paso, did not think that an attack by Villa was at all probable, but to allay local fears he asked the Department Commander [Funston] to transfer a battery of artillery from Douglas, Arizona, to El Paso. Pershing remarked also that Villa's prestige was waning rapidly. Several weeks later, concurrent with the wave of raids in the Lower Valley, rumors of an uprising by the Mexican population of El Paso disturbed the people of that city. Pershing promptly concentrated his available troops in order to be able to suppress quickly any attempt at armed revolt.[17]

As for President Wilson's appeal, it had no effect whatever, except, possibly, to arouse Mexican antagonism, as an interference in Mexican domestic affairs. Villa's reply and refusal were diplomatic and polite; Carranza's refusal was so curt as to be almost rude. It was probably at this time that a *corrido*—a popular song or ballad—was composed by some unknown Mexican minstrel. The first stanza indicated clearly the feeling of the Mexican people:

> ¡Madre mía Guadalupana,
> échame tu benedición,
> yo ya me voy a la guerra,
> ya viene la Intervención!

> (My Mother of Guadalupe,
> Give me your blessing,
> I am going soon to the war,
> For intervention is coming!)[18]

In the summer and fall of 1915, Villa was losing more than prestige. After the Battle of Leon, in which his casualties were heavy, his army began slowly to disintegrate. The legend of

Villa's invincibility had been shattered; his name had lost much of its magic. Many of his war-weary veterans wanted nothing so much as to return to their humble homes. Obregón's victory, moreover, cut Villa off from regions from which he might still have obtained supplies and recruits. As Villa's strength declined and his authority and influence became less and less, it was logical to see Carranza as the ultimate victor—the man whose party would be able to bring peace to Mexico.

In July and August, 1915, the new U.S. Secretary of State, Robert Lansing, had been exploring various ways and means of solving the Mexican problem. With the consent of their respective governments, he assembled in Washington the diplomatic representatives of Argentina, Brazil, Chile, Guatemala, Uruguay and Bolivia to discuss the Mexican situation and decide which regime there seemed most worthy of recognition. After several sessions, extending over a period of several weeks, the diplomats decided unanimously to recommend that their governments recognize Carranza. The United States led the way; on October 19, 1915, Secretary Lansing announced, "This Government today recognized the de facto Government of Mexico, of which General Venustiano Carranza is the Chief Executive."[19]

The same month, October, 1915, found Villa in Chihuahua, reorganizing his forces and preparing for the next campaign. In spite of his defeats and the loss of a large part of his strength, he still commanded a formidable force. His next objective was an open secret. He had lost all access to the sea and to all border ports except Juarez. Carranzistas had held Agua Prieta, opposite Douglas, Arizona, since 1914, completely isolated from other Carranza forces. The garrison of Agua Prieta was a standing threat to Villa's rear. The capture of the place would revive some of his lost prestige, would afford him an additional port of entry, and would give him a broad base along the border from which future campaigns could be launched.

With a strength variously estimated as from ten thousand to fifteen thousand men, Villa vanished from Chihuahua, moving westward. In the meantime, the Carranzistas were not idle. Since it was no part of President Wilson's policy to abet opposition to the de facto government that he had recognized, a request from

Carranza to be permitted to reinforce Agua Prieta through the United States was quickly approved. Train after train, carrying soldiers, arms, munitions, supplies and matériel of all sorts poured through Douglas and across the boundary to Agua Prieta. Under the driving command of General Plutarco Calles the garrison surrounded the town on three sides with deep and well-constructed trenches covered by aprons of barbed wire, with machine gun emplacements so located that the weapons could sweep the entire front. A great searchlight was placed on top of a wooden tower so that its beams could reach any part of the city or the anticipated zones of attack.[20] By the time the first Villistas appeared in the mountain passes to the east, Agua Prieta had been converted into a nearly impregnable fortress.

Knowing that trouble was more than likely when Villa attacked, General Funston reinforced the American troops at Douglas until they included three regiments of infantry, a regiment of field artillery and several troops of cavalry. Working as hard as the Carranzistas, the Americans constructed a series of entrenchments from Douglas to a range of low hills several miles to the east. It was not a continuous line of trenches but rather a system of mutually supporting strong points, each point protected by barbed wire and with machine gun emplacements so located as to be able to enfilade any approaching enemy.

The first definite information about Villa's whereabouts and movements came on October 30, 1915, when Villista troops were observed opposite Slaughter's Ranch, some eighteen miles to the east of Douglas. Villa himself soon appeared, and it was here that he was first informed (by an American newspaperman) of President Wilson's recognition of Carranza. He was obviously hurt and angry, although statements made from time to time that he raged like a madman, swearing vengeance against the United States, are uncorroborated by anyone who saw him at the time.[21]

Through October 31, 1915, the Villistas continued to debouch from the mountains. Before daybreak, on November 1, the Americans occupied their trenches and positions. Because of the critical situation, General Funston assumed personal command of the American forces at Douglas. The Villistas, having completed their deployment, advanced across the open plain east of their objective. The movement was clearly visible from the American positions, and American officers watching it were favorably impressed with the steadiness and discipline it revealed. It was equally visible from the Carranzista position. Shortly after noon the defending artillery opened fire; Villa's guns responded, and for the rest of the day there was an artillery duel, apparently with little damage being done by either side. At one thirty in the morning, Villa launched a massive assault, his men advancing and fighting with desperate courage and determination. Villa was the only commander in the Mexican Revolution who habitually attacked at night, and much of his previous success can be attributed to this practice. At Agua Prieta, however, he learned what the Allies and the Germans had discovered on the battlefields of Europe—an attack against an entrenched position, covered with barbed wire, defended by cross-firing machine guns, and supported by artillery, is usually doomed to failure. The Carranzista searchlight, too, made concealment difficult, if not impossible. The attacking waves were decimated before they could reach the Carranzista lines.[22]

Hundreds of bullets struck in the United States during the battle, causing several casualties among the people of Douglas. Although Funston was authorized by the War Department to fire on the Mexicans, if necessary, to prevent firing into the United States, he did not do so, because, as he reported, it was an "evident fact that both commanders were doing all they could to prevent injury to Americans." In another report he stated that he could not prevent some firing into the United States unless he were given authority to cross the boundary and drive the combatants out of rifle range.[23]

At first no one in the United States had any inkling how disastrous Villa's repulse had been. It was taken for granted that he would renew the attack within a few hours. Instead, he passed his army around Agua Prieta to the south, skillfully screening his movement from the town, and marched westward to Naco, where several days were spent in resting while Villa matured his plans for the next step. This proved to be a march southward and an attack upon Hermosillo, the capital of the state of Sonora.

The assault on Hermosillo (in daylight this time), delivered in the old, slashing Villa style, was even more disastrous than the attack at Agua Prieta. The garrison had ample warning of Villa's approach and was well prepared. Attacking boldly, even desperately, Villa's men were cut down in swaths by hidden machine guns and by riflemen firing by scores from the flat roofs of the adobe houses. Unable to take more losses and punishment, the Villistas panicked and broke and fled, their terrified flight spurred on by long-range artillery fire from heavy Carranzista guns in the town. The shattered remnants of Villa's army, disorganized, without any semblance of discipline, straggled northward toward Nogales, ravaging, looting and murdering as they went.[24]

As the disorganized fragments of what had once been a powerful army staggered northward toward the international boundary, the men began to build up a deep resentment toward the United States and for all Americans. Americans were responsible for all their troubles. The gringos had recognized Carranza; the gringos had allowed Carranza to reinforce Agua Prieta through the United States; by this time, in Villista belief, the famous searchlight was firmly mounted on United States soil and manned by United States soldiers. By the time the bedraggled, hungry, hard-core of Villistas who remained with their leader arrived at Nogales, they were in a murderous and dangerous mood. On reaching Nogales a small group, probably drunk, and filled with hate, madly galloped across the boundary, shouting insults and obscenities, and waving their pistols threateningly. For some reason the small detail of American soldiers on duty at the customs house did not shoot. Fearing further and more serious trouble, Funston at once reinforced the garrison on the United States side of the line and issued clear and explicit orders: any armed Mexican who crossed the boundary would be shot on the spot; if Mexicans fired upon United States soldiers from the Mexican side of the line, the fire would be returned at once. Villa's men made no more forays across the boundary, and as for firing at Americans from what they supposed was the safety of Mexico, they quickly abandoned the practice. They learned, for the first time apparently, the deadly accuracy of American rifle fire.[25] Within a few days, Villa himself and his handful of faithful followers vanished into the wilds of the mountains and were not heard from until after the new year.

Simultaneously with the decline of Villa's power and his unhappy campaign in Sonora, a situation was developing on the West Coast of Mexico that threatened, for a time, to bring about a repetition of the Vera Cruz affair. A number of American settlers as well as other foreigners were located in the fertile valley of the Yaqui River, in northwestern Sonora. A little farther to the south, in the vicinity of Topolobampo, the same was true. The Yaqui region had been the source and scene of trouble for centuries. The Yaquis were fiercely independent and determinedly attached to their country. Numerous attempts by the Spanish colonial government, and its successor, the Mexican Republic, to evict them were always met with ferocious resistance. Under Spain, according to tradition, large numbers of Yaqui prisoners were exiled to the Philippine Islands (which were technically a province of Mexico); under Díaz there was a continual stream of Yaqui prisoners to the distant state of Yucután and the unhealthy territory of Quintana Roo, where they were sold into slavery and quickly died.

On November 13, 1915, a dispatch was received in the State Department from the Acting American Consular Agent at Guaymas, relaying a message he had received from an American construction company saying that the Indians had killed four Mexicans nearby on November 10. The Indians were reported to be approaching, and the de facto government of Venustiano Carranza had furnished no military protection whatever. On the same day, November 13, Admiral Winslow, commander-in-chief of the Pacific Fleet, reported to the Secretary of the Navy from his flagship, at San Francisco, that he had received a message from the U.S.S. *Annapolis*, at Guaymas, saying, "Indian trouble feared Yaqui valley." Winslow added that because of the disbandment of Villa's army the Indians were more numerous than in 1914, when there had been trouble with them. He urged that pressure be put on the Carranza government to furnish protection, or that he be authorized to form an expeditionary force within his command and to land it if necessary.[26]

Secretary Daniels refused permission to land any forces from the fleet and transmitted all available information to the State Department, which, in turn, directed its special agent with Carranza to make strong representations. But while all this was going on, the Indians continued to advance. On November 17, 1915, a radiogram to Admiral Winslow from the *Annapolis* said that the town of Los Mochis had been raided that morning by a mixed band of Indians and Villistas. Four Mexicans were reported killed, and American properties in the vicinity had been looted. The commanding officer of the *Annapolis* stated that he was urging all Americans, "particularly the women and children," to come to Topolobampo for refuge. Later the same day another radiogram from the *Annapolis* reported that thirty-three refugees, mostly women and children, had come aboard the ship. American civilians in the town had organized themselves as outposts and patrols to safeguard the place. The Mexican officials and the few Carranza soldiers who had been there had boarded a schooner and sailed for an unknown destination.[27]

There was a flurry of telegrams from the State Department to the several consuls and consular agents in Sonora; strong representations were made to Carranza, but none of the officers or American officials on the spot had any confidence that action would be taken. On November 21 Winslow relayed another message from the *Annapolis*, saying that a band of Villistas at Los Mochis had run off stock belonging to Americans and that the local Carranzista commander, a Colonel Escobar, had abandoned the place and retired to San Blas, after looting a warehouse belonging to the United Sugar Companies. "It is hard to say," the American naval officer remarked, "which are the worst, the Indians or the Carranza forces."[28]

On November 23, 1915, Washington issued what amounted to an ultimatum to Carranza. Consul Alonzo Garrett, who was with Carranza at the time, was directed to point out to him that he had been allowed to transport his soldiers and great quantities of munitions and supplies through the United States at the time of Villa's advance on Agua Prieta, It seemed, then, that if he was unable to furnish protection to the Americans at Los Mochis and other places threatened by the Indians, he should have no objection to the landing of American Marines for that purpose. On the same day, November 23, the Secretary of State requested that the Secretary of the Navy prepare at once to send three hundred Marines to Topolobampo.[29]

Carranza, however, curtly turned down any suggestion of the landing of American forces on Mexican soil. General Muñoz, the local Carranza commander, even asserted that the Americans themselves were responsible for their own troubles: they had unwisely armed themselves, thereby giving provocation to the Indians and Mexicans. Muñoz also charged that landing forces from the *Annapolis* had been put ashore without any authority, an allegation that was flatly denied by the ship's commander.

To be nearer the scene of the troubles and to take immediate control of the American forces in the Gulf of California, Admiral Winslow sailed for Topolobampo in his flagship, the U.S.S. *San Diego*, on November 25, embarking the 1st Battalion of Marines before sailing. Another battalion was embarked at San Diego aboard the U.S.S. *Buffalo*. Before the end of the affair Winslow had with him four cruisers, an armed transport, and the two battalions of Marines, an impressive naval force.

Winslow held a series of conferences with Mexican officials. Like his subordinates, he soon felt completely frustrated. The Mexican officers and officials listened politely and made courteous promises that remained just that and nothing more. On December 11 he informed the Secretary of the Navy that he was completely unable to get an answer to a telegram he had sent to General Dieguez (the senior Carranza commander in Sonora and Sinaloa) several days before. At a conference on the *San Diego*, the Admiral finally extracted a reluctant admission from General Muñoz that the Americans would be justified in landing in case of a serious emergency, but he was of the opinion that such an act would be unfriendly toward Mexico.[29] Winslow sent a message to the Secretary of the Navy, asking, "Am I to land troops if General [Muñoz] is willing?" Secretary Daniels, however, refused consent: "Troops will not be landed without instructions from the Department."[30]

Faced with another Vera Cruz episode, Carranza's government

was finally stirred to action. Admiral Winslow and General Obregón met at Guaymas for a personal conference. Above almost everything else, it seems, the de facto government feared another "invasion" by the Americans, and the presence of several warships and several hundred Marines indicated that such a possibility was not very remote. Obregón ordered additional troops into the area, and although many of them deserted promptly, enough remained to suppress the hostiles. The threatened "invasion" of Mexico did not occur; the Marines, after spending weeks in the cramped quarters aboard the ships, sailed away without having once set foot on Mexican soil.[31]

The year 1915 did not see any direct military action by Americans in Mexico, but during the year there were scores of skirmishes and small fights against Mexican "invaders" of the United States. The course of events within Mexico and the policies of the United States Government toward the factions and turmoil set the pattern for the near future. The leader of one faction was changed from a friend to a bitter enemy, without increasing the friendliness of the suspicious leader of the other. The events of the early part of 1916 were a direct outgrowth of 1915.

NOTES

1. National Archives, State Department File No. 812.00/13518, Oct. 6, 1914.
2. National Archives, State Department File No. 812.00/13279, Sept. 23, 1914.
3. Paul Fuller, "Memorandum for the President," National Archives, State Department File No. 812.00/14236, Sept. 18, 1914.
4. Allene Tupper Wilkes, "The Gentle Zapatistas," *Harper's Weekly*, LX (Jan. 6, 1915), 56.
5. *Ibid.*, pp. 56–57.
6. Allene Tupper Wilkes, "Villa Enters Mexico City," *Harper's Weekly*, LX (Jan. 16, 1915), 57. The blue and gold costume the author mentioned was probably the full-dress uniform of a *general de división* of the Mexican Army.
7. *New York Times*, Tuesday, Apr. 13, 1915, 3:6.
8. Mrs. Borden Harriman, "Matamoras—A War Film," *Harper's Weekly*, LX (May 22, 1915), 494–96.

9. Charles C. Cumberland, "Border Raids in the Lower Rio Grande Valley—1915," *Southwestern Historical Quarterly*, LVII (Jan., 1954), 287.

10. William M. Hager, "The Plan of San Diego. Unrest on the Texas Border in 1915," *Arizona and the West*, V (winter, 1963), 331; "Mexican Affairs," Senate Document 285, 66th Cong., 2nd sess., pp. 1205–7. The latter document is the report of the Senate Committee headed by Senator Albert Fall, to investigate Mexican affairs. This document must be taken with great caution, but there is no reason to doubt the word or judgment of the witness cited here, who was District Attorney of the 49th Judicial District of Texas. The report will be hereafter referred to as *Fall Committee Report*.

11. Commanding General, Southern Department, to The Adjutant General, Aug. 11, 1915, AGO 2311838, Add. I. Quoted by Cumberland, *op. cit.*, p. 294.

12. "Testimony of Mike Monahan," *Fall Committee Report*, pp. 1265–66.

13. National Archives, OTAG Project Files, 1917–23, RG 4, Box 270; *Foreign Relations, 1915*, p. 811.

14. John W. Roberts, "Personal Glimpses: Entrenched with Villa," *Literary Digest*, L (June 18, 1915), 1485–88.

15. *Independent*, LXXXII (Apr.–June, 1915), 451, 492. See also General Francisco L. Urquizo, "Las Campañas del General Obregón," introduction to Obregón's *Ocho Mil Kilómetros en Campaña*, 2nd ed. (Mexico City, 1959), p. cxiv. Obregón was, of course, not killed but was so badly wounded that the amputation of his arm was necessary to save his life.

16. *Foreign Relations, 1915*, pp. 694–95.

17. Pershing to Funston, June 4, 1915. The Pershing Papers, Manuscript Division, Library of Congress.

18. Vicente T. Mendoza, *El Corrido Mexicano* (Mexico City, 1964), p. 41.

19. *Foreign Relations, 1915*, pp. 771–72.

20. Some Mexican writers have asserted that the searchlight was furnished by the United States Army, was emplaced on the United States side of the line, and was operated by American soldiers. Not one of these allegations contains a grain of truth.

21. National Archives, State Department Files Nos. 812.00/16653 and 16679, dated Oct. 31 and Nov. 1, 1915, respectively.

22. Col. Abner Pickering, 11th Infantry, "The Battle of Agua Prieta," *United States Infantry Journal*, XII (Jan. 1916), 707–10. Colonel Pickering commanded one of the American regiments at Douglas and was an eyewitness of the battle.

23. National Archives, State Department File No. 812.00/16689, Nov. 1, 1915.

24. National Archives, State Department File No. 812.00/17053, Dec. 27, 1915. See also the *Literary Digest*, LI (Dec. 11, 1915), 1395, and the *Independent*, LXXXIV (Dec. 6, 1915), 381, and (Dec. 20, 1915), 463. An extraordinarily vivid account of the Battle of Hermo-

sillo, probably based on eyewitness statements, is given in Ernst Löhndorff, *Bestie Ich in Mexiko* (Bremen, 1927), pp. 314–18.

25. National Archives, State Department Files Nos. 812.00/16855, Nov. 24, 1915, and 16856 and 16868, dated Nov. 24 and 26, 1915, respectively.
26. *Foreign Relations, 1915*, p. 839.
27. *Ibid.*, pp. 840–41.
28. *Ibid.*, p. 845.
29. *Ibid.*, p. 847.
30. *Ibid.*, pp. 863–64.
31. *Ibid.*, pp. 857, 859, 860.

CHAPTER 10

The Vengeance of Villa: Santa Ysabel and Columbus

IT MAY BE SAFELY assumed that on the morning of January 9, 1916, the weather at El Paso was fair and warm, with a touch of spring in the air. It may be assumed also that the seventeen Americans and twenty Mexicans, most of them young, who assembled at the railroad station, were glad to see one another. They were the management personnel, the engineers, the accountants and technicians, along with the experienced and trusted Mexican employees, of the Cusi Mining Company, which owned and operated mines in the state of Chihuahua. When the United States Government, several months before, urged all Americans to leave Mexico, the Cusi Mining Company evacuated all its American employees and laid off the Mexican workers, most of whom seem to have preferred to spend their enforced vacation in the United States. At the railroad station there were hilarious greetings between old friends who had not seen each other for a long time. Before the train started from El Paso for the city of Chihuahua, there were friendly cups of coffee together, and it is not unlikely that something a bit stronger than coffee was passed around in celebration of the reunion.

In November, 1915, a few days after the Battle of Hermosillo, General Obregón urged American mining operators to resume their activities, assuring them that the Carranza government would guarantee their safety.[1] After the formal recognition of Carranza's government as the de facto government of Mexico, the directors of the Cusi Mining Company decided to reopen

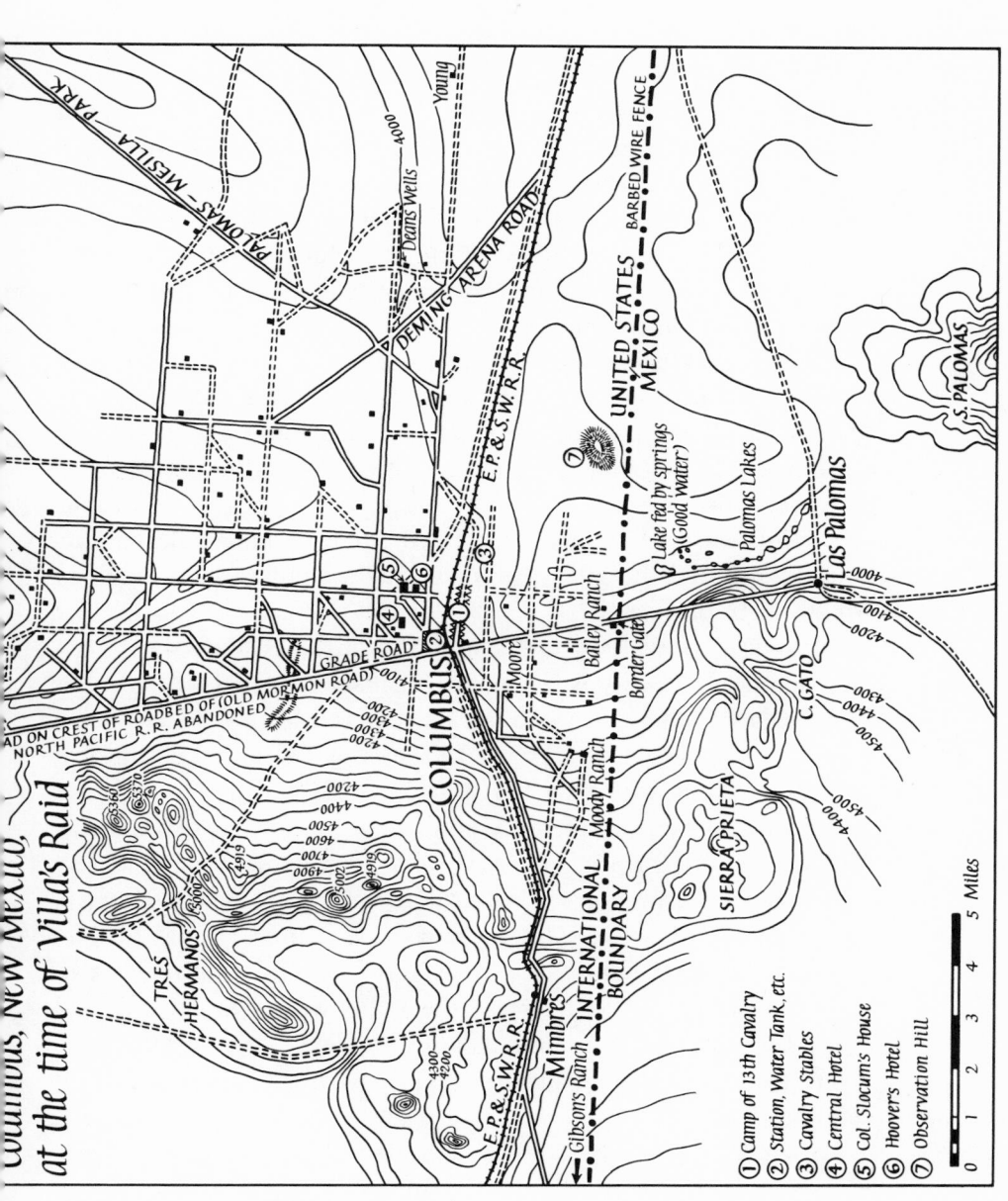

Columbus, New Mexico,
at the time of Villa's Raid

① Camp of 13th Cavalry
② Station, Water Tank, etc.
③ Cavalry Stables
④ Central Hotel
⑤ Col. Slocum's House
⑥ Hoover's Hotel
⑦ Observation Hill

0 1 2 3 4 5 Miles

their mines. The party of mine officials, engineers, technicians and their Mexican assistants rode from El Paso to Chihuahua without incident. At Chihuahua they changed to a train that was to carry them to their final destination. The Americans occupied one car; their Mexican assistants filled the next one. Nothing happened until the train reached a cattle-loading station west of the city of Chihuahua, known as Santa Ysabel. There the train was stopped by a barrier across the track, and as it lurched to a halt, a band of armed men, led by Colonel Pablo Lopez, of Villa's band, swarmed aboard. The scene that followed was horrible beyond description. The hapless Americans were herded off the train, roughly and brutally, and one by one, were shot beside the car. The Mexicans in the next car were robbed of all their possessions but were otherwise unmolested. Lopez called to them, "If you want to see some fun, watch us kill these gringos." And accompanied by shouts of *"Viva Villa!"* and *"Mueran los gringos!"* the massacre was accomplished quickly. One lone American escaped by feigning death in the chaparral. His account confirmed the later testimony of the helpless and horrified Mexican employees.

Although Villa's personal complicity in the Santa Ysabel atrocity has never been positively established, it probably could not have been done unless his followers believed fully that they were carrying out his wishes. Santa Ysabel was the culmination of a series of incidents proving that Pancho Villa had become a bitter and dangerous enemy of the United States and of all Americans. Villista hatred for the United States was demonstrated a few hours before Obregón's Constitutionalists occupied Juarez; a squad of Villistas, half a mile east of the international bridge, deliberately fired across the river into the United States, killing a car inspector as he went about his duties in the railroad yard. General Pershing immediately deployed troops along the river, with orders to shoot any Mexican firing toward American territory.[2]

As for Villa himself after the debacle at Hermosillo, his whereabouts and movements were a deep mystery. All sorts of rumors circulated, most of them indicating that he intended to retire from politics and take refuge in the United States. There is somewhat nebulous evidence that President Wilson might have agreed to give him sanctuary in the United States, and it is certain that both military and civil officers along the border were directed to be on the alert for him and grant him full protection.[3]

The Santa Ysabel massacre, horrible though it was, still did not provoke the President into aggressive action. Strong demands were made upon Carranza, who promised immediate action, but people on the border who were familiar with conditions had little hope that the de facto government of Mexico could, or would, do anything really effective. General Pershing reported to Funston that "there is little confidence in Carranza among Americans coming out of Mexico and many Mexicans are of the same mind."[4]

The horror of Santa Ysabel proved, however, that even though Villa's political and military fortunes were on the downgrade, *Villismo* was far from dead. A few days before the affair, when rumors of Villa's taking refuge in the United States were at their height, Felix Sommerfeld, who was supposed to be Villa's confidential agent in the United States, sent a telegram to General Scott, saying that reports of Villa's flight from Mexico were "fakes" and that an interview that Villa was supposed to have given to a correspondent of the New York *American* was fraudulent.[5]

The Carranza government promptly took such measures as it was able to take. The last thing that Carranza wanted was an American expedition into Mexico. That the measures his government took were ineffective was due not to unwillingness to punish the perpetrators of the massacre but rather to sheer inability. Peace was far from restored in the unhappy country. A large-scale operation against the Yaquis was under way; Zapata was still waging bitter war in the south, and the strong garrisons necessary in the major cities and other critical points absorbed a large part of the de facto government's troops. There were simply not enough Carranzista soldiers for all the missions. But because of Carranza's willingness to do what he could in this case, and in spite of pressure from President Wilson's political opponents and various interested parties, the United States took no military action. If it was Villa's intention to force American intervention, during which he might again become a great national hero, he failed.[6]

The indignation and excitement in the United States soon subsided, and the border settled down to its normal state of uneasiness. Villa's whereabouts were still unknown, but through the month of February rumors continued to circulate to the effect that he was coming to the United States. There were also rumors of plans for a grand massacre of all Americans in Mexico, but with all the fears and forebodings, February passed uneventfully.[7]

Late in the month, however, it became known, or was reported, that Villa and his band (no longer large enough to be called an army) were moving slowly northward. This bit of information probably came from Carranza sources, as neither the State Department nor the War Department had either funds or personnel for secret operatives in Mexico. The first definite and positive information was telegraphed to the State Department on March 3, 1916, by Zach Cobb, the Collector of Customs at El Paso. He informed the Department that Villa had left Madera, Chihuahua, on March 1, with about three hundred men. At the time Cobb sent his message, Villa was supposed to be someplace west of Casas Grandes. Cobb (who hated Villa bitterly) believed that he intended to cross the boundary, hoping to go to Washington.[8] On the other hand, General Gavira, the Carranzista commander in Juarez, told an Associated Press correspondent, George L. Seese, that Villa had no intention of taking refuge in the United States; he was coming north intending to make trouble—to do something that would force American intervention. Seese promptly passed this item of information to General Pershing, who replied that he had heard similar reports so often that he was inclined to be skeptical.[9]

On March 9, 1916, *The New York Times* repeated a brief news item from the El Paso newspapers, which said that Villa was reported to be at Palomas, Chihuahua, only a few miles from Columbus, New Mexico, and that he had killed two Americans, Edward J. Wright and Frank Hayden. The news item added that there was no information on the fate of Wright's wife and infant son.[10]

March 9, 1916, was a pleasant, sunny day, not too hot and not chilly. Young Charles Hoffman spent most of the day riding southward from Deming to Columbus, a distance of about thirty miles. He was on an important mission. He was an officer of the Indian Bureau, and he was looking for a man, believed to be heading for Columbus, who had committed a murder on an Indian reservation. Consequently, he was well armed with a high-power rifle (a Savage 250–3000) and a heavy revolver (as well as a pair of handcuffs and a warrant). Arriving at Columbus late in the afternoon (he was well known there), Hoffman soon found that his quarry was not yet there. At dusk, he retraced his steps back toward Deming for half a mile, tethered his horse behind an abandoned shack, where the animal would be invisible from the road, and bedded himself down in front, where he could hear, and be awakened by, anyone riding along the road at night. He slept soundly but was suddenly stirred into wakefulness by the staccato of shots, the sound coming from the direction of the town. Sensing that something terrible was occurring, he pulled on his boots and rode for the town. In a few minutes he saw figures in the road, people who were terrified at the sight of him, but he quickly reassured them. They were people whom he knew, a man, his wife and two young grandchildren. The woman was closely clutching a large clock, which she had snatched up in her panic and terror.

Hoffman decided that it would be suicidal to try to ride into Columbus. He tethered his horse loosely, so that the animal could break loose if necessary, and walked on afoot. A few seconds later a bullet cracked past, and someone shouted, "There's one of the bastards!" Hoffman hit the ground and rolled into the roadside ditch, yelling, "Don't shoot, I'm an American." By this time there was a red glow over Columbus from burning buildings. Hoffman crawled to an unroofed adobe structure near the railroad station and got inside. A few seconds later he was joined by a Mexican employee of the railroad, carrying a Winchester rifle. They could see a group of men on top of a rocky knoll (then known as Cootes Hill, now called Pancho Villa Hill), apparently setting up a machine gun. Both Hoffman and the Mexican (whose name is unknown) opened fire, then the Mexican crawled up into the railway coal chute, where he had unobstructed vision and a clear field of fire. The machine gun never came into action on Cootes Hill.[11]

Only a few seconds before Hoffman was awakened by the sound of firing, 1st Lieutenant James P. Castleman, of the 13th Cavalry, was sitting in the one-room adobe house assigned for the use of the Officer of the Day. He had taken off his belt and heavy pistol and laid them alongside him on the bunk. Probably intending to make the inspection of the guard required by regulations (at least one inspection was made after midnight), he rose and was buckling his belt, when there was the sharp crack of a rifle shot and a strangled cry, "I'm shot!" At the same instant a bullet smashed through the windowpane and mushroomed against the adobe wall. Castleman flung open the door and faced a strange Mexican, with a leveled rifle. The Mexican fired and missed; he had no chance for another shot, for Castleman's pistol practically blew his head off. By this time, although only a few seconds had elapsed, the camp echoed and re-echoed with firing and wild shouts of "*Viva Villa! Viva México! Muerte a los gringos!*"[12]

The 13th Cavalry had been stationed at Columbus for several months, although on March 9, 1916, only the regimental headquarters, the Machine Gun Troop and four rifle troops, totaling about 350 officers and men were actually located at Camp Furlong, as the post was named. A few days earlier the regimental commander, Colonel Herbert W. Slocum, had dispatched two troops, under Major Elmer Lindsley, to Gibson's Ranch, fourteen miles west of Columbus. A troop was stationed at the border gate, about three miles to the south of Columbus, and a troop was at Fort Leavenworth, Kansas, detached from the regiment. In a reorganization of border commands in January, 1916, the 13th Cavalry had been made responsible for patrolling and protecting a zone extending from Noria, New Mexico, on the east, to Hermanas, New Mexico, on the west, a distance of some sixty-five miles. The orders that forbade American troops to cross the international line were still in effect, and any information about activities and movements in Mexico which patrols might obtain was limited to what they could actually see from the United States side. Hence, for information from below the border, Slocum and all other border commanders were dependent entirely upon what was brought to them by civilians who could cross the line.

Because Camp Furlong was a temporary post, no quarters for married officers and soldiers were provided. The only officers who lived in the post were the unmarried ones; all married men had to rent whatever they could find in the town. This is a practice that was, and still is, quite usual in the United States Army.

Colonel Slocum was fully aware in the early days of March, 1916, that Villa was moving northward, although the information he received was vague and contradictory. The "fog of war" in which he was enveloped, and in which he had to make his decisions and dispositions, has seldom been thicker or more impenetrable, but nevertheless, he took such measures as were feasible and were indicated by common sense. Believing that Gibson's Ranch was a critical point because of its isolation, Slocum had strengthened his force there to two troops; at the same time, he had increased the guard at the border gate to a whole troop. On the evening of March 7 a Mexican employee of the Palomas Land and Cattle Company came to Columbus and informed Slocum that he and his foreman, McKinney, had seen Villa and about five hundred men in camp on the Casas Grandes River. The Mexican, who is known only as Antonio, managed to escape, but McKinney and another American were captured.

Antonio did not want to go back into Mexico; he was afraid of the Villistas, but Slocum finally persuaded him to return the next day for further observation. Antonio returned to Columbus late in the evening, March 8, with information that most of the Villistas had gone eastward toward Guzman, and that about 150 had marched toward Palomas but had later turned south. To add to the uncertainty and confusion, on March 8 George L. Seese, the Associated Press correspondent, received reports of Villa's presence in three widely separated places at the same time. The last of the three reports, which was accepted as probably true, placed him at Rancho Nogales, about sixty-five miles southwest of Columbus.[12]

Late at night on March 7, 1916, and before Antonio's first

information came in, Slocum, accompanied by Major Frank Tompkins, rode to the border gate to question the commanding officer of the small Carranzista detachment stationed there. The Mexicans sprang to arms when they heard the American party approaching, and Tompkins noticed that their trenches were so dug as to face an attack from the north, not the south. Of course, the Carranzistas knew nothing whatever about Villa, or so they professed.[13]

In contrast to the dark fog that covered and hampered the Americans, Villa was operating with full information on the situation in Columbus and the disposition of the American forces. Columbus was so small a place that the presence of any stranger was quickly noted, and several people commented on the number of strange Mexicans who appeared on the streets in early March. In addition, as became clearly evident later, a few of the Mexican residents of Columbus were Villista spies.[14]

Villa matured his plans carefully. The raid on Columbus was not decided upon hastily, nor was there anything hit-or-miss about it. Contemporary accounts of the raid mention certain papers that the Mexicans lost in their retreat, papers showing clearly that the attack was projected as early as January 6.

Following his usual custom, Villa planned to attack late at night. After crossing the boundary about two miles west of the border gate, he divided his band into two parts. One force moved, dismounted, northeastward until it was directly south of the camp, then it turned north and swarmed into the stable area. The Columbus–Palominas road was paralleled by a deep, wide ditch (sometimes described as an *arroyo*, although it was man-made), which provided perfect cover for the attackers. Before reaching the ditch, however, the invaders were further divided into two columns, one of which crept under cover of the ditch until it was right in the heart of town. The other subdivision attacked the camp directly from the west. Villa, with his staff, escort and the led horses, established himself at what a later military generation would call his command post, just outside the town, and in the vicinity of Cootes Hill.

When the assault started at three thirty or four o'clock in the morning (various accounts give slightly different times) almost the only Americans awake in the camp were the regular sentinels and the cooks and kitchen police. The mess-shack kitchens were adobe and were bulletproof. As the first invaders tried to crowd through the doors of the kitchens, they were met with cauldrons of scalding water, by cooks and kitchen police swinging butcher knives, cleavers, potato mashers and anything else that came to hand (the GI potato masher was a formidable weapon at close quarters; it could crush a skull as easily as an eggshell). In the stable area, the stable police, just starting to give the animals their morning feed, used pitchforks with deadly effect.

That the Villista attack was a tactical surprise, no one would deny, but in the end, it was the raiders who were really surprised. Villa had not dreamed of the resistance his men would encounter. Although the Americans were surprised, they reacted with a speed and vigor that reflected not only the training and discipline they had received but also intelligent initiative. Lieutenant Castleman, after his encounter with the armed Mexican at the door of his shack, raced to his troop (Troop F) and found that Sergeant Michael Fody had already assembled the troop and was moving toward regimental headquarters. Castleman assumed command and continued the movement. About two hundred yards to the north they came under rifle fire delivered at close range. Without command every man dropped to the ground and opened fire, shooting at the enemy flashes. The fire slackened; the enemy had had enough. Troop F, now joined by some soldiers from other organizations, advanced straight into the town. At first there were no visible targets; the enemy could not be seen in the dark, but within a few minutes the fire of the blazing Commercial Hotel and other buildings put the raiders in sharp relief, while the Americans were still covered by the night. In a short time, also, the comforting rattle of American machine guns was added to the din. Enemy casualties began to mount, while American casualties remained surprisingly low.[15]

1st Lieutenant John Lucas, the commanding officer of the Machine Gun Troop, returned to Columbus from El Paso on the midnight train. He trudged to the adobe shack that he shared with Lieutenant Clarence C. Benson. Acting on impulse, Lucas examined his pistol, found it unloaded, and, grumbling to himself, loaded it. Three or four hours later he was awakened by the sound of horses passing the cabin. Looking out the window, Lucas could see the silhouettes of men wearing the huge *sombreros* that only Mexicans wear. He seized his pistol, intending to sell his life as dearly as possible, but the horsemen rode on. Unable to find his boots in the darkness, Lucas ran barefooted to his troop. He directed the first sergeant to form the troop and bring it to the guardhouse (where the machine guns were kept). He ran ahead with two gunners, got out one gun, and set it up to sweep a railroad crossing.

The machine gun in use in the United States Army in 1916 was the Benet-Mercier, a complex weapon that jammed easily. This one promptly jammed. Another was brought from the guardhouse. At this time Lucas was joined by the rest of his troop and, like Castleman, was joined also by numbers of soldiers who could not find their own units in the darkness and confusion. The blaze of burning buildings illuminated targets for the machine gunners, and the raiders, caught in a deadly cross fire from riflemen and machine gunners, soon had their fill. As darkness began to give way to the first light of dawn, Mexican bugles began sounding, and the Villistas fled. The fight was nearly over, but not quite. Lucas and Castleman joined forces, firing on the fugitives. Colonel Slocum and other officers appeared, having finally escaped from their surrounded homes in the town.[16]

Shortly after the Villistas vanished from the town, Major Frank Tompkins searched for Colonel Slocum to ask permission to pursue. He found the colonel on top of the rocky knoll where Villa had, apparently, established his command post. Slocum was standing, calmly watching his men firing on the invaders, who were visible about four or five hundred yards to the west. Slocum approved Tompkins' request and told him to take Troop H. To assemble the troop and gather up enough horses to mount the men took fifteen or twenty minutes. Most of the horses had been turned loose by the raiders in hope of driving them to Mexico. Moving southwestward, Tompkins and his little force (thirty-two men at the start) could see the enemy heading toward the border. Tompkins moved parallel, to endeavor to cut them off. A short distance south of the boundary was a small hill, upon which the Villistas had stationed a covering detachment. Coming under fire from this hill, the Americans cut the fence, deployed into line at Tompkins' command, and increased speed until the command "Charge!" at the foot of the hill caused every man to drive in his spurs. As the charge approached, the enemy fired wildly, not a single shot taking effect. As the Americans surged up the hill, the Mexicans broke and fled. On reaching the crest, the Americans dismounted and opened fire. The Mexicans had not had time to run any great distance, and several were killed before they could mount.

Tompkins suddenly realized that he had crossed the boundary and was in Mexico. Hurriedly he sent a messenger to Colonel Slocum, asking for instructions and saying that the enemy had taken up a position along a ridge, about fifteen hundred yards south of the line. Slocum's reply was that Tompkins should use his own judgment.

Meanwhile the arrival of Castleman and his troop doubled the strength of the pursuing force. In addition, several officers who could be spared from the camp had joined as volunteers. Deploying with wide interval between troopers, and moving at a fast trot, the Americans resumed their advance. The Mexicans fired, but again their fire was wild. Some four hundred yards in front of the Mexican position there was a shallow depression that afforded cover from view and fire. Tompkins ordered the force to dismount, advance to a point where the enemy was visible, and there open fire. After suffering some losses the Mexicans (evidently a rear guard) quickly abandoned their position. The Americans remounted and took up the pursuit, regaining contact in about half an hour. Only once during the afternoon did the enemy show any signs of aggressiveness. A counterattack by a large group of Mexicans was launched but was not pushed home, especially as Tompkins promptly put his force into a defensive position. The Americans opened fire, the Mexicans hesitated, then drew away.

After awaiting attack for forty-five minutes, Tompkins decided to break off the pursuit. The ammunition was running rather low, and the men and horses were suffering from thirst, hunger and fatigue. Most of the men had been in action for fifteen hours. On the fifteen-mile march back to Columbus, the tired troopers had the satisfaction of seeing large numbers of enemy dead, along with abandoned weapons and the loot stolen from homes and stores in the town. The Americans *counted* at least seventy-five dead Villistas between the point where they abandoned the pursuit, and the international boundary.[17]

The fight at Columbus and the subsequent pursuit, by a force that was outnumbered by the retreating force, was unimportant as compared with the stupendous battles being waged in Europe at the same time. It was fought by small groups of soldiers and officers, sometimes fighting as individuals, and was so confused that to this day it is impossible to form a coherent picture of the whole. The fight might be compared aptly with the frontier battles in the early days of the British Colonies and the new United States, when communities of men, women and even children had to fight raiders for their own survival. The narratives of the citizens of Columbus who survived the shock and horror vary according to the experiences of individuals, but there is a unity among the accounts: all the people of the little town were surprised and terrified by the suddenness and unexpectedness of the raid. Dr. Roy E. Stivison, who was then a teacher in the local school, was awakened, with his wife and child, by the sounds of terrific rifle fire. They started to make a light but decided that to do so would be dangerous. They spent the next three hours listening to shouts of *"Viva Villa! Viva México! Muerte a los gringos!"* while occasional shots struck their house. The murders of the five guests in the Commercial Hotel (one of them a Sunday-school superintendent who had come to Columbus for a Sunday-school conference), who were dragged out of their rooms and shot, were examples of the brutality and savagery of the raiders.[18]

The narrow escapes, the almost unbelievable adventures of other townsfolk and members of the garrison, are so numerous that to repeat them in detail would be redundant. Lieutenant William A. McCain lived, with his wife and young daughter, in a house just south of the railroad track. That night his orderly happened to be staying at the house also. When the firing started, all four dashed out of the house and hid in the chaparral. They were joined, a few minutes later, by Captain George Williams. Williams had a pistol, and McCain and the orderly had a pistol and a shotgun. They were discovered a few minutes later by a Mexican straggler, but before he could give the alarm, McCain shot him with the shotgun, but since it was loaded with birdshot, he was not killed. The three men pulled him under a bush and choked off his cries. They were afraid to fire another shot for fear of attracting attention. One of the Americans tried to cut the man's throat with a pocket knife, but it was too dull; they finally bashed in his head with the butt of a pistol. And there was the horror endured by Mrs. J. J. Moore, who saw her husban killed before her eyes, saw her infant child murdered, and as a tragic finale, she herself was raped, although she was badly wounded.[19]

As was to be expected, there was a furor in the United States. Extreme pacifists and certain professional liberals immediately charged that the whole affair was a fake. Villa, some said, was not really responsible. The real responsibility rested on the bankers and industrialists of "Wall Street," who callously plotted the murder of American citizens and soldiers in order to force intervention and thereby safeguard their Mexican investments.[20] That most of the officers and many of the soldiers lived outside the camp came in for a great deal of ignorant criticism—criticism that ignored that no quarters for married people were provided at Columbus. Lieutenant Lucas was criticized because his machine guns were supposed to have jammed repeatedly during the action. The objection, of course, ignores the obvious: that Lieutenant Lucas had nothing at all to do with the design or adoption of the weapon. Any serious malfunctioning of the guns during the fight is amply refuted: the four guns fired more than twenty thousand rounds of ammunition. There were rumors, too, that because weapons and ammunition were kept under lock and key, the soldiers were unable to arm themselves. For good and sufficient reason, weapons and ammunition are always locked up, and there is no indication whatever that there was any delay in arming the soldiers. And finally, of course, there was a loud demand for a scapegoat, and Colonel Herbert Slocum was a natural target. It was quickly shown, however, that he had taken

every precaution that was possible with the small number of
men in his regiment and under the restrictions that government
policy placed upon his actions.[21]

During the fight a number of Villistas were taken prisoner,
and some of them were found to be local Mexicans, and in one
case, the man and his family had been living on the philanthropy
of the townspeople. The prisoners were duly tried for murder
under the laws of New Mexico, and in June, 1916, seven of them
were hanged in the jail yard at Deming. One prisoner, a boy of
about fourteen years of age, was not tried. He was taken to the
hospital, where an amputation proved necessary to save his life,
and upon recovery, was sent to school in Albuquerque.[22]

It is usually overlooked that the Columbus Raid was actually
a severe, almost disastrous, defeat for Villa. His band killed a
few soldiers and a few civilians; they obtained a few horses and
a small amount of loot from the stores and homes of the town.
And considering that the raiders achieved a complete surprise,
their losses in the ensuing fight were staggering. More than sixty
dead Mexicans were gathered up in the streets and byways of the
little town, and Major Tompkins' pursuit accounted for at least
seventy more. The most conservative estimate of the strength
of the raiding band is about four hundred men. Accepting this
as a reasonable figure, Villa's losses came to a full fourth of his
command—and that was in dead, with no information ever given
out on the number of wounded.

The most immediate effect of the raid was the reversal of
President Wilson's policy of "non-retaliation." The Punitive Expedition crossed the boundary within a few days, and from then
until Mexico finally settled down to internal peace, American
troops never hesitated to follow lawless raiders across the line.
And never again did Pancho Villa, or any other *caudillo*, seriously
threaten any American city or village of any size. "A burnt child
fears the fire," and Villa's followers had learned the hard way
that the American soldier is a very dangerous opponent. And
when the carping, the search for a scapegoat and the ignorant
criticism directed at the officers and soldiers of the 13th Cavalry
are viewed in their proper prespective, the record of the 13th
appears to be highly creditable.

NOTES

1. *Foreign Relations, 1915*, p. 954.
2. *Ibid.*, pp. 820–21; *Literary Digest*, LII (Jan. 22, 1916), 157–58.
3. Frank Tompkins, *Chasing Villa. The Story Behind the Story of Pershing's Punitive Expedition into Mexico* (Harrisburg, Pa., 1934), p. 41; Hugh Lenox Scott, *Some Memories of a Soldier*, (New York, 1928), pp. 517–18.
4. *Foreign Relations, 1916*, pp. 662–63.
5. The Hugh Lenox Scott Papers, Manuscript Division, Library of Congress. See also "Villa's First Aid to Washington," *Literary Digest*, LII (Jan. 1, 1916), 5. Felix Sommerfeld was a vague and shadowy character, of uncertain antecedents, who flits through the records of the time almost like a wraith. He was reputed to be Villa's personal and confidential agent in the United States. The writer has been informed, but has been unable to verify the statement, that Sommerfeld has been definitely proved to have been a German intelligence agent.
6. There was a widespread belief at the time that Villa was prompted by German intrigue and possibly by German funds. No positive evidence has ever come to light, but there is no doubt that Germany would have been very glad to see the United States involved in Mexico, in order to cut off the flow of munitions to the Allies. See Barbara Tuchman, *The Zimmerman Telegram* (New York, 1958), *passim*.
7. Tompkins, *op. cit.*, p. 41; Hugh L. Scott, *op. cit.*, pp. 517–18; *Congressional Record*, 64th Cong., 1st sess., pp. 1193–94.
8. *Foreign Relations, 1916*, p. 487.
9. *Ibid.*
10. *The New York Times*, Tuesday, Mar. 9, 1916, 1:4. Reprinted from an unidentified El Paso newspaper.
11. The foregoing narrative of personal experiences at Columbus was related to the writer in several personal interviews by Col. Charles W. Hoffman, U.S.A.R., Ret. Col. Hoffman also prepared a written memorandum covering the same ground. In August, 1967, the writer visited and explored the scene of the raid and estimated the distance from Hoffman's refuge to the top of the knoll as being from 250 to 300 yards—a very easy range for a good shot with a high-power rifle.
12. James Hopper, "What Happened in Columbus," *Collier's Magazine*, LVII (Apr. 15, 1916), 11; Tompkins, *op. cit.*, 42–44.
13. Tompkins, *op. cit.*, p. 45.
14. Ray E. Stivison, M.D., with Della Mavity McDonnell, "When Villa Raided Columbus," *New Mexico Magazine*, XXVIII (Dec. 1950),

18–19. Col. Hoffman pointed out to the writer, in a photograph of prisoners taken at Columbus, several who were local residents and were well known in the town.

15. Tompkins, *op. cit.*, pp. 48–50.

16. Narrative of Lt. John Lucas, quoted in Tompkins, *op. cit.*, pp. 50–53. Lucas commanded the American forces at Anzio, in World War II, and later was head of the military advisory group in Nationalist China.

17. Tompkins, *op. cit.*, pp. 55–57. Some critics who *were not there* have criticized Tompkins' account as "unreliable." Particularly, Gen. Alberto Salinas Carranza held it impossible for as small a force as Tompkins had in the pursuit to have killed as many as was claimed. The Mexican general was evidently unfamiliar with the stress the United States forces placed upon individual marksmanship.

18. Stivison and McDonnell, *op. cit.*, p. 19.

19. The murder of the Moore baby and the raping of Mrs. Moore are not mentioned in any account of the raid with which the writer is familiar. Col. Hoffman, however, assured the writer of the truth of the statement and pointed out one man in the photograph of the prisoners taken at Columbus who was subsequently convicted of the crimes and hanged.

20. See Edgcumb Pinchon, *Viva Villa! A Recovery of the Real Pancho Villa—Peon—Bandit—Soldier—Patriot* (New York, 1933), pp. 338–39, for a remarkable exposition of this theory. See also the speech made by Rep. Meyer London, a Socialist congressman from New York City, *Congressional Record*, 64th Cong., 1st Sess., pp. 5020–21. Congressman London charged, with pontifical authority, that Villa was merely the tool of "powerful interests."

21. For a full discussion of the charges and allegations, with full citations from appropriate records, see Tompkins, *op. cit.*, pp. 64–65.

22. Testimony of Jesus Paiz, *Fall Committee Report*, pp. 1616–20. The writer has been informed by someone whose identity he is now unable to recall that Paiz changed his name, became an American citizen, and is a highly respected businessman of the community where he lives.

CHAPTER 11

Marches, Wagons, Trucks and Dust: Opening Operations and the Base at Columbus

E VEN WHEN THEY had begun to recover from their stunned surprise, the people of Columbus were still terrified. In a tense situation all sorts of fantastic rumors develop and spread quickly, with few people questioning their truth. Before the day was over there were rumors, no one knowing where or how they started, but widely believed, that Villa would attack again that same night. Many of the frightened townspeople were allowed to spend the night in the camp hospital, or in the various mess shacks (which were of adobe and thus were bulletproof). The people were loaned blankets and pillows by the soldiers and from the camp stocks. They could not have slept comfortably, but at least they felt safe. Early in the morning of March 10 a welcome sight greeted their eyes—troop trains on the sidings and at the station, discharging hundreds of United States soldiers. For a people who were still suffering from shock and horror, it was the most comforting sight possible.[1]

All over the United States there was an immediate demand for the prompt punishment of the raiders. During the day, on March 10, the President and his Cabinet conferred at length, and early in the evening a warning order was telegraphed to General Funston, at San Antonio: "President has directed that an armed force be sent into Mexico with the sole object of capturing Villa and preventing further raids by his band, with scrupulous regard to sovereignty of Mexico."[2] This telegram was released to the press and in the hands of headline writers gave immediate rise to the myth that the Punitive Expedition was under orders to "get Villa, dead or alive." That Villa was not taken or killed has, in turn, given rise to another myth, that the Punitive Expedition was a most humiliating failure. As a matter of fact, the actual order for the Expedition, which followed quickly after the warning order, did not even mention Villa by name.

In Washington, the morning of March 10, 1916, provided a rough introduction—a regular hazing—to a "freshman" Secretary of War who had assumed office that same morning. Secretary of War Lindley M. Garrison had resigned from the Cabinet the month before; in the interim General Scott was Acting Secretary of War in addition to fulfilling his regular duties as Chief of Staff. President Wilson finally nominated a noted attorney and well-known political liberal from Cleveland, Ohio, Newton D. Baker, for the office. Baker was suspected in many quarters of being a pacifist, and it was certain that he had no military background whatever. His first official act as Secretary of War was to attend the Cabinet meeting that was called to determine a course of action regarding Villa. When the meeting adjourned, Secretary Baker went directly to the office of the Chief of Staff. According to General Scott's memory of the occasion, the Secretary said, "I want you to start an expedition into Mexico to catch Villa." Scott replied, "Mr. Secretary, do you want the United States to make war on one man? Suppose he should get onto a train and go to Guatemala, Yucatan, or South America; are you going to go after him?" In a few minutes' discussion, it became clear that the expedition's objective was not Villa himself but rather his band, or bands, and General Scott drew up a directive accordingly.[3]

In the United States it was assumed, both popularly and in official circles, that Carranza would welcome American assistance in eliminating his bitterest and most dangerous enemy. No one north of the international boundary seemed to realize the depth and passion of Mexican hatred for and suspicion of the "gringo." Virtually all Mexicans, of all classes and factions, feared the "Colossus of the North" and believed implicitly that the United States was merely biding its time before the seizure of more Mexican territory. This suspicion was confirmed by the wild statements and demands of the more immoderate interventionists in the United States.

As a matter of fact, Carranza feared the United States more than he feared Pancho Villa. Upon receiving news of the Columbus raid, he telegraphed orders to his commanding general at Vera Cruz, warning him that there was danger of a landing by American Marines and that such a landing should be resisted to the bitterest end. In the evening of March 10, the day after the raid, Collector Zach Cobb, at El Paso, who seems to have spent as much time as a volunteer State Department representative as he did as a Treasury official, telegraphed to the Secretary of State: "Indications are that Carranza authorities will resent American troops entering Mexico. They are rushing troops to Juarez as, I think, predicate to claiming ours unnecessary. Ours are necessary."[4] And on March 11, Carranza sent a cablegram to his representative in Washington in which he said, "It is necessary that the Department of State should be caused to understand that it would be unjust to attribute to the Government and people of Mexico the responsibility for the acts committed by a band of brigands whom this Government has placed beyond the law, and that there would be no justification for any invasion of Mexican territory by an armed force of the United States, not even under the pretext of pursuing and capturing Villa. . . ." Carranza suggested a reciprocal agreement similar to that which had been entered into during the Apache wars, under which the troops of either country might cross the border in "hot pursuit."[5]

On March 13, Secretary Lansing sent a dispatch to the State Department's representative with Carranza, freely giving the de facto government the right to send troops across the border; it was assumed that Carranza would at once concede the same privilege to the United States. But Carranza had no intention of authorizing the entry of United States troops into Mexico, and Washington completely overlooked that he proposed to grant such a privilege only in case of *future* raids.[6] From this misunderstanding, or misinterpretation, came many of the difficulties that General Pershing and the expedition encountered in the ensuing months. Additional instructions sent to General Funston on March 13 stressed that the expedition's actions "be scrupulously confined to the object already mentioned," and further instructions on March 17, when the expedition was already far into Mexico, emphasized that there must be nothing in the conduct of the expedition or its members that might bring criticism.[7]

Beginning early in the morning of the day after the raid, March 10, troop train after troop train steamed into Columbus. For several days trains discharged soldiers, wagons, horses, mules, supplies of all kinds—all the impedimenta needed by a force taking the field. From garrisons along the Border, troops entrained for Columbus, or marched in that direction as soon as they were replaced by soldiers from other regions.

General Pershing opened his headquarters and issued his General Orders, No. 1, at Columbus on March 14. The force that was assembling was designated as the Punitive Expedition, U.S. Army, and was organized as a provisional division, comprising three brigades. The 1st Provisional Cavalry Brigade, commanded by Colonel James Lockett, 11th Cavalry, consisted of the 11th and 13th Cavalry Regiments and Battery C, 6th Field Artillery. The 2d Provisional Cavalry Brigade included the 7th and 10th Cavalry Regiments and Battery B, 6th Field Artillery, all under Colonel George H. Dodd, 7th Cavalry. The 1st Provisional Infantry Brigade, commanded by Colonel John H. Beacon, 6th Infantry, was composed of the 6th and 16th Infantry Regiments, two companies of Engineers, an ambulance company, a field hospital, two wagon companies, Signal Corps detachments and the 1st Aero Squadron. Pershing appointed Lieutenant Colonel De Rosey C. Cabell, 10th Cavalry, as his chief of staff. The staff, incidentally, included at least two officers who were destined to rise to high command in the future. One was Major John L. Hines, who succeeded Pershing himself as Chief of Staff of the United States Army; another was Pershing's aide-de-camp, 1st Lieutenant George H. Patton.

In 1916 General Pershing was not widely known outside the army itself. Within the army he was known as a man who was a soldier through and through. He had received his first lessons in actual campaign in the later phases of the war against Geronimo's Apache outlaws. In the Spanish-American War he had had little opportunity to distinguish himself but on one occasion had attracted the favorable attention of his superiors by his utter fearlessness under fire. In the Philippines he made his mark professionally when he commanded, in the grade of captain, a large expedition against the hostile Moro bands in Mindanao. On this occasion Pershing's force was actually large enough to be considered as a brigade. The campaign was brief and was conducted with cool relentlessness, resulting in the speedy surrender of the Moros. For this, President Theodore Roosevelt nominated Pershing for the next vacancy that occurred in the grade of brigadier general, passing over scores of officers who were senior to him by many years.

Pershing was a natural leader, who wore his authority without ostentation. He was affable in manner and had the happy faculty of putting subordinates at ease, but he was merciless with the inefficient or anybody who did not render a satisfactory performance of duty. He demanded and received unwavering loyalty from his subordinates and exact compliance with his orders. From the very start of the Punitive Expedition the impact of his personality and authority was felt in every unit—even in those that were located far from his headquarters and his personal observation. It is hardly accidental that the expedition of 1916 is usually referred to as "Pershing's Punitive Expedition."

Pershing's initial plan was for the expedition to enter Mexico in two columns; the 1st Cavalry Brigade and the Infantry Brigade were to march south from Columbus, while the 2d Cavalry Brigade moved from Culberson's Ranch, near the southwest corner of New Mexico. The two columns were to converge and join at Ascensión. It was hoped that Villa might be caught between the two jaws of a nutcracker, but before the movement started, information came in that Villa had already passed Casas Grandes and was hurrying southward. The plan was therefore modified slightly; the western column was directed to march on Casas Grandes by the shortest practicable route. Casas Grandes would then become the expedition's advance base.

On March 13, however, before any movement of American troops took place, and a few hours before Pershing opened his headquarters at Columbus, an unexpected complication arose.

The commanding officer of the small Carranzista detachment at Palomas, only a few miles from Columbus, let it be known that he would resist any crossing of the border by American troops. He was told that the two governments had reached an agreement, but he was obdurate: he would resist any invasion of Mexican territory by the Americans. This led to a flurry of telegrams between the two capitals, with no solution for the problem in sight. His patience finally exhausted, General Funston ordered Pershing to move at once. If the Carranzistas at Palomas resisted, it would be too bad for them!

Meanwhile, the concentration of troops for the movement into Mexico was going on. At Naco, Arizona, were two troops of the 10th Cavalry, commanded by Major Elwood Evans, guarding the border and endeavoring to enforce the United States neutrality laws. One of the officers of the Naco detachment was Captain George Brydges Rodney, who had just joined after a tour of duty in the Philippines. On the evening of March 9, 1916, he and his wife, and the other officers and ladies of the small garrison, were Major Evans' guests at a dinner dance at the Warren Country Club, a few miles distant. About midnight, Major Evans, holding a piece of paper in his hand, caught Captain Rodney's eye and motioned for him to step outside. "Get all of the officers out here quietly," he said, "don't let anybody see you." Wondering what it was about, the five or six officers present gathered outside. Major Evans was suddenly transformed from the genial and hospitable host into one hundred per cent soldier. "Get your wives and leave at once for camp," he said curtly. "Villa jumped Columbus this morning. . . . The Regimental Adjutant wired me to stand by for orders. The regiment leaves at daybreak. We can't go till we're relieved, but we will follow the regiment and join it later."[8]

The next morning the main body of the 10th Cavalry passed Naco, having marched the afternoon before and spent the night at Hereford. In the afternoon two companies of infantry detrained, and the two troops under Major Evans followed in the wake of the regiment. Captain Rodney had had no previous service with Negro troops and started his troop's preparations for the coming march by closely supervising everything himself, as he was accustomed to doing. His first sergeant and supply sergeant listened to him respectfully, and then, with the same respect and with great determination, insisted that the captain leave all preperations to them. The troop commander, they said, had enough to do in getting himself and his own things ready. They would take care of everything else, even to selecting a suitable mount for him.[9]

At Douglas the two 10th Cavalry troops from Naco joined with the 7th Cavalry for the march to Culberson's Ranch. The march took three days, and the troops had a foretaste of what was in store for them in Mexico. The days were blazing hot; the nights were bitter cold. The road was dry and dusty, and hundreds of pounding hooves raised almost impenetrable clouds of dust. On arriving at Culberson's, on March 14, 1916, officers and men wrapped themselves in their blankets and lay on the ground. Shortly before midnight the Regimental Adjutant routed the officers out from their blankets: "We're breaking the camp in an hour. Turn out your troop. Three days' rations and all the ammunition you can carry. Have your wagons report to the quartermaster. They'll go to Columbus and will rejoin us later. We're crossing into Mexico."[10]

In the altitude of southern New Mexico the nights are likely to be cold in March, and this night was freezing. Nevertheless, some unidentified "brain truster" had decided that since Mexico is a tropical country, overcoats were unnecessary. They were bundled into the wagons to be taken to Columbus. During the weeks that followed, the shivering officers and soldiers, huddled about fires made of anything that was combustible, mentally (and probably orally, as well) cursed the military genius who was responsible for such an asinine order.

Although the troops were routed out of their blankets to march shortly after midnight, the departure was delayed for several hours. General Pershing had elected to march with that column, and while en route to join, he was involved in a motor accident. Fortunately, he was unhurt, but the march was delayed until the small hours of the morning. Dusk the next day found the troops at Ojitas, fifty-eight miles south of the boundary. Bivouacking for the night, they munched on the rations they carried in their saddlebags, fed the animals from grain carried on the saddles, and tried to sleep. The next day's march was sheer misery. There was no water all day; clouds of choking, alkaline dust filtered into clothes and coated the men's faces. Captain Rodney, glancing over his shoulder at his troop, was faintly amused to note that the faces were all dead white—only when a man blinked could the natural brown of his skin be seen momentarily. But there is an end, even to misery. Just before dark the force arrived at Colonia Dublán, which was a veritable oasis in the desert.[11]

Colonia Dublán was one of several Mormon colonies established in Mexico late in the nineteenth century. The industry and agricultural skill of the Mormons had produced a prosperous farming region—that is, it was prosperous before the Mexican Revolution. The Mormons, as foreigners, were not permitted to bear arms, and they had been subjected to all sorts of annoyances from all Mexican factions. After the Columbus raid, they were in fear of their lives; they were completely helpless against Villa and his hate-filled followers. They had actually seen the glow of the Villista campfires in the distance, but, by the intervention of Divine Providence, as they devoutly believed, Villa had passed them by. One of the elders of the colony wrote: "What a relief when a long line of United States troops toward evening filed down the western slopes and established camp near the colony. So rapidly had they come that Mormons and Mexicans were not aware of their approach. Knees bent in gratitude."[12]

The eastern column, from Columbus, marched at eleven thirty on the morning of March 15. Major Tompkins' squadron of the 13th Cavalry was given the honor of being the advance guard, but there was a brief halt at the boundary to allow the 6th Infantry to be the first American unit actually to cross the line. This was in commemoration: in the War of 1846–47, the 6th was the first regiment to cross the Rio Grande.[13] After this brief ritual, the advance guard moved out, with Troop K galloping to gain the necessary lead. The hamlet of Palomas was approached with due caution because of the Carranzista commander's threat, but the place was deserted except for one aged couple who had been unable to flee.

Palomas was an uninviting place, consisting of some thirty adobe houses, scattered unevenly about a spring and along an alkaline stream flowing from the spring. Tompkins quickly formed an outpost, and the remainder of the column closed up and went into bivouac. Because of the late start, the first day's march was unusually short, unlike the first day's march of the western column, which was unusually long. The night was frigid. The next morning the uncomfortable soldiers found the water in their canteens frozen solid, and there was ice on the surface of the stream.

The next few days' marches were more than uncomfortable. Freezing nights in bivouac were followed by blazing hot days. There had been no rain for months, and hundreds of animals and men stirred thick clouds of corrosive dust that penetrated nostrils and throats, inflamed eyes, and settled on everything like a blanket of snow. To add to the discomfort, March and April are the season for violent windstorms in northern Mexico and the southwestern part of the United States. Major Richard McMaster, of the 4th Field Artillery, marching over the same route a few days later, noted laconically in his diary, "Disagreeable, dusty march," and two days later he entered, "Dust storm blowing."[14]

To add to the discomfort and difficulties, supply was uncertain at its best; at its worst, it was simply nonexistent. This was especially true for the western column, which had been ordered to send its wagons to Columbus, there to be loaded with supplies. The western column was accompanied by a packtrain (probably two—the records are not clear), but the amount carried by a pack animal was a mere fraction of what was needed. General Pershing had ordered the column to take five days' rations, and all the ammunition and forage that could be carried, but evidence indicates that only three days' rations were available. The rations consisted of hardtack, bacon, coffee and sugar, carried in the soldiers' saddlebags. In addition to the forage carried by the packtrains, oats for two days were carried on the saddles, and every soldier had 120 rounds of ammunition in his belt.[15]

In a letter to a friend, written years later, when in a reminiscent mood, by a man who was a private in the 7th Cavalry, the trials and tribulations of the men of the western column were aptly summarized:

> The long days of marching, shortage of water for man and animal. When we had to cook out of the mess kit, bacon and hardtack, coffee, some sugar being passed along the line. Where the horse throwing a shoe, and a new shoe added by the rider (The extra being carried in the saddle bag with nails). Where the hair was long, beards long, some with six months growth.[16]

It must not be supposed that General Pershing and his military superiors at San Antonio and in Washington were unaware of conditions, or were indifferent. Nevertheless, it appears that one important detail had escaped attention entirely: no funds were provided to enable commanding officers and supply officers to make local purchases in Mexico, and since no formal state of war existed, "requisitioning" was forbidden. Although northern Mexico was devastated by years of revolution, forage and food for human beings were occasionally available. Quite understandably, the Mexican farmer or storekeeper was reluctant to accept a receipt—a mere piece of paper—in exchange for his produce, even though he was assured that the paper would be exchanged for cash by any American paymaster. Officers were frequently under the necessity of using their personal funds to purchase necessities for their men and animals. Later in the campaign, Colonel William C. Brown, of the 10th Cavalry, was able to cash a substantial personal check at the office of an American mining company. He turned five hundred dollars of it over to his supply officer and loaned each of his officers ten dollars.[17]

While the troops plodded southward, going deeper and deeper into Mexico, Columbus was becoming the scene of feverish activity, as supplies accumulated and as new organizations detrained. In his initial general orders, General Pershing had designated Major William R. Sample, of the 20th Infantry, as Base Commandant. Sample and his improvised staff worked energetically, and very quickly something like order was established, but they were handicapped by the utter lack of facilities. Railroad sidings were inadequate, there were no warehouses, and there was nothing but brawn and muscle to handle equipment.

Civilian laborers were hired by the score, messes were established to feed them, and tents were erected to house them. Lieutenant Vernon G. Olsmith, of the 23d Infantry, which had been suddenly moved from Galveston to El Paso, was ordered to Columbus to manage the messes. On his arrival, he found "a madhouse of activity. Over a thousand civilian laborers were employed, and they were a tough bunch of thugs."[18]

Temporary relief for what threatened to become a bottleneck was afforded by the arrival of the newest organization in the United States Army, the 1st Aero Squadron, Aviation Section, Signal Corps. The squadron received orders at Fort Sam Houston, Texas, on March 12, 1916; the rest of the day was spent in dismantling the airplanes and in packing and loading equipment. It was the only organization in the army that was wholly motorized, but it still did not have its full complement of trucks. At El Paso, on March 14, the local quartermaster added two hired trucks to the squadron's train and furnished ten days' rations. The squadron reached Columbus in the middle of the morning on March 15. One airplane was at once assembled and sent aloft on a twelve-minute test flight. The remaining airplanes were assembled the next day, and since the squadron's equipment had been unloaded from the cars, it was possible to lend seven trucks to the base quartermaster to haul supplies within the camp. On March 17, five flights were recorded, and nine trucks were loaned to the quartermaster to carry supplies into Mexico. On the next day, March 18, an aviation truck was dispatched to Boca Grande, Mexico, carrying twenty miles of field wire for the Signal Corps, and four trucks were sent to Ascensíon, bearing rations and forage. On the eighteenth, also, Captain Benjamin D. Foulois, the commanding officer of the squadron, was placed temporarily in charge of all transportation for the expedition—an arrangement that was logical, since his organization was furnishing all the long-range transport.[19]

It was hoped and planned originally to supply the expedition by the Northwestern Railroad of Mexico, which could transport supplies from El Paso to Chihuahua, or some other convenient railhead, from which they could be taken by wagon or packtrain to the final destination. This hope and plan, however, was balked at once by Carranza himself. He had no intention of cooperating with the "invaders," and to every request or suggestion by the United States he either turned a deaf ear or interposed such objections as to negate everything. When he finally (weeks later) made some grudging concessions, he interposed such reservations as to make the concessions valueless.

It was speedily apparent that something drastic, or radical, must be done if the expedition were not to fail from hunger. It was impossible to procure adequate supplies from the country, and animal transportation could not carry sufficient provisions over the vast distances of northern Mexico to serve the number of men and animals in the expedition. The standard army vehicle of the time (and for years thereafter) was the "escort wagon," drawn by four mules and capable of carrying three thousand pounds, fully loaded. But "fully loaded" assumed decent roads and fairly easy gradients, and the roads in Mexico were not decent roads, nor were the gradients easy. In short, wagons could not travel from the base into Mexico fully loaded, and for a trip of the length that would be necessary, a considerable part of the cargo capacity of each wagon must be taken up with forage for the wagon's own mules. And the same considerations applied to supply by packtrain. Each mule, when adequately fed and not overworked, could carry two hundred pounds, but as with the wagons, a considerable part of the cargo capacity of each packtrain must necessarily be taken up with forage for the mules themselves.

When it was apparent that an impasse had been reached in negotiations with Carranza for the use of the railroad, the State Department seemed to wash its hands of any further responsibility. General Scott went personally to the Department to plead with some of the officials whom he knew; he left with his face red with anger at their apparent indifference to the straits to which American soldiers would be reduced within a few days. Returning to his office, he sent at once for The Quartermaster General, Brigadier General Henry G. Sharpe, whose bailiwick included all army transportation. Ever since the 1911 maneuvers the army had been buying a few trucks annually, but most of them were assigned to posts and stations for local use, and Scott did not know, offhand, how many were available. He asked Sharpe if there were enough trucks to supply Pershing's force from Columbus. The reply was "No." Scott then asked about the cost of a sufficient number of trucks. Sharpe replied, "About four hundred and fifty thousand dollars." "All right," said Scott, "send right out and buy those trucks with the necessary traveling garages and mechanics; put a chauffeur on every truck and send them by express to Columbus. . . ." As soon as Secretary Baker appeared, Scott confessed that he had just committed a serious crime—one for which a penitentiary sentence was prescribed by law. He had spent government funds without an appropriation by Congress. Baker's reply was brief and to the point: "If anybody goes to jail, I'll be the man."[20]

On March 18 the first trucks arrived at Columbus, although it is probable that these were purchased before the incident just related. The shipment consisted of twenty-seven Jeffery "Quads" (four-wheel drive vehicles). With them came knocked-down escort wagon bodies, in lieu of regular truck bodies. There were no tools or equipment for assembling the wagon bodies or for anchoring them to the truck chassis. Again, the infant air force was called on for help. In their portable machine shop the aero squadron mechanics worked far into the night, making bolts, drilling holes, and assembling completed vehicles.[21] Trucks soon began arriving at Columbus in increasing numbers, as General Sharpe's agents bought whatever was available for sale and immediate delivery. According to tradition, they moved boldly in and practically seized a shipload of trucks on the docks at New York City, awaiting shipment to Europe. Trucks of all makes and models—Whites, Jefferys, Macks, Packards, Locomobiles, Peerlesses, Velies and probably others whose names now appear only in the advertising pages of forgotten magazines—were rolled down the unloading ramps at Columbus. The purchases included tank trucks, machine-shop trucks, wreckers and other special vehicles. In fact, beginning on March 14, 1916, a total of 588 cargo trucks, fifty-seven tank trucks, twelve machine-shop trucks and six wreckers were purchased by General Sharpe's office, and all but twenty-two of these were assigned to the Border. During the same period seventy-three passenger cars were purchased and sent to the Border. Most of them were Dodges, but there were also Fords, Chevrolets, Studebakers, Oaklands and possibly other makes as well.[22]

The army had never before used motor transportation on an extensive scale. There were no facilities for maintenance and repair at Columbus; the army had horseshoers, saddlers, wheelwrights and farriers, but it had no motor mechanics except for the handful in the aero squadron. The base quartermaster immediately established a motor transport division, which included a truck battalion, repair shops and a motor transportation shipping office. The Locomobile Company furnished an overseer for the first repair crew, and the civilian drivers who accompanied the first shipment of Jefferys were drafted as mechanics. For months there were no shop buildings; all repair work was done in the open, in spite of cold weather and the never-ending sand storms.[23]

From improvised and confused beginnings, the expedition's base at Columbus soon became a working organization. Its activities even extended beyond the mere receipt and forwarding of supplies and equipment. On a minor scale it engaged in manufacturing. The aero squadron had difficulty with propellers; the propellers designed for use at lower altitudes were unsatisfactory at the elevations from which the airplanes had to take off in New Mexico and Chihuahua. Experts were called into consultation, and a propeller-making plant was established at Columbus, thereby eliminating the delay that would have resulted had the manufacturing been assigned to civilian manufacturers in the industrial East.[24]

At an unspecified time while the expedition was in Mexico Major Sample was relieved of his duties as Base Commandant, probably because he was much junior to officers who were nominally under his authority. He was replaced by a full colonel. The Columbus base was the first example in recent American military history of such an installation, and to the first Base Commandant must go the credit for its success. It is well known that General Pershing was a hard and exacting taskmaster; had he been the least bit dissatisfied with Major Sample's performance of his difficult duties, Sample would almost certainly not have been placed in command of a much greater base in France less than two years later with a brigadier general's stars on his shoulders.

Even though the first troops to cross the border in March, 1916, suffered hardship and discomfort, and some of the difficulties were caused by the ignorance of some anonymous staff officer in a higher echelon of command, the supply of the Punitive Expedition soon settled into a working routine. At first the troops moved so far and so fast that no organized supply system could have kept up with them. The only solution was to live off the country, and that was impossible in revolutionary Mexico, except where certain items were concerned. For example, the troops never suffered from shortage of beef, despite the devastation of the country. At the start of the expedition, the General Staff was still viewed with a degree of enmity by some of the elderly die-hards, and by some members of Congress. Nevertheless, it was a far cry from the ineptitude of 1898 to General Scott's firm order to The Quartermaster General to go out at once and buy motor trucks, with no "back talk" or argument from The Quartermaster General himself.

Once an adequate number of motor vehicles had been procured, the serious hardships of the Punitive Expedition were over, although it must be admitted that the soldiers and officers never received the comforts and amenities of the American Expeditionary Forces in either World War, or in the wars that followed in Korea and Vietnam. But because of the carefully, although hastily, organized Columbus base, and the reforms of the early years of the twentieth century, adequate supplies flowed in a never-ending stream from the Border to American soldiers scattered over a hundred thousand square miles of hostile and forbidding territory.

NOTES

1. Roy E. Stivison and Della Mavity McDonnell, "When Villa Raided Columbus," *New Mexico Magazine*, XXVIII (Dec., 1950), pp. 41, 43.
2. *Foreign Relations, 1916*, p. 483.

3. Hugh Lenox Scott, *Some Memories of a Soldier* (New York, 1928), p. 519.

4. *Foreign Relations, 1916*, p. 484.

5. *Ibid.*, p. 486.

6. *Ibid.*, p. 493.

7. *Ibid.*, pp. 486–89; Scott to Funston, in the John J. Pershing Papers, Manuscript Division, Library of Congress, dated Mar. 17, 1916.

8. George Brydges Rodney, *As a Cavalryman Remembers* (Caldwell, Id., 1944), p. 250.

9. *Ibid.*, pp. 250–51. Col. H. D. Queen, U.S.A., Ret., who was then a sergeant in the 10th Cavalry, informs the writer that while the regiment was at Hereford a meteor of unusual size and brilliance flashed across the sky, startling the men and frightening the horses. Some of the more superstitious probably took it as an omen.

10. Rodney, *op. cit.*, pp. 254–56.

11. *Ibid.* The Rev. John Jeter, of Vallejo, Cal., who was then a corporal in the 10th Cavalry, informed the writer that the main body marched from Fort Huachuca without overcoats.

12. Thomas Cottam Romney, *The Mormon Colonies in Mexico* (Salt Lake City, 1938), pp. 240–41.

13. Information given to the writer by Col. Carroll A. Bagby, U.S.A., Ret., who was then a lieutenant in the 16th Infantry.

14. Tompkins, *op. cit.*, pp. 74–75; Rodney, *op. cit.*, pp. 254–56; Maj. Richard H. McMaster, 4th Field Artillery, "An Artilleryman in Mexico, 1916. Extracts from the [unpublished] Diary of Major R. H. McMaster, 4th F.A.," entries for Mar. 19 and 21, 1916. In addition to the above citations, further evidence of the rugged character of the march into Mexico is found in the diaries and journals of Colonel Jerome W. Howe, U.S. Army, Ret., and in a narrative of his personal experiences in the expedition given to the writer by Dr. Thorne Dueul, of the Illinois State Museum. Dr. Dueul was then a lieutenant in the 10th Cavalry. The late Col. Thomas L. Sherburne once remarked to the writer, "I have been in three wars, and for unmitigated hardship, the Punitive Expedition was the worst of all."

15. Statement to the writer by the Rev. John Jeter; Jerome W. Howe, "Chasing Villa," *The Journal of the Worcester Polytechnic Institute*, XIX (July, 1916), 380. Colonel Howe was then a lieutenant in the 10th Cavalry and was acting as aide-de-camp to the Brigade Commander, Col. George A. Dodd, 7th Cavalry.

16. Maj. G. L. Van Norman, U.S.A.R., Ret., in a letter to an unnamed friend, a copy of which he gave to the writer.

17. George Francis Brimlow, *Cavalryman Out of the West. Life of General William Carey Brown* (Caldwell, Idaho, 1944), pp. 352–53.

18. Vernon G. Olsmith, *Recollections of an Old Soldier* (San Antonio, Tex., 1963), p. 14.

19. War Diary, 1st Aero Squadron, entries for Mar. 12–18, 1916. The writer obtained a copy of this war diary through the courtesy

of Colonel John W. Cotton, U.S. Army, Ret., who was the sergeant major of the 1st Aero Squadron.

20. Scott, *op. cit.*, pp. 530–31.
21. War Diary, 1st Aero Squadron, entry for Mar. 18, 1916.
22. "Report of the Quartermaster General," *War Department Annual Reports, 1916*, I, 440–49.
23. Thomas and Allen, *Official History*, Chap. V, p. 4.
24. "Report of the Chief of Staff," *War Department Annual Reports, 1916*, Vol. I, 201; also "Report of the Chief Signal Officer," pp. 882–83.

CHAPTER 12

The Three Columns

THE ACTIVE CAMPAIGN to corner Villa's band could not stand still while supply difficulties were being ironed out in Washington, San Antonio and Columbus. In spite of the hardships and discomforts to which the troops were subjected, the search went on. One of the major military difficulties was the impossibility of gaining reliable information. From the start most Mexicans were resentful of United States troops being on the soil of their country. This was especially true in the state of Chihuahua, where a large part of the people were Villista in sympathy, and most of those who were not pro-Villa were afraid to give the Americans information, even if they were willing. Probably most anti-Villa Mexicans hated the Americans more than they hated Villa.

Not only was it impossible to obtain information about Villa, but it was almost equally difficult to obtain information about the country. There were virtually no maps, and the few that were available were highly inaccurate. The only reliable guides were occasional American cattlemen or prospectors, and a number of Mormons from the colonies of northern Chihuahua. In the main, it was necessary to depend on Mexican guides, whose reliability, at best, was very uncertain. The situation was far different from what it would be today, when highly accurate "photomaps" could be ready within a few days at most.

Before proceeding further, it is desirable to challenge or refute certain myths that have grown up about Villa and the

Part of
Chihuahua,
Mexico

0 10 20 30 40 50 Miles

Columbus, N.M.
Palomas
El Paso
Juarez
Culberson
Ranch
Vado de
Fusiles
Lake Guzmán
Guzmán
Lake Santa Maria
Carriza Spgs.
Ojitos
Ascensión
Ojo Frederico
Vuelto de Alamos
Colonia Dublan
Casas Grandes
Corralitos
Lake Patos
Ahumada
Carrizal
RIO GRANDE
CHIHUAHUA
TEXAS
Corrales
Pearson
El Rucio
Galeana
Angostura
San Miguel
El Valle
San Lorenzo
MEXICAN
NATIONAL R.R.
SIERRA
MADRE
Rio Casas
Rio Santa Maria
Rio Carmen
Cumbre
Colonia
Chuichupa
Grandes
Musica
Las Cruces
San Largo
Chaves
Animas
Namaquipa
Santa Catarina
MEXICAN
NORTHWEST R.R.
San Geronimo Ranch
Santa Ana
Providencia
Tepehuanes
Agua Caliente
Rubio
KANSAS CI.
MEXICO & ORIENT R.R.
Antonio Ranch
Bachiniva
Sta. Ysabel
Chihuahua
Guerrero
La Junta
Minaca
San Antonio
Arisiachio
Tomochic
Cusihuiriachic
Carreyas
Yoquiyo
Ojo Azules
Satevó
Sta. Rosalia
Tres Hermanes
S. Francisco de Borja
Sta. Ana
Ojitos
Sauz
SIERRA TARAHUMARE
Los Extados
Naica
S. Jose del Sitio
Valle de Zaragose
Sta. Cruz
Sapien
Doredo
S. Matio
Sta. Cruz
of Villegas
Jiminez
Parral
Agua Caliente
OLD BOUNDARY (1916)
DURANGO

Punitive Expedition and have become so much a part of the folk-lore of the time that they are accepted unquestioningly by reputable historians, as well as by more "popular" writers. It is almost an article of faith that the Punitive Expedition was a ponderous, slowly moving column, hampered and handicapped by its wagons and wheeled artillery, and about which the swiftly moving Villista guerrillas rode at will. Typical of such opinions is the following:

> Pancho Villa cannot keep away from the Expedition. It fascinates him. He can see it coming in that wide land a hundred miles. The order, method, discipline, transportation of the commissary, ammunition, water, are matters he wants to study; also he covets those new Springfield rifles! Expert at taking cover, knowing the country as a man might know his own yard, Pancho Villa and his men ride alternately point, flank and drag on the toiling column.[1]

Another writer who was much more familiar with Mexico than the one just quoted, has this to say: "Villa and his seasoned rebels and his intimacy with the hills, against Pershing and several thousand lumbering, cannon-hampered recruits, playing Mexican mountain cat to American domestic rat. The battles were a farce. Villa would squat in high caves and review the Pershing army regularly."[2]

Such examples could be multiplied but would serve no useful purpose. They are simply not true. As for "Mexican mountain cat to American domestic rat," the actual situation was the direct opposite. It was a game of hare and hounds, with Villa and his bands in the uncomfortable position of the hare.

After leaving Palomas the eastern column continued its march southward. The day's march was uneventful, except for finding the body of a man, evidently an American, beside the road. He had been blindfolded, with his hands tied behind him, and shot through the back of the head. The force paused long enough to bury him and "murmur a prayer for the repose of his soul."[3] On March 17 a message arrived from General Pershing, directing the column to join him in the vicinity of Casas Grandes, as he needed the wagon companies. The column reached the Casas Grandes River on March 19. Here, for the first time since leav-

ing Columbus, there was water, and to spare. Soldiers and officers splashed in the shallow water, enjoying their first bath since
leaving Columbus and the last that most of them would have
for many a day. Some of them even washed their underclothes.
Across the river, opposite the bathing place, there was a heavy
thicket that might easily conceal Villista snipers. To discourage
any who might be lurking there, two field guns were rolled to
the riverbank, pointed directly into the brush, and loaded. If
any Villistas were there, they did not reveal themselves.[4] On
March 20 the eastern column arrived at Colonia Dublán, where
General Pershing, his staff and some units from the western
column awaited the force.

General Pershing had received information that Villa was at
San Miguel, some fifty or sixty miles to the south, where he was
said to be commandeering horses and supplies and "drafting"
inhabitants into his ranks. Pershing decided to send three fairly
small, highly maneuverable, fast-moving cavalry columns, to
march on roughly parallel routes, so that Villa could be intercepted if he moved either eastward, toward the railroad, or westward toward Sonora. The first force to move out was the 7th
Cavalry, under immediate command of Colonel James B. Erwin.
The 7th marched out from Colonia Dublán late in the afternoon, March 18. On March 21 Pershing ordered Colonel Dodd,
who was in command of the 2d Brigade, but was still assigned to the 7th Cavalry, to rejoin his regiment and take command of the whole operation. Dodd overtook the regiment a few
miles south of Galeana but did not supplant Erwin as regimental
commander. To coordinate and direct the operations of the three
columns was full-time duty in itself. About noon, on March 22,
as the force was passing the little town of El Valle, where there
was a small Carranza garrison, Dodd sent an officer into the
town with a message, asking for an interview with Colonel Salas,
the Carranzista commander.

When Dodd and Salas met, a short time later, the Mexican's
attitude, at first, seemed to preclude any possibility of cooperation. Curtly, he asked Dodd by what authority American troops
were in Mexico. Dodd showed him a copy of the letter that
presumably authorized American entry into the country. Salas

remarked that he had already seen the document, but he had not received it through proper channels, from his military and civil superiors. Although Salas' attitude, at first, seemed to be unfriendly, he soon thawed, and in the conversation that followed he frankly admitted that he had been badly defeated by Villa only a few days before. His troops had been driven through Cruces to El Valle, where he was occupying a defensive position in anticipation of another Villista attack. Salas added the information, voluntarily, that Villa was at Namiquipa and had said that he intended to remain there until driven out.[5] When the interview ended, Salas sent one of his staff officers to accompany Dodd's party through a defile that was lined on both sides with Carranzista soldiers.

On the next day, March 23, the 7th Cavalry marched hours before daylight. The town of Cruces was bypassed at a considerable distance, for it was reputed to be a hotbed of Villista sympathy, and Dodd hoped to pass unobserved. His plan was to surround Namiquipa at dawn the next morning, after spending the night in a concealed bivouac several miles distant. But before the regiment reached the place tentatively selected for the bivouac, the American civilian scouts, who had been cautiously reconnoitering the town, brought word that Villa was not there. On March 20, shortly after he defeated Colonel Salas, he had been, in turn, defeated and driven from Namiquipa by Colonel Cano. What was more, the scouts reported that Villa had been badly wounded in the fight.

There was no information on the direction the Villistas had taken from Namiquipa, but Dodd picked up a vague rumor that Villa had passed through Oso Cañon. The men of the 7th Cavalry, from the Old Man himself down to the newest recruit, were bitterly disappointed that they had not caught Villa at Namiquipa, but everyone was so tired that a few hours' rest at the nearest water point was more than welcome. While soldiers and horses were resting, Dodd sent a message to General Pershing, relaying the scanty information he had; he sent another message to Colonel Cano, requesting that the Carranzistas block the mountain passes while the Americans tried to place themselves south or west of the quarry.

Meanwhile, one of the civilian scout-guides, a man named Barker, had gone boldly into Namiquipa, where he was apparently well known. He returned to the bivouac, several miles south of the town, with the information that three of Villa's most trusted subordinates had left the town with their chief. They were Hernandez, Cervantes and Tarongo. Pablo Lopez, the perpetrator of the Santa Ysabel atrocity, was wounded at Columbus and was reported to be hiding somewhere in the mountains. Candelario Cervantes was the actual leader of the assault at Columbus.

The next morning, March 24, 1916, somewhat to the amazement of the Americans, three Carranzista soldiers arrived, bearing a message from Colonel Brown, of the 10th Cavalry. He was at Babicora, a ranch belonging to William Randolph Hearst. He had received information, on fairly good authority, that Villa had fled from Namiquipa toward San Geronimo and might have gone even farther. Brown added that Villa was expecting reinforcements to join him at a point some twenty-three miles east of Namiquipa and that Colonel Cano would move a Carranzista force at once to Santo Tomás and from there march to block Villa's southern exit.

The 7th Cavalry's march on March 24 was brutal. A gale was blowing that seemed to come directly from the North Pole. The road was nothing more than a rough trail winding up and down the steep, rocky hills. Men shivered and tried to keep warm; horses turned their tails to the blast, and put their heads down. Scout Tracy, who had been off on an undisclosed mission assigned by Colonel Dodd, rejoined during the day with information that confirmed what the three Carranzista messengers had brought from Colonel Brown. At dusk, the tired, miserable soldiers made an uncomfortable bivouac in a cañon on the eastern slope of the Sierra Madres. In spite of the weather, they slept the sleep of utter exhaustion, but before daybreak the next morning, March 25, 1916, they were aroused, saddled the shivering horses, and began the steep climb westward. They were in the same general area in which, almost forty years before, the Apache scouts and the troopers of Crook's and Miles's forces had hunted Geronimo.

Like their predecessors of the past century, Dodd's men found
that the trail upward was so steep, narrow and rough that it was
necessary to dismount and lead—a measure that also conserved
the waning strength of the underfed and overworked animals.
The hardships of the day were momentarily forgotten, however,
when the tired force arrived at Babicora, the Hearst ranch. The
manager, Maximiliano Marques, who was also a Carranzista
colonel, proved cordial and hospitable. There was fodder for the
animals, corn and hay to fill their bellies. There were tortillas
and frijoles and other things for the men to eat. While they
were still at Babicora, late in the afternoon of the twenty-fifth,
an officer-messenger arrived from General Pershing with information about Villa that Dodd knew already. The messenger
also had information that the 10th Cavalry was marching on
Chavez.

The marches of the next two days were easier, except for short
stretches on the road. On the twenty-sixth a Carranzista messenger brought word that the 10th Cavalry had searched Oso
Cañon and found no indication that Villa had passed through,
as had been reported. By this time, Dodd had come to the conclusion that Villa was headed for Guerrero. Accordingly, he
ordered that the march be continued toward Bachineva. During
the day, on March 28, a Carranzista officer brought information
that Villa had turned eastward and was now twenty-five miles
to the east, on the Northwestern Railroad. This was at such
variance with what Dodd had already concluded that he paid
little attention to it. Information from a Mexican who was seized
and questioned a little later in the day seemed much more probable—that Villa had been at Bachineva two or three days before
and that he had been in a battle at Guerrero only the day before.

Just before the American column arrived at Bachineva an
airplane, 1st Lieutenant Herbert A. Dargue piloting, skidded
to a landing alongside the column. Dargue brought a message
from General Pershing, saying that Major Robert L. Howze,
with a squadron of the 11th Cavalry, was on the march to
relieve the 7th Cavalry. Dodd was directed to go into camp
near Namiquipa and give his exhausted horses and soldiers a
chance to recuperate. General Pershing, as an old cavalryman,

was well aware of the strain to which they had been subjected.

There was some indignant muttering in the 7th, a regiment always noted for its *esprit de corps*. Officers and soldiers were alike slightly irritated, and Dodd, feeling that Villa was within striking distance, was reluctant to let go. Several days must elapse before Howze could overtake the 7th. He decided to continue. At Bachineva he was informed that Villa was still at Guerrero, with five or six hundred men. The report that Villa had been wounded was confirmed. Dodd sent a message back to General Pershing saying that he was sure that Villa was near; he would continue until he made contact and then attack, unless Howze arrived sooner.

Except for the few hours at the Hearst ranch at Babicora, the entire march had been, so far, a grim experience. Men and horses were suffering from inadequate food and from the intense cold of "tropical" Mexico. Nightly, the men's canteens were frozen solid; icicles formed on the men's beards. Dodd had already found it necessary to leave at Santa Ana a number of men and horses that were incapable of continuing the march, along with his only medical officer, to care for them. Between Bachineva and Guerrero, where Villa was supposed to be, lay a high range of mountains that were unknown to Dodd's American guides. To obtain the services of a *reliable* Mexican guide was impossible. Not even the offer of a large sum of jingling silver money would tempt a single citizen of Bachineva to admit that he knew anything at all about the routes to Guerrero. Possibly violating President Wilson's policies, Dodd forcibly impressed two local men, trusting to their fear of immediate execution to keep them in line.

The column slipped quietly out of Bachineva at eleven o'clock at night. It was an arctic night. Officers and men rode with their blankets wrapped about them, like so many Indians. In spite of the cold, at the five-minute rest halts each hour, men dropped to the ground and fell asleep so soundly that they had to be shaken and even kicked into wakefulness at the end of the five minutes. Hour after weary hour the march went on. Whether deliberately, or from ignorance, no one can say, the impressed Mexican guides led the force by a long, roundabout path. Before daylight, the guides' scanty knowledge and their courage evaporated simultaneously, and there was a delay while other local men were found and pressed into service. Dodd had hoped to be able to attack at daybreak, but it was six thirty, well after the sun rose, before Guerrero came into view.[6]

The town of Guerrero lies in the bottom of the Guerrero River Valley, walled on the east and west by high escarpments. On the east, the direction from which the Americans came, the escarpment is so steep that the town cannot be seen until one is almost directly over it. The bluffs are cut by deep, wooded *arroyos* cutting far back into the mesa. The road from the east winds down a hogback between two *arroyos*, but the impressed guides did not lead the Americans to it. Instead, the force lost precious time "heading" the *arroyos*, hunting for a practicable trail down into the valley, where numbers of armed Mexicans could be seen.

A path down the bluff was finally found, and at about eight o'clock, Dodd was ready to launch his attack. He gave his orders orally. The 2d Squadron, under Major Edwin B. Winans, would descend into the valley, cross the river, and cut off any attempt by the Villistas to escape into the gullies and ravines on the western side. The remainder of the regiment would attack directly from the east. As the first troops of Winans' squadron started down the slope, the Villistas became aware of their approach. Captain Samuel F. Dallam, whose troop was at the tail of the column, could see mounted men galloping out of the town, heading for the eastern side of the valley. Dallam swung his troop toward the town, to prevent the escape of more fugitives. At this moment, firing from the head of the column showed that the battle had started. Major Winans, galloping by, approved Dallam's action. Between Dallam and the town there was a deep, narrow ravine, which was a natural exit. Dallam's men blocked it; a few minutes later a large number of men tried to rush through, led by an officer. A blast of fire from Dallam's men decimated the men and killed the officer, who proved to be no less a person than General Hernandez, one of Villa's right-hand men and the commander of the Villista force.

Meanwhile, the rest of the 7th Cavalry, still on the mesa, was moving north, delayed by the *arroyos* extending deep into the land. It was obvious that the Villistas were trying to escape. Dodd's immediate purpose became that of preventing their escape. Several troops were dismounted and the machine guns set up, opening fire at the fugitives at long range. Many of them could be seen running northward out of the town and then turning east, although the Americans were east of them. Lieutenant Colonel Selah R. H. Tompkins (an elder brother of Major Frank Tompkins, who has been mentioned often) hurried with one troop to cut them off before they could escape into the hills. A few minutes later he was reinforced by the machine guns and three more troops. He was too late to be able to head off the fugitives, but he pressed the pursuit. The jaded horses, however, could not be moved faster than the trot, even under whip and spur.[7]

During the next three or four hours there were numerous exchanges of fire with scattered bodies of the enemy, who made no serious stand. The only thing the Villistas wanted was to get away, as far and as fast as possible. By noon it was apparent that they had split into such small fragments that the band was disrupted beyond the possibility of immediate reassembly. Shortly after noon, the 7th Cavalry was brought together and a count was taken. The American casualties amounted to only five men wounded, none of them seriously. On the other hand, thirty-five dead Villistas were counted, and there were undoubtedly others scattered in the brush, unseen by the Americans. Inevitably, the enemy must have had a number of men wounded, but none were seen or captured. The spoils that fell into American hands included two machine guns, forty-four rifles, thirteen horses and twenty-three mules. The 7th Cavalry had present in this fight a total strength of 370 officers and men; the Villistas are variously estimated at from 500 to 600 men.[8]

At this point we must digress briefly and review what is known about the movements of the elusive Pancho Villa himself. After the Columbus raid he seems to have moved steadily and swiftly south until he reached San Isidro, the point from which he launched his attack upon Guerrero. At San Isidro he was reinforced by General Nicolas Hernandez (or Fernandez) with an undetermined number of men, and the ensuing attack upon Guerrero was successful. There is some doubt about when and where Villa was wounded. As noted earlier, the wound was at first reported to have been incurred in the fight with Colonel Cano's force, but it is also said that he received the injury at Guerrero. For reasons that need not be discussed, the latter account seems more probable. That he was really wounded seriously was confirmed at Guerrero when the Americans interrogated a doctor who had treated him; one leg was badly shattered by a shot. His hard core of devoted "Dorados" carried him out of the town only a short time before the Americans appeared on the mesa above. But for the delay caused by the ignorance (or deliberate misleading) of the impressed Mexican guides, it is extremely likely that Villa would have been taken or killed that morning. His Dorados took him to a cave, well hidden in the mountains but from which, it seems, it was possible for him to view much of the valley below. Here, according to the weight of evidence, he spent most of the next two months.

Villa was in great pain much of the time, and at times he was sure he was about to die. His iron constitution, the devoted care of two or three men whom he kept at his side, aided, possibly, by the simple, country remedies they applied, finally triumphed, and he began to walk, aided at first by a cane.

During this period his whereabouts were completely unknown. Rumors circulated, possibly started by his own people, but carefully fostered by the Carranzistas, that he was dead. If the Americans could be convinced of Villa's death, they would have no excuse to linger in Mexico.[9]

The fight at Guerrero was the first contact between the Punitive Expedition and Villa's forces. Their feeble resistance, together with the element of surprise, even though the surprise was not as complete as Dodd had hoped for, gave the measure of their combat quality against American Regulars. In fact, the Villistas offered almost no resistance: their one ambition was to escape. Their fire was wild and uncoordinated, their cohesion almost nonexistent.

In addition to the complete smashing of the Villista band at Guerrero, the fight had an incidental effect. Colonel Dodd was nearing the age of retirement. As a result of the Guerrero fight, he pinned on the stars of a brigadier general and spent the last few weeks of his active service as second in command to General Pershing.

The other two forks of the trident were from the 10th Cavalry. One force was the 1st Squadron of the regiment, commanded by Major Elwood Evans; the other comprised the remainder of the regiment, consisting of the regimental headquarters, the 2d Squadron, and the Machine Gun Platoon, under direct command of the regimental commander, Colonel William C. Brown. The plan was for both forces to leave Colonia Dublán by rail; Colonel Brown's column was to detrain at Cuevitas and march from there to San Miguel, one of the several places where Villa was rumored to be. Major Evans' force would continue by rail to Las Varas, near Madera, there detrain and march south to Babicora, to prevent Villa's escape in that direction, or to cooperate with the other forces, as occasion might demand.

The rail journey was expected to take no more than a few hours. A train consisting of twenty-five freight and stock cars, with three flatcars, was assembled. The cars were veterans of several years of warfare. Some of them had holes burned through the floors, where the Mexican *soldaderas* (soldiers' women) had built fires and cooked for their men; other cars had no floors at all, and many were without doors. The single locomotive to haul the train was also a war-weary veteran that had seen better days. It was a wood-burner and consumed staggering amounts of fuel. The soldiers labored for hours, improvising repairs, constructing crude doors, making floors and otherwise making the ancient relics usable. They tore down part of the cattle pens at Colonia Dublán to fill the engine's tender with firewood. By herculean efforts the repairs were finished, the train loaded, and the command entrained at five o'clock in the afternoon, March 19, 1916. Thirty minutes later the locomotive wheezed and puffed, and the train moved slowly ahead.

It was planned to pause at Casas Grandes and load more firewood, but the engineer refused to stop. He feared trouble with the Carranzista garrison. At Don Luis, several miles beyond Casas Grandes, he applied the brakes, and the soldiers dismounted and pulled down the stock pens for fuel. At eight o'clock the engineer again stopped the train; he had just discovered that the water was dangerously low. The locomotive was uncoupled and rolled ahead to Pearson for water. This consumed several hours. The engine was again coupled to the train, and chugged on without further incident to a point past Pearson, where, for reasons that are not clear, the train again stopped. This time Colonel Brown mounted into the cab, and the engine returned to Pearson, where, after some time and effort, Brown located and aroused the superintendent. The superintendent was amazed. He had received no information at all about the Americans' train! Brown tried to get two locomotives, but the superintendent refused; he could not take the responsibility without instructions from higher up. At four o'clock in the morning the train was once more put into motion, but two miles north of El Rucio the train crew announced that the train could go no farther. The load was too heavy for the engine. The train was then split into two parts. The first half, carrying Colonel Brown's force, crept along to El Rucio, where Brown ordered detrainment. The locomotive then wheezed back to the halting point to pick up Major Evans' part.

Before tracing Colonel Brown's movements, it will be worth while to follow briefly the journey of Major Evans' 1st Squadron. Several miles past El Rucio, where Brown had detrained, the locomotive again ran out of fuel. The soldiers got off, and for an hour pulled up mesquite roots and scavenged anything else that was combustible. But the locomotive was not only out of fuel; by this time it was out of water again. It returned to El Rucio, filled its tanks and returned, but this effort had used up all the fuel. Finally, with its tanks and tender full, the train crept ahead once again. It seemed that trials and tribulations might be over, but instead there was tragedy ahead. As the train crawled up a steep switchback near the Cumbre tunnel, there was suddenly a crash and rumbling roar as the worn-out roadbed gave way, and the two last cars jerked loose and rolled down a steep bank. Eleven soldiers were injured, two of whom died within a few hours.[10] Somehow, the train was reconstituted. The injured were bedded down in the caboose, attended by Sergeant Doudy, of the Hospital Corps (as it was then called), although he was painfully injured himself. The train moved slowly for a few miles more, but at Musica the antique locomotive gave up the ghost and refused to move farther. Evans was forced to detrain, just twenty-four hours after he was supposed to arrive at his detraining point, and miles short of where he hoped to be.

Colonel Brown's force, after detraining at El Rucio, fed and watered the horses, and the men had a hot meal, the last they were to have for many days. At one o'clock in the afternoon the horses were saddled and the march for San Miguel started. The trail (it could not be called a road) was narrow, steep and rocky. Several hours were lost during the afternoon when a packmule strayed from the packtrain and evaded all efforts to capture it. Late in the afternoon, when the mule and its precious pack were safely recovered, two Mexicans were encountered on the trail. They were questioned and assured the Americans that they knew nothing at all about Pancho Villa. Because it was patently impossible to reach San Miguel that day, Colonel Brown ordered the force to camp for the night. After starting early the next morning (March 21), the column approached San Miguel at noon. The place (which was a ranch) was carefully surrounded and a patrol sent forward to search. There were no Villistas. The manager said that he had heard that Villa had been seen at El Valle two days earlier. Other than that, he insisted, he knew nothing.

That night, after the force had settled into a bivouac, an officer-messenger arrived from Colonel Erwin, with information about the 7th Cavalry's position and movements. Brown sent a return message, in which he suggested that the 7th continue southward, while the 10th marched for Chavez. At Chavez, late in the afternoon of March 23, the 10th Cavalry found a fortunate abundance of good hay and corn, and the hungry animals were able to fill their bellies. The men were not quite so fortunate. They had left Colonia Dublán with only two days' rations, and these were now exhausted. It is not mentioned in any of the published accounts, but it was probably at Chavez that Colonel Brown commenced reaching into his own pocket to get food for his men by purchasing several cattle for slaughter. In fact, beginning at Chavez, for more than thirty days the men and officers of the 10th Cavalry literally lived off the country. Not a single wagon or packmule ever caught up with them. They subsisted on whatever they could forage in a war-devastated country.

In the meantime Colonel Brown had learned from the officers of the Carranzista garrison at San José de Babicora that Villa had been defeated by Colonel Cano and also that Villa was supposed to be at Namiquipa. On March 23, while the column marched for El Toro, Brown himself rode into San José de Babicora to confer with the officers of the garrison, who proved to be courteous and friendly. With their assistance, he was able to send a telegram to Dodd (via Pershing's headquarters), giving his own location and the latest information (or rumor) about Villa. On March 24 Major Evans' force rejoined the regiment, and on that day and the next, Brown was able to confer with Colonel Cano, at Namiquipa. At Namiquipa he ordered a halt of several hours while his supply officer collected flour, corn, beans and forage, all of which were paid for from Brown's personal funds.

By this time, in addition to being hungry, the 10th Cavalry troopers were suffering from the harsh climate and the hardships of the march as much as were their compatriots of the 7th Cavalry. They had encountered the same bitter winter winds and alkaline dust. Lips were swollen and bleeding, faces and hands were chapped and raw.

Colonel Brown suggested to Cano that the Carranzistas scout for and locate Villa; the Americans would then be the striking force to attack. Cano agreed readily, and Brown decided to give his men and animals a day of rest, while the Mexicans pinned Villa down. But at the end of the day, March 26, there had not been a single report from Cano. On the twenty-seventh, Brown again visited Cano and came away with the conviction that the Carranzista, despite his promises, had not sent out a patrol or scout. Cano had deluded the Americans with promises that he had no intention of keeping.

Having learned thus that the Carranzistas were not to be relied upon, Brown resumed his southward march. He planned to leave at three thirty in the morning, in order to surround Santa Catalina (or Caterina) at daybreak, but a raging prairie fire that threatened the camp, at one o'clock in the morning, delayed the start. The column arrived at Santa Catalina at six o'clock. Not a Villista was found there, but there was information that Villa had been at Rubio on March 26, two days earlier.

At Santa Catalina, Brown detached Evans' squadron, with instructions to march eastward to Tepehuanes, then south, paralleling the main column. At Tepehuanes, Evans found a workable telephone system, connecting the principal ranchos of the region. He was able to get Brown on the wire and received further orders to march the next day for Rubio. Using the telephone line as a guide, Evans marched south, carefully searching all the villages and ranches en route, without finding any trace of the enemy. He did, however, pick up the information that Villa had moved toward Guerrero on March 25 and had been badly wounded. This seems to have been the first information received about Villa's wound.

Before leaving Santa Catalina, Brown ordered the telephone lines cut, to insure that no information about the Americans would be sent ahead. The march from Santa Catalina to La Quemada was uneventful, but the road was unusually rough and rocky, even for Mexico. Brown later told Colonel Dodd that it was the worst he had ever seen. There were no Villistas at La Quemada, but it was found later that, as the Americans approached, a lone Villista officer had slipped out and hid himself in the brush on the far side. Brown decided to remain at La Quemada until March 30, in order to grope for more definite and satisfactory information than he had been able, so far, to obtain, and also to give the men and animals a few hours of badly needed rest. As he informed Dodd, "No use killing horses running aimlessly until more definite information is secured."[11]

From La Quemada, the 10th Cavalry marched to San Diego del Monte, where Evans' squadron rejoined and Brown learned of Villa's wound. Brown sent two soldier-messengers, accompanied by a Mexican guide, to take this important bit of information to Dodd. In spite of the dangerous character of their mission, riding through unknown country that, presumably, was populated by men who would cut an American throat with real pleasure, the two messengers reached their destination without adventure—at least, they never mentioned any. An attempt to communicate with General Pershing by telegraph failed. Lieutenant Joseph F. Richmond, with two or three soldiers as escort, rode to San Antonio, the nearest point where there was a telegraph station. Richmond was compelled to return without having sent the message; the railroad was blocked and the telegraph was inoperative.

The campaign of the three columns may be said to have ended when Brown decided to concentrate his regiment at La Quemada and to remain there for a short time. One phase of the campaign of the Punitive Expedition was now over, and another about to start. One of the three columns had struck the enemy a devastating blow. The other two saw no combat, but that is not to say that their efforts were useless. Their presence was a guarantee that Villa's band would not escape to the north or east. Their presence, also, undoubtedly had a quieting effect on the pro-Villa part of the local population, who might, otherwise, have engaged in sniping or other guerrilla activities against the Americans. And finally, since Villa's actual whereabouts were completely unknown until Dodd decided that he was at Guerrero, the efforts of the 10th Cavalry showed positively where Villa was *not* located. In war, negative information is often as revealing and useful as positive intelligence. Discovering where the enemy is not helps point to where he is. Those historians who believe that a military force has done nothing useful unless it fights spectacular battles are wrong. The two columns of the 10th Cavalry played an important part in the campaign.

NOTES

1. Edgcumb Pinchon, *Viva Villa! A Recovery of the Real Pancho Villa —Peon—Bandit—Soldier—Patriot* (New York, 1933), p. 341.
2. Anita Brenner, *Idols Behind Altars* (New York, 1929), pp. 211–12.
3. Tompkins, *op. cit.*, p. 75. Col. Harrison C. Brown, U.S.A., Ret., of San Antonio, Texas, who was a lieutenant in the 16th Infantry, in a letter to the writer, tells of the same incident.

4. *Ibid.*, p. 76.

5. *Ibid.*, p. 79; George R. Cole, "Brush Fire War, 1916 Style," unpublished thesis (M.A.), Louisiana State College, Lake Charles, Louisiana, 1963, p. 77.

6. Tompkins, *op. cit.*, p. 84; Col. Jerome W. Howe, U.S.A., Ret., "Chasing Villa," *Journal of the Worcester Polytechnic Institute*, XIX (July, 1916), 383; also, Col. Howe's unpublished memoirs, "My Military Career, 1909–1924," pp. 32–33. Howe was Dodd's aide-de-camp during the campaign.

7. Tompkins, *op. cit.*, p. 87; Col. Dodd's *Report*, pp. 14–15. Lt. Col. Selah R. H. Tompkins, familiarly and affectionately known known throughout the cavalry as "Tommy" Tompkins, was one of the most colorful characters ever to wear the United States uniform. He was known especially for the originality and vehemence of his profanity.

8. Tompkins, *op. cit.*, pp. 78–87. Maj. Edwin B. Winans, upon whose squadron the brunt of the fighting fell, later became a major general and held, among other assignments, that of Superintendent, United States Military Academy.

9. *Ibid.*, p. 87; Gustavo Casasola, *Historia Gráfica de la Revolución*, 3 vols. (Mexico City, nd.), III, 1023–24. Gen. Bernardo Mena Brito advances the startling theory that during the period of Villa's disappearance, he was actually in Washington, conspiring with President Wilson! See Bernardo Mena Brito, *El Lugarteniente Gris de Pancho Villa* (Mexico City, 1938), p. 288.

10. Tompkins, *op. cit.*, pp. 89–91, 95. In a personal interview, the Rev. John Jeter, of Vallejo, Cal., who was a corporal in Troop C, 10th Cavalry, in the Punitive Expedition, informed the writer that the bank over which the cars rolled was at least fifty yards high. Jeter was on the part of the train that was not wrecked and helped take the injured from the wrecked cars.

11. Tompkins, *op. cit.*, p. 93.

CHAPTER 13

Flying Columns—Manhunt
in Chihuahua

G ENERAL PERSHING'S ORGANIZATION of the search for
Villistas was essentially the same as that used by Crook
and Miles in the hunt for hostile Apaches—small, highly maneuverable forces that could move swiftly and, in a pinch, live off
the country for days, barren and wasted though it was. Simultaneously with the three forward columns, other forces moved
out from the base area around Colonia Dublán to comb the
country, prevent Villa's escape from the regions where he was
believed to be, and reinforce the advance columns if necessary.
The operations of these smaller forces, usually referred to as the
"flying columns," may, for convenience in discussion, be considered as a distinct phase of the Punitive Expedition. It must be
understood that there was actually no sharp line of distinction
between their activities and those of the three major forces; there
was no line of geographical demarcation, nor was there any
delineation in time. The two phases of the hunt in Chihuahua
overlapped and intermingled. And the story of the experiences
of the officers and soldiers in the flying columns does not differ
from what has already been related in recounting the experiences
of Dodd's and Brown's troops.

There were four such forces. The first to march from the
base was a small column consisting of two troops of the 13th
Cavalry, totaling twelve officers and seventy-five soldiers, commanded by Major Elmer Lindsley. Lindsley received orders late
in the afternoon of March 20, 1916, to march at once for Chui-

chupa, seventy or eighty miles distant, on the other side of the Continental Divide. On reaching Chuichupa, he would ascertain if Villa had passed that way. If so, Lindsley would pursue and attack at the first opportunity. If not, he would endeavor to locate Villa by patrolling and by contact with other American forces.

The squadron (for such it actually was) was allowed no transportation—not even a single packmule. Nothing was to be taken that could not be carried on the saddles. And from this occurred an initial difficulty. Each trooper was issued five days' rations and grain for his horse. In several regiments, including the 13th Cavalry, there were two types of saddle equipment in use in 1916. About half of the men had the old and proven McClellan saddle, but the others had an experimental type, designed in 1912 or 1913, commonly known as the Whitman saddle. The men who had the Whitman found it almost impossible to cram ten packages of hard bread, plus their bacon, coffee and sugar into their saddlebags, whereas the McClellan saddlebags easily held the rations, and the men's mess kits, spare horseshoes and currycombs as well.[1]

Lindsley marched at eight o'clock at night; the force climbed hundreds of feet to the top of the Continental Divide and bivouacked the next day in a deep cañon on the other side. After another night march, across another mountain range, the column arrived at Chuichupa shortly after noon on March 22. The two night marches were almost replicas of the march made by the 7th Cavalry in its night approach toward Guerrero. The nights were bitter cold, with temperatures far below freezing; the trails were steep, rough, rocky and narrow. To add to the discomfort of many of the men, one of the troop commanders, to save weight, had ordered the shelter tents and slickers left behind. Not a single human being was encountered on the march, and not a head of cattle was seen. The whole region was blasted by war.

Chuichupa was an old Mormon colony that had been ravaged and abandoned early in the Revolution. It was found to be deserted and falling into ruin, with no signs that Villistas or anybody else had been there for a long time. Lindsley decided to remain there for two or three days while he sent patrols to investigate the surrounding country. Before the reconnaissance was complete, however, the troopers were beginning to run out of rations, so Lindsley varied the patrolling by sending out two or three hunting parties. One of them returned to camp triumphantly with a deer and a wild turkey. This was probably the last instance in which an American military unit has had to depend on game for food.

A patrol sent to Musica, twenty-five or thirty miles distant, almost miraculously established communication with headquarters by hitching a field buzzer onto the Mexican telegraph line. The first incoming message was for Lindsley to move on. There was an almost harrowing march of four days, part of it through a raging mountain blizzard that drove the snow and sleet with stinging force. The soldiers discovered a way to thaw themselves and keep warm at night. They dug slit trenches just large enough to enable a man to stretch out, filled them with brushwood, and set fire to the wood. When the fire burned itself out, the ashes and hot coals were raked away, and the men crawled in, huddling under their blankets and saddle blankets.

The squadron approached the ranch of San Miguel cautiously, prepared for a fight, but there were no Villistas at San Miguel. The manager and the *vaqueros* were friendly but extremely noncommittal when questioned about Villistas.[2] Only very scanty supplies were procurable at San Miguel, so Lindsley sent a strong patrol under command of an unnamed young lieutenant to El Valle, some thirty miles away, to search for food and forage. He found a strong American outpost at El Valle; he was unquestionably startled when no less a person than General Pershing himself suddenly appeared out of the darkness, unexpected and unannounced. Pershing questioned the lieutenant, then directed him to return to the squadron and inform Major Lindsley that a packtrain was on the way, loaded with everything the troops needed and also carrying relief orders. The lieutenant arrived back at the squadron to find that the packtrain had already arrived; men and horses were feasting.

At first glance Major Lindsley's small operation may seem to have been futile, a blow in the air. The squadron did not fight; it did not see a single Villista. But nevertheless, in an important respect, its results were positive. Lindsley's search showed that Villa was not in the part of Chihuahua which he had covered, and showed, moreover, that not even a Mexican guerrilla force would be able to maintain itself there for any length of time.

It is desirable to digress briefly at this point from the flying columns. General Pershing's sudden appearance at El Valle is illustrative of his methods of command. He had assembled a competent staff whose members he trusted; he left all routine matters and most detail to them. He himself was "on the prowl" almost constantly. Little mention is made in any official record of this habit, but letters and diaries of veterans of the expedition frequently speak of his sudden appearances, usually after dark, observing closely, questioning closely, and occasionally giving terse orders. People who were "on their toes," and performing their duties to the best of their abilities had nothing to fear, but his tongue was a sharp goad to all others. He traveled without any sort of escort except the driver of his car and one of his aides-de-camp, even though the country was hostile. He and his staff lived as uncomfortably as the soldiers, even though they had the luxury of wall tents. During the early days of the expedition he established his headquarters near Casas Grandes, where he was located by a newspaper correspondent on March 23: "A Sand-storm [sic] . . . was raging. We came to a snarl of tents and wagons and dirty men, a Futurist creation in brown and green. Overhead were the cottonwoods on the banks of the Rio Casas Grandes, and nearly everywhere was desert. That was splotched by what appeared to be innumerable triangular little piles of sand. These were the troopers' pup-tents, double staked and stone-weighted, to prevent their blowing away."[3]

General Pershing quickly found that Casas Grandes was too far away from the "front" for him to be able to keep in touch with the troops, know what was going on, and exercise direct command. The distances in northern Mexico were too great for the relatively primitive signal communications of the time. Consequently, he decided to establish a forward headquarters, or command post, as it would now be called, at Namiquipa. The newspaper correspondents accompanied him on the move south. His motor convoy consisted of three small cars (probably Dodges), in the leading one of which he rode with an aide. The two other cars carried eight soldiers (drivers, clerks and orderlies) and the general's colored cook, who had been with him for many years. The three official cars were trailed in the dust by "a battered second-hand car," bearing two newspaper correspondents; the convoy was overtaken shortly by a still more ancient vehicle, driven at mad speed by Floyd Gibbons, the correspondent of the Chicago *Tribune*. It was alleged that Gibbons had bought the venerable wreck some place along the line (probably in New Mexico) and had given in payment a check written on a piece of wrapping paper. The trip to Namiquipa was uneventful, except that the general once had to "scrounge" food from the newspapermen, and at a night bivouac in wild and strange country, the general himself directed the preparations for possible defense.[4]

The second of the flying columns left Colonia Dublán on March 21. It was a composite group, commanded by Major Frank Tompkins, and consisted of Troops K and M and the Machine Gun Platoon of the 13th Cavalry, together with Troops I and K of the 10th Cavalry. As the force neared Casas Grandes a messenger from the Carranzista garrison of the town informed Tompkins that any approach toward the town would be resisted. This was significant as the first overt act of hostility on the part of the Carranza troops. At Galeana, the next day, there was clear evidence that the people of the town were unfriendly, so Tompkins established the night's bivouac at a considerable distance away.

On March 23 there was a violent gale all day, with thick clouds of dust blinding men and animals and obscuring everything. Early in the morning, an airplane was seen coming from the north in the midst of the storm. As it was descending, a gust caught it; it turned three or four somersaults and plunged to the ground. Men raced to the rescue, feeling sure that the aviator must have been killed or badly injured. Instead, they met him, calmly walking toward the camp, unscratched and his machine undamaged. His first question was, "Got anything to eat?"[5]

The aviator, 1st Lieutenant Arthur R. Christie, brought orders for Tompkins to march at once for El Valle and there establish a new advance base for the expedition. Arriving at El Valle the same day, the troops found the population to be deeply hostile, although there was no trouble. The gale, meanwhile, had increased to such force that it was impossible to light fires for cooking. (The organization cooks had been left behind. Each man cooked his own rations individually. This was the practice throughout the expedition for several weeks.)

On March 24 Tompkins left the two troops of the 10th Cavalry to guard the supplies for the new base, which were already coming in by truck train, and continued southward with the 13th. The trail was all but impassable, winding through deep cañons, and zigzagging up and down precipitous slopes on which the horses were barely able to keep their footing. That night, March 24, the command bivouacked at an elevation of over seven thousand feet. The guides chased a wild steer into the middle of the camp and shot it there. The men had fresh beef (somewhat tough, but edible), and the uneaten portion of the carcass was hung upon a tree. In the morning it was frozen solid. A night or two later, going into camp at the village of Cruces, Tompkins decided that it would be well to give a glimpse of the steel beneath the glove. He sent for the head man of the village and told him solemnly and impressively that if a single shot was fired at the Americans during the night, his house would be burned. Fortunately for all concerned, the people of Cruces seemed to be friendly.

The force arrived at Namiquipa on March 26. At some place along the line Tompkins had been issued, or had acquired, a small sum in Mexican silver pesos. He invited his officers to dinner at a restaurant in the town and found that silver coin was an "open sesame." Food, liquor and everything that the Americans desired appeared as by magic. Although the people of Namiquipa seemed to be friendly, Tompkins again took the precaution of warning the town's officials as to the consequences of hostile acts.

The next day, March 27, Major Robert L. Howze arrived at Namiquipa with the force from the 11th Cavalry that was supposed to relieve the 7th Cavalry. He had been unable, so far, to overtake the 7th, because, as has been noted, Colonel Dodd had no intention of being relieved. Howze's force was a provisional squadron, which consisted of men and horses selected from the regular troops of the regiment. It was accompanied by an overstrength packtrain of seventy-five mules, loaded with forage and rations. The toughened troopers of the 13th looked at the newcomers with regimental prejudice, remarking openly and caustically that Pancho Villa now did not stand a chance. Their prejudice was deepened when it became known that Howze refused a request from Tompkins for some rations from his ample supply. On departing, however, Howze had to leave a considerable quantity of rations behind, which Tompkins promptly seized, an occurrence that Howze probably anticipated.

On March 31, on orders brought by 1st Lieutenant George S. Patton, one of Pershing's aides-de-camp, the whole day was spent reconnoitering the vicinity of Providencia, without finding any trace of the enemy. Before returning to the bivouac Tompkins proposed to search Bachineva (there was ample time before dark), but Patton, as General Pershing's personal representative on the spot, overruled him. This was unfortunate, for it was later found that General Beltrán, one of Villa's principal leaders, was at Bachineva at the time.

Late in the evening of April 1 General Pershing made one of his unheralded appearances. In a campfire discussion, later in the evening, Tompkins expressed the opinion that Villa was probably headed for Parral, in the midst of his old "stamping grounds," where he was well known, had many supporters, and could obtain surgical treatment for his wounds. Pershing made no comment except to ask how many mules Tompkins would need. Tompkins replied that he would need twelve. At noon the next day Pershing sent for him and gave the brief order: "Go and find Villa, wherever you think he is."[6] But the adventures of Tompkins' squadron on its roving mission are a story that must be held temporarily in abeyance.

The story of the early operations of Major Howze's provisional squadron of the 11th Cavalry is largely a repetition of those already told. The 11th was not a "border" regiment. It was in a comfortable eastern garrison until it was hurried to Columbus to join the expedition. Its horses, after being crowded into stock cars for five days before they were unloaded at Columbus, were not in good condition for the long marches into Mexico. Howze marched from Colonia Dublán only three days after arriving there and before his animals had had any real chance to recuperate and recover their strength. When the squadron arrived at Namiquipa, where the 11th and 13th met, men and animals were showing signs of fatigue. After leaving Namiquipa, Howze spent several days in an abortive hunt for Beltrán, and arrived at Bachineva on April 2 with men and horses on the verge of collapse, even though he was one of the ablest leaders and best horsemasters in the army.

The fourth of the flying columns was also from the 11th Cavalry, under Lieutenant Colonel Henry T. Allen. Like Howze's force, it was a provisional squadron composed of selected men and horses from each troop of the regiment, and was accompanied by a large packtrain, the extra mules for which were taken from the 4th Field Artillery. Marching southward from the base, Allen's men endured the same discomforts as the other soldiers of the expedition, except that they did not have to go hungry, as did the men of Lindsley's force. Allen spent some time reconnoitering Oso Cañon and the vicinity of Los Tanques, where Villistas were reported to be lurking. None were found, but while returning toward Namiquipa the force was fired upon by snipers hidden in the brush, not far from the town. No one was hit; a fast thrust into the thicket failed to bring the enemy to bay. They vanished without a trace. This was the first encounter of any of the flying columns with the enemy.[7]

After combing out the weakest animals and men, Allen marched for San Antonio on April 6. Pausing for a brief afternoon rest at a village called Sitio las Varas, Allen noted that the people were surly and unfriendly and that there were two wounded men, who might easily have been wounded at Columbus or Guerrero. This was pure surmise, however, and he took no action about them. One of the wounded men warned the Americans, "There is danger ahead." The squadron halted for the night at Lake Itascate, described by a lyrical newspaper correspondent who was with the column, as "a sapphire spot

. . . on the limitless dead plain." The same correspondent drew
a not unpleasant verbal picture of the bivouac and the evening's
activities:

> "Jones, kill the cow!" was the colonel's signal to stop. [Jones was
> a Mormon guide who spoke English with a Spanish accent.] In
> a moment a black steer from the untended herd near the water
> was careening at the end of the Mormon's rope. The clink-clink
> of a hammer on steel pegs, laying out the horses' picket line,
> after they had grazed for an hour, rose on the still air. The men
> spread the long lines of their kits; a dozen sweet-smelling fires
> outlined scores of troopers' legs. Soon Chavez [the squadron's
> Mexican guide], in his dirty, pajama-loose white clothes, like a
> Korean, came and threw a rib on the colonel's and my fire.

A few minutes later, there was a flurry of excitement. Lieutenant Harding Polk, who was in command of the packtrain,
rode in, his face livid with rage. He had been fired upon while
passing the village.

"They shot at me, sir!" he reported to the colonel. "At the
rear of the packtrain. Two bullets between Brown and myself."

"By the very fellows who 'warned' us, eh?" weighed [sic] the
colonel. "That's like them."[8]

After spending several days in fruitless search of Pablo Lopez,
the perpetrator of the Santa Ysabel massacre, Allen decided that
his animals were nearing the limit of their endurance. The
squadron struggled into Satevo on April 10, where General
Pershing was on hand, and watched the tired troopers ride in.
But in spite of the jaded condition of the horses, the search and
pursuit must go on; Pershing assigned a new task, and the next
morning Allen marched for Zaragoza. A few hours after leaving Satevo the column was overtaken by a motor car carrying
Captain William O. Reed, of the 6th Cavalry, who was an acting member of Pershing's staff. A report had come to headquarters that Colonel Brown and the 10th Cavalry had run into
trouble at Parral; Reed was hastening with orders for Brown.
Actually it was Tompkins who had met trouble, but that fact
was still unknown at headquarters. Allen decided instantly to
march to Brown's assistance. Pushing the tired men and horses
through a long night march, he arrived at Santa Cruz de Ville-

gas early the next morning, where he found Colonel Brown and the 10th Cavalry, and also Major Tompkins with his force. A few hours later Howze's squadron arrived, making a total force equivalent to a brigade.

Two weeks earlier, when Brown and his regiment were at San Diego del Monte, he vainly tried to open communication with General Pershing's headquarters, or with Colonel Dodd. In the absence of orders, Brown decided to march for Guerrero, knowing that the 7th Cavalry was moving in that direction. After an unusually disagreeable and uncomfortable night in bivouac, with a gale driving sleet and snow, the regiment marched at daybreak. Through the morning the march was uneventful, but shortly after noon, as the advance guard (Troop E) neared the village, or ranch, of Aguas Calientes, there was a sudden burst of rifle fire. Troop E dismounted and opened fire. The other troops quickly deployed and fired. The Villistas (for such they proved to be), seeing the size of the force that was moving against them, began to evacuate the cluster of adobe buildings and retreat to the south and east. Major Charles P. Young, with two troops, galloped to cut them off; his troops dismounted, and firing rapidly, killed two of the enemy at once. A considerable number of the Villistas ensconced themselves behind a stone wall, from which they could not be dislodged by fire alone. Colonel Brown, watching the action from a position slightly to the rear, sent word to Young to charge and drive them out. Young's troopers, on his shouted command, raced to their horses and remounted. Then, with raised pistols, they were formed into a "line of foragers" (the cavalry version of the infantry's line of skirmishers), and trotted toward the enemy, down a long slope. At a signal from Young, who was well out in front, the troopers drove in their spurs; the trot became a rushing gallop, while every man yelled at the top of his lungs. Not a man fired a shot; seconds before they were within shooting range, the enemy had vanished, every man for himself.[9]

The 10th Cavalry's little fight at Aguas Calientes saw an innovation in combat in America, overhead machine-gun fire. Captain Albert E. Phillips, commanding the regimental machine guns, laid his guns to fire directly above the advancing soldiers.

It had been known for some time that this was theoretically possible, but until this moment, it had never been put to an actual test in the United States Army.

The Villistas, estimated at about 150 men, and supposed to be Beltrán's command, scattered and fled. Temporarily abandoning the march for Guerrero, the 10th spent the next two days following dim trails of fugitives and investigating rumors. The enemy abandoned several items of equipment, including weapons and a machine-gun packsaddle. A two-man patrol sent out with a Mexican guide returned a few hours later with two prisoners, several rifles, three mules and a horse. This haul was the last, except for two more prisoners who claimed that they were Carranzistas who had been captured by Beltrán but had escaped. Since there was no way to disprove their statement, they were released after being questioned. No more Villistas were encountered; they had run too fast and too far.

At a telegraph station on the railroad line, Brown attempted to send a telegram to headquarters. The Mexican operator refused to accept a receipt, and Brown had no cash; he finally obtained enough for the telegram by selling his pocketknife to one of his soldiers, who coveted it. No answer to the telegram was forthcoming, so the march southward was continued. At Cusihuiriachic, a mining camp owned and operated by an American company, the manager cashed Brown's personal check for over a thousand dollars—money with which he purchased supplies for the regiment. On April 6 an American airplane passed overhead, but the pilot did not see the column below him. He was seen to land a long distance away, and several hours were spent before locating him. Brown surmised that he carried orders for the 10th; the surmise was correct. The orders were for the 10th to march to Parral over a specified route, in order to shield Tompkins and Howze and prevent Villa's possible escape to the north. The message also informed Brown that a supply of money was being sent to him and that he was authorized to hire guides, interpreters and spies, but above all, he was to reach Parral quickly.[10]

At Santa Rosalia the 10th Cavalry found Tompkins and his force from the 13th; after a few hours the two organizations parted company, Tompkins on his roving mission, the 10th moving toward Parral as fast as the exhausted condition of the animals would allow. For several consecutive days it had been necessary to destroy animals that could go no farther. On April 12 the regiment reached Media Ranch, near Sapien, and went into bivouac late in the afternoon. About six thirty, Captain Rodney wandered from camp to the road, a few hundred yards distant. Suddenly three American soldiers came galloping wildly along the road. They did not pay any attention to him or even see him. He yelled, but they continued; only when he fired his pistol over their heads did they become aware of him and come back. The 13th had been ambushed at Parral, they said, and they were riding for help. Rodney grimly accused them of running away but believed the rest of their tale. Within two or three minutes the buglers of the 10th Cavalry began sounding "Boots and Saddles." The news that the 13th was in trouble raced through the camp, and within fifteen minutes after the first bugle signal, the regiment was in the saddle and on the way. It was well after dark before the 10th could arrive at Santa Cruz de Villegas, where Tompkins' squadron was. Knowing that Tompkins' men would probably shoot without challenging, Brown halted the regiment and had a bugler sound two peculiarly American calls, "Officers' Call" and "Attention." A moment later an answering call came from the 13th, and the 10th rode into the inclosure in which the 13th was barricaded.

There is a story, probably true, that as Tompkins saw the colored soldiers of the 10th ride in, he exclaimed to Major Young, "By God, Young, I could kiss every black face out there." Without cracking a smile, Young replied, "Well, Tompkins, if you want to, you may start with me."

The story of the trouble that Tompkins encountered at Parral is complex, and there are phases of it that are still not clear half a century later. After meeting with the 10th Cavalry at Santa Rosalia, he continued to march southward on his search for traces of Villa. At Santa Rosalia he had been able to purchase enough food and forage for his men and horses "to take the wrinkles out of their bellies."[11] On April 11 there was a brief skirmish with a group of Mexicans, identified as Carranzistas, who escaped through the brush. There were no casualties on either side. At Valle de Zaragoza, Tompkins was able to purchase some clothing, not regulation, but necessary, for those of his men who were nearly naked.

Late one afternoon, probably April 11, Captain Antonio Mesa, of the Carranzista garrison of Parral, rode into the squadron's bivouac. Several days before, Mesa had acted as a liaison officer with the 10th Cavalry and had proved to be helpful and reliable. It is possible, although not certain, that Tompkins had met him when the two organizations met at Santa Rosalia. Mesa assured Tompkins that the Americans would be welcome at Parral and that he would send a messenger ahead to arrange for a campsite and for the delivery of food and grain. On Wednesday, April 12, 1916, the squadron, totaling less than a hundred officers and soldiers, marched to Parral, anticipating hot baths, hot meals and some of the amenities of civilization. But contrary to what the Americans expected, there was no welcome. There was no guide and no one to meet them. The scowls of the people on the streets were anything but friendly. Tompkins finally found someone to guide him to the headquarters of General Lozano, the Carranzista commander, who was deeply perturbed and very much amazed at the Americans' arrival. He had no inkling that they were coming. Captain Mesa's messenger, he said, had never reached him but had been captured, probably, by the Villistas. Lozano urged Tompkins and his troops to leave the city at once. Tompkins agreed but said that he wanted to obtain supplies before he left. Lozano sent for a merchant, who promised to deliver the supplies immediately.

The conference took about an hour. Meanwhile, the troopers of the 13th were lined up in the plaza facing Lozano's headquarters. A crowd began assembling, and before long it was apparent that trouble was brewing. By the time Tompkins and Lozano came out of the latter's office, the crowd was becoming a mob. Mexicans were catcalling and jeering at the Americans; a runaway mule hauling a wagon raced from a side street straight for the American line, obviously released to cause damage. Some of the crowd was shouting "Viva Villa!" along with insults and obscenities that Tompkins understood but fortunately his troopers did not. Prominent was a man whom Tompkins took to be a German, who was urging the crowd to violence.

Led by General Lozano and some of his staff officers, the Americans marched out of the plaza, followed by the jeering mob. There was a shot, and another, then a fusillade.

Although Tompkins noticed a man who was egging the mob to attack the Americans, there was another person whom he did not see and who probably fired the first shot—a woman named Elsa Griensen de Alvarado. She was an Alsatian, a German national by birth, married to a Mexican who was an ardent Villista. What her motives and purpose were, no one can ever know. She might have been a burning Mexican patriot, trying to defend her adopted country; she might have been trying, as a German sympathizer, to foment trouble between the United States and Mexico. Be that as it may, she was a troublemaker. She came into the plaza while Tompkins and General Lozano were closeted together, screaming insults at the Americans and berating the Mexicans for allowing the vile gringos to defile their city.[12]

As the Americans filed out of the town, General Lozano hurried back to try to stop the firing. So far, there had been no casualties, and the Americans had not fired a single shot in return. As soon as the squadron was clear of the narrow streets, Tompkins took immediate measures to assure the safe withdrawal of the command. He ordered Lieutenant Clarence Lininger to occupy a railroad embankment north of the town with the rear guard, a squad of eight men. He sent one of the small troops to seize a hill to the immediate west. About six hundred yards distant was another hill, which was already occupied by Mexican soldiers—Carranzistas—carrying a large Mexican flag. Soon the Carranzistas started to move toward the American flank. Tompkins was still hoping to avoid a battle; he stood up on the railway embankment and shouted for the Mexicans to go back. Their reply was a volley directed at him. He was unscratched, but a sergeant standing close beside him was killed instantly. By this time Lininger's small rear guard was firing with sharp effect, and the advancing Mexicans wavered. But because the Americans were heavily outnumbered and were in a position commanded by several hills that they could not occupy, Tompkins ordered a withdrawal, across country to the road. The withdrawal was accomplished at speed; on reaching the road there was a halt to enable animals and men to recover their breath. A quick check revealed that so far, one man had been killed and two more were very seriously wounded.

Tompkins knew that the 10th Cavalry could not be far distant; he knew, too, that the ranch at Santa Cruz de Villegas was defensible. As his column moved northward small groups of mounted Mexicans, Carranzista soldiers (the mob stopped following as soon as the Americans opened fire), moved parallel, trying to pass, but the stone walls between the fields delayed them until they saw that it was impossible. A detachment tried to pursue directly. Lininger's rear guard dropped behind a stone wall and opened fire on them. Here occurred a small incident that could have happened, probably, only in the United States Army. Major Tompkins, staying with the rear guard, had dismounted, watching the action. Two soldiers, with their reins looped over their arms, were firing close beside him. Every time a shot was fired nearby, their horses tossed their heads, thus disrupting their aim. "Here, Major, hold my horse," one of them said, tossing his reins into the major's hand. The other soldier did likewise. The commanding officer willingly acted as horseholder for two privates of his command. And far from being an act of indiscipline, as some pedants might have interpreted it, it was proof of the men's confidence in him.

As the rear guard was leaving its position, a horse was hit, leaving its rider on the ground. Under a hot fire from the advancing Mexicans, Lieutenant Lininger picked him up. Another horse, terrified, broke away before its soldier could mount; Tompkins himself galloped after the runaway, caught it, and raced back to the dismounted man, with every Mexican in sight shooting at him. He was struck in the shoulder but, fortunately for him, sustained only a flesh wound.

After a brief halt to enable the doctor to give first aid to the wounded, during which a squad of riflemen kept the enemy at a respectful distance, the withdrawal continued. From time to time Tompkins dismounted one of the troops to hold the enemy at a distance. Private Ledford, one of the men who was wounded at the first exchange of fire, hanging onto his saddle in agony, was hit again and killed. Lieutenant Ord, the squadron adjutant, caught a bullet through his ear—a close shave and very painful, but not serious.

It was soon apparent that the Mexicans were about to launch a serious attack. Mounted men could be seen forming for a charge. Twenty men of Captain Frederick Turner's troop were dismounted behind a small ridge to await the onset. In a few minutes the Mexicans came surging forward, spurring their horses, yelling and waving their pistols. Turner waited until they were within two hundred yards, then gave one word of command: "Fire!" Horses and riders piled into a confused mass of struggling horses and writhing men. Turner's men continued to fire into a target that even a recruit could hardly miss. The survivors turned and raced away, sped along by following shots from the American riflemen. Information received later by the Americans indicated that more than forty were killed and many wounded. The dead included a Carranzista major.

The pursuers lost their enthusiasm; the Americans gained a respite; the squadron watered the horses in a roadside irrigation ditch, then moved in and seized the ranch. The entrances were quickly barricaded, and Tompkins placed riflemen on the flat roofs of the two main buildings. The enemy fired an occasional long-range shot, but the Americans did not reply; they had to save their ammunition, which was becoming dangerously low. After a while a detachment of the enemy could be seen beginning a cautious move forward. A group of mounted men, with a man in front leading, began to approach. Captain Aubrey Lippincott, a "Distinguished Marksman" (the highest qualification for marksmanship) took a soldier's rifle, estimated the range as eight hundred yards, carefully set the sights, with due allowance for the wind, lay prone, and slowly squeezed the trigger. A sharp report, and a second later the leader of the advancing party fell heavily to the ground and lay inert. The others turned abruptly and galloped away.

A short time later a messenger from General Lozano arrived

under a flag of truce. Lozano urged that the Americans withdraw at once; he could not restrain his soldiers much longer.
Tompkins sent a reply, saying that he would withdraw only if
his force was guaranteed freedom from interference. Otherwise
he intended to "remain here to await the arrival of other American forces."[13] But before an answer could come from Lozano, the
welcome music of the 10th Cavalry bugles announced the arrival of the other American forces.

Colonel Brown, assuming command of the combined American forces, listened to Tompkins' account of what had happened,
then sent a curt message to Lozano saying that he intended to
remain at Santa Cruz de Villegas until his own military superiors ordered him to leave. If the Mexicans started anything,
the responsibility would be theirs alone. He then sent a dispatch
to General Pershing, and in this is one of the oddities of the
situation. The message was carried to Parral by a Captain
Treviño, a Carranzista liaison officer who had been with the
10th Cavalry for several days. From Parral it was sent by
General Lozano himself to the American consul at Chihuahua.
The arrival the next day of Allen's and Howze's squadrons of
the 11th Cavalry, as has been mentioned before, gave Colonel
Brown a force that would give pause to any Carranzistas or
Villistas who might be disposed to make trouble. And when
Brown sent for Lozano and other local dignitaries, they did not
stand on their dignity; they came.

Before concluding the story of the four flying columns, it is
necessary to return briefly to Major Howze. He marched from
Bachineva on April 2 and for several days forced his tired men
and horses southward. There was a narrow escape from a fight
with Carranzistas when his advance guard, a squad under Lieutenant Sumner M. Williams, rounding a point on the train,
found itself face to face with a Carranzista band commanded
by one General Cavazos. Cavazos was truculently anti-American,
and although it has not been mentioned previously, Tompkins
had had difficulties with him. Seeing only a handful of Americans, Cavazos prepared to attack, but by the time the maneuver
was completed, Williams' men were ready to open fire, and

the other troops of the squadron had closed up and were preparing for action. Major Howze galloped forward, waving his hat. Cavazos realized that there were more Americans than he had bargained for; he was on the point of "grabbing a tiger by the tail." He turned his men about and vanished quickly.

Near San José del Sitio, the bivouac was fired into during the night. Howze took no retaliatory action. Apparently the shots came from the same village from which Allen's packtrain had been fired upon, although Howze had no knowledge of that incident. About noon the next day the head of the column was fired into from heavy brush along the road, near La Joya. The advance guard fired back; the enemy retreated without having been seen. One dead Mexican, later identified as a Captain Silva, a Villista, was found in the thicket. In the afternoon of the same day a heavy fire was opened on the packtrain from both sides of a narrow cañon through which the column was threading its way. No soldiers were hit, but two mules were so badly wounded that it was necessary to destroy them. An hour later the squadron was again attacked from both sides of another narrow defile. The enemy was driven away within a few minutes, but one soldier was killed and three were wounded. It was a full and exciting day for the soldiers of Howze's force.

After bivouacking for a few hours the squadron resumed the march in the early hours of the morning, and at three thirty surrounded the little town of Santa Cruz de Herrera. The Villistas in the town were on the alert, however, and began to escape before the encirclement was complete. There was a quick flurry of rifle fire; one dead man was found and another who was mortally wounded. The dead man was identified as a son of Beltrán, and the townspeople said that Beltrán himself was badly wounded in the brief skirmish but had escaped.

By this time Howze's squadron was approaching utter exhaustion. He noted in his war diary that the animals "were low in flesh, lame and footsore; our men were nearly barefoot; the country was devoid of food, and wherever we turned we found less horse feed."[14] Knowing nothing of the trouble that Tompkins had just run into, Howze decided to march for Parral, where he hoped to obtain supplies. On April 14, as the squadron approached the city, a deputation of citizens, carrying a white flag, came out. They told Howze what had happened and urged him to go to Santa Cruz de Villegas, where the other Americans were. Realizing that to go on into the city would cost lives and accomplish nothing, Howze turned northward. A few hours later he reported to Colonel Brown and placed himself under his orders.

Since marching southward from Columbus, Howze's provisional squadron of the 11th Cavalry had marched over a thousand miles. It had been in action several times and had lost one soldier killed and three wounded. It had lost thirty-two horses and five mules. Such a campaign would have been a remarkable achievement for an organization in which the men and animals were in the pink of condition, and the 11th Cavalry, due to no fault of its men and officers, was far from in the pink at the start of the march.

The story of the flying columns and a definite phase in the history of the Punitive Expedition comes to its end with Howze's arrival at Santa Cruz de Villegas. It was apparent to everyone that the political and military situation had changed. At the start of the expedition it was assumed that the Carranzistas would be friendly; indeed, there were numerous examples of Carranzista cooperation, but the Parral fight proved that the Carranzistas were essentially as hostile as the Villistas. There was now little prospect of damaging further any surviving Villista bands in a region where every man, woman and child was an enemy of the Americans. General Pershing must now make a new estimate of the situation, new plans and a new disposition of his forces.

Colonel Brown, meanwhile, had an ample force at his disposal to enable him to take care of any situation likely to arise while he "sat tight" and waited for General Pershing's wishes to become known. With his own regiment, and Tompkins', Allen's and Howze's squadrons, he could ignore any threat from the Mexicans. He intended to remain where he was until General Pershing ordered otherwise. If the Mexicans started anything, the responsibility would be theirs.

NOTES

1. Tompkins, *op. cit.*, p. 12.
2. *Ibid.*, pp. 103–8. The narrative of the operations of the 2d Squadron, 13th Cavalry, is from the account written by Col. John W. Converse, a Pennsylvania National Guardsman who was authorized to accompany the Punitive Expedition as a volunteer and who was with Lindsley's force during the entire march. Tompkins quotes the account *verbatim* and at full length.
3. Frank B. Elser, "General Pershing's Mexican Campaign," *Century Magazine*, XCIX (Feb., 1920), 437.
4. *Ibid.*, pp. 438–39.
5. Tompkins, *op. cit.*, p. 112.
6. *Ibid.*, p. 118.
7. Robert Dunn, "With Pershing's Cavalry," *Collier's Magazine*, LVIII (Sept. 23, 1916), 8; Tompkins, *op. cit.*, p. 125.
8. Dunn, *op. cit.*, p. 8. The place where this incident occurred is referred to both as Cienegas and Sitio las Varas. They seem to be identical.
9. Tompkins, *op. cit.*, pp. 145–46. Maj. Charles P. Young was one of the few Negro officers in the Regular Army before World War I. He was a graduate of West Point (Class of 1889) and before the Punitive Expedition had had a distinguished career in diplomatic assignments for the United States in both Haiti and Liberia, where his responsibilities were far beyond those usually assigned to the position of military attaché. His abilities and personality were such that white officers considered it a privilege to be allowed to serve under his command. Unless otherwise attributed, everything concerning the operations of Tompkins' squadron is based upon his own account, *Chasing Villa*, pp. 137–44.
10. *Ibid.*, p. 150.
11. *Ibid.*, p. 133.
12. Haldeen Braddy, *Pershing's Mission to Mexico* (El Paso, 1966), pp. 30–31.
13. Tompkins, *op. cit.*, p. 154.
14. From Maj. Howze's War Diary, quoted in Tompkins, *op. cit.*, pp. 166–67.

CHAPTER 14

End of the Active Pursuit

IT WAS OBVIOUS that if the de facto government of Mexico became openly hostile, and a full-scale war should result, the long lines of communication of the advance units of the Punitive Expedition would be dangerously vulnerable. Upon receiving word of the Parral affair General Pershing sent an order to Brown, who was still at Santa Cruz de Villegas: "On account of the difficulties of supply in your present locality you move your force, which now includes Major Tompkins' squadron and Lieutenant Colonel Allen's squadron, by easy marches to Satevo, taking advantage of any supplies or grazing along the line that may be necessary to put your command in better condition."[1] Pershing issued this order on April 15, but Brown did not receive it until April 20. By this time all the expedition's airplanes were out of action, and Brown was far beyond the transmitting range of the wireless sets of the time.

Before complying with the order, Colonel Brown invited General Herrera, who was in supreme command of the Carranzista forces in the region, to a conference, along with General Lozano. Brown made the meeting as impressive as possible. Seated at the conference table with him were all the field officers; behind him were the regimental standards of his regiment, the 10th Cavalry. After the preliminaries, Brown presented Herrera with a written demand for an explanation, an apology and a disavowal. Herrera was informed that his reply would be sent to General Pershing for transmittal to Washington. Herrera answered that he would send his reply the next morning.[2]

Late in the afternoon, after the conference, Lieutenant Colonel Cabell, the expedition's Chief of Staff, arrived by motor with orders directing Brown to march to Satevo, this confirming the orders previously received. The two squadrons of the 11th Cavalry marched at midnight; the 10th Cavalry and Tompkins' squadron moved out the next morning. Shortly after the Americans departed from Santa Cruz, General Herrera's reply to Brown's demands arrived. By inference, he placed the whole blame on the Americans and particularly on Tompkins, for having entered the city without prior permission from the *Jefe de Armas* (Lozano). He denied that any Carranzista soldiers were involved in the affair but admitted that the trouble was started by Mexican civilians, and admitted, also, that Tompkins and his men had conducted themselves with great restraint. He refused to apologize because he said that his explanation took up so much room that there was insufficient room on the paper for an apology.[3]

Colonel Brown and Major Tompkins arrived at Satevo after a three-day march. Orders were awaiting for Brown to continue on to Carretas. He ordered Tompkins to take the sick and wounded and men who were dismounted because their horses were played out or had been destroyed, and march via a fairly easy route to the same destination, taking three days to cover the distance. Near Santa Ysabel, Tompkins column of the sick, halt and lame ran into a force of Carranzistas who were in an ugly mood. "Our men had their magazines, both rifle and pistol, full, and we were ready to cut loose at the slightest sign of treachery."[4] By putting on a bold front, they bypassed the Carranzistas, and the detachment arrived at Carretas on April 27, with no further incident. After a couple of days of rest, the united force marched to San Antonio, arriving there on May 1, 1916. General Pershing was there when they arrived, as were two battalions of infantry and part of the 11th Cavalry. The next day the remainder of the 11th arrived, as well as the rest of the 13th Cavalry and a squadron of the 5th. It was the biggest aggregation of American troops in one place since the expedition crossed the border. The toughened soldiers and officers of the spear-point squadrons were happy to be reunited with their regiments; they were even happier to regain their personal effects, such as toilet articles and officers' bedding rolls, and to find that skinny, half-starved horses would now receive ten pounds of grain (five of oats and five of corn) daily, with seven pounds of hay. Welcome, also, were the troop cooks and field kitchens; no more frying bacon and hardtack in a mess kit.

It is necessary to return to Colonel Dodd and the 7th Cavalry, who had been in the vicinity of Guerrero through most of the month of April. General Herrera protested against the presence of American troops and said that Dodd's proposed movements would interfere with his own plans. Dodd, not knowing what the situation was outside his immediate vicinity, and thinking it possible that something had occurred of which he was ignorant, sent a dispatch to Pershing. Whether in response to Dodd's message or not (the records are not clear), the Acting Chief of Staff, Major James A. Ryan, came to Dodd's headquarters on April 9. Dodd took him to General Herrera, who, after a private interview, withdrew his objections to Dodd's movements.

In the meantime Dodd had received information that a detachment of Carranzistas northwest of Guerrero had mutinied and were about to join the Villistas, supposedly because of their hatred of Americans. Dodd sent two troops (K and M) to investigate and take action. While the troops were saddling their horses, on the morning of April 8, there was a sudden sound of rifle fire from the north. Captain William J. Kendrick, who was in command, marched toward the sound and in a short time came upon some thirty Mexicans, who were busily firing at a ranch house. There was a brief fire fight, and the besiegers decamped. They proved to be the disaffected Carranzistas; the ranch house was defended by two Americans and nine Carranzista soldiers, who probably owed their lives to the fortunate arrival of the Americans. Kendrick pursued for several miles but was unable to come up with the fugitives in the heavy brush and thicket. The Americans suffered no casualties; the enemy's losses were unknown, but it was believed that at least two were wounded.[5]

Information came from Mexican sources that a large force of Villistas was quietly asembling near Agua Caliente. This information was confirmed by the discovery of a heavy trail near that place, leading northeast. The discovery was made after a long, grueling night march. The trail was followed, but after a few miles it became apparent that the band was dissolving; small parties broke away here and there until it was no longer worth while to try to follow. A report reached Dodd that Villistas (probably the band that the 7th had been following) had just looted Yoquivo and were holding two foreigners—an American and a Frenchman—for ransom. On April 17, the 7th Cavalry was joined by a small Carranzista detachment, commanded by a Major González, who agreed to assist. For three days the force pushed through the mountains. On the evening of the twentieth the Americans and Carranzistas bivouacked in a cañon seven or eight miles from Yoquivo and marched again as soon as the moon rose, about eleven o'clock. Americans and Carranzistas took different routes on their approach. At daylight, as soon as it was possible to see, the Americans advanced to the attack—but found their erstwhile ally, Major González, stretched comfortably before a fire in one of the town's huts. The Villistas had left several hours before, having had full information of the American advance. The two prisoners had been released, having been able, somehow, to raise part of the ransom. Dodd suspected his ally of treachery but had no proof.

At Yoquivo it was ascertained that the Villista commander was Candelario Cervantes and that the band numbered about two hundred men. Dodd was sure that Cervantes could not be far away. Major González declined an invitation to remain with the Americans, and Dodd decided to go ahead without the benefit of allies. The Americans started at three thirty in the afternoon and marched all night. "The trail proved to be about the most difficult this outfit had yet encountered, while it seemed as if the horses could not stand another day's march."[76]

Up and down hill, and through rocky chasms, the trail followed a veritable corkscrew route over the mountains. After a short halt for breakfast, at dawn, the march continued. Once more men fell asleep in the saddle and had to be aroused forcibly at the hourly halts. It seemed that Dodd himself, a man almost sixty-four years of age, was the only man in the column who was not too tired to go on. He habitually rode well out in front with the advance guard, where he could get first information, but also where he would be the first to receive enemy fire. At three o'clock in the afternoon the column topped a high ridge, and the troopers of the 7th found themselves staring down at the village of Tomochic. Some thirty or forty Mexicans, presumably Villistas, could be seen straggling toward the hills to the north.

The trail down the ridge was so steep and rough that it took an hour to get to the level of the town. Once on the floor of the valley, two troops under Major Winans galloped into the town to take possession. The enemy fired, but as usual, his shots were wild. Fleeing from the town as Winans came in, the Villistas opened a hot fire from the hills to the north and south. Dodd sent a platoon to take care of the Villistas on the narrow plain to the east of Tomochic. The remainder of the regiment rode to support Winans.

Soon a heavy fire came from the wooded hills to the east; the Americans occupied a small knoll between the town and the hills. The single machine gun the 7th Cavalry had at the moment was brought into action. Parties of the enemy could be seen on the trail leading to Minaca; rifle and machine gun fire speeded them on their way. Pursuit was impossible; darkness was coming on too rapidly. The Americans bivouacked where darkness found them, with outguards ready to go into action on a second's alarm. It was taken for granted that the action would be renewed at daylight, but at dawn it was found that the Villistas had vanished during the night. They had retreated along the Minaca trail for two or three miles, and then scattered. Candelario Cervantes' band was effectively broken up.

American casualties were two killed, three wounded and several horses that died of exhaustion. As for the Villistas, thirty-one corpses were counted, and Dodd later received information that the number was actually very much larger. No account was taken of probable enemy wounded. Captured enemy equipment included several saddles, a few rifles, a quantity of dynamite, ten horses and fifteen mules.[7]

General Pershing decided, as a result of the political and diplomatic situation after the Parral affair, to reorganize the command and change the method of search. His decision was to establish five military districts, each occupied by a regiment, the commanding officer of which was responsible for the search within his district. He was to be allowed the greatest possible freedom of action. District commanders were not to be restricted to operating within their own areas but were free to send troops into any district, especially on a "hot pursuit" or in search of information.

The districts were as follows:

Namiquipa	10th Cavalry	Major Ellwood Evans
Guerrero	7th Cavalry	Colonel George A. Dodd
Bustillos	13th Cavalry	Colonel Herbert J. Slocum
Satevo	5th Cavalry	Colonel Wilber E. Wilder
San Borja	11th Cavalry	Colonel James E. Lockett[8]

On May 4, 1916, while the regiments were on the move to occupy their respective districts, a frantic request came from people at Cusihuiriachic for protection. Julio Acosta, a Villista general who was prominent on the list of men badly wanted by the Americans, with one Cruz Dominguez, was in the vicinity of Cusihuiriachic, threatening the town and the mines and boasting that he had more than a thousand men and was going to attack the American camp at San Antonio.

In response to the plea for help and to break up this Villista band (estimated at about two hundred men, in spite of Acosta's boasts), Major Howze marched from San Antonio at dusk, May 4, with six rifle troops of the 11th Cavalry, the regimental machine guns and the detachment of Apache Indian scouts. The force, with the Indians in front, arrived at Cusi (as the place was commonly called) about midnight. It was learned that Acosta was at Ojos Azules, about thirty miles distant. There was a delay of two or three hours while guides were located and persuaded to join.

At some time during the night's march (it is uncertain whether before or after arriving at Cusi) the Apache scouts sighted a Carranzista detachment that had also been threatened by Acosta. For a few minutes Lieutenant James Shannon, who commanded the Apaches, had a difficult time. To the Indians a Mexican was a Mexican; Sergeant Chicken, the first sergeant of the Scouts, was full of enthusiasm: "Heap Mexican. Shoot 'em all!" he exclaimed, fingering his rifle. Shannon managed to restrain his warriors, and after briefly interrogating the Carranzistas, the column marched on.[9]

Howze had hoped to strike Ojos Azules at daybreak, but because of the delay at Cusi, it was almost six o'clock and the sun was well up before the force arrived. The plan was for the Scouts to bypass the settlement (or *rancho*) and go to the hills to the west, in order to cut off the enemy's retreat. The Villistas' horses were grazing in a pasture east of the place and at some distance. As the scouts appeared, the herd guard caught sight of them and opened fire. The scouts should have disregarded the fire, which was totally ineffective, and gone at the gallop to their objective, but it was against Apache nature to be shot at without shooting back. The scouts piled off their horses and opened fire, and no amount of persuasion or even blasphemy could move them at that moment; they were too excited and too happy. The Villistas in the buildings swarmed out as soon as the first shots alarmed them and raced in disorder for the hills to the south and southwest. Twenty-five or thirty got onto the flat roofs and opened fire on the Americans from there. The leading troop of the column dashed through with raised pistols, ignoring the fire from the Mexicans on the roofs, and went after the fugitives. The following troops, in accordance with Howze's plan and orders, fanned out to the right and left at a fast gallop. A number of Villistas tried to make a stand on a small hill a few hundred yards southwest of the ranch. They were soon driven off and, running down the reverse slope, were caught squarely by Americans coming around the south side of the hill.[10]

The pursuit continued relentlessly until the American horses were ready to drop; the enemy had broken into such small groups that there was no target large enough to justify further action. Howze reported to General Pershing, "Those who escaped us did so as individuals."[11] More than sixty dead Villistas were counted; the number of wounded was never ascertained, but it must have been large. On the American side not a single man was scratched; the only casualties were several overworked horses that died of exhaustion.

As soon as the fight was over, or possibly even before, the ranch

buildings were searched and the Mexicans found there rounded
up. It was impossible to tell which were Villistas and which were
pacíficos, so they were all released. Among them, however, were
four Carranzista soldiers who had been slated for execution later
in the morning. Several undoubted Villistas were captured during the fight and pursuit. One of the Carranzistas volunteered to
execute them if some American would lend him a pistol for
a few minutes. His offer was not accepted.

Diplomatic relations between the United States and Carranza's
de facto government, meanwhile, were deteriorating. Carranza
was determined to get the Punitive Expedition out of Mexico,
and he was becoming increasingly truculent. It is possible that
he hoped, by adopting a stiff line with the United States, to rally
all Mexicans in support of himself and his government and
supplant Villa as a popular hero and patriot. To ease the mount-
ing tension, Secretary Lansing suggested a meeting between
Generals Scott and Obregón to endeavor to work out a *modus
vivendi*. They met at Juarez on April 30, 1916. General Funston,
who had been also directed to be at the conference, quickly
dropped out. In spite of the tact with which he had handled the
situation at Vera Cruz, he was no diplomat and knew it. He
had no patience with Latin indirection and circumlocution.

To all suggestions from Scott, Obregón returned one answer—
the immediate and unconditional withdrawal of the Punitive Expedition. To this, the United States would not consent, and it
took all of Scott's innate courtesy and loyalty to his orders from
the President to keep the conference going. And while the conferences were still under way, and before Funston excused himself from further participation, alarming information began coming in. It was noticed that Generals Gutiérrez and Calles, who
had been present at the first meeting, left suddenly for their
commands. General Scott heard from undisclosed sources that
he considered reliable that orders had been issued to crush the
Punitive Expedition unless the United States agreed upon immediate withdrawal. A report was received that General Arnulfo
Gómez, in Sonora, had received orders from Carranza, directing
him to "dispose your troops that they shall be in a position to
cut off the American expeditionary forces now in Chihuahua.

The action must be sudden and will take place after the Scott-Obregón conference."[11] The situation was so threatening that Funston sent orders to Pershing to draw in all scattered detachments and concentrate his whole force in order to be able to resist any sudden attack. At the same time he sent orders to all border commanders to increase their precautions.

Scott suspended the conferences under pretext of waiting for additional instructions from Washington. He and Funston, a few days later, sent a joint telegram to the Secretary of War saying that 150,000 additional troops were urgently needed on the border and recommending the immediate call of the National Guard of Texas, New Mexico and Arizona.[12]

General Obregón was actually as anxious as Scott to work out some solution for the difficulties that had arisen, and he probably did not feel any confidence in the ability of the Constitutionalists to expel the Americans by force, as some other revolutionary generals and politicians seemed to feel. Through a mutual friend, he sent word to Scott, suggestion that they meet privately and secretly at some place where they would not be subjected to pressure. Making their way, in the best "cloak and dagger" tradition, to a room in the Paso del Norte Hotel, they discussed the situation for a full night and a large part of the next day. Finally, both of them almost exhausted, they arrived at an agreement that seemed to them to be workable. The United States accepted the agreement immediately, but Carranza, while stating that he accepted it in principle, insisted upon certain changes that nullified the whole thing.[13]

On May 9 Funston sent orders to Pershing to withdraw all forces to the area of Colonia Dublán, as the situation made a concentration of the expedition imperative. Pershing replied that the situation did not yet justify a withdrawal that far, whereupon Funston modified his orders by directing that the troops be held where they then were and that Pershing should make such dispositions as he saw fit in the vicinity of Namiquipa.[14]

General Pershing was a careful commander who took no unnecessary chances. Plans were drawn up for an immediate offensive in case of an attack by the Carranzistas. Reconnaissance patrols kept a close eye on Carranzista movements, and before many days had passed, the expedition was so deployed that it could meet any situation that might develop.

As soon as the ban on search and troop movements was lifted, limited search within each zone was renewed. Villa's whereabouts were still unknown, and reports that he was dead continued to circulate. At least two of Villa's generals were known to be alive, Julio (or Julián) Cardenas and Candelario Cervantes. There was vague information that Cardenas was somewhere in the vicinity of Namiquipa. He was a native of that region, and his family owned a ranch known as San Miguelito, a few miles from Rubio (some say he owned it himself). About May 7, 1916, San Miguelito was searched by a patrol from the 16th Infantry, but before the "doughboys" could complete surrounding the place several mounted Mexicans burst out of the single gate and fled to the hills to the west. Later the same day San Miguelito was again searched, this time by a troop of the 11th Cavalry, but nothing was found. The troop was accompanied by General Pershing's aide-de-camp, First Lieutenant George S. Patton, who took this opportunity to familiarize himself with the ranch and its surroundings.

A week later, on orders from Pershing, Patton took three of the headquarters' Dodge cars, with several soldiers and two guide-interpreters, and drove east of Lake Itascate to buy corn at several *haciendas* that were believed to have supplies of the grain. Since San Miguelito was only a few miles distant, Patton decided to have a look before returning to headquarters. Placing a rifleman to cover each side of the quadrilateral, Patton and one of the guides ran to the gate. As they approached, three mounted men dashed out. Patton held his fire; General Pershing's orders about identifying Mexicans as enemies before opening fire were strict. The horsemen, finding themselves cut off by the riflemen at each corner, opened fire with their pistols. Patton instantly knocked one of them off his horse (Patton was a famous pistol shot, even then). The man scrambled through the gate into the patio. Patton's second shot killed a horse under its rider. The man extricated himself from his fallen animal, got to his feet, trying to fire; Patton dropped him. As for the man whom Patton knocked off his horse, accounts differ. There is a version that he

died from a wound from Patton's 45-caliber pistol while trying
to shoot at the Americans from inside the patio. A more probable
account is that he tried to lower himself from a window in the
outer wall of the ranch and was killed by Emil Holmdahl, one
of the guides. After searching the ranch thoroughly, Patton's
detachment lashed the three corpses onto the cars and returned
to Lake Itascate. As they passed through Rubio, a place that was
known to be a hotbed of Villista sympathizers, the sight of the
three dead Mexicans caused some excitement, but no violence
occurred. The Americans were obviously prepared for trouble,
and the three corpses were an object lesson. And, after arriving
at headquarters, the man whom Patton knocked off his horse,
and whom Holmdahl had killed, proved to be no less a person
that Julio Cardenas himself! One more Villista "bigwig" was
accounted for. The other two were identified as a Villista captain
and a private.[15]

About this same time General Candelario Cervantes, with a
small band of hard-core Villistas, began making small raids
upon ranches and isolated villages in the Namiquipa region. On
May 25, 1916, a small detachment of soldiers of the 17th Infantry, commanded by a lance corporal, and accompanied by two
engineer soldiers, a Signal Corps man and a Quartermaster man,
was a few miles south of Cruces. Their purpose was to get some
fresh beef and pork from the wild cattle and hogs seen about an
abandoned ranch. The two engineers were making road sketches.
Without warning, the party was attacked by a band of Mexicans
who charged from the thick underbrush, firing as they came
out. The lance corporal was killed instantly, and three soldiers
were wounded. Private George D. Huelett assumed command
and shot two of the assailants as they galloped by. The other
Americans opened fire, and the enemy became cautious. A soldier
who is remembered today only by his nickname, "Barney Old-
field," who was the driver of the wagon that had been brought
along to carry back the anticipated beef and pork, managed to
slip back to his wagon undetected. He cut loose one of his
horses and galloped to camp for help. Within a few minutes
(about five minutes, according to one of the participants), a
troop of the 11th Cavalry, a detachment of the 13th Cavalry

and one from the Machine Gun Platoon of the 17th Infantry were on their way. The relieving force arrived at the scene of the fight just one hour after leaving Cruces. The Villistas had been extremely cautious since Private Huelett dropped two of them and hurriedly took their departure as the relieving troops approached.

The two dead Mexicans were searched; the papers revealed that one of them was Candelario Cervantes himself! Cervantes, next to Villa, was probably the "most wanted" man in Mexico by the Americans. He was generally considered to be Villa's ablest lieutenant, and it was he who led the Villista column that penetrated into Columbus—the actual leader of the assault. General Pershing, who had high respect for Cervantes' military capabilities, said that killing him was "particularly important."[16]

The rescue party started in pursuit of the Villistas without a moment's delay. Lieutenant Berkeley T. Merchant's patrol from the 13th Cavalry was fired upon while threading its way through a deep, narrow cañon. The shots came from high up on the cañon walls. The Mexicans were so well concealed among the rocks that none were ever seen. There were no human casualties, but four animals were wounded. A day later, on May 26, 1916, Major John M. Jenkins, of the 11th Cavalry, had a brush with a Villista band (probably the same one) just at dusk, at a village called Ortega. Two Villistas were killed; the others scattered into the thicket, and no more was heard of Cervantes' band in the Namiquipa area.

While Scott and Obregón were conferring, Mexican raiders once again put in an appearance. At the tiny settlement of Glen Springs, Texas, not far from the Rio Grande, the 14th Cavalry had an outpost consisting of a sergeant and eight men. On May 5, 1916, raiders struck without warning. The soldiers barricaded themselves in an adobe hut but were finally forced out when the invaders set fire to the thatch roof. The soldiers managed to escape into the surrounding chaparral, from which they continued to shoot. During the two- or three-hour fight three soldiers were killed. The raiders, meanwhile, looted the local store and the storekeeper's house and killed his four-year-old son. From Glen Springs the bandits hastened to the Rio Grande, pausing long enough to loot a store at Boquillas, and forcing the store-keeper (a man named Deemer) and a Negro employee to go with them. They also seized seven American employees of the International Mining Company.

Glen Springs was so isolated that the outer world knew nothing of this raid for two days. General Funston was at El Paso. As soon as he received the news, on May 7, he ordered that two troops of the 8th Cavalry, under Major George T. Langhorne, with four wagons and four trucks, entrain at once for Marathon, Texas. From Marathon, Langhorne would march for the Rio Grande, pursue the raiders, and cross into Mexico if necessary. At the same time Funston telegraphed to Colonel Frederick W. Sibley, at Fort Clark, Texas, to take two troops of the 14th Cavalry, a packtrain, and wagons and motor trucks to Marathon by rail and from there follow Langhorne. The Department Signal Officer was ordered to run a buzzer line from Marathon to the Rio Grande to furnish communication of a sort.

From Marathon to Glen Springs was ninety-two miles. Langhorne's squadron detrained at about ten o'clock on Sunday, May 8, 1916, and within an hour was on the way south. It took two and a half days to reach the Rio Grande. There were no bandits on the United States side of the river, so Langhorne boldly forded the stream and struck into Mexico. At a place known as El Pilo (or El Pito), the Americans were glad to find the store-keeper, Deemer, and his Negro employee unharmed. It was gratifying, too, to learn that the seven kidnaped mining company employees had overpowered their guards and escaped, taking several of the guards as prisoners.

El Pilo was deep in Mexico, a hundred miles south of the boundary. Langhorne decided to establish his base there and then follow the same method that General Pershing had used—send out small, swiftly moving detachments to search and strike. The first detachment sent out, under command of Captain James C. Rhea, drew blood. Rhea surprised and surrounded the bandits at Santa Anita, some seventy-five miles south of El Pilo. There was a sharp fight that lasted only a few minutes; the band was utterly annihilated. Rhea marched triumphantly back to El Pilo with the horses of the 14th Cavalry that the raiders had taken at Glen Springs. The second detachment, under Lieutenant

Cramer, likewise returned to the base camp victoriously, having recovered most of the loot the raiders had taken at Deemer's store.[17]

It has become quite customary among historians to call the Glen Springs raiders Villistas and ascribe the responsibility for the raid to Pancho Villa himself. Nothing could be more unlikely. The raid occurred while Villa was still in hiding, recovering from his wounds, and hundreds of miles from where he actually was. It was in a region, moreover, where his forces never operated, except briefly, during the heyday of his power and authority. Americans on the border believed that the raiders were Carranzistas, or at least included some Carranzistas, but it seems probable that they were bandits, and nothing more, who thought they saw a chance to get some easy loot and kill a few gringos, with little risk to themselves.

Langhorne's small expedition remained in Mexico for two weeks, returning to the United States on May 26, 1916. Carranza sent a highly recriminatory protest to Washington, charging bad faith in sending troops into Mexico while the Scott-Obregón conferences were continuing. Carranza charged further that most of the border raids were actually fomented and planned in the United States. Mexico, he declared, was innocent.

The Carranzistas were becoming more and more openly hostile. In the zone of the Punitive Expedition two troops of the 7th Cavalry, which were still near Guerrero, learned that the bitterly hostile General Cavazos had ordered his troops to fire on any Americans they encountered. General Pershing found it necessary to send a curt note to the Carranzista commander of the Carranzista forces at Bachineva, warning him that any further advance of his troops toward Namiquipa would be regarded as an act of hostility that the Americans would resist. General Funston did not overrule Pershing in this matter, but directed him to "act conservatively. If a breach does occur the responsibility must be beyond question on the Carranza troops."[18] In the Lower Rio Grande Valley there were a number of "pinprick" raids into Texas. Luis de la Rosa, who has been mentioned as one of the promoters of the Plan of San Diego, reappeared, openly recruiting men for raids into the United States.[19] On June 10 a band, supposed to be Rosistas, crossed the Rio Grande a short distance above Laredo but ran into opposition. In the fight three were killed and six captured, one of whom was reported to be a Japanese. But significantly, papers found on one of the bodies showed the man to be a Lieutenant Colonel Villareal, of the Carranzista army.[20]

A few days later, on June 15, 1916, a 14th Cavalry outpost at San Ygnacio, about forty miles below Laredo, was struck at daybreak by raiders who had crossed the river during the night and infiltrated through the chaparral until they were very close. Three soldiers were killed and several wounded, but the outpost (consisting of a platoon) reacted quickly, and the raiders drew off, leaving eight of their number lying on the ground.

It so happened that Captain Edgar Sirmyer, with Troop I, 14th Cavalry, was on the road, marching for San Ygnacio to relieve the outpost with a platoon from his own troop. He was accompanied by Major Alonzo Gray, who was apparently going along just for the ride. Sirmyer and Gray had bivouacked on the night of June 14–15 about twenty miles from San Ygnacio. Early in the morning, as Troop I was breaking camp, a breathless messenger arrived from San Ygnacio. Major Gray, as senior officer present, assumed command and hurried the troop forward. On arrival at San Ygnacio, he found that the raiders had retreated into Mexico. He crossed the river in pursuit, but on finding that the raiders had scattered like quail, and that the local Carranzista commander was presumably hunting for them, he returned to the United States. It was a curious fact, however, that on one of the Mexican bodies at the outpost, there were papers identifying the corpse as a Major Cruz of the Carranzista army.

A curious detail of the San Ygnacio affair, revealing a certain bureaucratic mentality, shows in the unsuccessful effort by the regimental commander of the 14th Cavalry to get aid for his wounded men. Upon receiving information that several men were wounded at San Ygnacio, he telegraphed to Department Headquarters, requesting permission to send an ambulance for the men. To his utter amazement, the request was disapproved. A second telegram brought the same disapproval, whereupon the regimental adjutant telephoned to several public-spirited citizens of Laredo, who promptly climbed into their automobiles and drove over the primitive road to San Ygnacio to bring in the wounded men.[21]

Three days later, General James Parker, who will be remembered as the regimental commander of the 11th Cavalry in the mobilization of 1911, and who was now in command of the American troops in the Lower Rio Grande Valley, sent a small force across the river in pursuit of a gang of raiders. The next day he issued orders to return to the United States if the force had not yet overtaken the quarry. The troops had just mounted for their return to the United States when they were attacked by Carranzista soldiers. The Americans dismounted and returned the Mexican fire, killing and wounding several of the attackers. Then, upon a shouted command, the Americans remounted, and with pistols in hand, charged pell-mell into the enemy, who broke and fled. The Americans pursued for several miles, leaving the Mexicans demoralized and disorganized. Colonel Robert L. Bullard, of the 26th Infantry, on learning that there was trouble on the Mexican side of the river, promptly moved his regiment to a position where he could support the Americans in Mexico; in fact, one boatload of infantrymen reached the Mexican shore, but they were recalled. It was noted that after Parker's quick action, there was a marked lessening of raids and bandit activities in the Lower Rio Grande Valley.

The month of June, 1916, found relations between the two countries becoming more and more tense, with real danger of a full-scale war. Most Mexicans, regardless of their sympathies in their revolution, were united in their resentment against Americans and particularly against the Punitive Expedition. This resentment was manifested in the raids that have been recounted, and in many more that have not been mentioned. It appeared that the borderland was facing what a later generation would call a "blood bath."

NOTES

1. Tompkins, *op. cit.*, pp. 168–69. Major Howze's squadron joined before Brown started the march northward and was thus included in the command.

2. *Ibid.*, pp. 169–70.
3. *Ibid.*, pp. 171–72.
4. *Ibid.*, p. 187.
5. *Ibid.*, p. 174.
6. *Ibid.*, p. 177.
7. *Ibid.*, pp. 178–83; also the unpublished memoirs of Col. Jerome W. Howe, "My Military Career," pp. 35–41, and his field diary, entries for Apr. 20–23, 1916, inclusive.
8. Tompkins, *op. cit.*, pp. 189–90. Col. William C. Brown, of the 10th Cavalry, had been relieved of command, over his own vigorous protest, because of his health. This left Major Evans as the senior officer with the regiment.
9. James A. Shannon, "With the Apache Scouts in Mexico," *Cavalry Journal*, XXVII (Apr., 1917), 546. Shannon was killed in battle in France in 1918. Sgt. Chicken, whom the writer knew years later, with several other members of the Apache Scouts, was a veteran of the campaigns of Crook and Miles against Geronimo.
10. Sumner M. Williams, "The Cavalry Fight at Ojos Azules," *Cavalry Journal*, XXVII (Jan., 1917), 405–8. A soldier who was in this fight once told the writer, "They were on foot and we were mounted, but they ran so fast we couldn't catch them."
11. Quoted in Tompkins, *op. cit.*, p. 192.
12. Hugh Lenox Scott, *Some Memories of a Soldier* (New York, 1928), pp. 527–28.
13. Clendenen, *The United States and Pancho Villa*, pp. 270–75.
14. *Foreign Relations, 1916*, pp. 534–44.
15. Tompkins, *op. cit.*, p. 195.
16. *Ibid.*, pp. 200–203; Haldeen Braddy, *Pershing's Mission in Mexico* (El Paso, Tex., 1965, pp. 41–42, 75. See also Curtis G. Chezem, "Down Pershing's Highway to Pancho Villa Land," *Four-Wheeler*, Apr., 1966, 22–25. Dr. Chezem, who is a nuclear physicist at Los Alamos and a four-wheel–drive enthusiast, visited San Miguelito in 1965. He and his son were most hospitably received, and he says, "We were astonished to hear the story of Patton's assault almost exactly as reported in the U.S. Army records."
17. Braddy, *op. cit.*, pp. 43, 75. Braddy quotes from the Pershing Papers, Box 372. Also Tompkins, *op. cit.*, pp. 202–5.
18. *Foreign Relations, 1916*, pp. 540–41, 542, 543, 544–46; James Hopper, "A Little Mexican Expedition," *Collier's Magazine*, LVII (July 15, 1916), 4–6, 22; Report of the Chief of Staff, *War Department Annual Reports, 1916*, I, 193.
19. *Foreign Relations, 1916*, pp. 565–66.
20. *Ibid.*, pp. 567–73.
21. Information given the writer by Maj. Gen. Frederick Gilbreath, U. S. Army, Ret., who was then the adjutant of the 14th Cavalry.

CHAPTER 15

The National Guard
and the Border

THE EARLIEST English Colonists in North America brought with them as a part of their intellectual baggage, the concept, dating from Anglo-Saxon times, that every able-bodied male had an obligation to help defend the realm. In actual practice the theory had fallen into obsolescence by the time of King James I, but sheer necessity brought about a revival in the American Colonies. There was the ever present danger from Indians, and there was always a threat from the French in the north and the Spaniards in the south. At first the militia laws were strictly enforced, and training days were frequent, but as the frontier receded westward, less and less attention was paid to the militia, and as in the Mother Country, the system fell into the discard.

One of the early acts of Congress, under the new Constitution, was a militia law legislated in 1792. It was vague and general, and no machinery or organization for its enforcement was provided. Its broad terms specified that all able-bodied men between the ages of eighteen and forty-four, inclusive, were members of the militia. It provided, on paper, for the organization of companies, regiments, and even brigades and divisions, but the Federal government assumed no responsibility for weapons, ammunition, uniforms or other supplies. All that was left to the different states, and in most cases, the states "passed the buck" to the individual. There were a few states in which militia organizations grew up composed of men who had a taste for the military and who were able to arm and uniform themselves and drill with some degree of regularity. Such organizations were also social clubs, and often membership carried with it a high degree of social prestige. But over the country as a whole the militia system was moribund, and the "Federal Militia Act of 1792 had given America's obligated manpower a semblance of organization that was no more than a system for a continuing military census."[1]

The law of 1792 remained, unchanged, as the fundamental militia law of the United States until 1903. After the War of 1812 on only two occasions was the militia taken into Federal service, at the outbreak of the Civil War and of the Spanish-American War, both times on a purely voluntary, instead of an obligatory, basis. In fact, some of the militia organizations had so far become purely social organizations that the colonel of one famous regiment refused to answer the call, on the ground that he could not subject his officers and men to the indignity of taking orders from Regular Army officers, who were their social inferiors.

In the ferment following the Spanish-American War, Congress at last changed the fundamental law. The Dick Act of 1903 increased appropriations for the militia and provided for Federal pay when the militia was participating in maneuvers with the Regular Army and for uniformity of organization and equipment with the Regular Army. An important provision was that a sharp line of demarcation was drawn between the organized militia and the vast, unorganized reservoir of manpower included in the Act of 1792. The organized militia would henceforth be designated as the National Guard—a term that had been in use for years but had had no legal definition. The tug of war between the proponents of the National Guard and a strong group in the War Department who wanted exclusive Federal control over all military matters lies outside the scope of this discussion. It is enough to say that for the first time in American military history the militia (or National Guard, the term that will be used hereafter) became a definite component of the national military organization. In 1908 the Dick Act was amended to specify that the National Guard would be ordered into the Federal service before the issue of any call for volunteers and that when so ordered, it might be retained in the national service as long as the President considered necessary. In 1912, however, the effects of the Dick Act were weakened somewhat by an opinion of the Attorney General that the Guard could not be sent outside the territorial limits of the United States.[2]

The reader will recall than on May 8, 1916, Generals Scott and Funston sent a joint telegram to Washington urging that the National Guard of Texas, New Mexico and Arizona be ordered into the Federal service at once. The Regular Army was scraping the bottom of the barrel, and still there were not enough United States soldiers on the Mexican border to assure the safety of the people. Seldom in American history has such a recommendation been approved and acted on so quickly. On May 9, the next day, the Guard of the three states received the Presidential order.

Among the rank and file of the Guard there was some misunderstanding at the time. Officers and men were required to take an additional oath, this one directly to the United States government. Some men had the idea that they were enlisting in the Regular Army and would be held for a full term of enlistment, which they were loath to do. In a company that is unidentified, except that it was from Texas, one of the lieutenants talked informally to the objectors:

> "I just have this to say," he told the men as he came to them —not making a speech or anything of the kind, but talking quite informally. "I just want to say that if any man in this company shows a streak of yellow, I don't want him ever to speak to me again back home—because I surely don't intend to speak to him. I don't want him even to look at me on the street. I don't want to have anything to do with him, and I don't want my friends to associate with him either. If there's one thing I despise it's a quitter."[3]

The men were soon reassured about their enlistments; they were obligated only for the unexpired part of their enlistment in the National Guard. They were not enlisting for the Regular Army term of seven years (three years on active duty, four years in the reserve, according to the law of the time). Very few Guardsmen refused to take the required oath.

The mobilization of the Guard from the three border states brought out into strong relief some of its weaknesses and deficiencies, none of which surprised anyone who was familiar with the Guard, although it seems that newspapers overstressed and exaggerated many of them. It was alleged that more than a hundred Texans refused to be mustered in; that another organization reported for duty with some of the officers and soldiers wearing civilian clothes and "derby hats, and with feather beds for the officers."[4] Inasmuch as all three states made strenuous efforts to recruit their organizations after the Federal orders were received, and that uniforms and equipment were short, the allegation is not improbable, except that derby hats were not popular in the West. As for the feather beds, why not? They were not forbidden, and the best field soldier is the one who makes himself as comfortable as possible, not the one who deliberately cultivates discomfort.

The war in Europe and the imminent danger of war with Mexico had combined to make the American people more aware of national defense problems than ever before in American history. There were vociferous pacifists who opposed any military measures whatever, and in Congress, and probably the Cabinet as well, there was disagreement on what should be done. Before his resignation Secretary of War Lindley M. Garrison had sponsored and supported a plan for a "Continental Army," which would, in effect, have been a National Guard under purely Federal auspices. The existing National Guard would have been relegated to the status of a home guard. Quite naturally and understandably, the National Guard, with its long tradition, and its local pride and *esprit de corps*, fought back. The result was that in the National Defense Act of 1916, which became law on June 3 of that year, the National Guard would pass under complete Federal control in time of war or grave public emergency, as decided by the President.

In Mexico, resentment against the United States and the Punitive Expedition continued to mount. The situation became really threatening when, on June 17, information reached Washington that on the day before, General J. B. Treviño had notified General Pershing that thereafter the American forces would be allowed to move in no direction except to the north; any American troops moving south, east or west would be attacked. Pershing replied curtly, "You are informed that my Government has placed no such restrictions upon the movements of the American forces. I shall therefore use my own judgment as to when and in what direction I shall move my forces in pursuit of bandits or in seeking information regarding bandits."[5]

In case of a full war in Mexico, the attenuated forces on the border would be totally inadequate for defense, even though they had just been reinforced by approximately five thousand officers and men of the Guard of the border states. Not merely were the forces on the border inadequate for proper defense, but it would be impossible to undertake the offensive that would be necessary to bring the Mexican war lords to their senses. And the only reserve that the United States had was the National Guard. On June 18, 1916, the day after Washington was informed of General Treviño's threat, and less than three weeks after the passage of the National Defense Act of 1916, President Wilson ordered the National Guard of all the states into the national service.

Beginning the next day, June 19, National Guardsmen began assembling at their armories all over the United States, in every state except Nevada, which had no National Guard. The general plan was for the Guard of each state, after assembling at their various armories, to be concentrated at a central camp in each state and then moved to the Border. There was, naturally, much confusion, but actually much less than might reasonably have been expected. Many organizations were little more than cadres; in many, too, there was a lack of essential equipment. But the movement went on. It seems that the General Staff, expecting that Congress would approve something like Secretary Garrison's Continental Army scheme, had not prepared plans for a full mobilization of the Guard, but even so, and in spite of accusations and allegations that came up later, the Guard assembled and moved to the Border.

With surprising speed, in view of the lack of a basic plan and no previous preparation, the movement proceeded. On July 1, only twelve days after the Presidential call to arms, there were

122 troop trains on the way; four days later 101 trains were en route. The first National Guard unit actually to reach the Border was the 1st Illinois Infantry, which left its assembly camp at Springfield late in the evening of June 28 and detrained at San Antonio a few minutes after midnight, June 30. By midnight of July 4, 1916, National Guardsmen of fourteen states were at their assigned Border stations. By the end of July, no less than 112,000 men had been transported to four major assembly areas— San Antonio, Brownsville, El Paso, and Douglas, Arizona.[6]

In some instances there were delays in the departure of Guard units from their state assembly points because of understrength and inability to obtain essential items of equipment. In a few instances delay was caused by faulty liaison between the War Department and state military authorities. In West Virginia, for example, the Guard assembled at the state capital, Charleston, while Federal equipment and supplies were shipped to Terra Alta, the place that had been designated in a previous plan for the mobilization of the West Virginia Guard.

In spite of inexperience and the occurrence of the unforeseeable, troop trains rolled toward the Border in unbroken succession for days. Admittedly, some of the Guardsmen did not find the journey a pleasure trip. The more sensational newspapers, especially those that were opposed to the Administration, had a field day in recounting the hardships and terrors of the trip to the border. Floyd Gibbons, whom the reader has encountered briefly chasing General Pershing in a second-hand car in the depths of Chihuahua, was loudly indignant in the pages of the Chicago *Tribune* because of "overloaded day coaches" filled with "weary, sleepless, unwashed human freight."[77]

The reason, of course, why many of the troops had to ride in day coaches was simply that there were not enough tourist sleepers in the United States to accommodate the number of men being transported. The complaints about the rail accommodations for the troops were voiced so loudly that as early as July 5, while the movement was still under way, Congress called upon the Secretary of War for a statement. Baker ordered an investigation, which revealed that the Pullman Company owned 750 tourist sleepers, of which 623 had been turned over to the government.

As for allegations that many of the Guardsmen had to ride in coaches that were without lights, these were found to be figments of some journalist's imagination. Likewise, charges that the men were without food, and had to raid stores and restaurants at stopping places, were found to be without foundation.[8] It is clear that most of the alleged discomfort of the train journey occurred because neither officers nor noncommissioned officers knew yet how to handle the "travel ration," or how to expend "liquid coffee money," which they received before leaving their mobilization camps.

To the Guardsmen of the border states the scenery of the border country was familiar, but to the men from the green Middle West and the Atlantic Coast, the scene was one of desolation and horror. Many of them knew so little of what to expect, knew so little about the southwest of their own country, that when a train was delayed at San Antonio because of a broken rail, the officers immediately formed a defensive perimeter to repel the expected Mexican attack.[9]

Since there was no time to prepare camps and campsites in advance, the Guardsmen had to make shift with constructing their own living places. The 1st Kansas Infantry, for example, detrained at Eagle Pass, Texas, on July 2, 1916, and marched several miles to the regiment's assigned area. There the soldiers "laid out the camp from the primeval desert . . . grubbing out mesquite, cactus, and other undesirable features of the terrain, including rattlesnakes, tarantulas and scorpions, in 100-degree heat—it hadn't rained for nine months."[10]

Early in July the Assistant Chief of Staff, Major General Tasker H. Bliss, started on a detailed inspection of the Guard on the border, all the way from Brownsville to Nogales, Arizona. He took almost a month on it, going into detail and missing nothing. He found widely varying conditions. In some camps there were men sleeping on the ground, while others in the same camp had cots. Nearly all units were short of necessary items of equipment, but such shortages were being corrected as rapidly as possible. Most of the National Guard machine gun companies were lacking in either guns or horses, and sometimes in both. The campsites were good, except for two, which would be flooded and become quagmires in case of wet weather. The men were in good health, and sick rates were low. There were some cases of venereal disease, most of which were contracted before coming to the Border. With a few exceptions, the Guardsmen were properly clothed and shod. General Bliss found the training of the units generally unsatisfactory, but he realized that at the time of his inspection, there had not yet been enough time to whip into shape the number or raw recruits every unit had. And without exception, he found their spirit excellent.[11]

There is no denying that many of the amateur soldiers found the going rough. A New York Guardsman wrote in a letter to friends in the lushly foliaged East: "You have bought real estate in many parts of the country; but if you ever bought any here one would think you had lost your mind. This is the most forsaken country the Lord ever made. We ought to clean Mexico up, and for punishment make them take back this part of Texas."[12]

It goes without saying that most of the Guardsmen expected and hoped to fight the Mexicans soon after arriving, but such was not to be. Instead, they found themselves in a daily grind of drill, drill, shoot, shoot and fatigue, fatigue and more fatigue. There were long marches, designed to harden the men and instill march discipline so that they could be maneuvered if war should come. The marches were, at first, hard on men who were not accustomed to the summer temperatures of the Border, or to the dust and the complete absence of amenities that they took for granted in their homes. Rupert Hughes, a noted writer of the time, who was a captain in the famous old 69th New York Infantry, described, in harrowing terms, a "hike"—a practice march—that his regiment had to take as a part of its training. To a seasoned soldier the daily march schedules would appear almost ridiculously easy, being only six or seven miles a day, but to men who were accustomed only to the sidewalks of New York, they were frightful. And to city men the hours demanded of soldiers were pure tyranny:

> Reveille is a tune played by a pack of bugles all barking lustily. As Sergeant Madigan of my company would say in the big hike: "When I get home to New York, well, there's a man sharpens scissors used to come down my street blowin' a bugle!

I'm just waitin' for him when I get home. If he blows his bugle in my street, I'll wrap a horseshoe round his neck."[13]

To add to the discomfort of everybody, and especially to the relatively raw soldiers of the National Guard, in the middle of July a hurricane struck through all of lower Texas. Captain Hughes's company was on the target range several miles from San Antonio when the storm hit: "We shot lying down in bathtubs of water with the rain flogging our backs and filling the sights of the guns." On the return march to their camp the men "leaned" against the wind and floundered in the mud. The tents in the camp were blown down, and the men spent the night huddled around smoky fires that they were able to start and somehow keep burning.[14] In the 1st Kansas Infantry camp, near Laredo, the officers' tents had been pitched along the bank of a ravine, which quickly became a rushing, dangerous torrent that washed away many of the wooden tent floors; the soldiers' conical Sibley tents were blown flat, wooden mess halls were unroofed. Fortunately the storm lasted only a few hours. It was over by dawn, and the troops spent the day drying themselves and reerecting the sodden tentage.

Hughes, speaking rather cynically, quoted General Funston as saying that troops in a permanent camp decline in efficiency. The infantry, he said, must learn to march. Hughes observed, also, that Sir Isaac Newton had missed one undoubted law of gravity: that the longer an object such as a soldier's pack is carried, the heavier it becomes. The last day of the march was the worst of all. It was a hot day such as only the borderland knows. In the 69th New York Infantry no less than 130 men fell by the wayside, overcome by heat and exhaustion, but the morale of the 69th received a fillip when the soldiers learned that another New York regiment had left 340 men beside the road.[15]

Many observers, newspaper reporters and other writers, unaccustomed to soldier ways, took the men's griping and grumbling seriously: "Never again!" "I'm through. They'll never get me into uniform again as long as I live!" "I wanna go home!" And yet these same National Guard organizations, with many (probably most) of the same men, within the next two years, plunged ahead into flaming sheets of German machine gun fire and barrages to carry their objectives.

There was, however, a serious side to some National Guardsmen's complaints that posed a problem that has not been wholly solved as yet and possibly cannot be solved. Actually it is a problem as old as war itself—the problem of the soldier who leaves dependents behind. A succession of pitiful letters was addressed to the President, the Secretary of War and to the senators and representatives in Congress, pleading for the immediate release of the breadwinner, the sole support of a large family, or of sick children or aged parents. It was necessary for the military authorities to take a skeptical view of most of these complaints, as pitiful as many of them were. It was impossible to investigate each complaint and plea, and while many of them were exaggerated or spurious, others were genuine cases of hardship. To take care of worthy cases, on July 18, 1916, the Secretary of War authorized the discharge of any National Guardsmen who had dependent relatives and who applied for his discharge. A few weeks later Congress passed an act for financial assistance for Guardsmen with dependents. This was a measure that helped morale and also provided a precedent for similar legislation in more recent wars.[16]

Another personnel and morale problem arose from the numbers of college students who had enrolled, almost en masse on some campuses. At Yale a large number of students had formed themselves into the "Yale Battery" of artillery. Because there was no such thing as the R.O.T.C. at that time, in order to obtain necessary equipment (including the guns), the Yale Battery was integrated into the Connecticut National Guard and ordered into the Federal service with the rest of the Connecticut Guard. The National Guard artillery of most of the eastern states never went to the Border, but spent their time at Tobyhanna, Pennsylvania, where they underwent a summer of intensive training. The Yale Battery was but one of several similar organizations in different parts of the country, and there were large numbers of students in nearly all units. On August 2, 1916, Secretary Baker ordered the discharge of such students and student organizations as soon as practicable after September

1. This policy was modified within a few days, but nevertheless, there is no record of any student missing his school year because of enlistment in the National Guard. A little while later, orders were issued for the discharge of any bona fide student who intended to resume his studies and applied for discharge.

This order gave at least one young student an opportunity to discover for himself that senior Regular Army officers were not always the ogres that popular imagination often depicted. An undergraduate of a midwestern university, believing that nothing important was going to happen on the Border, applied for his discharge in September, so that he could reenter college. Several days later he asked the regimental adjutant about his discharge. The adjutant's reply was, "The colonel says that nobody gets a discharge," and with that, the soldier's discharge papers, which were lying on the desk, were crumpled up and tossed into the wastebasket. The young Guardsman, discouraged and depressed, took his courage in hand and walked into the headquarters of Major General George Bell, the district commander, and asked the adjutant there for permission to speak to the commanding general. The adjutant refused, but General Bell, overhearing the conversation, came to the door of his office, and said, "What's the matter? Come on in, soldier." Once in the general's office, the Guardsman poured out his troubles. General Bell listened quietly, then exploded, calling the adjutant: "Get Colonel Blank up here at once! I'll teach him who's running the army!" And to the soldier, "You'd better get out of here, son. There's going to be some fireworks." The soldier received his discharge the next day and went from there to a long and distinguished academic career.[17]

Although the ranks of the National Guard on the border were thinned somewhat by dependency and student discharges, the tight training and hardening schedules went on, along with some experiment and innovation. Early in September, 1916, it was decided to transfer the two Kansas infantry regiments to San Antonio, where they would be incorporated into the newly formed 12th Division, and for the first time in American military history a large body of troops was moved by motor, instead of by marching or by rail. To carry the two regiments

required 132 vehicles; the motor movement took two days to
cover a distance of approximately 180 miles. Moving by truck
was not as comfortable as moving in a limousine or a Pullman
car, but, "Oh well, it beats pounding the hard road with our
shoes."[18] Planks were placed across the side boards of the trucks
for the men to sit on, but the planks became uncomfortably
hard as the trucks bounced along the unimproved dirt roads of
the region. The soldiers soon found that their blanket rolls could
be used as cushions, and there was even a rumor that Guardsmen "liberated" a number of car seats from automobiles parked
along the road.

General Funston was at hand to watch the Kansas troops
move into San Antonio. He was a Kansan, and his Spanish-
American War regiment, the 20th Kansas Volunteers, was
considered to be the ancestral regiment of the 1st Kansas Infantry of 1916. He was pleased with what he saw, but the troops
were not allowed to rest very long. A practice march from San
Antonio to Austin and return was soon under way. On this
march the Guardsmen slogged along the road in the traditional
infantry way. Although the weather in southern Texas in September is usually oppressively hot, by this time the Guardsmen
were hardened. Not a man fell by the wayside. As an important
detail in their training, each man was limited to one canteen of
water per day while marching, and the daily marches were much
longer than those that had caused such consternation earlier in
the summer.[19]

No National Guard organizations crossed the boundary into
Mexico, although two regiments, the 1st New Mexico Infantry
and the 2d Massachusetts Infantry, were assigned to the Punitive Expedition and were carried in its station list. They were
kept at Columbus to provide guards and local security for the
base. Numbers of individuals from these two regiments, however, crossed the border on various duties. Officers from both
regiments were placed in command of truck trains, and National Guardsmen were frequently detailed as guards for the
trains. And it might be mentioned in passing that several soldiers
of the New Mexico regiment were tried by court-martial for
going into Mexico to hunt, without authority.

The medical arrangements for the health and well-being of

the troops on the border were exhaustive and thorough. It was a far cry from the conditions of 1898, only eighteen years before. In addition to the regimental and post dispensaries, large hospitals were established at Brownsville, San Antonio, El Paso and Douglas. In addition, the War Department was able to obtain a hospital train, the first in the American service, with cars specially fitted and equipped for hospital purposes. It was constructed at the Pullman shops in Chicago and sent to the border in August, 1916. The train consisted of ten cars and could care for 76 bed patients and 120 ambulatory patients. One car was fitted as a kitchen car, one car was living quarters for the medical personnel, one car was an operating and recovery room, four cars were for litter patients, one car was a combination of baggage car with additional recovery space, and two cars were for ambulatory patients. The train was staffed by three medical officers, twenty-five Hospital Corps soldiers, and seven nurses.[20]

The mobilization of the National Guard in the summer of 1916 was a direct outcome of the international situation that arose from Pancho Villa's raid and the Punitive Expedition. Thus, although no Guard units entered Mexico, and as far as available records show, none had a fight with raiders, the story of the National Guard in 1916 is quite properly a part of the history of American military ventures into Mexico. And, like the Punitive Expedition itself, the mobilization of the Guard was to have an effect in the near future that no one could foresee in the summer of 1916. Large numbers of men were hardened physically and trained; officers and noncommissioned officers gained priceless experience in actually handling men in the field, planning for them, and making them take care of themselves. Deficiencies in procedures and other weaknesses were revealed. Beginning in February, 1917, a start was made toward the demobilization of the National Guard, but with increasing tension with Germany, the demobilization was not entirely completed. When the final breach with Germany occurred, the remobilization of the Guard units that had been already discharged was far smoother and effected with less confusion than in June, 1916. It is quite true that the United States was woefully unprepared for a war against a major power in the spring of 1917, but not nearly as poorly prepared as it would have been had not the Punitive Expedition of 1916 brought about the first nation-wide mobilization of the National Guard.

NOTES

1. Jim Dan Hill, *The Minute Man in Peace and War. A History of the National Guard* (Harrisburg, Pa., 1964), p. 9.
2. *Ibid.*, pp. 185–90, 203–5.
3. Dallas *News*, date unspecified, quoted in *Literary Digest*, LVII (June 24, 1916), 1866, 1868.
4. "Our Unprepared Militia," *Literary Digest*, LVII (June 3, 1916), 1617.
5. *Foreign Relations, 1916*, p. 577.
6. *Report on Mobilization of the Organized Militia and National Guard of the United States, 1916* (Washington, 1916), p. 12. This is the official report of the Militia Bureau of the War Department. Hereafter referred to as *Militia Bureau Report*.
7. Hill, *op. cit.*, p. 239.
8. *Militia Bureau Report*, pp. 52–53.
9. Earle E. Perrenot, "The National Guard Fiasco," *Out West*, XLIV (Aug. 1916), 80.
10. Unpublished diary of Maj. Gen. Frank N. Roberts, U.S. Army, Ret., a copy of which General Roberts kindly gave the writer.
11. *Militia Bureau Report*, pp. 59–64.
12. "From a National Guardsman," *Outlook*, CXIII (Aug. 2, 1916), 773.
13. Rupert Hughes, "The Big Hike," *Collier's Magazine*, LVIII (Nov. 11, 1916), 5.
14. *Ibid.*, p. 6.
15. *Ibid.*, p. 26.
16. *Militia Bureau Report*, pp. 40–41.
17. In a personal letter from Dr. John Rufi, emeritus Professor of Education, the University of Missouri, to the writer.
18. Statement by Col. Edwin Wheatley, U.S. Army, Ret., in the Horton, Kansas newspaper. Colonel Wheatley gave the writer a copy of the article, but unfortunately both the exact name of the newspaper and the date of issue are missing.
19. *Ibid.* This motor movement is also mentioned in General Roberts' diary, cited earlier, and in a letter from L. E. Hervey to Leon B. Graves, of Ottawa, Kansas. Mr. Graves, who is an *aficionado* of Pancho Villa and the Border warfare, has made a collection of letters from Kansas Guardsmen who served on the border.
20. "The First American Hospital Train," *Review of Reviews*, LIV (December, 1916), 652–653; "Report of the Chief of Staff," *War Department Annual Reports, 1916*, I, 197–198.

CHAPTER 16

The Fight at Carrizal

GENERAL PERSHING was still moving his forces slowly northward to the vicinity of Casas Grandes and Colonia Dublán on May 16 when he received the extraordinary communication from General Treviño that said that the Americans would be attacked if they moved in any direction save north. Pershing's reply to Treviño has been related. On the same day Pershing was informed orally by the commander of the Carranzista garrison at Casas Grandes that the First Chief had ordered that the Americans would be allowed to move northward only. To this, Pershing replied by asking the Carranzista to inform his superiors that the Americans refused to be bound by such instructions.[1]

On May 22, 1916, the de facto government sent a lengthy communication to Washington that was almost unprecedented in diplomatic correspondence for its acrimonious tone and undiplomatic language. Carranza charged the United States with bad faith, and with making a serious invasion of Mexico for the purpose of seizing additional Mexican territory. Langhorne's pursuit of the Glen Springs raiders was denounced as an act of unjustifiable aggression against Mexico, and as for the Punitive Expedition, the note said bluntly, "In regard to the troops which are now in the State of Chihuahua and which crossed as a result of the Columbus affair, the Mexican government is forced to insist upon their withdrawal." It was added that in case of refusal, Mexico had no recourse but to take up arms—

a clear threat of war. Yet, inconsistently, a large part of the document was concerned with complaints that the United States had halted the delivery of a shipment of machinery for the manufacture of munitions which had been purchased by the de facto government.[2]

The Carranza note was so provocative and so inflammatory that the State Department decided not to make it public for fear that its insulting tones and terms might so arouse the public that calm consideration would be impossible. The Carranza government, however, felt no such qualms, for the note was given to the press in Mexico City. It was an opportunity for the Carranza government to capitalize upon the almost universal Mexican resentment against the United States by "plucking feathers from the eagle's tail."

As tension mounted, General Gabriel Gavira, who commanded the Carranzista forces at Juarez and the surrounding area, made the sensible suggestion that a large part of the difficulties arose because he and General Pershing were not in communication with each other and that a conference between the two might overcome much of the misunderstanding. Washington approved, and Gavira and Pershing met at Colonia Dublán on June 1. Without any apparent difficulty they reached an agreement whereby Gavira would reduce the Carranzista garrisons along the railroad in the zone occupied by the Americans and would remove the garrisons from towns on the American lines of communication. The United States approved at once, but nothing was ever heard from Mexico City. The earlier and more ambitious attempt to arrive at an understanding through the conferences between General Scott and Obregón had failed already because Carranza would accept nothing but the immediate withdrawal of the expedition.

Whether or not Pershing was aware of the orders sent from Mexico City to General Arnulfo Gómez in Sonora, to be ready to cut the American lines of communications, is unknown. It is more than probable that all information that came to Funston's headquarters, and to General Bell, at El Paso, was transmitted to him as quickly as possible. He had his own sources of information that kept him apprised of matters of local and im-

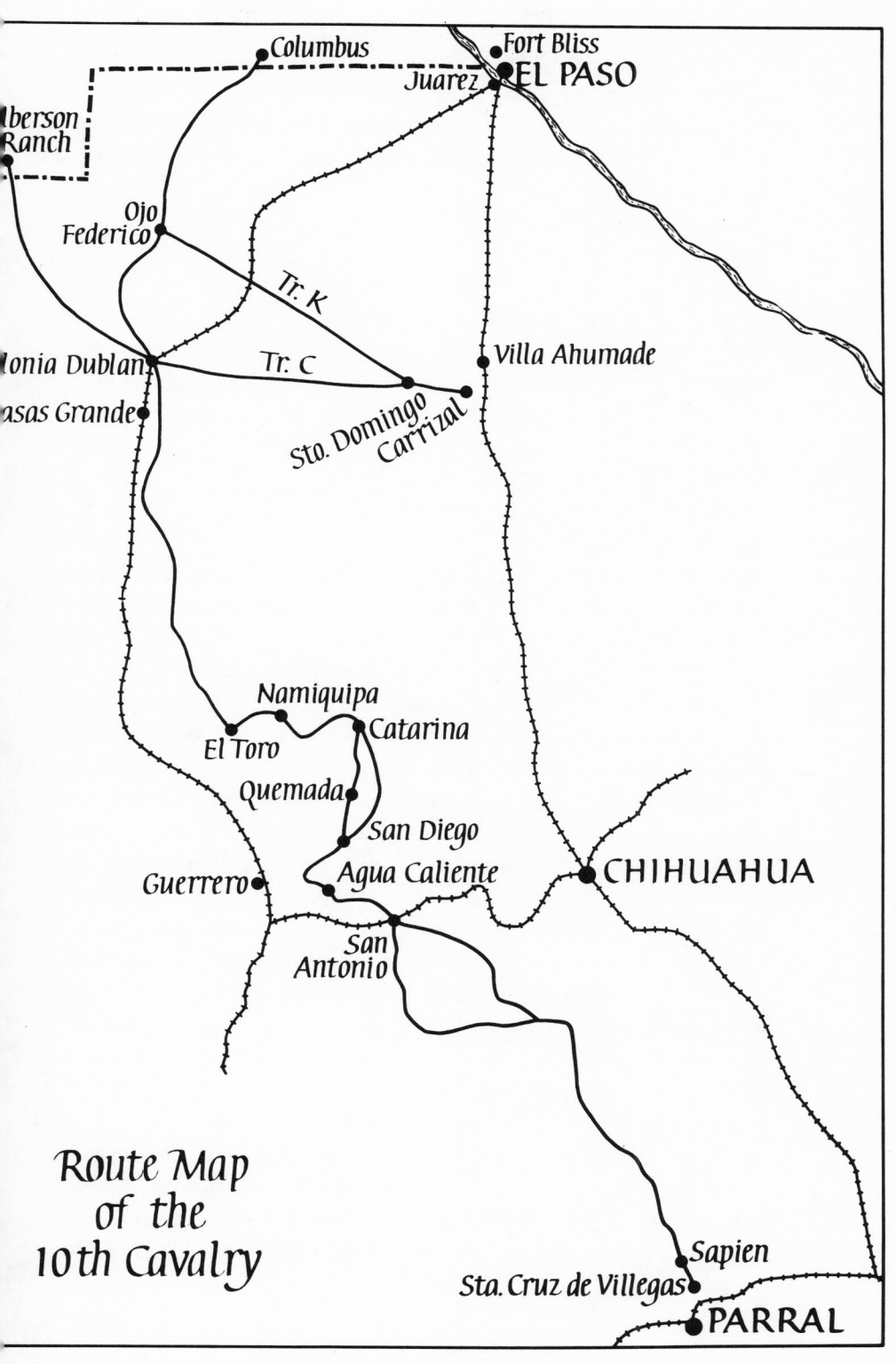

Columbus

Fort Bliss

Juarez

EL PASO

lberson
Ranch

Ojo
Federico

Tr. K

lonia Dublan

Tr. C

Villa Ahumade

asas Grande

Sto. Domingo
Carrizal

Namiquipa

Catarina

El Toro

Quemada

San Diego

Guerrero

Agua Caliente

CHIHUAHUA

San
Antonio

Route Map
of the
10th Cavalry

Sapien

Sta. Cruz de Villegas

PARRAL

mediate importance, and moreover, Pershing was not a commander to be caught napping. As the international situation
developed, he laid his plans with care for fast action in case of
open hostilities. In one of his pocket notebooks is an undated
entry entitled.

In case of hostilities

Dublan & [illegible]

1. Order cavalry to move south and capture garrisons at Pearson
   and San Diego.
2. Also destroy railroads south of those points and carry away
   rails. Also destroy telegraph line and seize instruments at
   both places.
3. To move one squadron south and destroy railroad [entry il-
   legible] only sufficiently to detain any enemy trains, but not
   so that it cannot be repaired by our own R.R. repair gangs
   with rails and ties.
4. Then to contract camp into a new compact size and construct
   it to protect supplies and lines of communication.
5. To make frequent patrols south and west and cause same to
   be made by other commands on line of communications.

This entry in Pershing's personal notebook seems to have
been made in the first week of June, 1916. In another pocket
memorandum book he noted a complete plan of action in case of
necessity—a plan in which each major unit of the expedition was
assigned a specific mision in a series of quick, smashing blows
with massed forces of cavalry, infantry and artillery against the
Carranzista forces. In short, he planned to take the offensive.[3]

On June 1, before Treviño's ultimatum to Pershing but after
the offensive Mexican note of May 22, President Wilson let it be
known that he had no intention of withdrawing the Punitive
Expedition simply because of Carranza's demands. It is probably not coincidental that the American reply to the note of
May 22 was forwarded to Mexico City on June 20, after the
mobilization of the National Guard was ordered. The American
reply to Carranza was almost an innovation in the long and
tortuous diplomatic correspondence between the two governments. Secretary Lansing did not mince terms, although he did
not step outside the polite phraseology of diplomacy. He did not

openly accuse the Mexican government of bad faith, and he did not openly call Carranza a liar, although the inference was clear. To the Mexican demand for the withdrawal of the Punitive Expedition, Lansing replied that "the request of the de facto Government can not now be entertained." If the Carranza government resorted to arms, as was so broadly threatened, "the Government of the United States would surely be lacking in sincerity and friendship if it did not frankly impress upon the de facto Government that the execution of this threat will lead to the gravest consequences."[4]

There the situation rested for a brief time—a situation that could be likened to an open case of dynamite with a careless smoker standing nearby. From late in May, General Pershing's standing instructions to all patrols were that the Americans must do nothing that would antagonize the Carranzistas. Patrols were ordered to avoid all places occupied by the troops of the de facto government: "Make every effort to avoid collision, but if attacked, inflict as much damage as possible, having regard for the safety of your own command."[5] On May 25 a small patrol from the 5th Cavalry had an otherwise unrecorded brush with Villistas at the Guadalupe River. There were no casualties, and no details are known. This was the last fight with Villistas by any unit of the expedition, but active patrolling and reconnaissance continued, as is attested by the war diaries of all organizations of the command.

On June 17, 1916, the day after Treviño's warning reached Pershing, Captain Charles T. Boyd, of the 10th Cavalry, was ordered to report to the Commanding General at his headquarters at Colonia Dublán. Boyd was the troop commander of Troop C, 10th Cavalry; he and Pershing had known each other for years. According to the statement that Pershing later made for the record, he told Boyd:

A large concentration of Carrancista [sic] troops is reported in the vicinity of Ahumada, one the Mexican Central Railroad. Information has been received that this force is being assembled in conjunction with other de facto forces from Pearson and Nueva Casas Grandes [sic]. Take your troop and reconnoiter in the direction of Ahumada and obtain as much information as you can regarding the forces there. This is a reconnaissance only, and you will not be expected to fight. In fact, I want you to avoid a fight if possible. Do not allow yourself to be surprised by superior numbers. But if wantonly attacked, use your own judgment as to what you shall do, having due regard for your command. I then went on to tell Captain Boyd of General Treviño's order to attack our troops if we should send them west, east, or south. And further told him that it would not be wise to go into any place garrisoned by Carrancista troops.[6]

Numerous items in General Pershing's papers show that he had the highest regard for Boyd, both personally and professionally. Boyd had a fine military record and was the author of a book on minor tactics. There is some indication that his regimental commander selected him for this mission because of his established reputation for firmness, courage, tact and diplomacy.[7] The 10th Cavalry, as has been mentioned before, was one of the four Negro regiments of the Regular Army before World War II. It had a splendid battle record in numerous Indian wars, in the Spanish-American War and in the Philippine Insurrection, and had an enviable *esprit de corps* and regimental pride.

On June 18, 1916, Captain Lewis Morey, of Troop K, 10th Cavalry, then at Ojo Federico, about midway between Colonia Dublán and Columbus, received an order in writing similar to that which Pershing had given to Boyd orally. But there is a discrepancy that is impossible to explain today. Morey was ordered to march to Santo Domingo ranch, and there report to and join Boyd. For some unfathomable reason, Boyd was not informed of this.[8]

The eastward march of the two troops, in direct defiance of General Treviño's warning, was without incident. The march across the flat desert was uncomfortable but without the grim hardship of the marches in the arctic winter of the Sierra Madre. The country was barren and dry, with "the outline of a distant plateau, plenty of mesquite and alkaline atmosphere."[9] The distance to be covered by each troop in its march from the starting point to the vicinity of Villa Ahumada was about a hundred miles, possibly more. (Existing maps of the region, to this day, are so inaccurate that it is impossible to scale the distances exactly.) At the end of the second day Troop K arrived at the Santa María River, with men and horses parched with thirst from the alkali dust. "The water was the worst I ever drank," one trooper said.[10]

The two troops were little more than skeleton organizations. The morning reports, preserved in the National Archives, show that on the morning of June 18, 1916, Troop C had two officers, twelve noncommissioned officers and twenty-nine privates for duty, a total of forty-three officers and men. Troop K had present for duty one officer and thirty-nine enlisted men. Several men and an officer from Troop K were on their way from Columbus, bringing a herd of remounts for the expedition.[11] In addition to the military personnel, Troop C had an unnamed Mexican guide and an American guide, Lemuel Spilsbury. There is no mention of a guide with Troop K, but there probably was one.

On the morning of June 19, the day after marching from Ojo Federico, Captain Morey assembled his noncommissioned officers and told them in substance that the destination was Villa Ahumada to ascertain if Carranzista troops were assembling there. "Our orders were that the troops would move into the town in a column of twos at the gallop, and if fired upon we would use our pistols, the men on the right firing to the right, and the men on the left firing to the left."[12] And Captain Boyd, before leaving Colonia Dublán, likewise assembled his noncommissioned officers and told them, "It is reported that the Mexicans say that they will attack us if we move any direction except to the north. We are going to test that."[13] Any attempt to reconcile the orders as actually recorded, and the interpretation placed upon those orders by both Captain Boyd and Captain Morey would be fruitless. It is sufficient that both officers interpreted their orders as requiring offensive action.

On June 20, after a long march of nearly fifty miles, and as Troop K was nearing Santo Domingo ranch, the corporal in command of the point (the foremost element of the advance guard) signaled "enemy in sight in large numbers." A few minutes' observation through field glasses disclosed, however, that it was not an enemy that had been sighted but Troop C.[14]

The two troops joined, and Captain Boyd, who as has been mentioned, knew nothing about Troop K, assumed command of the entire force. After supper the three officers, together with Lemuel Spilsbury, the Mormon guide, held a conference. The foreman of the ranch, W. P. McCabe, was questioned closely about Ahumada and the nearer town of Carrizal. During the conference Boyd told McCabe that his orders required him to go *through* Carrizal on the way to Ahumada. McCabe told Boyd that Carrizal, a typical adobe-built small Mexican town, was a perfect trap and that it was possible to pass around the main part of the town through a part where the buildings were wide apart. He would thus be complying with the letter of his orders with less danger than otherwise. Boyd replied that he was going *through* the town. Captain Morey protested mildly but added that if Boyd ordered him to go through the town first, he would do so, or he would go alone.[15]

Meanwhile, the presence of American soldiers at Santo Domingo ranch had become known to the Mexican forces at Carrizal, which were commanded by General Felix U. Gómez. A patrol from the Carrizal garrison, at an unspecified time during the late afternoon or early evening, came to Santo Domingo to obtain beef. The leader of the patrol had a talk with Boyd and Morey, the substance of which has never been revealed, but the Mexicans left Santo Domingo hurriedly. General Gómez made immediate preparations to attack the Americans but first telegraphed to Juarez for instructions. He was ordered to make no overt move, but if the Americans advanced, he was to resist them.[16]

The two small troops marched from Santo Domingo ranch at four o'clock in the morning, June 21, 1916, leaving their picket lines and other unnecessary impedimenta at the ranch. Each man carried a full canteen, a belt full of ammunition and a bandoleer of ammunition slung across his shoulder. In high spirits, the colored troopers swung into their saddles and rode forth. The distance to Carrizal was not long, but to prepare for what the day might bring, the horses were watered twice in irrigation ditches passed on the way. A few hundred yards short of the town Boyd halted the column and sent Spilsbury ahead to ask for permission to enter. Spilsbury was met by Lieutenant Colonel Genevevo Rivas Guillen, whom Spilsbury assumed to be the commanding officer. Rivas refused permission and insisted upon speaking to the American commander. He was taken to Captain Boyd, who could not speak Spanish, and it was decided to wait for General Gómez, who was summoned. What passed between Boyd and Gómez is still a mystery, but it seems that Gómez asked for a delay while he telegraphed to Juarez for additional instructions, but Boyd saw in this only an excuse for additional delay while Mexican reinforcements arrived. According to Spilsbury, Boyd terminated the interview by saying, "Tell the son-of-a-bitch that I'm going through!" A slightly different version, but not necessarily contradictory, was related by Sergeant Peter Bigstaff, who was stable sergeant of Troop C and who went forward with Captain Boyd to act as horseholder. Bigstaff was too far away to hear the conversation but said that suddenly Boyd rose to his feet (the two men were sitting down beside the road), shook his fist, and said, "God damn you! I've never disobeyed an order yet, and I'm not going to now. I'm going through your goddamned town!" And when he came back to the horses and mounted, he said, "Sergeant, we're going to have to fight."[17]

Captain Boyd then rode back to the two troops, which were some distance away. He spoke to them briefly. Colonel Queen remembers his remarks as: "I value each of you as ten Mexicans. Do not let it be said that the American troops fired the first shot. If they fire on us, we will answer them, shot for shot. The only thing I will not forgive is showing your back to the enemy. Troops will move forward in line of platoon columns." Guide-scout-interpreter Lem Spilsbury recalls Boyd's remark as, "My orders are to go east to Villa Ahumada on the other side of this town, and I'm going through and take all of you men with me," whereupon the soldiers cheered. The Reverend John Jeter remembers only that Boyd gave the drill-book command, "Fight on foot, action right."[18]

When American cavalry dismounted to fight on foot, the horses were held and led by the No. 4 man of each set of fours. Each horse was fastened to the animal on its left by a link strap on the cheek piece of the bridle, or by passing the reins to the horseholder. Thus, dismounted cavalry could normally put into action only three-quarters of its strength. The command "action right" or "action left" indicated on which side of the column of led horses the dismounted men would form.

The advance commenced, with Troop K on the right, echeloned back slightly in order to cover the right flank. Lieutenant Adair's platoon of Troop C was similarly echeloned back on the left. The led horses had been sent back several hundred yards to the rear. The Americans advanced steadily across an open plain, under full view of the Mexicans, who could also see the horses as they were taken back. For two or three hundred yards of the American advance, there was silence, then at about 250 yards the Mexicans opened fire. The first burst, apparently from the Mexicans' one machine gun, caused no casualties among the soldiers; it went over their heads, but the shot fell squarely into the midst of the animals; terror-stricken, they stampeded, breaking away from the horseholders, and vanished into the chaparral. The advancing American troopers instantly returned the fire. General Gómez was among the first to fall, killed by a shot into the brain. The Carranzistas learned what the Villistas had learned, the deadly accuracy of American rifle fire. Captain Daniel González Corella, who was in command of the machine gun and who was standing near General Gómez, later recorded the dismay and confusion caused by the American musketry:

> The noise of the fusillade drowned the last note of the bugle. General Gómez dropped instantly, with a bullet through his forehead. The most fearful disorder spread through our ranks, since many of our poor soldiers did not have time to dismount, nor draw their weapons. They did not know what to do or whom to obey. The horses were stampeded, entangled in their maguey rope reins and halters, running in all directions, many of them with their viscera dragging on the ground.[19]

Captain González' horse was hit just as he was dismounting. The animal plunged into the barbed wire fence and hung there. González directed the fire of the machine gun against Troop C. The Americans were momentarily checked but then continued their advance, "pulling themselves forward with their elbows, firing their 45-caliber pistols."[20]

In front of the Mexican position was a wide, deep irrigation ditch. Troop C's advance carried the troopers that far, in spite of the intense Mexican fire. Coming out of it on the far side, Captain Boyd, who had been wounded twice already, was killed. About the same time (no one can say whether it was after or before), Lieutenant Adair was killed, only a few yards from the machine gun. Boyd's dying words were, "I'm done, Sergeant. Take the troop forward and take the town."[21]

On the American right, Captain Morey was wounded early in the fight. The enemy worked gradually around the right flank, until, forty minutes after the fight started, the commander of the right-flank platoon (who was also wounded) reported to Morey that he could no longer hold the position. It appears, however, that Troop K had inflicted such punishment on the enemy that the Mexican attack was not pressed with any vigor. The two troops were separated by some two hundred yards; they were too far apart for either to give fire support to the other, and neither knew what was happening to the other.

Reluctantly, Morey gave the order to fall back and ordered his men to leave him, since he could not move rapidly because of his wound. That order, they refused to obey. But with heavy losses, and deprived of leadership, the little American force began to disintegrate. Some, with their ammunition exhausted, were taken prisoner. Still more refused to surrender and prepared to sell their lives dearly, "with a sharp and accurate fire on their attackers. Along with some others, the gallant young Captain Rodriguez, died in one of these isolated duels."[22]

Among the survivors, making their way grimly to the rear, there was suffering and hardship; there was also quiet heroism. Corporal John Jeter, of Troop C (who later became a minister of the Gospel), helping a wounded comrade to safety, took time and risked capture to search Captain Boyd's body and remove all his papers so that the enemy would not capture them. (These papers, with blood stains on them, are now in the National Archives.) Corporal Queen and Corporal Houston, of Troop K,

with their rifles and pistols, but without canteens or food, walked
steadily until about noon. Then they decided to turn north toward some trees they could see in the distance. During the night
they became separated; Queen continued, guiding himself by
compass. By pure chance, he and Houston encountered each
other the next morning. They found themselves near a ranch,
where they were able to buy some tortillas and beans and also
a Mexican pony. That night they slept in the open, and at daybreak they discovered three American cavalry horses, which
they were able to capture. Riding two of the animals and leading the third, they arrived at the Santa María River at a place
where Captain Morey had cached some rations. While they were
resting and eating, they were found by Troop M, of their own
regiment, which was scouring the country, hunting for fugitives. Their immediate troubles were over.[23]

Corporal Jeter and Sergeant Lyons, the wounded man, after
searching Captain Boyd's body, crossed an open space, where
they were sighted by a party of mounted Mexicans. They both
still had their weapons; Sergeant Lyon was not too badly
wounded to be able to shoot, and the two opened fire. They
believed that they caused some casualties among the enemy. At
any rate, the Mexicans sheered off and left them alone. With
great difficulty, they made their way on foot to Santo Domingo
ranch, where the foreman, McCabe, hid them until American
rescue forces arrived. On examining himself, Jeter found that,
unknown to himself, his clothing had been punctured by bullets
no less than three times. Being a devout man, he ascribed his
escape from death to the direct care of God.[24]

So ended the little battle of Carrizal. It was definitely a defeat for the Americans, but when one takes into account certain
factors that historians usually overlook, it was not a humiliating
defeat, except insofar as any defeat is humiliating. The Americans numbered less than a hundred officers and men, of whom
not more than sixty were in the firing line. Nevertheless, they
made such an impression on the enemy that Mexican estimates
of their strength run from two hundred to as high as four hundred. The American losses were two officers and ten soldiers
killed and one officer and ten men wounded. One noncommis-

sioned officer was missing, undoubtedly dead someplace in the mesquite, as he was known to have been wounded. On the Mexican side, estimates of the losses vary from a minimum of seventy-four dead and wounded to somewhat higher figures.[25] The total Mexican strength is unknown but would appear to have been in the neighborhood of three hundred officers and men.

The cavalry service as the men of the Punitive Expedition knew it, is a thing of the past, but there are certain lessons still to be drawn from the tragic little fight at Carrizal—lessons that are still pertinent in the days of air-transported cavalry and even of nuclear weapons. First, there was no attempt at concealment or surprise. The Americans went into dismounted action in plain view of the enemy and advanced across an open plain that afforded no cover from either sight or fire. The led horses and pack animals were sent a short distance to the rear, with the enemy watching, and were held in the open only 150 or 200 yards from the firing line, well within the range of the enemy's small arms. To transcribe what this means in more recent terms, a tank or a troop carrier in view and range of the enemy is a vehicle lost. A direct, frontal attack was launched against an enemy already in position, and other things equal, this is almost invariably a bloody failure. There was a complete lack of liaison between the two troops, and the over-all commander, instead of directing the operation as a whole, devoted himself exclusively to his own troop. The cavalry organization of the time was faulty in that there were no permanent platoons or squads. Consequently, when the officers were out of action and confusion began, the soldiers did not know where to look for leadership. And not the least, the three officers, instead of directing their units, got directly into the firing line with the men. They cannot be blamed for this, since it was the accepted practice of the time, but as someone has said, they were the highest paid corporals in the army, rather than captains and lieutenant.

Upon receiving reports of the Carrizal fight, General Pershing took immediate steps to attack as soon as authorized. Truck trains were assembled at Colonia Dublán, and all troops south of El Valle were ordered north immediately. Within a few days Pershing was ready to strike and strike hard. But the Carrizal fight had an effect that few, if any, historians have noticed. It was a tactical victory for the Carranzistas, but it was a Pyrrhic victory. The Mexican losses were such that the Carranza government's attitude softened preceptibly in the next few weeks. It is true that a number of disagreeable incidents occurred, but the immediate danger of a major war passed.[26]

In spite of their burning nationalism, and their resentment at what they regarded as an unjustifiable American infringement on their cherished sovereignty, it is unlikely that Carranza or any of his responsible officials actually wanted war. And there can be little doubt that they realized, after Carrizal, that such a war, especially in its initial stages in Chihuahua, would be what a later generation learned to call a "blitzkrieg." Thus, although the Carranza government loosened a diplomatic and propaganda offensive, accusing the Americans of all sorts of atrocities, including an allegation popular at the time, of using "dum-dum" bullets, the diplomatic communications from Mexico City began to lose their previous arrogance.

In fact, on July 4, 1916, Carranza took the initiative in suggesting that the two governments accept an offer of mediation, previously made by certain Latin-American countries. Mexico was willing to accept such mediation, or was willing to negotiate directly. The United States accepted at once, and it was quickly agreed to negotiate directly. Carranza almost reneged when President Wilson suggested that the conference might well consider "pending questions." His ingrained suspicion of the United States led him to fear that such a broad basis for discussion might too easily lead to a demand for the cession of Mexican territory. His fears were finally put to rest, and, after some delay, each government named three commissioners, to meet at New London, Connecticut, late in August or early in September.

The conferences were long-drawn; they lasted for more than six months, without accomplishing anything more positive than did the earlier Scott-Obregón conferences. The Mexican delegation had one demand and one reply to all suggestions—the immediate and unconditional withdrawal of the Punitive Expedition. The Americans insisted that security for the Border was an essential. The Mexicans maintained that Villa was now powerless, but their position was weakened by Villa's sudden reappearance at the head of an "army" in September, scattering the Carranzistas in Chihuahua. This, however, did not cause any change in their stand. Until weeks after the New Year, the delegates met and bickered diplomatically and politely, without any definite result.

The New London conferences were, nevertheless, not entirely negative in their result. They were a definite proof that Carranza did not want a war with the United States, and they provided a much needed "cooling off" period, during which passions and emotions could subside. At the beginning of the summer a full-scale war between the United States and Mexico seemed inevitable. It is perhaps not too farfetched to say that the forgotten little battle of Carrizal, by showing the de facto government the probable cost of a war with the United States, provided an impetus that caused war between the two nations to recede from the inevitable into the merely possible.

NOTES

1. *Foreign Relations, 1916*, p. 577; Tompkins, *op. cit.*, p. 208.
2. *Foreign Relations, 1916*, pp. 552–562.
3. John J. Pershing Papers, Manuscript Division, Library of Congress, Box 70. Fortunately for both Mexicans and Americans, it was never necessary to put these plans into effect.
4. *Foreign Relations, 1916*, pp. 581–82.
5. War Diary, 5th Cavalry, Punitive Expedition Records, National Archives, R.G. 120, Box 60.
6. "Memorandum from General Pershing for the Inspector General, Headquarters, Punitive Expedition, Camp Dublan, Mexico, June 30, 1916," National Archives, Punitive Expedition Records, Box 70.
7. Rodney, *As a Cavalryman Remembers*, pp. 274–78. See also H. B. Wharfield, *10th Cavalry & Border Fights*, p. 25.
8. Wharfield, *op. cit.*, p. 31.
9. In a written statement given to the writer by the Rev. John Jeter, who was then a corporal in Troop C, 10th Cavalry.
10. In a letter written by Corpl. H. C. Houston, of Troop K, 10th Cavalry, to the sister of Col. (then Lt.) Jerome W. Howe. The writer is indebted to Colonel Howe for a copy of this letter.
11. The figures cited are from the official returns of the two troops (the morning reports), in the Punitive Expedition Records, National

Archives, Box 70. Col. Albert B. Dockery, U. S. Army, Ret., who was then the lieutenant of Troop K, gave the writer a detailed narrative of his experiences on the way from Columbus with the remounts.

12. In a statement given to the writer by Col. H. D. Queen, U.S.A.R., Ret., who was then a noncommissioned officer of Troop K.

13. Told to the writer by the Rev. John Jeter, to whom reference has been made before.

14. In Col. Queen's statement. The signal "enemy in sight, large numbers," consisted of holding the rifle horozontally above the head in both hands, and raising and lowering it rapidly.

15. W. P. McCabe's affidavit, quoted in Tompkins, *op. cit.*, pp. 210–12.

16. 1st Capt. Daniel González Corella, "The Fight at Carrizal," included in Gen. Alberto Salinas Carranza, *La Expedición Punitiva* (Mexico City, 1936), p. 280. The article by Capt. González originally appeared in one of the Mexican military journals in 1933 or 1934. The writer translated it, but in the course of several transcontinental and intercontinental moves, has lost the reference. Gen. Salinas quotes it in full.

17. Told to the writer by Sgt. Bigstaff. Spilsbury's remark is quoted in Wharfield, *op. cit.*, p. 35.

18. The Rev. John Jeter's statement.

19. Capt. Daniel González Corella, quoted in Salinas Carranza, *op. cit.*, pp. 285–86; Wharfield, *op. cit.*, p. 36.

20. *Ibid.*

21. Lewis Morey, "The Cavalry Fight at Carrizal," *Cavalry Journal*, XXVII (Jan., 1917), pp. 449–56.

22. Capt. Daniel González Corella, *op. cit.*, pp. 286–87. General (then Lt. Col.) Genevevo Rivas Guillen's report on the fight is also included in Salinas Carranza's work. It agrees substantially with the foregoing account.

23. Col. Queen's statement to the writer. A firsthand account of the fight is also in the testimony of George Turner, *Fall Committee Report*, pp. 1561–68. Turner was a soldier in Troop C.

24. The Rev. John Jeter's statement to the writer.

25. González Corella, *op. cit.*, p. 287; Haldeen Braddy, *Pershing's Mission in Mexico* (El Paso, Tex., 1966), pp. 56–57; Tompkins, *op. cit.*, p. 209.

26. These unfortunate incidents, which helped inflame feelings at the moment, are covered in *Foreign Relations, 1916*, pp. 598–99, 602–3.

CHAPTER 17

Airplanes and Motors

WHILE THE Punitive Expedition was the swan song of the traditional cavalry that had fought Indians across the Plains and through the mountains of the Far West, as well as in the Philippines and China, it was, at the same time, the almost unnoticed forerunner of new methods and ideas. The expedition can be correctly called the last of America's nineteenth-century wars and the first of those of the twentieth century. Among the first units to arrive at Columbus was the 1st Aero Squadron, Aviation Section, Signal Corps. It should be explained that it had been customary to assign anything that was new and experimental to the Signal Corps, the army's scientific branch, for development. Thus, when Congress first authorized the purchase of one or two airplanes for experimental purposes, in 1907, it was logical to assign them to the Signal Corps.

As noted earlier, the squadron was at San Antonio when it received orders, on March 12, 1916, to move at once to Columbus for duty with the Punitive Expedition. Its personnel consisted of eleven officers, eighty-four enlisted men (including two Hospital Corpsmen) and one civilian technician. Its equipment included eight airplanes, ten trucks (one of which was a mobile machine shop) and one passenger vehicle. As the squadron passed through El Paso the local quartermaster added two trucks that he hired locally, but even then the motor train was only half of what was authorized in the tables of organization and equipment. Arriving at Columbus on the morning of March

15, the squadron at once unloaded from the train and commenced reassembling the airplanes. One was completed and put
into the air for a few minutes' test flight that same day. The
first reconnaissance flight over Mexico was made the next day,
with Captain T. F. Todd as pilot, and Captain Benjamin D.
Foulois, the squadron commander, as observer.[1]

Since supplies of all sorts were pouring into Columbus on
every incoming train, and the base quartermaster had no transportation but a few wagons, it was necessary for the squadron's
trucks to be used for several days to clear the congestion, and
Captain Foulois was put, temporarily, in charge of all transportation. The first shipment of motor trucks for the Punitive
Expedition arrived at Columbus on March 18. It consisted of
seventeen Jeffery "Quads" (four-wheel drive), with knocked-
down wagon bodies in lieu of truck bodies. The aero squadron,
with its portable machine shop and soldier-mechanics, was the
only organization then at Columbus that could make the necessary changes in the chassis and assemble the wagon bodies. The
aero squadron soldiers worked round the clock, drilling holes
and fitting the wagon bodies to the vehicles. It might be added
that until the arrival of civilian truck drivers, the men of the
aero squadron were the only ones at Columbus who were qualified truck drivers; driving a motor truck was a skill that the
army had not yet found necessary on any but the smallest scale.

In spite of interruptions in their normal and proper duties,
the men of the squadron managed to assemble all eight airplanes
and have them ready for flight on March 19, the day after their
arrival. On that day orders came from General Pershing to fly
all eight planes to Casas Grandes for immediate service. They
took off from Columbus at five o'clock in the afternoon. One
immediately developed engine trouble, but the pilot managed
to get it back to Columbus without mishap. The seven others,
overtaken by darkness, had various misadventures. Night landing facilities were virtually unknown in the United States and
Europe, let alone in Mexico. Three of the craft were successfully landed at Ascensión, one at Ojo Caliente, one at Janos,
while the seventh crashed near Pearson, a total wreck. Three

days later a small detail sent from the squadron to salvage whatever they could from the wreck was fired on by unidentified
Mexicans and was forced to return. The next day a stronger
party was sent, prepared to fight if necessary. This time there
was no opposition, and the wreck was stripped of everything
that might be useful. At the very beginning of the campaign
the destruction of one plane left the squadron with only seven.
The plane that landed in the dark at Ojo Caliente was damaged
in landing, but the damage was repairable. Still, several days
elapsed before the craft could be put back into the air.

It was very quickly found that the planes with which the
squadron was equipped were not at all suitable for operations
in the mountains and high plateau of northern Chihuahua. They
did not have enough power to overcome the erratic winds or to
climb to the altitudes needed to cross the mountains. On March
20, for instance, Captain Todd, with Captain Foulois as observer,
was ordered on a reconnaissance mission south of Casas Grandes
but was unable to go over twenty-five miles. Whirlwinds and
heavy air currents made it impossible for him to climb to the
height necessary to pass over the intervening mountains. On the
same day Lieutenant T. S. Bowen was caught by a whirlwind
while landing. His plane was wrecked beyond possibility of repair, leaving the squadron with only six aircraft. During the
next few days several missions were flown successfully, but it
was clear to everyone that the squadron, if it was to perform
its duties successfully, would have to be reequipped with more
powerful machines.

Captain Foulois submitted an urgent request for the immediate purchase of ten more machines, specifying in detail just
what he wanted and including in the request a sufficient number
of extra engines and spare parts for quick repairs. But even if
this requisition successfully ran the gantlet of Washington bu-
reaucrats and other "red tape" artists, it would be some time
before the new airplanes could be delivered. To make the maxi-
mum and most efficient use of the remaining six planes, Foulois
submitted four alternative plans to General Pershing, who approved No. III, which, in substance was as follows:

1. To discontinue the use of airplanes to carry messages between Casas Grandes and Namiquipa, except in emergency, as soon as radio communication was established;
2. To use airplanes for communication between Namiquipa and El Valle only when all other means failed;
3. To concentrate the six available airplanes at Namiquipa for communication with troops that were beyond the range of other means.

The use of airplanes as attack weapons, that is, as bombers, was in its infancy in Europe, although the great war had been raging for two years, and in the United States it had not yet been tried. The airplane was still primarily for reconnaissance and observation. None of the aircraft with which the 1st Aero Squadron was initially equipped was armed or fitted for use as a bomber. Since their effectiveness for reconnaissance was limited, as has been mentioned, they became, in effect, vehicles for the rapid delivery of messages.[2]

Plan No. III was ordered into effect on April 1. A large number of flights were made, including some reconnaissance flights made primarily to locate American units, the whereabouts of which were unknown at headquarters. On April 6 another airplane was so badly damaged in landing at San Geronimo that it had to be destroyed. To recount the fate of each individual aircraft in the squadron would be tedious. By April 20, only a month after entering Mexico, the 1st Aero Squadron did not have a single operative airplane. The planes had not been new to start with; they had been in use in the United States for months. They had insufficient power and were too frail in construction to cope with the conditions under which they had to operate.

This brief summary of the active operations of the 1st Aero Squadron in the early days of the Punitive Expedition may seem to be a record of failure, but the squadron's performance was far from negative in its total and final results. In spite of the handicap imposed by the nature of the equipment, the daring, skill and initiative of the handful of pilots who then constituted the entire United States Air Force produced results far beyond what might reasonably have been expected. Vital messages and orders were carried from Pershing's headquarters to units that were "lost" in the Mexican wilderness. All roads leading to the city of Chihuahua were reconnoitered, and numerous photographs were taken. The squadron experimented with an automatic camera that could photograph strips of the country over which an airplane was passing. This was the first serious aerial photography in American history, and was probably abreast of similar developments in Europe at the time.

It is remarkable that even with night landings, the flimsy airplanes (made of canvas and bamboo) and crash landings, that there was not a single fatality, and only two instances in which pilot or observer was slightly injured. But aside from their occupational hazards, the pilots and observers of the 1st Aero Squadron had their moments of excitement. On April 11 the squadron's truck train was fired upon by Villistas while passing through the village of Cienegas, a few miles north of Satevo. It must be assumed that the soldiers of the train returned the fire, although the report does not so state. There were no casualties. On April 7, 1916, two planes were sent to the city of Chihuahua, carrying duplicate messages for the American consul in that city. By previous understanding, Lieutenant Dargue landed on the south side of the city, and Lieutenant Carberry on the north. Captain Foulois, who had flown with Dargue, told him, after landing, to fly his plane to the north side and join Carberry. As Dargue started to take off, several Mexicans opened fire on him with rifles, from a considerable distance. Captain Foulois, hearing the firing, returned to the plane, whereupon the four riflemen took him into custody and to the city jail, accompanied by a jeering mob. En route to the jail, Foulois managed to call to a bystander who looked like an American to go to the American consul. On arrival at the jail, Foulois insisted that General Gutierrez, the Military Governor, be notified. After some delay, Foulois was taken to Gutierrez, who ordered his immediate release and also, upon Foulois' request, ordered that a guard be placed over the planes. Foulois delivered his dispatches, and then, accompanied by the Mexican Chief of Staff, returned to the airplanes. The guard had not yet arrived, and the mob, including Carranzista soldiers and officers, had slashed the fabric of the wings, burned holes in them, and had taken off many nuts and bolts. The Americans decided to fly to the American Smelting and Refining Company's plant, a few miles away, rather than risk having the machines completely wrecked. Carberry took off without difficulty, but Dargue took off under a shower of stones. A few minutes later the top of his fuselage blew off, and he had to make a quick turn and a forced landing. This time the mob stayed at a distance, from which it may be inferred that Dargue displayed his pistol. A few minutes later the guard arrived, and he was able to make temporary repairs without interruption. He flew then to the American Smelting and Refining Company's plant, where the two pilots patched the holes in the fabric, replaced nuts and bolts, and were able, the next day, to fly back to their base. They carried with them the knowledge that the Mexican masses were distinctly hostile, Carranzistas as well as Villistas.

In at least two instances American pilots had to make forced landings in unknown country, far from the nearest American forces. Lieutenant Dargue's plane made its last flight on April 19, when his motor failed far from any road and deep in enemy country. The plane was smashed beyond any possibility of repair. Almost miraculously, Dargue was uninjured, but his observer, Captain Robert H. Willis, was pinned beneath the engine. Fortunately, his injuries, although painful, were not serious. Dargue extricated him, set fire to the plane, and the two started to walk to San Antonio, the nearest American base of which they were sure. Two days later, suffering from hunger, thirst and fatigue, they staggered into San Antonio, where Willis' injuries were treated. Three days later they were sent by car to headquarters, where they reported to General Pershing personally.

Lieutenant Edgar S. Correll made a forced landing at night in unknown country. He crawled away from the wreck on his hands and knees to avoid being seen. About two o'clock in the morning, he fell asleep, and slept until sunrise. At noon, with the sun beating down full force, and with the water in his canteen half gone, he turned back. He became almost delirious: "Ahead I seemed to see a lake, full of cool, splashing water with waves and whitecaps. I started to run, and the beautiful lake disappeared. I tried my canteen, but it was empty. . . . Several times I fell and lay stupefied."[3] After dark, by pure chance, he stumbled and fell into a water hole, with real water in it. After drinking his fill, and dousing his head and burning shoulders, he fell asleep. On waking the next morning, he came upon a humble Mexican who proved to be a friend. He threw a saddle on a horse and led Correll toward the Americans; shortly they met an American patrol that took him to Ascensión, and his troubles were over. Actually, he had a narrow escape and was doubly fortunate that the single Mexican whom he encountered was not hostile.

The first four of the airplanes that Foulois had requested arrived at Columbus late in April. They were much more powerful than the planes with which the squadron was originally equipped, but even then they were not altogether satisfactory for service in Mexico. They promptly developed several "bugs," the most serious of which was in the propellers. It was soon found that propellers designed for air densities at seacoast level did not function properly in the altitudes of the New Mexico and Chihuahua plateau. The squadron constructed a propeller-testing stand at the Columbus base and tested propellers from practically all of the manufacturers in the United States. All were unsatisfactory, so three technicians of the Curtiss Aeroplane Company were sent to Columbus, and, as has been mentioned, the Columbus Base added the manufacture of airplane propellers to its multifold activities.

The squadron continued experiments with the automatic camera that could take a continuous series of photographs of the country over which the craft was flying—a series from which a mosaic could be constructed, giving a detailed picture that was superior to any existing map. And not the least important among innovations, the squadron received twelve Lewis guns with which to arm the airplanes, and a supply of 100-pound bombs. It is not recorded whether or not the squadron had gunnery and bombing practice, but it is not unreasonable to suppose that exercises in both were carried out.

In summarizing the work and accomplishments of the tiny

aviation force of the United States in its first actual campaign, it can be said that the occasional expression of disappointment by observers and newspaper correspondents and editorial writers was unjust. Probably no one except the pilots and their ground crews knew the handicaps under which the 1st Aero Squadron operated. It was understrength, and its airplanes, already old, were entirely unsuited for conditions in Mexico. Nevertheless, between March 15, 1915, and August 15, of the same year (months before the expedition was withdrawn), the squadron flew 540 missions. The experience and knowledge gained were basic in the tremendous expansion that took place after the United States entered the war against Germany. The dozen pilots and less than a hundred soldiers of the 1st Aero Squadron were the seed from which the present United States Air Force has grown.

The use of motor vehicles to supply the Punitive Expedition was an innovation that was as revolutionary in its way as the introduction of the airplane. The stubborn refusal of the Carranza government to allow the expedition to make full use of the railways, as has been mentioned, made the use of motor trucks necessary. The expedition could not have existed without them, and it became speedily apparent that the new transportation provided a mobility and flexibility of supply that was impossible when supply depended entirely upon railroads for major shipments. The army was convinced quickly of the desirability of replacing older and more traditional forms of transport by motors; that the substitution was not complete until the 1930s was not due to military conservatism. It was due to lack of funds during the several Presidential administrations that stressed "economy" above everything else. There were no appropriations (or appropriations were insufficient) for the purchase of new vehicles, spare parts, gasoline, oil and tires.[4]

General Scott's morally courageous action in ordering the purchase of enough trucks to supply the expedition without waiting for congressional action has already been related. Trucks were purchased wherever they were available for immediate delivery, trucks of a half-dozen or more different makes. Truck companies were quickly improvised, with civilian drivers. As described earlier, a repair shop was established at Columbus, and before long the motor section of the Punitive Expedition was a working organization. This was a real achievement, especially when one considers the haste with which everything was thrown together, and that the army had had no previous experience with motor transportation, except on the scale of single vehicles.

A total of ten truck companies was formed during the Punitive Expedition; the first one actually to be organized and function was Truck Company No. 3, which was "activated" (to use a present-day term) at El Paso on March 16 or 17, 1916, with civilian personnel. It was equipped with White trucks, which, like those that first arrived at Columbus, were sent with wagon bodies that had to be fitted to the truck chassis. To put the vehicles together and equip the men took two days. The drivers, although civilians, were issued rifles and pistols and other items of a soldier's equipment. As soon as these preparations were finished, the company was ordered to speed to Columbus, a distance of 125 miles from El Paso. It was estimated that the movement to Deming, New Mexico, would take about six hours, but in fact, it took almost twenty-four hours. The company commander recorded: "I marvel that we got there at all, considering our ignorance of trucking matters, and the lack of discipline, knowledge, and capacity of the civilian personnel with the truck train."[5]

Gradually, over several months, many of the civilian drivers were replaced by qualified soldiers. The better ones among the civilians were retained, and the matter of discipline was partly solved by a ruling of The Judge Advocate General of the Army that, although there had been no formal declaration of war by Congress, a state of war actually existed. Consequently, "followers to the camp" were subject to military law and trial by court-martial, if necessary. There is no record that any civilian ever was tried by court-martial in the Punitive Expedition, but the knowledge that it could be done undoubtedly had a quieting effect upon some of the more turbulent characters.[6]

Among the soldiers there was a certain amount of understandable jealousy toward the civilian truck drivers. The civilians were paid one hundred dollars per month, a very high rate of pay in 1916, and were not expected to risk their lives by fighting except in self-defense. The soldier was paid twenty-one dollars a month, and it was taken for granted that he would risk his life in combat and endure any hardship uncomplainingly. The soldier, pounding down the road on a horse, or upon his own two feet, envied the truckers, riding in their cabs.

The soldier, envying the driver because of the "soft job," did not realize that driving a heavily loaded truck was then the hardest kind of physical labor. In fact, driving over "washboard" dirt roads, full of ruts, jarring chuckholes, made of soft sand, in and out of narrow, deep, rocky ravines, was a man-killing job. In addition there were repairs to be made on the road, often major repairs. The ruts and chuckholes caused broken springs, and often even solid disc steel wheels collapsed under the strain and the constant pounding. The drivers became adept at making emergency repairs on the road, but even so, it was rather common for a truck train to be delayed for several hours by one repair after another. And when a truck train pulled into a bivouac area, the drivers had to do necessary maintenance on their vehicles (often including major repairs) before they could rest.[7]

The first truck train to go into Mexico, which went as far as San Geronimo, quickly learned tricks of the trade and worked out a field routine that others followed. Each truck was given a ten-gallon milk can for water. This made the truck trains independent of the uncertain water holes and rivers. Some unidentified genius devised a fireless cooker, using another milk can, so that the men of a truck train had a hot meal with plenty of hot coffee at the noon halt. Drivers then started the afternoon run refreshed and rested, and two or three cups of "soldier" coffee guaranteed that they would stay awake. (Some unknown wag has said that soldier coffee could lick Jack Johnson in a twenty-round bout.) Each truck train was authorized a field kitchen, but usually only the utensils were carried. A very satisfactory substitute for the field range was a radiator grill over a narrow slit trench. And truck company commanders soon learned that probably the most important individual in the company was the cook. A good field cook was a priceless asset, and company commanders probably connived at dishonesty and all sorts of skulduggery to lure good cooks into their companies.

Each truck train was accompanied by a squad of soldiers, under a noncommissioned officer, as guard and escort. On the road the soldiers rode on top of the cargoes, with loaded weapons. They were strictly forbidden to fire unless the train was attacked, but there are indications that they were sometimes rather loose in their interpretation of what constituted an attack. For instance, a group of Mexicans on a hill overlooking a defile and in a position to roll boulders down the slope onto the trucks were sent scurrying by a shot or two.

There was an occasion in which the soldier riding on the tail truck of a column dozed, and when the truck hit a chuckhole, fell off. He was knocked out momentarily by his fall, and when he came to, a few seconds later, an old Mexican woman was stooping over him, staring closely. She left, and the soldier groggily thought, "She's gone to get me some water." But a second or so later, when he was conscious enough to raise his head, he saw the old lady picking up a large rock. His complete recovery from his accident was almost miraculously instantaneous.[8]

Possibly the climax of the motor operations, at least from the soldiers' point of view, was at Thanksgiving, 1916. General Pershing had ordered positively that the turkeys for Thanksgiving dinner *must* arrive at Colonia Dublán the day before Thanksgiving. The trip from Columbus to Colonia Dublán normally took two days, but to get the turkeys to their destination on time necessitated a nonstop run. In the camp at Colonia Dublán interest ran high. The soldiers were paid regularly, but with no place to spend their money, their pockets were heavy. Hence, large bets were laid on whether or not the turkeys would arrive on time. On the afternoon before Thanksgiving Day hundreds of men, officers as well as soldiers, gathered at the northern perimeter of the camp area, scanning the northern horizon. Finally, just as dusk was descending, a faint dust cloud was seen in the distance, and finally, when the trucks rolled in with hundreds of pounds of turkey, the air was rent with cheers. In

the next few minutes thousands of dollars changed hands, and
the losers were as elated as the winners.[9]

As any old soldier knows, government property that is not
bolted down or under the eyes of a vigilant guard is likely to
disappear in the most mysterious and unaccountable way. On one
occasion a disabled truck was left at El Valle, with an earnest
request to the local commander to see that nothing happened
to it, as the necessary parts for its repair could be brought from
Columbus within a few days. But when the train commander
returned, all he could find was the bare frame of the chassis. He
finally identified a new searchlight on top of the guardhouse as
being from his truck, but nothing else was discoverable. He had
the cold comfort of knowing that the government had really
lost nothing, for everything that was missing was undoubtedly
still in the government service, but in ways not contemplated
either by regulations or by the manufacturers of the vehicle.

One further item should be mentioned in which the Punitive
Expedition pioneered. At some time during the summer of 1916
the government purchased a number of motorcycles with side-
cars—a new type of vehicle at the time. On each sidecar there
was a machine gun. At first glance it appeared that machine-gun
motorcycles might be very useful. They were highly mobile,
easily maneuverable, and could develop tremendous fire power.
They were turned over to the 1st Aero Squadron for use. After
a few days, however, the 1st Aero Squadron put them aside.
Such vehicles might be useful where roads were hard-surfaced
and gradients not too steep, but in Mexico they were of no use
whatever. They could not survive the rocky trails, the deep sand;
they could not move at all after a rainstorm, when the roads
became morasses. And as for their fire power, it was quickly
found that any sort of accuracy was impossible; the sidecar was
not firm enough to provide a stable base for the gun, and the
vibration caused a wild spray of bullets over the country, instead of a close and accurate cone of fire.[10]

The two great innovations in warfare—the airplane and the
motor vehicle—both had their first serious tests for the United
States Army in the Punitive Expedition. They had been tried
tentatively in the maneuvers of 1911 and were already common-

place in the war taking place in Europe, but their real development lay in the future, and they were destined to change the whole pattern of war. Old concepts, old methods, were to become obsolete within thirty years under the impact of these two innovations, but there is a definite link between the 1st Aero Squadron, Signal Corps, and the present United States Air Force; between Pershing's cold, hungry troopers, "grooming and growling," and the helicopter-riding cavalrymen of the present. It is no exaggeration to say that the Punitive Expedition of 1916 gives continuity between the American soldier of the Civil War and the Indian wars, and the American soldier of World War II, Korea and Vietnam.

NOTES

1. Everything concerning the 1st Aero Squadron and air operations in Mexico, unless otherwise noted, is taken from two basic sources. The first is Capt. Benjamin D. Foulois' "Report of the Operations of the First Aero Squadron, Signal Corps, with the Mexican Punitive Expedition, for Period March 15 to August 15, 1916." This is in Tompkins, *op. cit.*, Appendix B, pp. 236–45. The other is the War Diary, 1st Aero Squadron, to which reference has been made.
2. Foulois, *op. cit.*, pp. 238–39.
3. "Flying into Mexico," *Literary Digest*, LII (Apr. 15, 1916), 1103. Quoted from the New York *American*.
4. All material on motor operations is taken, unless otherwise indicated, from Capt. Francis H. Pope, Quartermaster Corps, "Motor Transport Experiences with the Mexican Punitive Expedition," Appendix C, Tompkins, *op. cit.*, pp. 246–54. The writer has also talked to officers and soldiers who served with the truck trains in the expedition.
5. Pope, *op. cit.*, p. 247. The writer has had, personally, several similar experiences.
6. War Diary, Camp Headquarters, Ascensión, Chihuahua, entry for June 6, 1916. National Archives, Punitive Expedition Records, R.G. 120, Box 59.
7. Pope, *op. cit.*, pp. 249–50.
8. Told to the writer by Col. Charles W. Hoffman, who was the non-commissioned officer commanding the guard.
9. Told to the writer by Maj. Gen. Donald C. Cubbison, who was an eyewitness of the occasion.
10. Information given by Col. John W. Cotton, U.S.A., Ret.

CHAPTER 18

Colonia Dublán—The End of the Expedition: Odds and Ends

THE TENSION of May and June that brought the two nations to the brink of open warfare caused Pershing to draw his forces into a fairly restricted area in the vicinity of Casas Grandes and Colonia Dublán. The only detachments were those that were necessary to safeguard the lifeline linking the expedition with the base at Columbus. The region was barren, dusty, and subject to violent windstorms and to equally violent rainstorms during the short rainy season. There was a small degree of excitement from the frequent discovery of unwelcome local fauna, such as rattlesnakes, scorpions, centipedes, vinegaroons and tarantulas. Lieutenant George S. Patton wrote to his wife in May, saying, "Here we are back at the windiest place in the world." He had just killed two rattlesnakes outside his tent and was being "ribbed" by the other officers because he had used his pistol instead of his sword.[1] Captain Martin L. Crimmins, of the 16th Infantry, who was an enthusiastic amateur naturalist, especially interested in rattlesnakes (upon which he became a recognized authority), found plenty of specimens to study and to ship to the New York zoo, including some very rare species.[2]

The troops concentrated around Colonia Dublán, with nothing but field equipment, had to use all their ingenuity to make themselves even passably comfortable. For cover, they had nothing but their shelter tents.[3] For eating, they had only their aluminum mess kits. To be more comfortable while eating, Captain Crimmins had his men dig parallel slit trenches, two or three feet apart, into which they could put their feet while

using the bank between as a table.[4] At Colonia Dublán, however, they were spared the necessity of cooking bacon and hardtack in their mess kits; the field kitchens were there, with the
organizational cooks. With the truck trains arriving regularly
from Columbus, there was no longer any shortage of rations.
There was plenty to eat, although "kitchen police" resumed its
place in necessary but disliked daily activities. Firewood for the
numerous troop kitchens was shipped from Columbus on the
truck trains; the country around Colonia Dublán was too barren
to afford a sufficient supply.

There was no timber, but there was an unending supply of
the basic building material of northern Mexico, adobe. The
soldiers built small, two-man adobe huts, using their shelter
tents for roofing. They improvised bunks, using all sorts of
scrap and salvaged material. In lieu of mattresses or bedsacks
they softened the bunks with brush or (it is to be suspected)
straw stolen from the picket lines. Lieutenant Cubbison, of the
artillery, was placed in charge of the twenty odd Villista prisoners who had been captured at various times. His orders were
to keep them busy, which was difficult to do at first, until it
occurred to him that they knew how to make adobe bricks. He
had just finished building a fine adobe house for the artillery
headquarters when the Chief of Staff, Lieutenant Colonel Cabell,
noticed it, and the prisoners were at once transferred to the expedition's headquarters to make bricks there.[5]

The soldiers' worst enemy after the active pursuit of Pancho
Villa ceased, was boredom and monotony. Recreational facilities
were practically nonexistent. There was no United Service Organization; the Y.M.C.A., the Salvation Army, Knights of
Columbus and Jewish Welfare did not start recreational work
among the soldiers until after the United States entered the war
in Europe. Baseball diamonds and boxing rings appeared all
over the area, almost spontaneously. The regiments of the expedition included chaplains of nearly all denominations; religious
services were conducted regularly, but there is no evidence that
many of the soldiers were especially interested. There were no
Bob Hopes, no touring theatrical troops or motion picture stars
to entertain the troops.

A few officers, after the expedition had settled for an indefinite stay at Colonia Dublán, managed to have their shotguns and other hunting weapons sent to them. There was good water-fowl-shooting in the vicinity, at two or three places. Hunting was difficult, however, because any hunting party had to be accompanied by an armed escort of sufficient strength to discourage possible interference by the Mexicans. Nevertheless, occasional hunting parties were authorized, and the escorting soldiers thoroughly enjoyed these occasions. They were hunting, too. Especially fortunate was the hunter who was able to get his escort from the Apache scouts, for then game was guaranteed. One officer who went out with the Indians brought back seven deer. A few days later the same officer went with a detachment of soldiers from his regiment; the party did not see a single deer. Lieutenant James Shannon, the commander of the scout detachment, remarked, "The amusing thing was that he did not seem to realize that the presence of the Indians had anything to do with finding the deer."[6]

The Apache scouts had other uses. In August, Lieutenant Shannon and a detail of Indians were sent in pursuit of three deserters. For two days the Apaches followed the deserters' trail like hounds. Finally, Sergeant Chicken announced, "We see 'em about five minutes." Ten minutes later the three deserters were in custody.[7]

To return from this brief digression to the circumstances of the camp at Colonia Dublán, the army has never condoned gambling, but has never forbidden it, knowing that any attempt to enforce a prohibition would be a sheer waste of time and effort. The soldiers of the expedition were paid regularly and were paid in coin—money that clinked and jingled. There was almost no place where the soldiers could spend it, and it burned holes in their pockets. The result was that gambling became a major evening diversion, and as long as the games kept the men entertained and no disorder resulted, General Pershing and his staff saw no reason to interfere.[8]

But in spite of having fairly weatherproof huts, and regular rations, the men were never completely comfortable. The weather was unpredictable, except that it was safe to forecast disagreeable weather. The clouds of dust, the swarms of flies, as long as warm weather prevailed, could not be escaped. The Thanksgiving dinner seems to have been a success, but Christmas dinner, which was keenly anticipated, and for which elaborate preparations were made, was a dismal failure. The cooks of the 10th Cavalry were barbecuing whole steers when a cold norther, driving a fog of dust, swept through the camp. Within a few minutes everything, including the roasting steers, was so covered with a thick layer of grit and sand that it was inedible. All festivities were canceled; the dust was so penetrating that many men were unable to eat for twenty-four hours. Fires could not be lighted, and men huddled in their huts, vainly trying to keep warm.[9]

Rather oddly, one legitimate outlet for the soldiers' pay came about as a result of Pancho Villa's reappearance upon the Mexican political scene, in September, 1916. He vented upon the hapless Chinese of Chihuahua the same bloody fury that he had once turned on the Spaniards. In any place he captured, the Chinese were murdered in cold blood. Scores of them (possibly hundreds) fled for safety and refuge to the Americans. Captain Pope, in his report on motor operations, noted that an "interesting feature was the rapidity with which Chinese stores and restaurants would appear on the fringes of the little stations along the trail" to Columbus.[10] In the Colonia Dublán area, General Pershing assigned space for the use of the Chinese, who opened their shops, restaurants and laundries under the close supervision of the Provost Marshal. No one could figure out they obtained the stock for their enterprises, but they did somehow, and the soldiers were able to purchase knickknacks and small articles that were unobtainable otherwise, and at prices that the Provost Marshal fixed.[11]

The intelligence activities of the Punitive Expedition are necessarily still shrouded in considerable mystery, mainly because no record of such measures is usually maintained. It is apparent, however, that an intelligence organization was quickly set up and operated throughout the time that the expedition was in Mexico. The expedition's intelligence officer (now called the Assistant Chief of Staff, G-2) was Major James A. Ryan, of the 13th Cavalry, who was succeeded eventually by Captain

Nicholas W. Campanole, of the 6th Infantry, an officer of Spanish-American descent who spoke Mexican Spanish as his native language.

Military intelligence was a subject that the United States Army almost studiously neglected before World War II. In 1916 there was virtually no information about northern Mexico available in the War Department. There were no reliable maps, and in fact, much of the country in which the Punitive Expedition was to operate was practically unexplored, as far as the Americans were concerned. From the outset, the expedition was dependent upon guides to find its way about the country. Most of the guides were Americans who had spent years in Mexico, but also, the knowledge of most of them was limited to the regions in which they had lived.

For information about Villista activities the expedition was practically limited to the interrogation of inhabitants and the occasional Villista prisoner who was captured. There was no way of knowing whether or not these people were telling the truth, but it was possible, by questioning a sufficiently large number, and comparing their separate stories, to arrive at an approximation of the truth.

For combat intelligence—the information needed by troops in contact with or close proximity to, the enemy—active patrolling has always been the most reliable source. Patrolling for information was actively and energetically carried on. For example, a patrol sent out by the 6th Infantry early in May is interesting. It consisted of forty soldiers, with an American guide, commanded by Lieutenant Richard Wetherill. The orders were to investigate reports that groups of Villistas were in the habit of visiting certain ranches, and to arrest and bring in several wounded Mexicans reported to be at La Cienega Grande ranch. The patrol drew a blank, except for the wounded men. Wetherill found two; he arrested them, and also eighteen others who were found at the ranch. They were taken to the ranch owned by the American guide, where the foreman identified and gave a clean bill of health to eleven. The remaining seven were held as prisoners.[12]

The existence of an espionage organization can be inferred

from a number of records, although it is impossible, from the evidence available, to do more than conclude that such an organization existed. In April, 1916, Captain Campanole cited several reports by agents, referring to them as "Agent A," "Agent G," and "Agent J" and "Messenger O." And it is interesting to note that three of the "scouts" who reported regularly to headquarters, and who were regarded as trustworthy, were named Suzuki, Sato and Dyo. In September, 1916, two of Pershing's agents, two brothers, managed to get into Villa's camp. Unsuspected, they saw and talked to Villa himself and noted that he was able to mount and dismount without any apparent difficulty, and reported that his forces amounted to about eight hundred men. A third one also penetrated Villa's lair, but there seems to be no record of what he reported.[13]

It would be fascinating to follow the adventures of the American intelligence agents, but they did not leave any written records. Any agent who left written documents of the kind that the conscientious and conventional historian looks for, would not last long. Those unknown men who worked in the dark, whether Mexican, American or Japanese, took their lives in their hands, and they knew it. It is not unreasonable to suppose that a great deal of what went on in Villa's bivouacs, and among his supporters, was known very quickly to Pershing and his headquarters. One final bit of evidence, however, is a letter written at Colonia Dublán in August, 1916, addressed "To Whom it may Concern." The bearer, said the letter, had rendered most valuable services to the Punitive Expedition, for which he had been compelled to take refuge in the American lines; he was now en route to the United States and hoped to become an American citizen. All American officials were requested by General Pershing to give him every possible assistance.[14]

A weak point in the Punitive Expedition, from first to last, was in its signal communications. The radio sets of 1916 were crude and untrustworthy. The pack sets that accompanied the cavalry were as temperamental as the proverbial prima donna, and when they functioned, they had an operating range of only about twenty-five miles. The more powerful sets that were carried in wagons could not keep up with the fast-moving cavalry columns and were almost as undependable as the pack sets. When the expedition marched into Mexico there was no telegraphic system at all except the railway telegraph lines, which were under Carranzista control. A buzzer line was laid on the ground by the Signal Corps from Columbus to the Casas Grandes region, but it was frequently broken by horses plowing across it, or by grazing cattle. It was not until some time in the summer of 1916, when active pursuit of Villa was over, that the Signal Corps was able to install a regular telegraph system between Columbus and the troops in Mexico. An auxiliary means of communication was in the use of carrier pigeons, but although it is known that they were used occasionally, there is no record of performance; there is no information about the numbers used, the locations of pigeon lofts or any messages that were transmitted by this age-old means.[15]

For carrying secret and confidential messages, General Funston "drafted" seven or eight young lieutenants from regiments under his command. These officer-messengers traveled by rail from San Antonio to Columbus. From Columbus to General Pershing's headquarters they had to depend on their own ingenuity. In other words, they had to hitch-hike, although the expression was not then in use. Their trips to Colonia Dublán were not without adventure. Colonel Paul Davison recalls that on one of his trips (he made a dozen) he flew with a Lieutenant Richardson in a Curtiss plane. Halfway to their destination the engine failed, and they made a forced landing. They were seen by bandits (presumably Villistas), but managed to make their way to the road through the heavy brush and "finished the trip on the tail gate of an eight-mule wagon."[16]

There was one feature of the camp at Colonia Dublán that has never received any public notice and yet was an important factor in maintaining discipline and morale. It is well known to all soldiers and students of military history that women follow armies. The Punitive Expedition was no exception, and it was followed into Mexico by numerous ladies of the night from El Paso and other places. General Pershing knew full well the truth of Kipling's saying that "Single men in barracks [or in camps] don't grow into plaster saints."[17] If the soldiers of the expedition went prowling into Mexican villages or through the countryside they were likely to get into serious trouble and even have their throats cut. So the camp followers were rounded up and placed under guard. A high, tightly constructed barbed-wire stockade was erected, with an adobe hut for each woman. There was but one gate, at which there was a guard and a prophylaxis station. A soldier desiring to enter had to show the guard that he had the necessary fee, which was regulated by the Provost Marshal, Captain Julien Gaujot, of the 11th Cavalry, who was the commanding officer of the establishment. At the end of a half-hour, if the soldier had not come out, the guard went in and got him. Every man coming out was required to take a prophylactic. The result was that the venereal rate in the Punitive Expedition was one of the lowest the army has ever known. Possibly the high point in the history of the Punitive Expedition's stockade was Thanksgiving dinner, prepared by the girls themselves, and at which Captain Gaujot was the guest of honor.[17]

Taken all in all, the health of the officers and men of the Punitive Expedition was excellent, in spite of the hardships of the first few weeks and the distinctly unsanitary conditions under which officers and men frequently had to live for extended periods. The Surgeon General remarked in his annual report, "During all this arduous service the troops were maintained in an exceptional condition of health and efficiency."[18] In the mid part of August there were several cases of malaria in the 13th Cavalry, which was then stationed on the Santa María River, at Las Galeras. The whole regiment was required to take quinine twice a week, and as soon as possible the regiment was transferred to Colonia Dublán, where there were no mosquitoes. A few cases of paratyphoid appeared in the 11th Cavalry in September, and later that month the whole expedition was inoculated against the disease, which was not prevented by the regular antityphoid inoculations. But no epidemics of any sort developed; the army had learned much since 1898.[19]

The force assembled at Colonia Dublán was the largest American military force concentrated in one area since the maneuvers of 1911, and with six full regiments of cavalry and a squadron of another, it was the largest American cavalry force since the Civil War. General Pershing at once instituted a training program that was stiff, thorough and realistic. A series of experiments was carried out to develop new methods and new tactical concepts. There were practice marches, but with one difference from marches in the United States. In Mexico the soldiers carried live ammunition in their belts and were ready to go into action at a second's notice. The advance and flank guards were vigilant against a real enemy who might appear at any moment—but never did. There were endless maneuvers and field exercises, one-sided, against an imaginary or outlined enemy, and two-sided, with troop pitted against troop, or regiment against regiment. Target ranges were constructed, and in July orders were issued that every man who had not fired for record would fire at 100, 200 and 300 yards. The order remarked that "unfortunately, the theory to some extent prevails in our army that the fire efficiency of a company of average or even untrained shots is as high as that of a company of trained shots, but this theory has not stood the severe test of real war conditions abroad."[20] Other orders required the appointment of athletic officers at each station, and a few weeks later, prescribed at least ten minutes of vigorous calisthenics at the beginning of each drill period.

The intensified training, the maneuvers and field exercises were closely and carefully observed by the Commanding General and his staff; mistakes and errors were pointed out in no uncertain terms. The period of marking time at Colonia Dublán was a period of training for war. No one could foresee, but within a year the training lessons learned at Colonia Dublán were to prove invaluable in the hasty training of a huge army for a major war.

In experimenting in new combat methods and new uses for weapons already in use, the camp at Colonia Dublán anticipated, to some extent, the various branch boards (the Infantry Board, the Cavalry Board, etc.) that were set up as a permanent part of each branch school after World War I. An example of the kind of experiment that was carried out was the use of the 45-caliber automatic pistol as a mounted weapon. American mounted troops had always been trained to use firearms on horseback, but there were certain limitations. The revolver could be fired only to the right or left but not to the front. Thin slivers of lead scraped off the bullet between the cylinder and barrel of the weapon would strike the horse in the neck, making the animal gun-shy. A series of exhaustive experiments showed quickly that this danger did not occur with the automatic pistol; it could be fired in any direction and at any gait. Firing regulations were revised, and from 1916 until the horse cavalry passed from the scene, the American trooper was trained to fire his pistol mounted, front, right, left and to the rear, all at the fast gallop.

As mentioned before, in August of 1916, Pancho Villa, with his wounds healed and still full of ambition and hatred for Carranza and the United States, exploded from hiding. Late in August the Carranzistas reported that they had defeated him near Satevo, but Collector Zach Cobb, at El Paso, learned something quite different: the Carranzistas had fled from the battle in disorder. Three weeks later, on the night of September 15–16, the people and garrison of the city of Chihuahua awoke to find Villa in their very midst. He opened the penitentiary and liberated some two hundred prisoners. General Treviño, on being awakened, started for the scene of the trouble, but his personal bodyguard deserted and joined Villa, as did most of the Carranzista artillery. After several hours in the city Villa withdrew in a leisurely way, taking with him a large augmentation to his forces and sixteen automobile loads of ammunition and small arms.[21]

On October 24 Pershing reported to Funston that Villa was in complete control of a large part of central Chihuahua and that the Carranzistas seemed unable to stop him. Pershing believed that many Carranzista officers were merely waiting for an opportune moment to change sides, and hinted broadly for permission to go after Villa. "If further operations on our part should be contemplated, the occupation of the city of Chihuahua by . . . this command would be very advantageous."[22]

On November 23, Villa, with his old audacity, again swept into the city of Chihuahua. This time he ran into opposition, and it took five days of heavy fighting to gain full possession. The Carranzista resistance finally collapsed, and Villa occupied the city for several days. At first it was reported that great numbers of foreigners, including many Americans, were killed, but it was found later that only the unfortunate Chinese had suffered. Scores of them were butchered.[23]

General Pershing was champing at the bit. He wrote to Funston: "A swift blow delivered by this command should be made at once against this pretender. Our own prestige in Mexico should receive consideration at this time. In the light of Villa's operations during the past two weeks, further inactivity of this command does not seem desirable, and there is no longer doubt as to the facts." Funston forwarded Pershing's recommendation to the Secretary of War, urging approval, but the approval never came. The Administration's policy was to avoid becoming more deeply involved in Mexico. The Punitive Expedition continued to mark time.[24]

It appeared before long that the de facto government was regaining control in Chihuahua. General Murguía recaptured Chihuahua city without much trouble, but this was partly offset by Villa's capture of Torreón, just before Christmas. He made no effort to hold Torreón, but evacuated within a few days. In fact, he made no effort to hold any of the cities he captured. His campaign was a series of "hit and run" raids to keep the Carranzistas off balance, and to obtain arms, munitions, funds and recruits (often by impressment).

But in spite of Villa's renaissance, President Wilson decided, late in January, 1917, to withdraw from Mexico. On January 30, 1917, General Funston telegraphed to the Secretary of War that the withdrawal had started; on February 5, at three o'clock in the afternoon, the last man of the Punitive Expedition marched across the international boundary south of Columbus, and the Punitive Expedition was no more. General Pershing stood in the bandstand in Columbus and watched his soldiers march past. They were ragged (for various reasons the issue of clothing had been irregular), but they were lean and hard and marched with the unconscious swagger of thoroughly trained troops. It was a tightly knit, keen, fighting force, and Pershing's heart must have swelled with pride as he looked at the men. And it is possible that even the tight-lipped Pershing smiled inwardly when, as the 10th Cavalry marched by, a trooper's pet snake poked its head through a hole in the Negro soldier's shirt and stared about with its beady eyes.[25]

Several complications arose with the evacuation of the American forces from Mexico. The ladies of the stockade were among the first to go. They rode gaily out on a train of freight cars, waving merrily to their acquaintances. Inevitably, in the poker and crap games that had flourished every night, the greater part of the payroll of each company had wound up in the hands of a few men. To transport their winnings was a serious problem to those individuals. The soldiers had been paid in coin, and coin is heavy. One sergeant, who had accumulated around twenty thousand dollars, asked his battery commander to take care of it for him. Reluctantly, and with the clear understanding that he assumed no responsibility for the safety of the treasure, the battery commander consented; the money was wrapped in his bedding roll and carried on the battery baggage wagon. The money arrived safely, and the sergeant eventually established himself in business in El Paso with his chance-won capital.[26] How other heavy winners brought out their winnings is unrecorded, but there are no buried-treasure legends connected with the Colonia Dublán campsite. The twenty odd Villista prisoners were turned over to the state of New Mexico for trial. The unfortunate Chinese who had taken refuge with the Americans posed a special problem. The entry of Chinese into the United States was forbidden by law, but common decency and humanity demanded that they be not left to the mercies of the Mexicans of either faction. General Funston took the legal bull by the horns and ordered Pershing to bring them to the United States, regardless of the exclusion law. They were sent to Fort Sam Houston, at San Antonio, and in a short time the Bureau of Immigration consented to their remaining in the United States, provided that the army would guarantee that they would not become public charges. This was easy, for they included numerous skilled cooks and men with other useful crafts, and their services were snapped up.[27]

From Columbus the troops of the Punitive Expedition were quickly scattered to posts and stations over the United States, but mostly on the Border. The dismantling of the base at Columbus commenced immediately, and by the end of May, 1917, all the machinery had been shipped to other places where the war with Germany made it necessary. The hundreds of motor vehicles that had served the expedition were shipped to El Paso and San Antonio for reconditioning, after which they were sent to the numerous cantonments that were being built to house the huge army that was being formed.

The Punitive Expedition was so overwhelmed by events immediately following that historians have given it little attention, and of those who have noted it, many have made egregious errors, such as that made by a recent writer who said that the infantry rode on trucks going into Mexico. The various infantry adjutants, who daily noted the number of men who were suffering from sore feet, did not know that they were riding in trucks. The commonest assumption is that the Punitive Expedition was a humiliating failure because it did not bring Pancho Villa back, "dead or alive." This assumption is shared by reputable historians, as well as by "popular" writers to whom Villa has become a figure of romance. Actually, the major Villista bands were smashed with dispatch and with crippling losses in every encounter. As for the supposed superiority of the Villistas in guerrilla warfare, it need only be pointed out that *they were surprised in every encounter* and not once were they victorious. And as for the single American defeat, at Carrizal, it is enough to say that two understrength troops of the 10th Cavalry, with their officers killed or wounded, inflicted casualties almost equal to their own total strength, and that the Carranza government changed its tone immediately after the fight. It should be noted, also, that when Villa reappeared on the scene, he never came within reach of the expedition, nor did he, as far as available records show, offer violence to Americans, in spite of his bloodcurdling threats. The expedition was far from a failure, even though it did not capture or kill Villa. And who can say what the outcome would have been if it had not entered Mexico?

An unquestionable result of the Punitive Expedition which cannot be evaluated exactly, but is nonetheless real, was that it provided a hard core of trained and experienced soldiers who were available for the war against Germany. General Pershing emerged as a driving field commander and a skillful trainer of troops, often ruthless in his methods but satisfied with nothing less than perfection. Because of his handling of the Punitive Expedition, he was the logical choice as a commander of the American Expeditionary Forces in Europe. The Adjutant General of the expedition, Major John L. Hines, swiftly rose to command of a division, then a corps, in France, and succeeded Pershing himself as Chief of Staff of the United States Army. The units that had comprised the Punitive Expedition and the thousands of National Guardsmen who cursed the Border and sweated through months of training, formed a nucleus around which the National Army of 1917 and 1918 was assembled and trained with a dispatch that utterly surprised the methodical Prussians, who had convinced themselves that the United States was impotent. It is not too much to say that the Mexican Punitive Expedition of 1916 and 1917 was a training school for the greater war that was soon to follow.

NOTES

1. Patton was a noted swordsman and was the designer of the saber that was standard cavalry armament in the United States Army until it was abolished as a weapon in the early 1930s. His pre-World War II nickname was *not* "Blood and Guts" but was "Saber" Patton.
2. Chris Emmett, *In the Path of Events with Colonel Martin L. Crimmins, Soldier, Naturalist, Historian* (Waco, Tex., 1959), pp. 311–312.
3. Told the writer by Maj. Gen. Donald C. Cubbison, U.S. Army, Ret. The terms "pup tents" and "dog tents," which were popular with reporters and correspondents, were never used in the service. The tents were always referred to as "shelter tents" or "shelter halves," since each soldier's equipment included one-half of a complete tent.
4. Emmett, *op. cit.*, p. 310.
5. Related to the writer by Maj. Gen. Cubbison.
6. Lt. James A. Shannon, "With the Apache Scouts in Mexico," *Cavalry Journal*, XXVII (Apr., 1917), 544.

7. *Ibid.*, p. 556.
8. Told to the writer by Maj. Gen. Cubbison. Other veterans of the Punitive Expedition have commented on this.
9. Tompkins, *op. cit.*, p. 214.
10. Pope, "Motor Transport Experiences," included in Tompkins, *op. cit.*, p. 253. Maj. Gen. Cubbison also commented at length on the Chinese refugees.
11. Told to the writer by Maj. Gen. Cubbison.
12. Punitive Expedition Records, National Archives, R.G. 120, Box 2-F.
13. *Ibid.*, Box 2-I.
14. *Ibid.*, Box 2-F.
15. *Ibid.*, Box 422; George McAdam, "The Life of General Pershing," Part VII, *World's Work*, XXXVIII (June, 1919), 151.
16. Letter from Col. Paul Davison, U.S. Army, Ret., to the writer, July 30, 1966.
17. From Kipling's "Tommy." Information about this unpublicized feature of the camp at Colonia Dublán was given by several people, including (many years ago) the late Col. Julien E. Gaujot, who was the Provost Marshal.
18. "Report of The Surgeon General," *War Department Annual Reports*, *1917*, I, 349.
19. *Ibid.*, pp. 482–83.
20. Punitive Expedition Records, National Archives, R.G. 120, Box 58.
21. *Foreign Relations, 1916*, pp. 609–10.
22. *Ibid.*, pp. 612–13.
23. *Ibid.*, pp. 616–23.
24. *Ibid.*, p. 623.
25. Related to the writer by Col. Charles W. Hoffman, who was an eyewitness of the incident.
26. Related to the writer by Maj. Gen. Cubbison.
27. Related to the writer by Maj. Gen. Cubbison. See *Foreign Relations, 1917*, pp. 1088–92. The Palo Alto *Times*, on May 17, 1966, carried a news item about an elderly Chinese who died of a heart attack in Denver, Colorado, a few days before, with a large sum of money on his person. He had told friends that General Pershing had rescued him from Mexico.

CHAPTER 19

The Last Battles

WITH PANCHO VILLA LOOSE in Chihuahua, Mexico was
still far from showing any signs of settling down, but in
the United States, in the spring of 1917, Mexico became a minor
issue because of the war with Germany. Raids from across the
border into Texas, New Mexico and Arizona still occurred frequently, and life was hazardous for borderland ranches and
farmers. The attitude of the Administration in Washington had
changed, however, and on February 18, 1917, only a few days
after the Punitive Expedition returned to the United States, the
Secretary of War sent confidential instructions to the Commanding General, Southern Department (then Pershing himself, as
General Funston had died of a heart attack)

> that in the event of the repetition of such raid by Mexican bands
> crossing the border into the United States as recently occurred
> in the vicinity of Arroyo del Tigre and Corner Ranch you will
> take action as follows:
> You will direct the nearest Commanding Officer of United
> States troops who has a suitable and sufficient force for the
> purpose to immediately pursue the raiding band with a view to
> its capture or destruction.

The order specified that United States troops would not remain in Mexico more than three days, or go more than sixty
miles beyond the Border. Pursuit must take place within seven
days after a raid, and if the pursuers met troops of the de facto

government, they would turn over such information as they had and return to the United States.[1]

Through 1917, 1918 and 1919 the raids from Mexico went on. Raiders were pursued across the Rio Grande, and there were numerous skirmishes, usually with some Mexicans killed and often with casualties on the American side. The Carranza government never failed to protest against these "invasions" of Mexican soil and offenses against Mexican sovereignty. On December 27, for example, Indio Ranch, below Del Rio, Texas, was raided. There were no casualties in the raid, but the raiders stole about one hundred goats, which they took across the river into Mexico. A small force of American troops crossed the boundary on December 29 in pursuit. They came up to the bandits at a village named San José, where they were fired upon. In the ensuing scrimmage, several bandits were killed. The de facto government, in its protest, several months later, accused the Americans of wantonly murdering the peaceful inhabitants of the village, an allegation that the Americans denied.[2]

The Mexican protests were received in Washington so regularly, and many of them were so vehement, that the Secretary of State, on July 29, 1918, suggested to Secretary of War Baker that to avoid further embarrassment, American troops be ordered not to fire into Mexico or cross the boundary without express authority from Washington. Secretary Baker dryly replied that "it would be most undesirable from a military standpoint to instruct our men that when they are being shot at themselves from the Mexican border they were not to return the fire but to ask the War Department for permission to do so."[3]

A few of these raids and the ensuing pursuit were especially noteworthy. On March 25, 1918, bandits raided Nevill's ranch, about twenty-five or thirty miles from Van Horn, Texas. Nevill, a widower, lived with his son and had a Mexican housekeeper-cook whose husband was a ranch employee. Nevill had been away until late in the afternoon. On returning to his ranch, and after supper, he and his son were talking, when they heard the sound of horses outside and suddenly rifle bullets smashed through the ranch house. Nevill and his son both picked up their Winchesters. Nevill himself escaped, but his son was killed

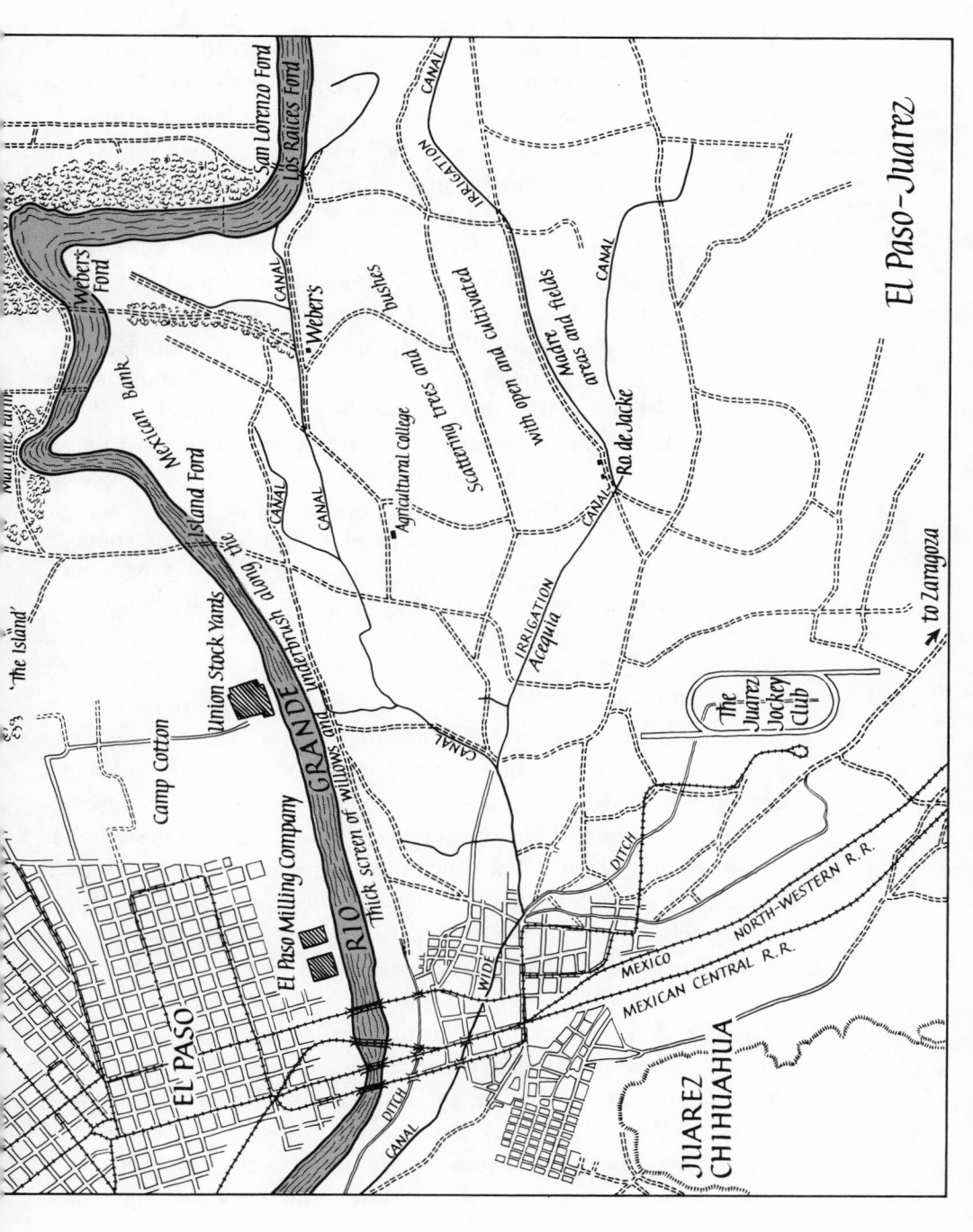

El Paso-Juarez

EL PASO

JUAREZ
CHIHUAHUA

The Island

Mad Chez Farm

Weber's Ford

Mexican Bank

San Lorenzo Ford

Los Raíces Ford

Island Ford

Camp Cotton

Union Stock Yards

El Paso Milling Company

RIO GRANDE

Thick screen of willows and underbrush along the

Weber's

Agricultural College

Scattering trees and bushes

with open and cultivated areas and fields

Madre

CANAL

CANAL

CANAL

CANAL

CANAL

CANAL

IRRIGATION

CANAL

Ro. de Jacke

IRRIGATION Acequia

CANAL

CANAL

WIDE

DITCH

DITCH

The Juarez Jockey Club

to Zaragoza

MEXICO NORTH-WESTERN R.R.

MEXICAN CENTRAL R.R.

CANAL

trying to get from the house to the chaparral. Nevill, while dashing for a deep ditch nearby, killed two of the invaders.

The raiders stripped the corpse of young Nevill, then looted the house, killing the Mexican housekeeper but sparing her three small children.[4] News of the raid reached Colonel George T. Langhorne, of the 8th Cavalry, after midnight that night. He immediately ordered two troops of his regiment, with a pack-train, to follow the raiders and destroy them. The Americans came up with the bandits at Pilares ranch, several miles south of the international boundary. The bandits attempted to escape, and in the running fight that followed, covering some eleven miles, thirty-three were killed. Young Nevill's chaparejos were found on one of the dead raiders; his horse was found among the captured animals, and his saddle was identified. A large quantity of ammunition and dynamite were found at Pilares, which had been reputed among the Americans for a long time to be an outlaw rendezvous. The ranch was burned to the ground, but whether from accident or design does not show in any available records. During the pursuit, General Murguía, the local Carranzista commander, notified Colonel Langhorne that he was sending troops, not to capture the bandits, but to resist the Americans.[5]

The raid on Nevill's ranch and the subsequent pursuit were typical of many Border incidents in 1917, 1918 and the early part of 1919 but was somewhat more important than other such incidents because of the numbers involved, the drastic destruction of the bandits' hideout and the almost complete destruction of the raiding band. The outstanding incident on the Border during the period mentioned was, however, not a bandit raid, but a pitched battle between Americans and Mexicans on a part of the Border that had always been relatively quiet, at Nogales.

Late in the afternoon of August 27, 1918, Lieutenant Colonel Frederick J. Herman, of the 10th Cavalry, who was commanding officer of the subdistrict of Nogales, while driving to Nogales from camp, stopped an army truck that was exceeding the speed limit. The truck driver was on his way to camp in a hurry, because Americans and Mexicans were firing at each other at the international line. When the noise of the motor stopped, Herman could hear the firing himself. He turned and dashed back to camp, finding that the cavalry squadron was already mounted and ready to move.

Herman got his own weapons and equipment and returned to town, arriving at the same time as the cavalry. Holding the troopers under cover of some buildings, he went forward to reconnoiter. He found that a string of railroad cars had been drawn up on the Mexican side, affording cover for a large number of riflemen, that heavy fire was coming from a hill just south of the town and that General Obregón's residence, which fronted on the boundary, was occupied by Mexicans, who were firing out of every door and window. Herman ordered the cavalry troops to clear the commanding position just southeast of the town and to drive the Mexicans out of the houses facing the international boundary, taking care not to kill any women or children.

Troop C, on the extreme left, the same troop that was in the Carrizal fight, attacked up the hill in waves of a squad at a time, shooting to the right and left as the men saw targets. At some time during the attack the troop commander, Captain Joseph D. Hungerford, was shot through the head and killed instantly. Troop A, under Captain Roy V. Morledge, swept across the international line into the houses. In one of them, the "Concordia Club," one of the girls caused a laugh in the midst of the battle excitement by addressing a soldier by name.

Meanwhile, Major Herbert E. Marshburn arrived with three companies of the 35th Infantry in trucks—any truck that Marshburn could get his hands on. Two companies extended the American line and opened fire immediately. One company was held in reserve. Troop A sent a report to Colonel Herman that it could go no farther until the enemy was cleared from a hill to the south. Herman, going forward to see the situation personally, was shot in the leg by a sniper in a second-story window. Herman's wound was painful but not disabling; the sniper had exposed himself a second too long. He slumped down, with several American bullets in him.

Shortly before dark, a white flag appeared above the Mexican customs house, and Herman was persuaded to accompany the American consul to his office on the Mexican side of the line.

There was a conference between Herman, the Carranzista commander and several Mexican and American civil officials. It was quickly agreed to stop the firing. Herman's bugler sounded "Cease fire," and the firing from the American side died down. From the Mexican side it continued until officers and messengers were dispatched with the commandant's orders. The Americans who were on the Mexican side of the boundary returned to the United States, and the battle of Nogales was over. On the American side two officers, three soldiers and two civilians were killed; on the Mexican side the losses are unknown, but American military intelligence agencies reported that 129 were buried, including two individuals who appeared to be Germans.

When the shooting started, there were a number of American officers and soldiers in Nogales for various reasons who did not belong to the local garrison. Without exception they reported for duty—any duty. Captain James Duke was directed to take command of Troop C, replacing Captain Hungerford, who was killed. Lieutenant William Scott, of the 10th Cavalry, drove his motorcycle to the top of a hill overlooking the Mexican position and from there became a sniper, picking off several riflemen on the Mexican side. He was a former Texas Ranger and an expert rifleman. A sergeant from the ordnance warehouse, driving a truckload of ammunition and spare rifles into Nogales, overtook a 10th Cavalry soldier wearing a hospital bathrobe and pajamas, riding a horse bareback, with only a halter for control. The "sick" man begged for a rifle and some ammunition; he was trying to join his troop. Contrary to all regulations, the ordnance man let him have the rifle and a bandoleer of ammunition but made him sign a receipt for them.

As for the causes of the little battle of Nogales, all accounts agree that it started at the customs house gate when somebody tried to get through without stopping. Some say that the Mexican customs men fired first; others say that the Americans fired the first shot, but regardless of who started it, or why, it quickly developed into a full battle. Herman had received information several days before that there was likely to be trouble, as the Carranzista garrison was being increased by soldiers who had not been paid for a long time and were hungry. They had been told that food and wealth were to be had for the taking on the American side of the line. Herman had been skeptical of these reports, but nevertheless, had succeeded in obtaining reinforcements, including some machine guns. There was to be no repetition of Columbus.[6]

During this same period, the 10th Cavalry fought the last of the Indian battles. Although not, strictly speaking, a part of the long story of American military adventures in Mexico, it is so closely related as to warrant mention. After the Punitive Expedition, one of the major duties of the 10th Cavalry was patroling the long stretch of desert wasteland extending northwest from Nogales. An outpost was maintained at Bear Valley, about thirty miles from Nogales, and troops were rotated on duty there. The Yaquis of northwestern Sonora were in their perennial struggle to maintain their independence and their ancestral lands. Bands of them, driven from their own country, drifted northward and began to cross the boundary into Arizona in the wilderness northwest of Nogales. Ranchers began to find slaughtered cattle, with the hide cut into strips to make Yaqui sandals. A prospector riding to his claim suddenly found himself surrounded by Indians. They offered him no violence, and after a few minutes conversation in halting Spanish, he turned and rode away. Another independent miner encountered a band of Yaquis at night, while he was coasting around a curve in his Model T Ford.

In January, 1918, Troop E, 10th Cavalry, commanded by Captain Frederick H. L. Ryder, took over the outpost at Bear Valley. Overlooking the camp was a small peak that commanded a view over a vast distance. Because reports of "Indian sign" were coming in with increasing frequency, Captain Ryder established an observation post on the peak. On the morning of January 9, 1918, on receiving a report from a rancher that one of his cattle had been killed and skinned by Indians, Ryder reinforced the observation post and included an officer with a powerful pair of field glasses. The officer was Lieutenant William Scott, who has been mentioned already as a volunteer sniper in the battle at Nogales. About the middle of the afternoon Scott signaled "enemy in sight" from the observation post. He pointed to a low ridge a quarter of a mile west of the camp. A long column of Indians was plainly visible on the ridge.

In the camp a shout from the first sergeant brought every man racing to his horse with his saddle and weapons. The troop galloped to the top of the ridge and dismounted in a gully on the other side. The horses were circled by squads and left immobile, with a small guard. Forming the troop into a skirmish line, Captain Ryder gave the order to move up the side of the cañon. Nothing was found, so the order was given to return to the horses by another route. Halfway down the cañon the soldiers found hastily abandoned Indian packs, and at the same moment the hidden Indians opened fire. Fortunately for the Americans the fire was wild, and no one was hit. Ryder ordered an advance, the soldiers to fire as they moved. The Yaquis kept falling back, taking advantage of every boulder and bush. One Indian was seen to fall, but he kept on going. In about half an hour the Indian fire lessened and seemed to come from a small group. The troopers concentrated their aim on the group's position. After a few minutes an Indian stood up and waved his arms as a signal for surrender. Cautiously the cavalrymen moved forward and surrounded the group, ten warriors, one of whom was a young boy, who had fired a rifle as long as he was. One Indian was badly wounded; he died while being taken to the military hospital at Nogales.

The 10th Cavalry sustained no casualties in this last Indian battle. The Yaqui prisoners were held by Troop E while their fate was decided in higher echelons. They proved to be hard workers, who kept the camp immaculate, and they were so impressed with three substantial meals a day and a warm place in which to sleep, that they wanted to enlist in the United States Army. The de facto government of Sonora attempted to extradite them to Mexico, but since this would have been nothing but judicial murder, the United States authorities declined. Eventually they were tried in a Federal court on a purely technical charge of violation of the United States neutrality laws and were given nominal sentences. This precluded their deportation. Their subsequent fate is unknown, but it is not at all improbable that they joined the colony of Yaqui Indians that was forming in the outskirts of Tucson, Arizona, and which was, for many years, a source of industrious, hard-working, dependable laborers.[7]

During 1918 and 1919, Pancho Villa continued his efforts to reestablish his power and authority. Despite his fulminations against the United States he was careful to avoid any violence to foreigners, and some of his measures recalled the days when he was believed by many liberals to be the answer to Mexico's problems. In May, 1919, for instance, it was reported that he had ordered the schools in Parral to be reopened at once. The Mexican inhabitants of the city were taxed to support the program; the American residents were not required to contribute.[8] Before this, in May, 1917, Villista forces had attacked Ojinaga. The outnumbered and outfought Carranzistas did exactly as the Huertistas had done when Villa attacked a few years earlier: they took refuge in the United States. The Villistas evacuated very shortly, and in due course the Carranzista garrison returned from the United States. The Villistas made no effort to cross the boundary during the time they occupied Ojinaga. But there was no rest for the Carranzista garrison. In early November, 1917, Villa struck again, and once again scores of refug es and Carranzista soldiers streamed across the Rio Grande.[9]

As time went on and his forces increased, Villa became bolder. His power extended through most of the state of Chihuahua, but the major port of entry, Juarez, was still occupied by Carranzistas. Early in June, 1919, reports were received that Villa was gradually moving northward, with Juarez as his probable objective. On June 10, 1919, the United States Chief of Staff, General Peyton C. March, sent a "Very Confidential" communication to the Commanding General of the Southern Department, Major General De Rosey C. Cabell, who had been the Chief of Staff of the Punitive Expedition:

> Press reports indicate possibility of Villa attacking Juarez. Secretary of War directs that if Villa takes Juarez you will close the border. Should Villa men fire into El Paso you will cross the border and disperse his troops but will on no account undertake an expedition into Mexico. As soon as you have accomplished your purpose and the safety of the citizens of El Paso

is assured you will withdraw to the United States side of the river. It is highly important these instructions remain confidential. . . .

General Cabell acknowledged his receipt of the order on June 12 and at the same time informed the War Department that he had ordered the 24th Infantry to El Paso from Columbus.[10] Tension increased as Villa's forces, almost as strong, it seemed, as in 1914, moved steadily northward. On June 11 Juarez was cut off from the rest of Mexico, and Villa's brilliant artilleryman and principal professional adviser, General Felipe Angeles, was reported to be only eight miles to the south. Nevertheless, the district commander, Brigadier General Erwin at El Paso, for some reason, did not anticipate a Villista attack. He reported successively on June 11, 12 and 13 that everything was quiet. Erwin, however, was taking no chances. Even though he discounted the probability of an attack by Villa, he kept his troops at the alert, and ready to move.

Shortly after midnight on June 14–15, 1919, a heavy Villista attack thrust quickly into the heart of Juarez. The Carranzista garrison, outnumbered, retreated into the citadel of Fort Hidalgo, on the hills overlooking the city. At four o'clock, still fighting in the dark, the Carranzistas counterattacked, driving their enemies out of a large part of the city, but were unable to drive them completely away. Late in the afternoon of June 16, Villa again launched an attack, and the fighting seesawed back and forth through the city.

On the American side, plans had been laid long in advance for just such a contingency, and as soon as General Erwin realized that his belief that Villa would not attack was vain, he moved his troops to their assigned positions. At Fort Bliss and in bivouac between El Paso and Ysleta was the 2d Cavalry Brigade, commanded by the already legendary "Tommy" Tompkins. It consisted of the 7th Cavalry and two squadrons of the 5th Cavalry. Other troops of Erwin's command were the regimental headquarters and two battalions of the 82d Field Artillery, two battalions of the 8th Engineers (mounted), the 7th Field Signal Battalion, the 24th Infantry, one battalion of the 9th Engineers, a field hospital, and a searchlight section of the

8th Engineers, which was emplaced on the mesa above El Paso High School.

Colonel Thomas E. Merrill, commanding the Field Artillery, established his headquarters at the stockyards office building and put four batteries into position to fire into Mexico. Other batteries of the regiment were with the cavalry brigade. Ever since the Villistas moved in to attack Juarez, there had been sporadic firing that struck into the United States. By nightfall, June 16, several soldiers and civilians in El Paso were killed or wounded by shots from the Mexican side (incidentally, most of the wounded civilians were Mexicans). At Colonel Merrill's artillery headquarters shots began hitting early in the afternoon. At ten thirty at night one soldier had been killed and another wounded. Colonel Merrill called the district Chief of Staff, Colonel Francis W. Glover, who was at his office in the Mills Building, to inform him. Colonel Glover went to artillery headquarters at once. He, Colonel Merrill, with a captain and a soldier, went to the roof of the building and purposely exposed themselves, watching for a flash on the Mexican side. In a matter of seconds there was a bright flash of a rifle across the river and a shot took off the mortar on the chimney beside which they were standing. It could not have been an accidental shot, and it came from a part of Juarez that Glover knew was held by Villistas.

A few hours later Glover telephoned to the headquarters of the 24th Infantry, in the customs house, and inquired about the situation. The reply was that it was unsafe for anybody to stick his head out of a door or window, the bullets were flying so fast. On orders from General Erwin, Glover went to the Santa Fe Street bridge and stood in the open on the bridge, observing where the fire was coming from. He quickly ascertained that the fire was coming from Carranzistas, who were attacking and firing northward, so that their shots were striking into the United States.

General Erwin decided to move into Mexico and drive the Villistas away from the boundary. The cavalry brigade was ordered, in accordance with previous plans, to cross the Rio Grande at a ford a few miles below Juarez, to cut off the enemy's retreat. The 24th Infantry was ordered to cross at the Santa Fe Street bridge and drive the Villistas out of Juarez. A message was sent to General González, telling him to get his troops out of the way. Colonel Glover crossed with the advance guard. At the Mexican end of the bridge there was a small Carranzista detachment, who appeared to be pleased at the Americans' arrival. Glover learned from them that the Carranzista forces distinguished themselves by rolling up the left trouser leg and both sleeves. He then told them to get out of the way if they did not want to get hurt, and the Americans deployed and advanced, with fixed bayonets.

Meanwhile, four batteries of American artillery were firing with a speed and accuracy previously unknown in Mexican warfare. According to tradition the first salvo burst on the Juarez race track, where a large number of Villa's men were known to be encamped. The water tower mushroomed under the impact of high explosive shells and spewed out thousands of gallons of water, flooding the field and almost literally washing the Villistas away.

Down the river, the cavalry brigade crossed at three fords, San Lorenzo, Cinecue and Zambrone. There was no difficulty, except that an artillery caisson overturned in the middle of the river and had to be abandoned temporarily. Once across the river the cavalry turned to the right, up the river road. The Americans were fired upon from the underbrush, but the fire caused no casualties. The main body of the Villistas was not yet located, and since it appeared that they had eluded the pincers between the infantry on the north and the cavalry to the south, Tompkins pulled the brigade back to the San Lorenzo ford to feed and water the horses and wait for daylight. A little after nine o'clock in the morning, a patrol from the 7th Cavalry found the main Villista force just west of Zaragoza. Ten minutes later the brigade attacked. The terrain was so cut up by irrigation ditches that mounted movement was difficult, but the enemy had no stomach for rifle, machine-gun and artillery fire from the Americans. The Mexicans broke and fled wildly from their bivouac, abandoning equipment and weapons in their haste to get away. The official report of the action by Colonel Tompkins says that they "scattered like quail."[11] The brigade pursued as vigorously as the waterlogged ground and the maze of ditches allowed. By noon the enemy had vanished. The absence of dust clouds showed that the Villistas had broken into very small groups or were escaping as individuals. Since General Erwin's orders were not to pursue more than fifteen miles into Mexico, and there was no longer a profitable target, the troops were assembled and marched back to the United States. By five o'clock in the afternoon there was not an American soldier in Mexico. The cavalrymen returned to their own country dry-shod; the 8th Engineers had erected a ponton bridge across the river. The overturned caisson was recovered, and the battle of Juarez was over.

Of course, the Mexicans protested. From his refuge in Fort Hidalgo, General González sent a note of protest. Days later the de facto government protested formally and asserted that the Villistas were already beaten and had provoked American intervention by deliberately firing into the United States. And for his firmness in maintaining the sovereignty and dignity of his country, General González was promoted to *general de división*, (major general,) the highest rank in the Mexican Army.

As for Pancho Villa's army, which he had carefully rebuilt and nurtured ever since the Punitive Expedition, it simply ceased to exist. It lacked the toughness and resiliency of his earlier forces and could not stand defeat. Probably most of the rank and file were unwilling conscripts, impressed by force and fear from the villages and ranches of Chihuahua, men who wanted nothing so much as to return to their homes. Under the shattering impact of the American artillery and the pistols of the American troopers, they vanished, leaving some two hundred of their number lying motionless in the fields and through the mesquite. It was impossible to gather them together again. As a serious threat to the Border and the de facto government, Villa was finished, even though he made determined attempts through the remainder of 1919 and into 1920 to rebuild his forces. His name had lost its magic and all Mexico was war-weary.

The battle of Juarez was the last major American military

venture into Mexico. That is not to say that there were no further bandit raids and retaliatory pursuits by American troops crossing the boundary. There were numerous minor incidents, all following the pattern that has been related many times. But with the revolution that swept Venustiano Carranza out of office and to his death, and the establishment of firm control by General Álvaro Obregón, the Border gradually became quiet. The last incident worthy of mention occurred in 1930, during an attempted revolution, when a group of rebels had a skirmish with a patrol from the 10th Cavalry near Naco. As for the future, no one knows.

NOTES

1. Punitive Expedition Records, National Archives, OTAG Project Files, 1917–25, Box 269.
2. *Ibid.*
3. *Ibid.*, Box 270.
4. Testimony of E. W. Nevill, *Fall Committee Report*, pp. 1510–14.
5. Testimony of Col. George T. Langhorne, *Fall Committee Report*, pp. 1633–35; *Foreign Relations, 1918*, pp. 556–57.
6. Testimony of Capt. Frederick J. Herman, *Fall Committee Report*, pp. 1811–16; Wharfield, *10th Cavalry & Border Fights*, pp. 16–23.
7. H. B. Wharfield, "A Fight with the Yaquis at Bear Valley, 1918," *Arizoniana*, IV (fall, 1963), 1–8. The writer has also heard accounts of this last Indian fight from Col. F. H. L. Ryder (recently deceased) and several soldiers who were in it.
8. El Paso *Times*, May 15, 1919.
9. *Foreign Relations, 1917*, pp. 940–44.
10. Punitive Expedition Records, National Archives, OTAG Project Files, 1917–25, Box 269.
11. For information on the last battle against Villa, the writer is indebted to Col. Geoffrey Galwey, U.S. Army, Ret., who was in the fight and who made an extensive collection of excerpts from the National Archives and from contemporary newspapers, all of which he made available.

Conclusions

F ROM THE MEXICAN WAR of 1846–48 the borderlands between Mexico and the United States have been a region of turbulence, lawlessness and disorder until recent times. Throughout most of the latter half of the nineteenth century and until the end of the Mexican Revolution there was a continual succession of raids from one country into the other by Indians and outlaws. By far the greater number of such raids were from the Mexican side of the international boundary, although, admittedly, converse incursions were not unknown. Because of the inability, and in some instances the unwillingness, of Mexican authorities to take action to prevent or punish such raids, the United States felt forced, on numerous occasions, to take military action. Usually American expeditions into Mexico were regarded with deep hostility by Mexicans, although the several expeditions against hostile Apaches in the Sierra Madre range of Chihuahua and Sonora were welcomed.

Mexican raids into the United States reached their climax during the years of the Mexican Revolution, with Francisco Villa's descent upon the hamlet of Columbus, New Mexico, as the most spectacular and disastrous of all. It resulted immediately in General Pershing's Punitive Expedition, which was the largest American force to enter Mexico since the Mexican War.

Because the Punitive Expedition did not kill or capture Pancho Villa himself, it is usual for both serious historians and romancers to regard and treat it as a humiliating failure. It is generally depicted as a slowly moving, lumbering column of heavy-footed men, weighted down with equipment and handicapped by long lines of wagons and wheeled artillery, plodding through the endless wastes of northern Mexico, while Villa's guerrillas danced in circles about them, slashing in and retreating at will.

Nothing could be farther from the truth. It is true that the Punitive Expedition did not attain the dramatic success of bringing Pancho Villa to the United States in handcuffs, but the Americans quickly destroyed Villa's principal bands. That was Pershing's actual assigned mission—not to capture Villa "dead or alive." As for the imagined superiority of Villa's followers as guerrilla fighters, it should be sufficient to point out that the Villistas were *surprised in every single encounter*. The Punitive Expedition was *not* a single slow column plowing through the Mexican wilderness. Pershing's method of operation, rather, was a series of small, mobile forces that moved as fast as the Mexicans, or faster, and could live off the country for long periods of time.

The conclusion is inescapable that the Punitive Expedition of 1916 accomplished its major mission, and was, therefore, successful. And its success was attained in spite of unfamiliarity with the country, the opposition, both passive and overt, of the de facto government's forces and the difficulties of supply. It may be noted, also, that when Villa emerged from hiding, after his wounds were healed, he carefully kept himself beyond reach of the Americans and never again threatened an incursion across the boundary.

Possibly even more important than the actual destruction of Villa's main bands was the unintended role of the Punitive Expedition as a school that prepared officers and soldiers for the greater expedition of 1917 and 1918 and as an experimental laboratory in training and in new equipment. Pershing's rugged and intensive training program at Colonia Dublán was the prototype for the training schedules that enabled the United States to launch a huge army into Europe months before the Germans believed that such was possible. The experiences of the Punitive Expedition led to changes in armament (such as machine guns, for example) and proved the value of motor transportation. The experiences of the 1st Aero Squadron were invaluable to the handful of young aviators who constituted the entire United States Air Force of the time, and it is noteworthy that most of them later rose to high command.

Last, but not least, General Pershing emerged from the Punitive Expedition as an experienced field commander who could handle large organizations scattered over a vast region and who was bold without being rash, and ruthlessly determined—a combination of qualities that made him the logical choice when President Wilson had to decide upon a commander-in-chief for the American Expeditionary Force in Europe. And like Pershing himself, the Punitive Expedition brought out such men as John L. Hines, who would command a division and corps with conspicuous success in France, and would succeed Pershing himself as Chief of Staff of the United States Army, and Lieutenant George S. Patton, who would, in a second world war, become famous as one of the "fightingest" generals who ever wore the American uniform.

Bibliography

During the course of research and preparation, the writer interviewed the following persons:

> Col. John W. Cotton, U.S. Army, Ret.,
> Maj. Gen. Donald C. Cubbison, U.S. Army, Ret.,
> Maj. Gen. Ernest J. Dawley, U.S. Army, Ret.,
> Col. Albert B. Dockery, U.S. Army, Ret.,
> Col. Geoffrey Galwey, U.S. Army, Ret.,
> Col. Charles W. Hoffman, U.S.A.R., Ret.,
> Rev. John Jeter,
> Maj. Gen. William O. Ryan, U.S. Air Force, Ret.,
> Sra. Luz Corral viuda de Villa.

In addition, as a lieutenant in Troop C, 10th Cavalry, the writer conversed many times and at length with men who were in the Punitive Expedition, whose recollections and experiences made a deep impression upon a young officer.

GOVERNMENT PUBLICATIONS

Annual Reports of the Secretary of War, 1843, 1852, 1854, 1860, 1877, 1881–1882.

Committee on Foreign Relations of the United States Senate, *66th Cong., 2nd sess., Senate Document No. 285,* 2 vols.

Congressional Globe, 30th Cong., 1st sess.

Congressional Record, 64th Cong., 1st sess.

"Diplomatic Correspondence," *40th Cong., 2nd sess., H.R. Executive Document No. 1, Pt. 2.*

"Difficulties on Southwestern Frontier," *36th Cong., 1st sess., H.R. Executive Document No. 52.*

"Mexican Affairs," *66th Cong., 2nd sess., Senate Document No. 285* (The Fall Committee Report).

Official Records of the Union and Confederate Armies in the War of the Rebellion, Series I, Vols. XV, XXVI, XXXIV.

"Report and Accompanying Documents of the Committee on Foreign Affairs of the United States House of Representatives," *45th Cong., 2nd sess., H.R. Report No. 701.*

Papers Relating to the Foreign Relations of the United States, 1871, 1872, 1877, 1882, 1911, 1912, 1913, 1914, 1915, 1916, 1917, 1918, 1919.

"Mexican Border Troubles," *45th Cong., 2nd sess., H.R. Misc. Document No. 64.*

"Report of General Crook to Hq., Military Division of the Pacific, July 23, 1883, *48th Cong., 1st sess., H.R. Executive Document No. 1.*

Report on the Mobilization of the Organized Militia and National Guard of the United States, 1916.

Navy Department Annual Reports, Fiscal Year 1916.

"Texas Frontier Trouble," *44th Cong., 1st sess., H.R. Report No. 343.*

"Troubles on Texas Frontier," *36th Cong., 1st sess., H.R. Executive Document No. 81.*

"Report of the Committee on Military Affairs," *45th Cong., 2nd sess., H.R. Misc. Document No. 64.*

War Department Annual Reports, 1911, 1912, 1913, 1914, 1915, 1916, 1917.

STATE OF CALIFORNIA

Orton, Brig. Gen. Richard C., *Records of California Men in the War of the Rebellion, 1861 to 1867.* Sacramento, The State Printer, 1890.

STATE OF CONNECTICUT

Biennial Report of The Adjutant General to the Governor for the Two Fiscal Years ended September 30, 1916.

MEXICO

Reports of the Committee of Investigation Sent in 1873 by the Mexican Government to the Frontier of Texas. Trans. from the Official Edition made in Mexico. New York, 1875.

ARCHIVAL MATERIALS

National Archives, Old War Records.

National Archives, Punitive Expedition Records.

National Archives, State Department Records, 1914–1919.

Library of Congress, Manuscript Division:

The John J. Pershing Papers.
The Hugh Lenox Scott Papers.
The Woodrow Wilson Papers.
War Diary, United States Expeditionary Force, Vera Cruz, 1914, *Records of the War Department, Records of the Adjutant General, Record Group No. 94.*

UNPUBLISHED MANUSCRIPT MATERIAL

(Now in the writer's possession, to be deposited in the Hoover Library, Stanford University.)

Bagby, Col. Carroll Armstrong, Punitive Expedition diary.

Carruth, Col. John H., Letter on experiences in the Punitive Expedition.

Davison, Col. Paul R., Letter on experiences as an officer-messenger in Mexico.

Deuel, Dr. Thorne, Statement of his memories and experiences, Mexico, 1916.

Drake, Brig. Gen., Charles C., Diary kept while at Vera Cruz, 1914.

Gilbreath, Maj. Gen. Frederick, Letter on the San Ygnacio raid.

Herman, Col. Fred W., Letter on experiences in the Punitive Expedition.

Hoffman, Col. Charles W., Reminiscences of the Columbus raid; Personal account of the execution of the prisoners taken at Columbus; Personal narrative of Service; Numerous letters.

Howe, Col. Jerome W., Field diary kept during the Punitive Expedition; Operations of Col. Dodd and the 7th Cavalry; My Military Career, 1909–1924; Letter from Cpl. H. C. Houston, Troop K, 10th Cavalry, to Colonel Howe's sister, describing the Carrizal fight.

Jeter, Rev. John, Narrative of experiences in the Carrizal fight.

Johns, Brig. Gen. Dwight F., Letter on experiences in the Punitive Expedition.

King, Col. Joseph Choate, Diary.

"Let's Get Acquainted" (mimeograph), annual dinner, Company K, 7th California Infantry, 1955.

Lewis, Harry C., Narrative of experiences in the Punitive Expedition.

McMaster, Maj. Richard H, 4th Field Artillery, "An Artilleryman in Mexico, 1916" (diary).

Queen, Col. Howard, Narrative of experiences in the Punitive Expedition and the Carrizal fight.

Rhodes, Maj. Gen. Charles D., Diary of a special mission to Mexico.

Roberts, Maj. Gen. Frank N., Service diary.

Ryan, Maj. Gen. William Ord, U.S.A.F., Diary kept during the Punitive Expedition.

Van Norman, Maj. George L., Troop history of Troop D, 7th Cavalry, Jan. 1, 1916–Dec. 31, 1916. Numerous letters on experiences in the Punitive Expedition.

Velarde, Col. C. Julian, Narrative of experiences in the Punitive Expedition.

Wood, Col. Otis, Letter on experiences on border service with the 1st New Mexico Infantry.

Autobiographies, Memoirs, Monographs, Etc.

Aguirre Benavides, Luis, *De Francisco I. Madero a Francisco Villa (Memorias de un Revolucionario)*, Mexico City, 1966.

Ashburn, Percy M., *A History of the Medical Department of the United States Army*, Intro. by Surgeon General Merritte W. Ireland, Boston and New York, 1929.

Atkinson, Donald T., *Texas Surgeon. An Autobiography*, New York, 1958.

Bailey, L. R., *Indian Slave Trade in the Southwest. A Study of Slave-taking and the Traffic in Indian Captives*, Los Angeles, 1966.

Baker, Ray Stannard, *Woodrow Wilson, Life and Letters*, IV, Garden City, N. Y., 1931.

Banners and the Glory, The. The Story of General Douglas MacArthur, New York, 1965.

Barnes, Will C., *Apache Longhorn. The Reminiscences of Will C. Barnes*, Los Angeles, 1941.

Barney, James M., *Tales of Apache Warfare. True Tales of Massacres, Fights, and Raids in Arizona and New Mexico*, np., 1933.

Betzinez, Jason, with Wilbur Sturtevant Nye, *I Fought with Geronimo*, Harrisburg, Pa., 1959.

Biddle, Ellen McGowan, *Reminiscences of a Soldier's Wife*, Philadelphia, 1907.

Blaisdell, Lowell L., *The Desert Revolution. Baja California, 1911*, Madison, Wis., 1962.

Bourke, John Gregory, *An Apache Campaign in the Sierra Madre. An Account of the Expedition in Pursuit of the Hostile Chiricahua Apaches in the Spring of 1883*, New York, 1886.

———, *On the Border with Crook*, New York, 1892.

Braddy, Haldeen, "Pancho Villa at Columbus. The Raid of 1916," *Southwestern Studies*, Texas Western University, III, No. 1, El Paso, Tex., 1965.

———, *Pershing's Mission in Mexico*, El Paso, Tex., 1966.

Brandenburg, Frank, *The Making of Modern Mexico*, Intro. by Frank Tannenbaum, Englewood Cliffs, N. J., 1964.

Brenner, Anita, *Idols Behind Altars*, New York, 1929.

Brenner, Anita and George R. Leighton, *The Wind That Swept Mexico. The History of the Mexican Revolution, 1910–1942*, New York and London, 1943.

Brimlow, George Francis, *Cavalryman Out of the West. Life of General William Carey Brown*, Caldwell, Id., 1944.

Bush, Ira Jefferson, *Gringo Doctor*, Foreword by Eugene Cunningham, Caldwell, Id., 1939.

Callcott, Wilfred Hardy, *Liberalism in Mexico, 1857–1929*, Stanford, Cal., 1931.

Calzadiaz Barrera, Alberto, *El Fin de la División del Norte*, Mexico City, 1965.

———, *Villa Contra Todo . . . y en Pos se la Venganza sobre Columbus*, N. M., 2 vols., Mexico City, 1960 and 1963.

Carter, William Harding, *The American Army*, Indianapolis, 1915.

———, *The Life of Lieutenant General Chaffee*, Chicago, 1917.

Carter, Robert Goldthwaite, *On the Border with Mackenzie, or, Winning West Texas from the Comanches*, New York, 1961, reprint from the 1935 ed.

Casasola, Gustavo, *Historia Gráfica de la Revolución*, 5 vols., Mexico City, nd.

Cleland, Robert Glass, *A History of Phelps Dodge, 1834–1950*, New York, 1952.

Clendenen, Clarence C., *The United States and Pancho Villa. A Study in Unconventional Diplomacy*, Ithaca, New York, 1961.

Cline, Howard F., *Mexico, Revolution to Evolution, 1940–1960*, New York and Toronto, 1962.

Cole, George D., "Brush Fire War, 1916 Style," unpublished M.A. thesis, Louisiana State College, Lake Charles, La., 1962.

Cook, James H., *Fifty Years on the Old Frontier as Cowboy, Hunter, Guide, Scout and Ranchman*, New Haven, 1923.

Cooper, Herbert H., "Arizona Border Towns and the Huerta Revolution of February, March, and April, 1913," unpublished M.A. thesis, University of Southern California, 1942.

Cosio Villegas, Daniel, *História Moderna de México. La República Restaurada*, Vol. I, 2nd ed., Mexico City, 1959.

Creel, George, *The People Next Door. An Interpretive History of Mexico and the Mexicans*, New York, 1926.

Creelman, James, *Diaz, Master of Mexico*, New York and London, 1911.

Cremony, John C., *Life Among the Apaches*, San Francisco, 1868.

Crook, George, *General Crook: His Autobiography*, Martin F. Schmitt, ed., Norman, Okla., 1960.

Cruse, Thomas, *Apache Days and After*, ed. and Intro. by Eugene Cunningham, Caldwell, Id., 1941.

Cumberland, Charles Curtis, *Mexican Revolution: Genesis Under Madero*, Austin, Tex., 1952.

Daniels, Josephus, *The Wilson Era. Years of Peace—1910–1917*, Chapel Hill, N. C., 1944.

Davis, Britton, *The Truth About Geronimo*, Milo Milton Quaife, ed., Chicago, 1951, reprint from the 1929 ed.

Dobie, J. Frank, *A Vaquero of the Brush Country*, Pref. by Lawrence Clark Powell, Boston, 1929.

Domenech, Abbé Emmanuel Henri Dieudonne, *Missionary Adventures in Texas and Mexico. A Personal Narrative of Six Years' Sojourn in Those Regions*, London, 1858.

Donnell, Guy R., "The United States Military Government at Veracruz, Mexico," in *Essays in Mexican History*, Thomas E. Cotner and Carlos E. Castañeda, eds., Austin, Tex., 1958.

Downey, Fairfax, *Indian Fighting Army*, New York, 1941.

Dupuy, R. Ernest, *The Compact History of the United States Army*, New York, 1956.

Emmett, Chris, *In the Path of Events with Colonel Martin Lalor Crimmins, Soldier—Naturalist—Historian*, Las Vegas, N. M., 1959.

Erwin, Allen A., *The Southwest of John H. Slaughter, 1841–1922: Pioneer Cattleman and Trail-driver of Texas, the Pecos, and Arizona and Sheriff of Tombstone*, Glendale, Cal., 1965.

Fain, Samuel S., "The Pershing Punitive Expedition and Its Diplomatic Backgrounds," unpublished M.A. thesis, University of Arizona, 1951.

Flandrau, Charles Macomb, *Viva Mexico!* C. Harvey Gardiner, ed., Urbana, Ill., 1964, reprint of the 1908 and 1937 eds.

Ford, John Salmon, *Rip Ford's Texas*, Stephen B. Oates, ed., Austin, Tex., 1963.

Fornaro, Carlo de, *Diaz, Czar of Mexico. An Arraignment by Carlo de Fornaro, with an Open Letter to Theodore Roosevelt*, New York, 1909.

Forsyth, George A., *Thrilling Days in Army Life*, New York and London, 1900.

Freeman, Douglas Southall, *R. E. Lee. A Biography*, Vol. I, New York and London, 1934.

Friedel, Frank, *The Splendid Little War*, Boston and Toronto, 1958.

Ganoe, William Addleman, *The History of the United States Army*, New York and London, 1924.

Gibson, A. M., *The Kickapoos. Lords of the Middle Border*, Norman, Okla., 1963.

Gillett, James B., *Six Years with the Texas Rangers, 1875 to 1881*, Milo Milton Quaife, ed., Chicago, 1943.

Godoy, José F., *Porfirio Diaz, President of Mexico. The Master Builder of a Great Commonwealth*, New York and London, 1910.

Goede, William H., *American Occupation, Vera Cruz, 1914*, Galveston, Tex., nd.

González Ramírez, Manuel, *La Revolución Social de México. Las Ideas —La Violencia*, Vol. I, Mexico City and Buenos Aires, 1960.

Greer, James Kimmins, *Colonel Jack Hayes. Texas Frontier Leader and California Builder*, New York, 1952.

Gruening, Ernest, *Mexico and Its Heritage*, New York, 1928.

Gurney, Gene, *A Pictorial History of the United States Army in War and Peace, from Colonial Times to Vietnam*, Foreword by Gen. Harold K. Johnson, Chief of Staff, U.S. Army, New York, 1966.

Guzmán, Martín Luis, *Memoirs of Pancho Villa*, Virginia H. Taylor, trans., Austin, Tex., 1965.

Hagood, Johnson, *The Services of Supply. A Memoir of the Great War*, Boston and New York, 1927.

Hannay, David, *Diaz*, London, 1917.

Harrera E., Celia, *Francisco Villa ante la História*, Mexico City, 1964.

Harris, Larry A., *Pancho Villa and the Columbus Raid*, El Paso, Tex., 1949.

Hein, Otto L., *Memories of Long Ago, by an Old Army Officer*, New York and London, 1925.

Heinl, Robert Debs, Jr., *Soldiers of the Sea. The United States Marine Corps, 1775–1962*, Annapolis, Md., 1962.

Hill, Jim Dan, *The Minute Man in Peace and War. A History of the National Guard*, Harrisburg, Pa., 1964.

Horn, Tom, *Life of Tom Horn, Government Scout and Interpreter, Written by Himself Together with His Letters and Statements by His Friends. A Vindication*, Intro. by Dean Krakel, Norman, Okla., 1964.

Howard, Oliver O., *My Life and Experiences Among Our Hostile Indians. A Record of Personal Observations, Adventures, and Campaigns Among the Indians of the Great West, with Some Account of Their Life, Habits, Traits, Religion, Ceremonies, Dress, Savage Instincts, and Customs in Peace and War*, Hartford, Conn., 1907.

Hughes, W. J., *Rebellious Ranger. Rip Ford and the Old Southwest*, Norman, Okla., 1964.

Huidekoper, Frederic Louis, *The Military Unpreparedness of the United States. A History of American Land Forces from Colonial Times Until June 1, 1915*, New York, 1915.

Jennings, N. A., *A Texas Ranger*, Foreword by J. Frank Dobie, Dallas, Tex., 1930.

Johnson, Virginia Weisel, *The Unregimented General. A Biography of Nelson A. Miles*, Boston, 1962.

King, Rosa E., *Tempest Over Mexico. A Personal Chronicle*, Boston, 1935.

Knight, Oliver, *Following the Indian Wars. The Story of the Newspaper Correspondents Among the Indian Campaigners*, Norman, Okla., 1960.

Knox, Dudley W., *A History of the United States Navy*, Intro. by Vice Admiral William L. Rodgers, New York, 1936.

La Farge, Oliver, with Arthur N. Morgan, *Santa Fe. The Autobiography of a Southwestern Town*, Foreword by Paul Horgan, Norman, Okla., 1959.

Lansford, William Douglas, *Pancho Villa*, Los Angeles, 1965.

Leech, Margaret, *In the Days of McKinley*, New York, 1959.

Lejeune, John A., *The Reminiscences of a Marine*, Philadelphia, 1930.

Lister, Florence C. and Robert H., *Chihuahua, Storehouse of Storms*, Albuquerque, N. M., 1966.

Lockwood, Frank C., *Pioneer Days in Arizona from the Spanish Occupation to Statehood*, New York, 1932.

Lummis, Charles F., *The Land of Poco Tiempo*, New York, 1893.

———, *General Crook and the Apache Wars*, Flagstaff, Ariz., 1966.

McIntyre, Benjamin F., *Federals on the Frontier: The Diary of Benjamin F. McIntyre*, Austin, Tex., 1963.

McKee, Irving, *"Ben Hur" Wallace. The Life of General Lew Wallace*, Los Angeles, 1947.

McWilliams, Carey, *North from Mexico. The Spanish-Speaking People of the United States*, Philadelphia and New York, 1949.

Martin, Percy F., *Mexico in the Twentieth Century*, 2 vols., London, 1907.

Mattes, Merrill J., *Indians, Infants and Infantry. Andrew and Elizabeth Burt on the Frontier*, Denver, Col., 1960.

Medina Ruiz, Fernando, *Francisco Villa. Cuando el Rencor Estalla. . .* , Mexico City, 1960.

Mena Brito, Bernardo, *El Lugarteniente Gris de Pancho Villa (Felipe Angeles)*, Mexico City, 1938.

Mendoza, Vicente T., *El Corrido Mexicano. Antología, Introducción y Notas de*, Mexico City, 1954.

Merrill, James M., *Spurs to Glory. The Story of the United States Cavalry*, Chicago, New York and San Francisco, 1966.

Meyer, Michael C., *Mexican Rebel. Pascual Orozco and the Mexican Revolution, 1910–1915*, Lincoln, Neb., 1967.

Miles, Nelson A., *Personal Recollections and Observations of General Nelson A. Miles, Embracing a Brief View of the Civil War, or, From New England to the Golden Gate, and the Story of His Indian Campaigns with Comments on the Exploration, Development and Progress of Our Great Western Empire*, Chicago and New York, 1896.

Miller, Francis Trevelyan, *General Douglas MacArthur, Fighter for Freedom*, Chicago, Philadelphia and Toronto, 1942.

Millis, Walter, *The Martial Spirit. A Study of Our War with Spain*, Boston and New York, 1931.

National Park Service, *Soldier and Brave. Indian and Military Affairs in the Trans-Mississippi West, Including a Guide to Historic Sites and Landmarks*, Intro. by Ray Allen Billington, New York, Evanston and London, 1963.

Nelson, Otto L., *National Security and the General Staff*, Washington, 1946.

Obregón, Álvaro, *Ocho Mil Kilómetros en Campaña*, 2nd ed., Mexico City, 1959.

O'Connor, Richard, *Black Jack Pershing*, Garden City, N. Y., 1961.

———, *Sheridan the Inevitable*, Indianapolis and New York, 1953.

Olmsted, Frederick Law, *A Journey Through Texas; or a Saddle-trip on the Southwestern Frontier; with a Statistical Appendix*, New York, 1857.

Olsmith, Vernon C., *Recollections of an Old Soldier*, San Antonio, Tex., 1963.

O'Reilly, Edward S., *Roving and Fighting: Adventures Under Four Flags*, London, 1918.

O'Shaughnessy, Edith, *A Diplomat's Wife in Mexico*, New York and London, 1916.

———, *Intimate Pages of Mexican History*, New York, 1920.

Palmer, Frederick, *Newton D. Baker: American at War*, 2 vols., New York, 1931.

Paré, Madeline Ferrin, with Bert M. Fireman, *Arizona Pageant. A Short History of the 48th State*, Phoenix, Ariz., 1965.

Parker, James, *The Old Army: Memories, 1872–1918*, Intro. by Lt. Gen. Robert L. Bullard, Philadelphia, 1929.

Pinchon, Edgcumb, *Viva Villa! A Recovery of the Real Pancho Villa, Peon—Bandit—Soldier—Patriot*, New York, 1933.

Post, Charles Johnson, *The Little War of Private Post*, Boston and Toronto, 1960.

Puente, Ramón, *Hombres de la Revolución: Villa*, Los Angeles, 1931.

———, *Vida de Francisco Villa, Contada por El Mismo*, Los Angeles, 1919.

Quirk, Robert E., *An Affair of Honor. Woodrow Wilson and the Occupation of Vera Cruz*, University of Kentucky, 1962.

———, *The Mexican Revolution, 1914–1915. The Convention of Aguascalientes*, Bloomington, Ind., 1960.

Remington, Frederic, *Frederic Remington's Own West*, ed. and Intro. by Harold McCracken, New York, 1960.

Richardson, Rupert Norval, *The Comanche Barrier to South Plains Settlement. A Century and a Half of Savage Resistance to the Advancing White Frontier*, Glendale, Cal., 1933.

———, *The Frontier of Northwest Texas, 1046 to 1876. Advance and Defense by the Pioneer Settlers of the Cross Timbers and Prairies*, Glendale, Cal., 1963.

Rickey, Don, Jr., *Forty Miles a Day on Beans and Hay. The Enlisted Soldier Fighting the Indian Wars*, Norman, Okla., 1963.

Rister, Carl Coke, *Border Captives. The Traffic in Prisoners by Southwestern Plains Indians, 1835–1875*, Norman, Okla., 1940.

———, *Border Command. General Phil Sheridan in the West*, Norman, Okla., 1944.

———, *Southern Plainsmen*, Norman, Okla., 1938.

———, *The Southwestern Frontier, 1865–1881. A History of the Coming of the Settlers, Indian Depredations and Massacres, Ranching Activities, Operations of White Desperadoes and Thieves, Government Protection, Building of Railways and the Disappearance of the Frontier*, Cleveland, O., 1928.

Rodney, George Brydges, *As a Cavalryman Remembers*, Caldwell, Id., 1944.

Rolle, Andrew F., *The Lost Cause. The Confederate Exodus to Mexico*, Norman, Okla., 1965.

Romney, Thomas Cottam, *The Mormon Colonies in Mexico*, Salt Lake City, 1938.

Russell,, Don, *One Hundred and Three Fights and Scrimmages. The Story of General Reuben Bernard*, Washington, 1936.

Rynning, Thomas H., *Gun Notches. The Life Story of a Cowboy-Soldier, as Told to Al Cohn and Joe Chisholm*, Foreword by Rupert Hughes, New York and Chicago, 1931.

Salinas Carranza, Alberto, *La Expedición Punitiva*, Mexico City, 1936.

Scott, Hugh Lenox, *Some Memories of a Soldier*, New York, 1928.

Sears, Joseph Hamblen, *The Career of Leonard Wood*, New York and London, 1919.

Semmes, Harry H., *Portrait of Patton*, New York, 1955.

Shadley, Frank William, "The American Punitive Expedition into Mexico, 1916–1917," unpublished M.A. thesis, College of the Pacific, 1952.

Sheridan, Philip Henry, *Personal Memoirs of P. H. Sheridan, General, United States Army*, 2 vols., New York, 1888.

———, *Report of Operations of the United States Forces, and General Information of the Condition of Affairs in the Military Division of the Southwest and Gulf and Department of the Gulf, Major General P. H. Sheridan, U.S.A., Commanding, from May 29, 1865 to November 4, 1866*, New Orleans, 1866.

Silva Herzog, Jesús, *Breve Historia de la Revolución Mexicana; los Antecedentes y la Etapa Maderista*, Mexico City and Buenos Aires, 1964.

Sonnichsen, C. L., *The Mescalero Apaches*, Norman, Okla., 1958.

Spaulding, Oliver Lyman, *The United States Army in War and Peace*, New York, 1937.

Spring, John A., *John Spring's Arizona*, A. M. Gustafson, ed., Tucson, Ariz., 1966.

Stimson, Henry L., *On Active Service in War and Peace*, New York, nd.

Summerhayes, Martha, *Vanished Arizona. Recollections of My Army Life*, Milo Milton Quaife, ed., Chicago, 1939, reprint from the 1908 ed.

Taylor, Paul Schuster, *An American-Mexican Frontier. Nueces County, Texas*, Chapel Hill, N. C., 1934.

Thomas, Lowell, *Old Gimlet Eye. The Adventures of Smedley D. Butler*, New York, 1933.

Thomas, Robert S. and Inez V. Allen, *The Mexican Punitive Expedition under Brigadier General John J. Pershing, United States Army, 1916–1917*, Washington, 1954.

Thord-Gray, I., *Gringo Rebel (Mexico, 1913–1914)*, Coral Gables, Fla., 1960.

Thrapp, Dan L., *Al Sieber, Chief of Scouts*, Norman, Okla., 1964.

———, *The Conquest of Apachería*, Norman, Okla., 1967.

Tompkins, Frank, *Chasing Villa. The Story Behind the Story of Pershing's Punitive Expedition into Mexico*, Harrisburg, Pa., 1934.

Toulmin, H. A., *With Pershing in Mexico*, Harrisburg, Pa., 1935.

Turner, John Kenneth, *Barbarous Mexico*, Chicago, 1910.

Tweedie, Ethel Brilliana, *Mexico as I Saw It*, London, 1901.

———, *The Maker of Modern Mexico, Porfirio Diaz*, New York, 1906.

Urquizo, Francisco L., *Origen del Ejército Constitutionalista*, Mexico City, 1964.

Utley, Robert M., *Frontiersmen in Blue. The United States Army and the Indian, 1848–1865*, New York, 1967.

Vandegrift, A. A., *Once a Marine. The Memoirs of General A. A. Vandegrift, United States Marine Corps, as Told to Robert B. Aspery*, New York, 1964.

Villegas, Daniel Cosio, *The United States versus Porfirio Diaz*, trans. by Nettie Lee Benson, Lincoln, Neb., 1963.

Wallace, Ernest and E. Adamson Hoebel, *The Comanches, Lords Of the South Plains*, Norman, Okla., 1952.

Warrior: The Story of General George S. Patton, New York, 1967.

Webb, Walter Prescott, *The Texas Rangers. A Century of Frontier De-*

fense, 2nd ed., Foreword by Lyndon B. Johnson, Austin, Tex., 1965.

Weigley, Russell F., *The History of the United States Army*, New York, 1967.

Wellman, Paul I., *Death in the Desert. The Fifty Years War for the Great Southwest*, New York, 1935.

————, *Death on the Prairie. The Thirty Years' Struggle for the Western Plains*, New York, 1934.

Wharfield, H. B., *10th Cavalry and Border Fights*, El Cajon, Calif., 1964.

————, *Apache Indian Scouts*, El Cajon, Calif., 1964.

————, *Cooley, Army Scout, Arizona Pioneer, Wayside Host, Apache Friend*, El Cajon, Calif., 1966.

Whitman, S. E., *The Troopers. An Informal History of the Plains Cavalry, 1865–1890*, New York, 1962.

Wilson, Edmund, *A Prelude. Landscapes, Characters and Conversations from the Earlier Years of My Life*, New York, 1967.

Wiltsey, Norman B., *Brave Warriors*, Caldwell, Id., 1963.

Woodman, Lyman L., *Cortina, Rogue of the Rio Grande*, San Antonio, Tex., 1950.

ARTICLES

"Achievements of Diaz, The," *Review of Reviews*, XLIII (Apr., 1911), 401–4.

Adossides, N. C., "Victoriano Huerta, the Man, the Soldier," *Review of Reviews*, XLIX (June, 1914), 695–702.

————, "Pancho Villa, Man and Soldier," *Review of Reviews*, XLIX (May, 1914), 566–73.

"An American Army to the Border," *Review of Reviews*, XLIII (Apr., 1911), 405–6.

"An American Woman's Letters from Mexico," *World's Work*, (Jan., 1914), 268–71.

"Apache Scouts with the Punitive Expedition," *Collier's Magazine*, LVII (Apr. 29, 1916), 18.

"As to Catching Anarchy," *Harper's Weekly*, LX (May 29, 1915), 506.

"A Vain Appeal," *Outlook*, CX (May 15, 1915), 1–2.

Avirette, John A., "Diaz and His Peons," *Everybody's Magazine*, XXIV (Jan.–June, 1911), 758–60.

————, "Mexico's Trouble Maker," *Collier's Magazine*, XLVIII (Feb. 14, 1912), 15.

————, "The Situation in Mexico. Political Skies There Presage a Storm," *Collier's Magazine*, XLVIII (Jan. 27, 1912), 14.

Archer, William, "The Collapse of the Diaz Legend," *McClure's Magazine*, XXXVI (Aug., 1911), 395–411.

"A Pacifist Secretary of War, Newton D. Baker," *Literary Digest*, LII (Mar. 9, 1916), 701.

Barnes, W. C., "In the Apache Country," *Overland Monthly*, IX, Ser. 2 (Feb., 1887), 172–80.

Barra, Leon de la, "Present Conditions in Mexico," *Independent*, LXX (Mar. 16, 1911), 545–46.

Barzini, Luigi, "Villa's Style of War," *Literary Digest*, XLVIII (June 27, 1914), 1537–38.

"Battle of Agua Prieta, The," *Review of Reviews*, XLIII (May, 1911), 535.

Beaumont, Eugene Beauharnais, "Over the Border with Mackenzie," *United Service Review*, XII (1885), 281–88.

Bennett, James A., "A Dragoon in New Mexico, 1850–1856," Clinton E. Brooks and Frank D. Reeves, eds., *New Mexico Historical Review*, XX (Jan., 1947), 51–97; (Apr., 1947), 140–76.

Beringer, Pierre N., "General Felix Diaz," *Overland Monthly*, LVI (1910), 136–37.

———, "The Awakening of a Nation. Marvelous Mexico and the Muck Raker. A Study on the Spot," *Overland Monthly*, LVI (1910), 2–22.

Bonebrake, Percy Locke, "The Apache Kid," *Brand Book, 1951*, Los Angeles Corral, The Westerners.

Bourke, John Gregory, "General Crook in the Indian Country," *Century Magazine*, XLI (Mar., 1891), 643–60.

Braddy, Haldeen and John H. McNeely, "Francisco Villa in Folk-songs," *Arizona Quarterly*, X (spring, 1954), 5–16.

Brayer, Herbert O., "The Cananea Incident of 1905," *New Mexico Historical Review*, XIII (1938), 387–415.

Breeden, Marshall, "The Task of the National Guard," *Overland Monthly*, LXVIII (Aug., 1916), 99–111.

Browne, Porter Emerson, "The Mexican Mess," *Collier's Magazine*, LVII (July 22, 1916), 11.

"Bullets Across the Border," *Literary Digest*, XLII (Apr. 29, 1911), 823–25.

"Calling Out the Guard," *World's Work*, XXXII (Aug., 1916), 437–52.

Carol, William, "The North and South War in Mexico," *World's Work*, XXVII (Jan., 1914), 298–312.

"Carranza Mentions the Door," *Literary Digest*, LII (June 10, 1916), 1689–90.

Carson, John, "The Captain Who Wouldn't Stay Buried," *Brand Book, 1963*, Denver Posse, The Westerners, pp. 98–104.

Carter, William Harding, "The Border Patrol," *Outlook*, XCIX (Dec. 23, 1911), 972–78.

———, "The War Department—Military Administration," *Scribner's Magazine*, XXXIII (May, 1902), 661–73.

———, "Will America Profit by Its Recent Military Lessons?" *North American Review*, CLXXIV (May, 1902), 658–71.

Chezem, Curtis, "Down Pershing's Highway to Pancho Villa Land," *Four Wheeler. The Magazine of Back Country Cars* (Apr., 1966), pp. 22–25.

Clendenen, Clarence C., "Mexican Unionists: A Forgotten Incident of

the War Between States," *New Mexico Historical Review*, XXXIX
(1964), 32–39.

Connolly, James B., "The Seagoing Flyers," *Collier's Magazine*, LIII
(June 20, 1914), 12.

"Continuing Mexican Trouble, A," *World's Work*, XXXII (June, 1916),
137–38.

Cremony, John C., "The Apache Race," *Overland Monthly*, I (Sept.,
1868), 201–9.

Crimmins, Martin L., "Colonel Buell's Expedition into Mexico in 1880,"
New Mexico Historical Review, X (1935), 133–42.

Cumberland, Charles C., "Border Raids in the Lower Rio Grande Valley
—1915," *Southwestern Historical Quarterly*, LVII (July, 1953–Apr.,
1954), 285–311.

Daly, Henry W., "The Capture of Geronimo," *American Legion Monthly*,
VIII (June, 1930), 30.

Davenport, Harbert, "General José María Jesús Carabajal," *Southwestern
Historical Quarterly*, LV (July, 1951–Apr., 1952), 475–83.

De Ellen, Fritz Arno von, "Mexican Camp Followers," *Harper's Weekly*,
LVIII (May 2, 1914), 19.

"Drifting Toward Intervention in Mexico," *Literary Digest*, LII (May
27, 1916), 1515–17.

Dunn, Robert, "With Pershing's Cavalry," *Collier's Magazine*, LVIII
(Sept. 23, 1916), 8.

Ellis, Richard N., "Copper-skinned Soldiers—The Apache Scouts," *Brand
Book, 1963*, Denver Posse, The Westerners, pp. 151–62.

Elser, Frank B., "General Pershing's Mexican Campaign," *Century Magazine*, LXXXIX (Feb., 1920), 433–47.

Emerson, Edwin, "The Rurales of Mexico," *Century Magazine*, LXXXII
(June, 1911), 271–78.

"End of the Chase after Villa," *Current Opinion*, LX (May, 1916), 304–5.

"Flying into Mexico," *Literary Digest*, LII (Apr. 15, 1916), 1103.

"Folks They Left Behind Them, The," *World's Work*, XXXII (Oct.,
1916), 690–95.

"Funston and Pershing, The Generals in Charge of the Chase after
Villa," *Current Opinion*, LX (May, 1916), 318–20.

"Funston's Men at the Front," *Collier's Magazine*, LIII (May 23, 1914),
12.

Fusco, E. Miles, "The Tragic Death of Captain Crawford," *Brand Book,
1963*, Denver Posse, The Westerners, pp. 91–96.

"General Staff Bill of 1902," *Public Opinion*, XXXII (Feb. 20, 1902),
229.

"German Scorn for Our Army," *Literary Digest*, XLII (Apr. 1, 1911),
617–18.

Goodwin, Grenville, "Experiences of an Apache Scout," *Arizona Historical Review*, II (Jan., 1936), 31.

Greene, Francis Vinton, "The United States Army," *Scribner's Magazine*,
XXX (July–Dec., 1901), 593–613.

Hager, William A., "The Plan of San Diego, Unrest of the Texas Frontier in 1915," *Arizona and the West*, V (1963), 327–36.

Hanna, Robert, "With Crawford in Mexico," *Arizona Historical Review*, VI (1935), 56–64.

Hare, James H., Letter describing the battle of Juarez, *Collier's Magazine*, XLVII (May 28, 1911), 5.

———, "The 'Rebuke with Flames of Fire' at Vera Cruz," *Collier's Magazine*, LIII (May 16, 1914), 8–10.

Harriman, Mrs. Borden, "Matamoras—A War Film," *Harper's Weekly*, LX (May 22, 1915), 494–96.

Hart, Albert Bushnell, "Mexico and the Mexicans," *World's Work*, XXVII (Jan., 1914), 272–89.

Heiliger, Edward M. "La Revolución Mexicana en la Prensa de Lengua Inglesa, 1910–1952," *História Mexicana*, III (1953–54), 451–72.

"He Showed Them How" [Gen. Crook], *New Mexico Electric News*, XVI, No. 1, 8.

Hopper, James, "A Little Mexican Expedition," *Collier's Magazine*, LVII (July 15, 1916), 1.

———, "Browsing on the Border," *Collier's Magazine*, LVII (May 27, 1916), 1.

———, "New Columbus and the Expedition," *Collier's Magazine*, LVII (May 27, 1916), 10.

———, "Pancho Villa," *Collier's Magazine*, LVII (Apr. 29, 1916), 8.

———, "Twin Towns on the Border," *Collier's Magazine*, LVII (Aug. 19, 1916), 1.

———, "What Happened at Columbus," *Collier's Magazine*, LVII (Apr. 15, 1916), 11.

———, "Wilson and the Border," *Collier's Magazine*, LVII (July 8, 1916), 7.

"Hospital Train, The First American," *Review of Reviews*, LVI (Dec., 1916), 652–53.

Howe, Jerome W., "Chasing Villa," *Journal of the Worcester Polytechnic Institute*, XIX (July, 1916), 380–87.

"Huerta's Arms Unloaded," *Independent*, LXXVIII (June 8, 1914), 444.

Hughes, Rupert, "The Big Hike," *Collier's Magazine*, LVIII (Nov. 11, 1916), 5.

———, "The Case of the National Guard," *Collier's Magazine*, LVII (May 20, 1916), 7.

———, "The Crisis in the National Guard," *Collier's Magazine*, LVIII (Dec. 9, 1916), 5.

"Intervention in Mexico," *World's Work*, XXX (Sept., 1915), 507–8.

"Invading Mexico to Avert Intervention," *Literary Digest*, LII (Mar. 25, 1916), 801–4.

"Jewish Press on Army Prejudice," *Literary Digest*, XLII (June 24, 1911), 1229–30.

Kurtz, Henry I., "Rip Ford, Lone-Star Giant," *Real West*, IX (Nov., 1966), 36.

Kyne, Peter B., "With the Border Guard," *Collier's Magazine*, LIII (May 9, 1914), 9.

Lazelle, Henry M., "Puritan and Apache: A Diary," Frank D. Reeve, ed., *New Mexico Historical Review*, XIII (Oct., 1948), 269–301; XIV (Jan., 1949), 12–53.

"Life of the Border—A Guardsman's Letter," *Outlook*, CXIII (Aug. 23, 1916), 936–37.

London, Jack, "Mexico's Army and Ours," *Collier's Magazine*, LIII (May 30, 1914), 5–7.

———, "The Red Game of War," *Collier's Magazine*, LIII (May 16, 1914), 5–7.

———, "With Funston's Men. Our Army and Navy in Peaceful Action," *Collier's Magazine*, LIII (May 23, 1914), 9.

McCormick, Medill, "Just Out of Jail," *Harper's Weekly*, LVII (May 30, 1914), 6–7.

———, "The Army in Vera Cruz," *Outlook*, CVII (May 30, 1914), 233–34.

———, "The Mexican Cactus," *Harper's Weekly*, LVIII (June 13, 1914), 6–7.

McDaniel, Ruel, "Juan Cortina—Hero or Bandit?" *The Best of True West*, 1964.

McGregor, "Huerta and Other Leaders," *Harper's Weekly*, LVIII (May 9, 1914), 12–13. This writer never signed himself otherwise than as "McGregor." The present author has been unable to ascertain his initials or given name.

———, "Villa's Right-hand Man," *Harper's Weekly*, LXI (July 24, 1915), 89–90.

MacAdam, George, "The Life of General Pershing," Part VII, *World's Work*, XXXVIII (June, 1919), 148–58.

"Madero's Camp, In," *Collier's Magazine*, XLVII (May 13, 1911), 17.

"Madero Gaining Ground," *Literary Digest*, XLII (May 20, 1911), 985–86.

"Making Over the Army of the United States," *Current Opinion*, LX (May, 1916), 308–11.

"Married Militiamen," *Outlook*, CXIII (July 19, 1916), 636.

Marvin, George, "Bandits and the Borderland," *World's Work*, XXXII (Oct., 1916), 656–63.

———, "Invasion or Intervention," *World's Work*, XXXII (May, 1916), 40–62.

———, "The First Line of Defense in Mexico," *World's Work*, XXXII (Aug., 1916), 416–24.

———, "The Quick and the Dead on the Border," *World's Work*, XXXII (Jan., 1917), 295–311.

Mason, Gregory, "Campaigning in Coahuila," *Outlook*, CVII (June 20, 1914), 391–97.

———, "Mexico—From the Inside Looking Out," *Outlook*, CXIII (May 10, 1916), 92–96.

———, "Our Citizens in Arms," Outlook, CXIII (July 5, 1916), 546–49.

———, "The Army of Protection," *Outlook*, CVII (July 18, 1914), 651–54.

———, "The Mexican Man of the Hour," *Outlook*, CVII (June 6, 1914), 292–306.

———, "With Villa in Chihuahua," *Outlook*, CVII (May 9, 1914), 74–78.

"Massacre of Americans in Chihuahua, The," *Current Opinion*, LX (Feb., 1916), 73–75.

Merritt, Wesley, "Three Indian Campaigns," *Harper's Magazine*, LXXX (1889–90), 720–37.

"Messages from Mexico," *World's Work*, XXXII (Aug., 1916), 430–36.

"Mexican Hostility," *Literary Digest*, XLI (Nov. 26, 1910), 965–66.

"Mexican Murders, The," *Literary Digest*, LII (Jan. 22, 1916), 157–58.

"Mexico," *Harper's Weekly*, LX (June 19, 1915), 577.

"Mexico," *World's Work*, XXX (July, 1915), 261–62.

"Mexico and Its Maker," *World's Work*, XXII (June, 1911), 14431–32.

"Mexico and the Militia," *Outlook*, CXIII (May 31, 1916), 233–34.

"Mexico—Viewed from Texas," *Literary Digest*, XLVIII (Mar. 14, 1914), 535–37.

"Mexico's Centennial," *World's Work*, XX (July, 1910), 132–37.

"Mexico's Centennial and Its Director," *Literary Digest*, XLI (Sept. 17, 1910), 461–62.

"Mexico's Insurrection," *Review of Reviews*, XLIII (Mar., 1911), 283.

"Mexico's Revolutionists," *Independent*, LXX (Feb. 9, 1911), 281.

Middleton, James, "Mexico, the Land of Concessions," *World's Work*, XXVII (Jan., 1914), 289–98.

Mills, Elizabeth H., "The Mormon Colonies in Chihuahua after the 1912 Exodus," *New Mexico Historical Review*, XXIX (July, 1954), 165–82; (Oct., 1954), 290–310.

"Mobilization of 1911," *Outlook*, XCVII (Mar. 18 and 25, 1911), 565, 613; (Apr. 15, 1911), 796.

Moran, George H. R., "Diary of George Moran in Arizona Territory, 1878," *Arizona and the West*, V (1963), 249–67.

Morey, Lewis, "The Cavalry Fight at Carrizal," *Cavalry Journal*, XXVII (Jan., 1917), 449–56.

Morris, Leopold, "The Mexican Raid of 1875 on Corpus Christi," *Texas Historical Association Quarterly*, IV (July, 1900–Apr., 1901), 128–39.

"Motor-cycle Machine Guns in Mexico," *World's Work*, XXXII (June, 1967), 237.

"Motor Truck in Mexico, The," *Literary Digest*, LII (May 27, 1916), 1599.

"Movement Toward Mexico, The," *Independent*, LXX (Mar. 16, 1911), 579–80.

Murray, Robert Hammond, "Porfirio Diaz at First Hand. What the Maker of Mexico Thinks of His Country and Its Future. A Character Sketch from Interviews," *World's Work*, XXII (July, 1911), 14571–91.

Nalty, Bernard C. and Truman R. Strobridge, "Captain Emmet Crawford,

Commander of Apache Scouts, 1882–1886," *Arizona and the West*, VI (1964), 30–40.

"National Defense and Villa's Raid," *Current Opinion*, LX (Apr., 1916), 231.

"National Guard, The, Demonstrates Some Facts," *World's Work*, XXXII (Sept., 1916), 485–486.

"National Guard, Helping the," *Outlook*, CX (Aug. 11, 1915), 830–31.

"National Guard, The, Under Fire," *Literary Digest*, LII (Apr. 22, 1916), 1132–33.

"Newton D. Baker, the Mayor Idealist of Cleveland Becomes the New Secretary of War," *Current Opinion*, LX (Apr., 1916), 246–48.

"Next Step in Mexico, The," *World's Work*, XXII (July, 1911), 14551–52.

Oates, Stephen B., "John S. 'Rip' Ford," *Southwestern Historical Quarterly*, LXIV (January, 1961), 289–314.

Opler, Morris E., "A Chiricahua Apache's Account of the Geronimo Campaign of 1886," *New Mexico Historical Review*, XIII (1938), 360–86.

"Our Debt to Villa," *Literary Digest*, XLVIII (May 16, 1914), 1166–67.

"Our Punitive Expedition into Mexico and Its Possible Consequences," *Current Opinion*, LX (Apr., 1916), 229–31.

"Our Task in Mexico," *World's Work*, XXX (Oct., 1915), 634–35.

"Our Unprepared Militia," *Literary Digest*, LII (June 3, 1916), 1617.

"Our Unpreparedness Revealed by Villa," *Literary Digest*, LII (Apr. 1, 1916), 883–86.

"Pacifist Secretary of War, A" *Literary Digest*, LII (Mar. 18, 1916), 701.

Palmer, Frederick, "Mexico. The American Spirit in Vera Cruz," *Everybody's Magazine*, XXX (June, 1914), 806–20.

Park, Joseph F., "The Apaches in Mexican-American Relations, 1848–1861," *Arizona and the West*, III (1961), 129–46.

Patullo, George, "Brother Bill on the Border," *Saturday Evening Post*, CLXXXIX (Aug. 5, 1916), 14.

———, "Once a Mexican Always?" *Saturday Evening Post*, CLXXXIX (Aug. 12, 1916), 3.

———, "Sentinel Rheumatism," *Saturday Evening Post*, CLXXXIX (Aug. 19, 1916), 23.

Perrenot, E. E., "The National Guard Fiasco," *Out West*, XLIV (Aug., 1916), 79–81.

"Personal Glimpses—Our Generals on the Mexican Border," *Literary Digest*, XLII (Mar. 25, 1911), 585–87.

Phelps, Frederick E., "A Soldier's Memoirs," Frank D. Reeve, ed., *New Mexico Historical Review*, XXV (1950), 206–21.

Philpott, William A., "A Stake-town in Seventy Hours," *Independent*, LXX (May 18, 1911), 1038–43.

———, "Life at the Big Khaki Town," *Independent*, LXX (June 15, 1911), 1307–12.

Pickering, Col. Abner, "The Battle of Agua Prieta," *United States Infantry Journal*, XII (Jan., 1916), 707–10.

Porter, Kenneth Wiggins, "The Seminole Negro-Indian Scouts, 1870–1881," *Southwestern Historical Review*, LV (July, 1951–Apr., 1952), 358–77.

"Possibilities on the Mexican Border," *Literary Digest*, XLII (Mar. 25, 1911), 535–36.

"President Diaz' Prompt and Efficient Remedy for Oppressive Trusts," *Arena*, XXVII (Feb., 1902), 210–11.

"Press and the 'War' in Mexico, The," *Review of Reviews*, XLIII (Apr., 1911), 401.

Pulido, Marco Antonio, "Cuando Pancho Villa Atacó a Columbus," *Contenido* [Mexico City], No. 38 (July, 1966), 44–66.

"Punishing Villa or Punishing Our Pride?" *Collier's Magazine*, LVII (Apr. 29, 1916), 18.

"Race Question in Camp, The," *Independent*, LXX (Apr. 13, 1911), 751–52.

"Real Revolution in Mexico," *Review of Reviews*, XLIII (June, 1911), 660–66.

"Rebellious Mexico," *Outlook*, XCVI (Dec. 3, 1910), 760.

Remington, Frederic, "On the Indian Reservations," *Century Magazine*, XXXVIII (1889), 394–405, 536–45.

"Revolt Against Diaz, The," *Literary Digest*, XLI (Dec. 3, 1910), 1019–21.

Rippy, J. Fred, "Border Troubles Along the Rio Grande, 1848–1860," *Southwestern Historical Quarterly*, XXIII (1919–20), 91–111.

———, "Some Precedents of the Pershing Expedition into Mexico," *Southwestern Historical Quarterly*, XXIV (1920–21), 292–316.

———, "The Indians of the Southwest in the Diplomacy of the United States and Mexico, 1848–1853," *Hispanic-American Historical Review*, II (1919), 363–96.

Roberts, John W., "Personal Glimpses: Entrenched with Villa," *Literary Digest*, L (June 18, 1915), 1485–88.

"Role of the Texas Rangers, The," *Literary Digest*, XLVIII (Mar. 28, 1914), 710–12.

Ruhl, Arthur, "Campaigning with Mr. Madero," *Collier's Magazine*, XLVIII (Oct. 28, 1911), 17.

———, "The Fall of Vera Cruz. When is a War not a War?" *Collier's Magazine*, LIII (May 9, 1914), 6.

———, "The Gallery at San Antonio, and Other Lighter Aspects of the Mobilization on the Texas Border," *Collier's Magazine*, XLVII (Apr. 29, 1911), 13.

———, "The Puzzle of Mexico in Revolt," *Collier's Magazine*, XLVII (Mar. 25, 1911), 17.

———, "The Unfinished Drama," *Collier's Magazine*, LIII (May 30, 1914), 7.

———, "What Is the Matter with the U.S. Army?" *Collier's Magazine*, XLVII (Apr. 15, 1911), 17.

Sabin, Edwin L., "The American Soldier and the American Sailor," *Lippincott's Magazine*, LXXXVIII (Dec., 1911), 892–93.

Sacks, Benjamin H., "New Evidence on the Bascom Affair," *Arizona and the West*, IV (1962), 261–78.

Schwatka, Frederick, "Among the Apaches," *Century Magazine*, XXXIV (May, 1887), 47–52.

"Secretary Garrison's Resignation," *Literary Digest*, LII (Feb. 19, 1916), 425–26.

Shearer, Ernest C., "The Carvajal Disturbances," *Southwestern Historical Quarterly*, LV (1951–1952), 201–30.

Sheppard, Morris, "The Mexican Situation," *Review of Reviews*, XLIX (Apr., 1914), 431–32.

Slayden, Ellen Maury, "The Grace and Gaiety of the Mexican Centennial," *Independent*, LXX (May 25, 1911), 1091–98.

Smith, Harry A., "The Texas Bandit Problem," *United States Infantry Journal*, VI (Mar., 1916), 845–52.

Smith, Ralph A., " 'Apache Ranching' Below the Gila, 1841–1845," *Arizoniana*, III (1962, No. 4), 1–17.

———, "The Scalp Hunter in the Borderlands, 1835–1850," *Arizona and the West*, VI (1964), 5–22.

Smythe, Donald J., S.J., "John J. Pershing, Frontier Cavalryman," *New Mexico Historical Review*, XXXVI (July, 1963), 220–43.

"Spirit of the Guardsman, The," *Outlook*, CXIII (Aug. 9, 1916), 815.

Stivison, Roy E. and Della Mavity McDonnell, "When Villa Raided Columbus," *New Mexico Magazine*, XXVIII (Dec., 1950), 17.

Stowell, Fred W., "On the Trail of Geronimo," *Overland Monthly*, VII (Apr., 1886), 348–56.

"Surrender of Diaz, The," *Literary Digest*, XLII (May 27, 1911), 1038–40.

"Swearing in the Militia, The," *Literary Digest*, XLII (June 24, 1916), 1866–67.

Tassin, A. G., "Among the Apaches," *Century Magazine*, XIV (July–Dec., 1889), 311–22, 374–79.

Temple, A. D., "Bandit Hospitality," *Harper's Weekly*, LVIII (Apr. 25, 1914), 10–12.

"Trouble for Madero," *Outlook*, XCIX (Dec. 2, 1911), 798.

Utley, Robert M., "The Bascom Affair; a Reconstruction," *Arizona and the West*, III (1961), 59–68.

———, "The Surrender of Geronimo," *Arizoniana*, IV (1963, No. 1), 1–9.

"Vera Cruz: A Crusade for Decency," *Outlook*, CVII (July 4, 1914), 527–28.

"Villa's American Allies," *Literary Digest*, LII (Apr. 8, 1916), 951–54.

"Villa's Lesson," *World's Work*, XXXII (May, 1916), 18.

Wallace, Edward S., "Border Warrior," *American Heritage*, IX, No. 4 (June, 1958), 22.

———, "General John Lapham Bullis, Thunderbolt of the Texas Frontier," *Southwestern Historical Quarterly*, LV (July, 1951–Apr., 1952), 77–85.

——, "General Ranald Slidell Mackenzie—Indian Fighting Cavalry-man," *Southwestern Historical Quarterly*, LVI (July, 1952–Apr., 1953), 378–96.

Wallace, Ernest and Adrian S. Anderson, "R. S. Mackenzie and the Kickapoos: The Raid into Mexico in 1873," *Arizona and the West*, VII (1964), 105–26.

"Warfare Worth While," *Independent*, LXXVIII (June 8, 1914), 441.

" 'War Game' on the Mexican Border, The," *Literary Digest*, XLII (Mar. 18, 1911), 497–99.

"War on the Rio Grande, The," *Literary Digest*, XLII (Feb. 25, 1911), 344–45.

Wharfield, H. B., "A Fight with Yaquis at Bear Valley, 1918," *Arizoniana*, IV (Fall, 1963), 1–8.

"What to Do with Mexico," *Literary Digest*, LII (May 20, 1916), 1438–40.

"What the Troops in Texas Have Learned," *Review of Reviews*, XLIII (May, 1911), 537–38.

"What War with Mexico Means," *World's Work*, XXXII (Aug., 1916), 425–30.

Whitaker, Herman, "The Childish Conquerors of Mexico," *Independent*, LXXVIII (June 15, 1914), 488–90.

——, "Villa—Bandit—Patriot," *Independent*, LXXVIII (June 8, 1914), 450–52.

Whitney, Caspar, "Why Mexico Is a Thorn in Our Side," *Outlook*, CX (May 5, 1915), 87–94; (May 19, 1915), 145–50; (May 26, 1915), 177–80.

Wilkes, Allene Tupper, "The Gentle Zapatistas," *Harper's Weekly*, LX (Jan. 16, 1915), 56–57.

——, "Hunger in Mexico City," *Harper's Weekly*, LXI (Aug. 14, 1915), 148–49.

——, "A Musty Fort in a Modern Crisis," *Harper's Weekly*, LXI (Sept. 18, 1915), 275.

——, "Villa Enters Mexico City," *Harper's Weekly*, LX (Jan. 16, 1915), 57.

"Wilson's Message to Congress," *Outlook*, CVII (May 2, 1914), 107.

Winski, Norman, " 'Bad Hand' Mackenzie (Custer's Avenger)," *Pioneer West*, I (July, 1967), 28.

"With the Army in Texas," *Outlook*, XCVII (Apr. 1, 1911), 726–29.

Woodward, Arthur, "Side Lights on Fifty Years of Apache Warfare, 1836–1886," *Arizoniana*, II (fall, 1961), 3–14.

Worcester, Donald E., "The Beginnings of the Apache Menace of the Southwest," *New Mexico Historical Review*, XVI (Jan., 1941), 1–14.

Index

Index

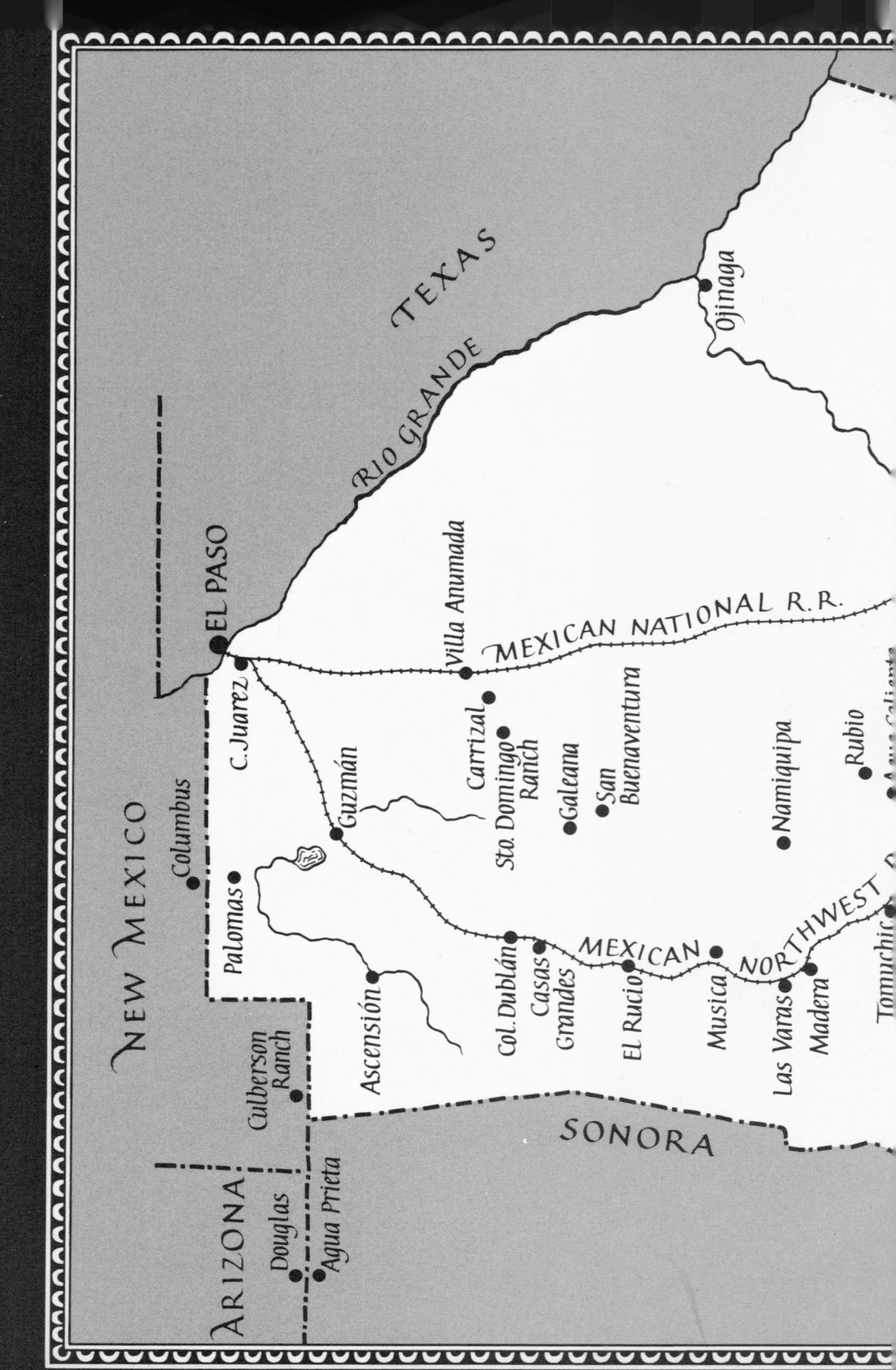